Yosemite & the
Southern Sierra Nevada

FIRST EDITION

YOSEMITE & THE SOUTHERN SIERRA NEVADA

David T. Page

The Countryman Press
Woodstock, Vermont

For my family.

We welcome your comments and suggestions. Please contact Great Destinations Guide Editor, The Countryman Press, P.O. Box 748, Woodstock, VT 05091, or e-mail countrymanpress@wwnorton.com.

ISBN 978-1-58157-077-9

Cover and interior photos by the author unless otherwise specified
Book design by Bodenweber Design
Composition by Susan McClellan
Maps by Mapping Specialists Ltd., Madison, WI © The Countryman Press

Published by The Countryman Press, P.O. Box 748, Woodstock, Vermont 05091

Distributed by W. W. Norton & Company, Inc., 500 Fifth Avenue, New York, NY 10110

Manufactured in the United States of America

10 9 8 7 6 5 4 3 2 1

GREAT DESTINATIONS TRAVEL GUIDEBOOK SERIES

Recommended by *National Geographic Traveler* and *Travel + Leisure* magazines.

[A] CRISP AND CRITICAL APPROACH, FOR TRAVELERS WHO WANT TO LIVE LIKE LOCALS.
— *USA Today*

Great Destinations™ guidebooks are known for their comprehensive, critical coverage of regions of extraordinary cultural interest and natural beauty. The authors in this series are professional travel writers who have lived for many years in the regions they describe. Each title in this series is continuously updated with each printing to ensure accurate and timely information. All the books contain more than one hundred photographs and maps.

Current titles available:

THE ADIRONDACK BOOK

ATLANTA

AUSTIN, SAN ANTONIO
& THE TEXAS HILL COUNTRY

THE BERKSHIRE BOOK

BERMUDA

BIG SUR, MONTEREY BAY
& GOLD COAST WINE COUNTRY

CAPE CANAVERAL, COCOA BEACH
& FLORIDA'S SPACE COAST

THE CHARLESTON, SAVANNAH
& COASTAL ISLANDS BOOK

THE CHESAPEAKE BAY BOOK

THE COAST OF MAINE BOOK

COLORADO'S CLASSIC MOUNTAIN TOWNS:
GREAT DESTINATIONS

THE FINGER LAKES BOOK

THE FOUR CORNERS REGION

GALVESTON, SOUTH PADRE ISLAND
& THE TEXAS GULF COAST

THE HAMPTONS BOOK

HONOLULU & OAHU:
GREAT DESTINATIONS HAWAII

THE HUDSON VALLEY BOOK

THE JERSEY SHORE: ATLANTIC CITY TO
CAPE MAY (INCLUDES THE WILDWOODS)

LAS VEGAS

LOS CABOS & BAJA CALIFORNIA SUR:
GREAT DESTINATIONS MEXICO

MICHIGAN'S UPPER PENINSULA

MONTREAL & QUEBEC CITY:
GREAT DESTINATIONS CANADA

THE NANTUCKET BOOK

THE NAPA & SONOMA BOOK

NORTH CAROLINA'S OUTER BANKS
& THE CRYSTAL COAST

PALM BEACH, MIAMI & THE FLORIDA KEYS

PHOENIX, SCOTTSDALE, SEDONA
& CENTRAL ARIZONA

PLAYA DEL CARMEN, TULUM & THE RIVIERA
MAYA: GREAT DESTINATIONS MEXICO

SALT LAKE CITY, PARK CITY, PROVO
& UTAH'S HIGH COUNTRY RESORTS

SAN DIEGO & TIJUANA

SAN JUAN, VIEQUES & CULEBRA:
GREAT DESTINATIONS PUERTO RICO

THE SANTA FE & TAOS BOOK

THE SARASOTA, SANIBEL ISLAND
& NAPLES BOOK

THE SEATTLE & VANCOUVER BOOK: INCLUDES
THE OLYMPIC PENINSULA, VICTORIA & MORE

THE SHENANDOAH VALLEY BOOK

TOURING EAST COAST WINE COUNTRY

WASHINGTON D.C., AND NORTHERN VIRGINIA

YELLOWSTONE & GRAND TETON NATIONAL PARKS
AND JACKSON HOLE

YOSEMITE & THE SOUTHERN SIERRA NEVADA

If you are traveling to, moving to, residing in, or just interested in any (or all!) of these enchanting regions, a Great Destinations guidebook is a superior companion. Honest and painstakingly critical, full of information only a local can provide, Great Destinations guidebooks give you all the practical knowledge you need to enjoy the best of each region. Why not own them all?

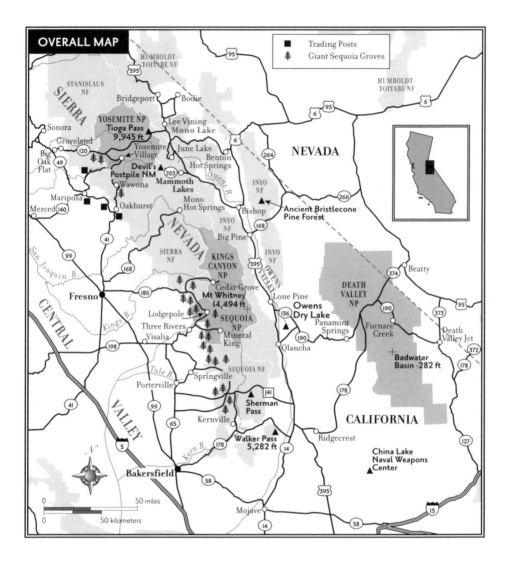

Contents

Introduction   9

The Lay of the Land   12

The Way This Book Works   13

Acknowledgments   15

1

Contexts
Making the Range
17

2

Into the Hills
Approaches, Traverses, Methods of Travel
51

3

Death Valley
Across the Great Sink
74

4

The Owens Valley & Eastern Sierra
True West
109

5

Mammoth Lakes & Mono Country
Under the Volcano
151

6

Sequoia, Kings Canyon & the Great Western Divide
Dominion of Giants
209

7

Yosemite
The Incomparable Pleasure Ground
261

8

Information
Resources & Practical Matters
317

General Index 330
    Lodging by Price Index 350
    Gear, Guides & Outfitters Index 351
    Spa & Golf Index 352

Maps
    Overall   6
    Regional Overview   52
    Approaches to the Sierra & Death Valley from the East   69
    Approaches to the Sierra from the West   70
    Death Valley National Park   81
    Eastern Sierra Overview   118
    Mammoth & Mono Overview   159
    Town of Mammoth Lakes   169
    Sequoia/Kings Canyon National Parks   213
    Great Western Divide Highway   242
    Kaiser Pass   247
    Yosemite National Park   269
    Yosemite Valley Detail   298

INTRODUCTION

The West of which I speak is but another name for the Wild; and . . . in Wildness is the preservation of the world. Every tree sends its fibres forth in search of the Wild. The cities import it at any price. Men plow and sail for it. From the forest and wilderness come the tonics and barks which brace mankind. Our ancestors were savages. The story of Romulus and Remus being suckled by a wolf is not a meaningless fable. The founders of every state which has risen to eminence, have drawn their nourishment and vigor from a similar wild source. It is because the children of the empire were not suckled by the wolf that they were conquered and displaced by the children of the northern forests who were.

—*Henry David Thoreau*, Atlantic Monthly, 1862

In the spring of 1868, less than a month before his 30th birthday, a wild-haired itinerant college dropout by the name of John Muir, "with incredibly little money" and no guide-book, stepped off a Panama steamer at the Port of San Francisco. He'd quit his job at a carriage-parts shop the previous fall and had walked a thousand miles from Indianapolis to the Gulf of Mexico, "holding a generally southward course, like the birds when they are going from summer to winter." He'd spent a few months in Cuba, looking at plants, had had a notion to go to South America—to wander up and then float back down the Amazon—but then crossed the Isthmus at Panama instead, and ended up in California.

The way he tells it, the first thing he did was walk up and ask a fellow for the best way out of town.

"But where do you want to go?" the fellow asked.

"To any place that is wild," said Muir.

The fellow pointed the way to the Oakland Ferry.

Muir got himself a pocket map of some kind, booked passage across the bay, took rough bearings from the sun, and then proceeded to wade across the Central Valley through a sea of waist-deep wildflowers—to what he would later describe as "the most divinely beautiful of all the mountain-chains I have ever seen."

Here he would spend the rest of his life—give or take a trip or three around the world. Here he would climb countless peaks, explore innumerable canyons, tally thousands of tree rings. He would write 10 books and hundreds of articles; ride an avalanche; climb to the top of a 100-foot-tall spruce tree in a gale-force windstorm; establish the Sierra Club as a force to be reckoned with; serve as personal tour guide to Ralph Waldo Emerson and Teddy Roosevelt. "His was a dauntless soul," wrote the President and onetime Rough Rider. At age 73 Muir finally made that trip to Brazil—it was 1911—as part of an epic, 40,000-mile, cross-country, cross-ocean, solo adventure that took him not only up the Amazon to the Andes, but to deep Africa and the headwaters of the Nile.

On the road to Ballarat, Panamint Basin, June 2007   Burke Griggs

Muir was not a big fan of guidebooks, especially of the stay-here, eat-this, buy-that variety. "Most people who travel," he wrote, "look only at what they are directed to look at." And yet he wanted people to see what he had seen: to see that it must be saved—and to save themselves in the process. His unique and enduring guidebook, *The Yosemite,* published upon his return from Africa (two years before his death), is one part fireside chat, one part travelogue, two parts natural history, three parts high-flown panegyric to "the great fresh unblighted, unredeemed wilderness" that had given his life its greatest purpose.

Thanks to Muir, and to the generations of "good wanderers" he inspired, a significant part of this wild country abides—in some ways even wilder than it was a century ago—not merely in Yosemite, but to the south: across the rugged, roadless, granite backlands of the Sierra, from the trickling glacier in the lap of Mount Lyell to the Minarets, and Mammoth Mountain; from Kings Canyon to the Whitney Crest; from Giant Forest to the Kern Plateau; and to the east, in the shadow of the range, across the Alabama Hills and Mary Austin's "Land of Little Rain," to Death Valley.

It is a place of extremes, of measurements and calculations of the sort that help define the edges of what we know: Here is the largest living thing on the planet. Here is the oldest. Here are the youngest volcanoes in North America. Here is the fastest-rising mountain range, and the longest. Here is the greatest plant and mammal diversity, the biggest snowfall, the tallest single-drop waterfall, the deepest valley. Here, they say, one can experience the greatest number of sunny days per year in the continental United States. Here, within a hundred miles of the lowest, driest, hottest basin (at 282 feet below a rising sea level), one can, in one long push, make his or her way to stand atop the highest peak (14,782 feet higher, also rising). Here, within a few hours' drive of the largest, fastest-growing cities in America, lies one of the world's last great wild frontiers, some of the most sparsely populated country in the West, whence one can still strike out on foot—or on horseback, or on skis—into the depths of one of the most extensive wildernesses in the Lower 48.

Of how the ordinary traveler might get to the edges of this country—where a decent breakfast might be had, or a good glass of wine, or 800-thread-count sheets, or a massage, or a miniature synchilla-mastodon Christmas ornament—there is precious little, nay nothing, in Muir (except a brief note that most accommodations had by 1912 burned down, and that what remained was woefully inadequate). Such was not his concern. "Only by going alone in silence, without baggage," he had once written to his wife, "can one truly get into the heart of the wilderness. All other travel is mere dust and hotels and baggage and chatter."

This book is not a guide to the wilderness, but to the half-devised landscape along its edges. What you will find in these pages, I hope, is dust and hotels and baggage and chatter—that these may in turn, along some road somewhere, provide glimpses of something else, something nourishing. "[E]ven if we never do more than drive to its edge and look in," wrote Wallace Stegner, back in the days (not so long ago) when lines were still being drawn around what was wild and what was not, ". . . it can be a means of reassuring ourselves of our sanity as creatures."

The preservation of the world—whatever that means, exactly—has yet to be determined. In the meantime, the wildness from which it may derive here awaits your pleasure in the Sierra Nevada and the Great Outback of California.

Cirrus plume from High Sierra over Death Valley. Note Mono Lake (top), thick forest belts on western slope, dry basin-and-range country to the east.   NASA

THE LAY OF THE LAND

The Southern Sierra is a vast region, held together mostly by its emptiness. By "Southern Sierra" I mean, somewhat arbitrarily, the mostly contiguous series of roadless areas from the northern boundary of Yosemite National Park, south along the highest parts of the range, some 250 miles, through Kings Canyon and Sequoia, to Walker Pass (the Tioga Road and Sherman Pass being closed in winter). From west to east I include the last access points in the Sierra Foothills, over the crest to the Owens River watershed, and the long rain shadow cast by Whitney and its fellows, to the Panamint Basin, Death Valley, and the Amargosa.

The Way This Book Works

. . . you may reach my country and find or not find, according as it lieth in you, much that is set down here. And more. The earth is no wanton to give up all her best to every comer, but keeps a sweet, separate intimacy for each.

—Mary Austin, Land of Little Rain, 1904

This book is divided into seven main chapters. The first aims to provide an overview of the natural and social history of the Southern Sierra, taken as a whole, as well as some contexts for understanding the place as it is today. The second chapter provides notes on means of transportation, weather, and climate considerations, and the logistics of getting there and getting around. There are five regional chapters, within each of which listings for lodging and points of interest are organized as much as possible according to a certain logic of geography—in other words, as you might come upon them, along the road, rather than in alphabetical order. For alphabetical reference use the index at the back of the book. Dining and food purveyors, on the other hand, wherever services are concentrated in one location, are listed alphabetically. An overview of recreational opportunities is provided at the end of each regional chapter, not as a detailed how-to guide but as an indication of where to get started. At the end of the book you will find the Information chapter, containing a detailed list of further reading, useful Internet resources, and contact information for a variety of visitors' services throughout the region.

Nuggets: At a site marked with the star symbol (✪), you will find something of significant historic and/or aesthetic value, worth traveling out of one's way for.

Prices

Prices for lodging are generally based on a per-room, double-occupancy rate at peak season. Peak season in Death Valley (November to April) is the opposite of peak season in Yosemite and Sequoia–Kings Canyon (Memorial Day to Labor Day). Prices are often significantly reduced during off-seasons. The peak in Mammoth Lakes comes during the two weeks around Christmas and New Year's, and over the Presidents' Day midwinter holiday, when prices are often double what they are during the rest of the year. The price code for lodging in Mammoth is based on an average nonholiday weekend rate. The dining code is based on the cost of a meal for one person, including an entrée and appetizer (or entrée and dessert) and a beverage. Tax and gratuities are not included.

Price Codes

	Lodging	Dining
Inexpensive	Up to $75	Up to $15
Moderate	$75 to $125	$15 to $30
Expensive	$125 to $200	$30 to $45
Very Expensive	Over $200	Over $45

"The Sierras" or "The Sierra"?

James Mason Hutchings, one of the earliest pioneers to set up business in the Yosemite Valley, and author of its first published guidebook, *Scenes of Wonder and Curiosity in California* (1862), habitually referred to these mountains as the "Sierras," following a long-standing tradition by which most other great and famous ranges—from the Rockies to the Smokies, from the Alps to the Andes to the Himalayas—are referred to in the plural. (California adds another tradition; appropriating original Spanish place names for their obvious romantic value, while ignoring their meaning. Thus have we inherited all manner of silly phrasings and redundancies; e.g., the La Brea Tar Pits, or the "the tar pit" tar pits.) Such habits prove hard to break. Joseph Starr King, another early promoter of the range; Joseph LeConte, one of the eminent patriarchs of the Sierra Club (note the singular form); Mary Austin; Teddy Roosevelt; Fred Eaton, of the great Los Angeles/Owens Valley land and water grab— all wrote of this collection of granite peaks as "the Sierras." The problem, alas, is that in pronouncing the word "Sierras" (plural), a person is saying "Ranges" in Spanish. And there is no disagreement that what we have here, however impressive, is but a single range: the *Sierra Nevada*, the Snowy Range, or as John Muir suggested, the "Range of Light." If it were multiple ranges it might have been called *Las Sierras Nevadas*. But it is not, and was not. Whitney had it right, and Muir, of course, and Ansel Adams. The Park and Forest Services these days generally get it right, and yet to this day it is not uncommon to overhear someone speaking of his or her latest fabulous weekend adventure in the "Sierras."

Acknowledgments

Anyone pretending to be a guide through wild and fabulous territory should know the territory. I wish I knew it better than I do. I am not Jed Smith. But Jed Smith is not available these days as a guide, and I am. I accept the duty, at least as much for what I may learn as for what I may be able to tell others.

—*Wallace Stegner*, Living Dry, *1987*

It was Lydia Prior who, by the innocent forwarding of an e-mail, planted the seed that would become a full-blown excuse to leave the city, uproot my family, and head for the High Sierra (not a moment too soon). I have since crossed paths with all manner of curious and extraordinary characters, each of whom shared with me, at one point or another—often without realizing it—his or her deeper sense of the place. These include but are by no means limited to: John Wentworth, Ed Laos, Fritz Bagget, Lindsay, Mike, Chris Miles, Andy Bourne, Jeremy, Joni, Nina Weissman, Robert Creasy, and quite a few others whose names I never got or couldn't hang on to. Eamon Briggs rallied me to get back up to Pear Lake, which proved a pivotal adventure. Paulette Helms got me to the season finale of Marta Becket's Sitting Down Show. Kenny Karst worked not a few small miracles in accommodations during the busiest season. As did Mona Mesereau. And Catherine Boire. Stacy Texara entertained us over dinner at the Tenaya Lodge. Linda Eade, having already organized the extensive collection of photos and materials at the Yosemite Research Library, made that part of life easy. Chris Langley made apparent the ghosts of Lone Pine. Brad Peatross and Laura Johnson helped track down rights and permissions for historic Mammoth photos. It was Burke Griggs who helped me pull the whole grand scheme together (in my head, anyway), mostly by sitting for 10 long days in the seat of a rental car, foil for my rants, sleeping little and taking many fine photographs along the way—for which images in the end, alas, there turned out to be unfortunately limited space. Sumell provided occasional, mostly healthy distraction. Allison did much tedious work sorting through and organizing hundreds of campground listings, and more importantly, for many months on end, covered my ass on every front. My mother, while sitting in the half-dark with her dying uncle, read many of these pages, and just when it was needed gave encouragement. My editors were patient above and beyond the call. My family and friends, willing or no, graciously tolerated my absence throughout. For a while I was on the road. And then I was not. "Whatcha doing, Daddy? Going to work?" said Jasper, age two, as daily I disappeared to the basement. And every time I came up for another cup of coffee, or another maté: "You done, Daddy?"

Now, yes, finally, for now, I have finished. Thanks.

P.S. For news, updates, and reader feedback, check www.sierrasurvey.com.

El Capitan, Yosemite National Park
Burke Griggs

CONTEXTS

Making the Range

No range among all the mountain chains which make up the Cordilleras of North America surpasses, if any one equals, the Sierra Nevada, in extent or altitude, and certainly no one on the continent can be compared with it in the general features of interest which characterize it—its scenery, vegetation, mines, the energy and skill with which its resources have been developed and the impetus which this development has given to commerce and civilization.

—Josiah D. Whitney, The Yosemite Book, *1868*

At just after 2:30 AM on March 26, 1872, anyone who had previously been asleep or otherwise about to doze off, anywhere near the Sierra Nevada—from, say, Winnemucca to Oakland, Los Angeles to Sacramento, in a bed, on the ground, or in the back of a freight wagon—was awakened by a rumbling in the earth, as of a train approaching.

Then the quake hit.

Clocks are said to have stopped as far away as San Diego. At the epicenter in the Owens Valley a crack opened in the earth that was 12 miles long. "Whether the land on the east was lowered or that on the west was raised no scientist ever took the trouble to announce," wrote local historian W. A. Chalfant in 1922, "but a difference of from four to twelve feet was made." Another fissure, between Big Pine and the base of the Sierra, measured "from fifty to 200 feet wide and twenty feet deep."

The shaking is said to have lasted for up to three minutes, at a magnitude now estimated between 7.4 and 8.3 on the Richter scale (comparable to the Great San Francisco Earthquake of 1906, which killed approximately 300,000 people). The aftershocks, some nearly as violent as the initial jolt, went on all night and into the next day, tapering off only over the course of the next few weeks.

Nearly every structure in the old pueblo of Lone Pine was leveled. Twenty-seven people were killed, mostly crushed by their own adobe-block houses. The original brick courthouse at Independence collapsed. One small lake disappeared; another was created. The course of the Owens River was shifted such that Bend City, site of the first county-constructed bridge across the river, was left standing on the bank of a dry wash. "Not far off," wrote Chalfant, "a horse's hoof protruding from the ground, where a crack had opened and then closed, gave reasonable inference as to where the rest of the animal might be found."

John Muir, working as winter caretaker at Black's Hotel in Yosemite Valley that winter, was one of the many shaken from his bed. "It was a calm moonlight night," he wrote, "and no sound was heard for the first minute or two save a low muffled underground rumbling and a slight rustling of the agitated trees." From behind one such tree he watched with delight as huge blocks of granite, 1,500 feet above him, gave way, shattered into thousands of smaller boulders, sparked and glowed with friction in the air, and crashed to the valley floor. "[I]f all the thunder I ever heard were condensed into one roar," he wrote, "it would not equal this rock roar at the birth of a mountain talus."

For two days the dust hung thick over the Sierra. An uncertain number of Lone Pine's dead—around 14, mostly Mexicans and Indians—were buried in a common grave on the north end of town. Without delay, the county of Inyo issued bonds, raised funds, and built—this time of wood harvested from the Sierra, instead of bricks—a new courthouse. On July 4, 1873, just 15 months after the great quake, the newly finished structure played host to "exercises of the greatest celebration the county had ever had."

NATURAL HISTORY

"The dynamics that have pieced together the whole of California have consisted of tens of thousands of earthquakes as great as that," writes John McPhee in *Assembling California,* "—tens of thousands of examples of what people like to singularize as 'the big one'—and many millions of earthquakes of lesser magnitude." As much as the earth beneath us is in any given moment the most solid and immoveable thing we know, or can imagine, it is, in fact, in constant motion. Every week, the U.S. Geological survey measures several hundred earthquakes in California alone. Of these only a handful will be felt by average citizens on the surface. Still, even as you read this, the plates beneath our elaborate system of roads and shopping malls and courthouses are shifting, pushing, and stretching; grinding against each other; building up and releasing pressure; bulging and subsiding and cracking at the seams. Here at the place where the state of California meets the state of Nevada, where at a distance of less than 80 miles the granite atop Mount Whitney has recently been lifted to a height of nearly 15,000 feet above the cracked salt pan at the bottom of Death Valley, the mountain- and basin-building that began more than 200 million years ago—the most dramatic of which has likely occurred within the last 3 or 4 million years—is still very much under way.

The Paiute Indians, who nowadays live in one of the driest places on the planet (the Owens Valley) and make the bulk of their communal income by the operation of a casino and gas station in the town of Bishop, are said to have an old story in which, once upon a time, the world was all water. "At that time," so the story goes, according to Chalfant, "the Great Wolf God, the God of Creation, with the assistance of his little brother or son, the coyote, planted the rock seeds in the great water, and from them the rocks and land grew." On the other side of the range, the Yokuts tell a similar tale with a different cast of characters: "Falcon and Crow," they say, according to historian David Beesley, "took some of the earth brought up by Duck from the mud beneath the primeval floodwaters . . . and as they flew they scattered grains of soil and told them to become mountains." Falcon made the

Eastern scarp of the Sierra Nevada from Lone Pine. In March 1872 the range lifted an average of 30 feet in less than three days. Burke Griggs

California coastal range, and Crow, who had somehow managed to get more dirt, made the Sierra Nevada.

A version told by contemporary geologists is not wholly at odds with these earlier tales, at least insofar as the primeval abundance of water is concerned. For most of the Triassic period—from, say, 240 to 200 million years ago, in the days when the first small dinosaurs were just starting to pop up amid the Big Trees, and Pangaea was only just beginning to consider subdividing into Gondwanaland and Laurasia—the coastline of what we now think of as North America ran right down the middle of Nevada. Out there to the west of Vegas, out beyond the sandy beaches, there was nothing: no California, no Paiutes or Yokuts, no nuclear test sites or proposed waste dumps, no Sierra Nevada, no Yosemite—just open water. The great ancestral Pacific Ocean.

Then came the Pacific plate crashing headlong into the North American. (And here the story diverges from the earlier traditions: it would be another 25 million years, it turns out, before the first proto-falcons and crows appeared on Earth; many millions more before wolves and coyotes.) There was some crumpling, of course, and raising of mountains to the east, on the continent, and accretion to the erstwhile seashore of considerable amounts of material—islands and such, ocean floor, crust, a whole mess of material formerly of the terrane Sonomia, of the Pacific plate—material which today makes up the

Exfoliating granite, Marble Fork of the Kaweah, Sequoia National Park Burke Griggs

oldest rocks in Death Valley. But the Pacific plate itself, having apparently nowhere else to go, dove eastward beneath the North American. Or, to look at it another way, the North American plowed westward, right over the top of the Pacific.

The friction created by such a move—geologists call it subduction—caused no small amount of melted rock between the two plates. This stuff—red-hot, highly pressurized magma of the sort one sees in *National Geographic* photo spreads, flowing and splashing from the vents on Kilauea in Hawaii—tried its best to get out into the air. And in some places it did, piling up huge volcanoes—"Stratovolcanoes," writes McPhee, "Kilimanjaros and Fujis," of an ancient California range, a range which in those days more closely resembled the Cascades than the present Sierra. The bulk of the stuff, however, rose beneath the surface in great trapped bubbles that together cooled and crystallized—like (to borrow an image) so many stale marshmallows in a bag. The result: the so-called batholith—150,000 cubic miles of plutonic igneous rock, the famously enormous and complex mass of granite (granodiorite) that today makes up the core, and most of the surface, of the Sierra Nevada.

One hundred and thirty million years of steady erosion later, the once-towering volcanic mountains at the edge of the North American continent had been worn down to a series of low, fertile rolling hills, thickly forested with ancestral cedars, redwood, and giant sequoia. The dinosaurs had begun to die off (coincidentally), and in places the batholith was starting to show through. From high inland plateaus, westward to the coastal plains, wide prehistoric rivers carried gravels laden with gold. Then suddenly the Pacific plate, still shoveling along under the North American but at a considerably diminished pace—having already piled up material enough to make the rest of California all the way to San Francisco—seems to have taken a hit, broadside. Or in any case to have changed direction. This was some 60 million years before the present.

At the margin between the two plates, the basic movement changed from subduction to a so-called strike-slip motion. Rather than the one plate sliding beneath the other (or the other pushing up over the top of the one), the two now ground against each other side-by-side like clashing half-stripped gears, the Pacific plate driving generally northward, the North American doing its best to push south. The result was drag, a build-up of pressure, and a sometimes-gradual, sometimes-violent stretching out of the western edge of the North American continent.

Across what we now call the Great Basin the crust began to pull apart, literally at the seams. Like cracks in an old fan belt, great rifts opened up—rift after rift after rift—valleys flat as elevator platforms dropping thousands of feet toward the level of the sea. At fault scarps along the rift edges, blocks of the original crust—now ridges made of old bedrock and the metamorphic stuff above it—thrust upward and tilted back like giant ship's hatches opening from below. From east to west into the slow-rising rubble the old rivers cut new and ever-deeper V-shaped canyons until they could no longer keep up; until they were cut off by the rising walls and rerouted. On the western slopes of the westernmost ranges, these rivers left only vast deposits of gravel as evidence of their passage—detritus of ancient, gold-rich beds—thereafter to be dredged by glaciers, sifted through by snowmelt creeks, and, finally, in the second half of the 19th century, to be called the Mother Lode and hauled off from the top down by assiduous hordes of prospectors and the increasingly industrial mining operations in their wake.

But it would be at least 3.5 million years, maybe more, before anyone was to see the glint of precious metal in the sunlight. In the meantime—so the story goes—the old Pacific plate once again altered its course, this time by 11 degrees to the northeast. The mechanics and timing of it all is still hotly contested. The results are undeniable: "The tectonic effect on North America," writes McPhee, "was something like the deformation that occurs when two automobiles sideswipe."

Volcanic hot spots of the sort that form island archipelagos began to migrate, punching holes through miles of crust and granite, spewing ash, leaking carbon dioxide and super-heated water, spilling magma to cool as andesite and basalt and obsidian—from Mono Hot Springs to Mammoth Mountain to Paoha Island in the middle of Mono Lake. Without much recorded ado—other than, say, the recent leveling and rearranging of Lone Pine—the Sierra Nevada, with its colossal heart of granite, crumpled upward nearly halfway to the jet stream. Erosion did its best, meanwhile, to crack apart the rocks, to wear them down even as they lifted. Clouds caught in the crest, gathering ever more snow and rain to feed the rivers along the western flank, while to the east, in the shadow of the new range, from the Owens all the way to the Great Salt Lake, and southeast across the Mojave, once verdant valleys dried up.

SOCIAL HISTORY

The First Pioneers

They came from the north, with families and dogs and all manner of equipment in tow. Their ancestors had traveled across the old Bering Land Bridge. (Had they seen the camels headed the other direction?) Season by season they multiplied, split into groups, sepa-rated, explored, learned which plants were poisonous, which salubrious, which could be counted on to intoxicate, which made the color red, which blue. They invented new ways to hunt, found water, made structures to sleep in from local materials, ate, had babies, mourned their dead, drew pictures on the rocks, named local landmarks, made up new languages and recipes (and lost track of the old ones), told stories about where they'd come from and where they were headed, sang, danced, played instruments, followed the herds. Season by season, without much need to consider the possible utility of the wheel, they made their way south.

Then one day, some ten thousand years ago, one of these people, traveling alone or with

Indian Bark House, Yosemite Valley, 1887 Taber Photo, courtesy NPS, YNP

a group of associates, became the first human being to gape upward at the Sierra Nevada.

The latest ice age had come and gone. Glaciers had piled up in the crevices between the peaks, had spilled down into the old V-shaped valleys, scooping them out, polishing their granite ribs, driving their crusty innards out onto the basins below in broad, damlike arcs of broken debris—and then had retreated. Where the glaciers had been there now tumbled clear perennial streams. There were lakes and waterfalls, rivers impossible to ford in springtime, tall-grass meadows ringed with granite domes, and deep forested canyons. All up and down the range, and east into the drier country, there were top-notch campsites for winter and summer. There was an abundance of game—deer, elk, antelope, rabbit, squirrel, quail, duck, partridge, turkey, golden and cutthroat trout, and so on—and for the making of spear and arrow points, the best obsidian anyone had ever seen. There were acorns in the foothills, for milling into flour; there were sturdy reeds for making arrow shafts and weaving into baskets; there were sweet berries, lettuce, wild grapes, and tobacco. There were hot springs to soak in on a cold night. The bugs, the snakes, and even the grizzly bears were eminently reasonable. And there was firewood to last until the end of time.

It wasn't long, of course, before the word got out.

Pretty soon there were people everywhere. There were people camped out above the shores of Mono Lake. There were people all along the Owens River, from June and Mammoth Lakes to Indian Wells, some in permanent villages. There were people living on the shores of an ancient lake in Death Valley, and later, when things dried up, at the springs at Saline and Furnace Creek. There were people at Darwin Falls and in the canyons above Ridgecrest—on land now reserved for the testing of weapons by the U.S. Navy. There were people up every fork of the Kern, every fork of the Tule, every fork of the Kaweah. There were people who passed their winters in bark huts in the foothills, their summers under the stars in Kings Canyon—or at Mono Hot Springs, or in the Valley of Yosemite, or at Hetch Hetchy—people who when the snow melted hiked up over well-worn paths to trade with the sometimes-friendly folks on the other side: acorns for pine nuts; arrow shafts for obsidian; lake perch for Lahontan trout; deerskins for salt.

There were quarrels, raids, and reprisals. There were territorial disputes. There were wars and drought and periods of hunger. People died, were afraid, got sad. But there were great feasts, too, and marriages and dances and games in the woods—games (by the description of A. L. Kroeber) "in which not sticks and luck, but the tensest of wills, the keenest perceptions and the supplest of muscular responses are matched." They built permanent roundhouses for ceremonies. They learned to use fire to clear the woods of brush, to propagate the black oaks across the foothills, to improve forage for deer, to make travel easier. Each month brought a return of the full moon. Each year brought a new crop of acorns, a new crop of pine nuts and blackberries, a fresh run of salmon up the San Joaquin.

Alta California

When Francisco Vásquez de Coronado wandered into Kansas in the early 1540s, looking for the Seven Cities of Gold, he carried with him a sense of geography that generally held California to be an island "on the right hand of the Indies," abounding with "gold and precious stones" and populated entirely by robust black women. Why Coronado did not endeavor to go there, instead of Kansas, is mostly a factor of his having been misled by a local guide. There was not a single city of gold upon the Great Plains, of course, nor riches of any sort that Coronado could see. He overlooked the buffalo herds and the farmland,

Fire

Maria Lebrado, granddaughter of Chief Tenaya, was among the last of the Ahwahneechee to be marched out of Yosemite by the Mariposa Batallion. She was 10 years old. Seventy-eight years later, in July 1929, she returned—and was less than pleased to see the way the place had been maintained. "Two young men drove us over the Valley she had not seen since her childhood," recorded her companion. "The wide open meadow of her day was covered with trees and shrubs. She shook her head, saying, 'Too dirty; too much bushy.'"

For thousands of years the Sierra tribes had practiced a regimen of annual controlled burning, thereby creating what John Muir would describe as "the inviting openness of the Sierra woods." The Park Service now estimates "that historically an average of 16,000 of Yosemite's 747,000 acres may have burned under natural conditions in the park each year." Beginning in the late 1850s, the valley's new caretakers, James Hutchings and others, planted orchards, cultivated gardens, built fences and hotels, and, for obvious reasons, did their utmost both to keep fires from starting and to keep those that had started naturally (i.e., by lightning) from spreading.

The U.S. Forest Service was established in 1905 by Teddy Roosevelt, with Gifford Pinchot as the first Chief Forester. "Since 1910," wrote Norman Maclean in *Young Men and Fire,* "much of the history of the Forest Service can be translated into a succession of efforts to get firefighters on fires as soon as possible."

By the early 1960s, decades of diligent and institutional fire suppres-

Prescribed burn, West Yosemite Valley, June 2007

sion had effectively removed fire from the scenario, the result of which, over time, was denser forests and "as much as 75–90% of meadows . . . lost to tree encroachment." The build-up of debris and underbrush—so-called ladder fuels—also created the potential for larger, more dangerous "crown" fires than had existed in earlier, tidier forests. "Today much of the west slope is a dog-hair thicket of young pines, white fir, incense-cedar, and mature brush," reported Park Service scientist A. Starker Leopold in 1963, "—a direct function of overprotection from natural ground fires."

In 1968 the Park Service designated 600,000 acres of Sequoia-Kings Canyon a natural fire zone, where wildfires are monitored but generally allowed to run their course. A prescribed fire program was initiated in Yosemite two years later, in 1970, and starting in 1972 naturally ignited wildland fires in the higher elevations were allowed to burn. Prescribed burning is now a common sight throughout the parks, in Giant Sequoia National Monument, and in some areas under the management of the Forest Service.

Giant sequoias are especially fire adapted: their bark is fire-resistant; fire aids in the opening of their cones and the scattering of their seeds, and keeps at bay competitive species.

and missed the petroleum reserves. He ordered his guide garroted on the banks of the muddy Arkansas and turned around for home.

Coronado made it back to Mexico City not much improved for the effort but with a much clearer notion—gleaned from another of his more trustworthy guides—of the "low sandy country" to the west. "[T]hat peninsula which was formerly held to be an island," wrote one of the expedition's most thorough chroniclers, ". . . is inhabited by brutish, bestial, naked people who eat their own offal. The men and women couple like animals, the female openly getting down on all fours."

It was another 230 years before the Spanish managed to establish missions at San Diego (1769) and Monterey (1770). The goal, by then, was not so much to find gold, but to muster as many tax-paying, Castilian-speaking, Church-fearing bodies in Alta California as possible—mostly to keep the Russians from acting on any territorial ambitions they may have had in the region—even if the only bodies available at the time were of the native "brutish, bestial, naked" variety.

In October 1775, Lt. Col. Juan de Anza, having already proved the feasibility of crossing overland from Mexico to the new mission at Monterey, undertook a second such expedition with a group of missionaries and colonists. By the beginning of April they stood, haggard and exhausted, at the crest of Tejon Pass (somewhere above what is now I-5). They looked out across the vast Tulare Lake (formerly the largest freshwater lake west of the Missouri, now mostly fields of cotton and rice and alfalfa) and saw some very big mountains. "[A]t a distance of about forty leagues," wrote friar Pedro Font, "we saw a great snow-covered range [*"una gran sierra nevada"*] whose trend appeared to me to be from south-southeast to north-northwest." It was more a vague description than a name, but there it was, written down in a diary and on a map: the future name of a best-selling microbrewed pale ale.

Sierra tribes are said to have had a highly efficient system of relays for communication of news and important information. Later, Indian Field Days became a popular feature for tourists. Telles family album, courtesy NPS, YNP

There were in those days anywhere from 30,000 to a quarter million so-called Indians living in the valley of the San Joaquin and in the foothills of the Sierra, beyond the direct influence of the growing Spanish settlements on the coast. The Spaniards did make occasional military forays into the wilds of the interior, at first for purposes of exploration and recruitment, then increasingly to bring back *indios* who had run away from the padres at the missions. ("They [the Indians] have no knowledge of benefits received," lamented one Spanish writer in 1822, "and ingratitude is common amongst them.") Whatever the purpose, it was in the course of such outings that many of the rivers flowing from the western slope of the Sierra received their names: the San Joaquin, the Calaveras, the Plumas (Feather), the Merced, el Río de los Santos Reyes (Kings). The Spaniards showed little interest in penetrating the range itself, preferring to let it stand as an imagined impenetrable barrier to the French and Americans, still a very dry continent away on the other side.

After the whole of California was ceded to Mexico in 1821, the "unconquered tribes" in the Central Valley began, with greater frequency, to organize expeditions of their own in the other direction, westward to the coast—to, in the words of one contemporary observer, "plunder the farms of the colonists of horses, which they [the natives] eat in preference to beef." These raids were often met with fierce vigilante-style reprisals. "[T]he last expedition which the citizens of this town made to the tulares," complained the Governor of Monterey in 1835, "they committed various atrocities against the heathen Indians without distinguishing between the innocent and the guilty. In addition to stealing their ornaments and personal effects they [the citizens] took away seven small boys to serve them and act as slaves, without informing this government of the occurrences."

The Pathfinders

Late in the summer of 1826, at the age of 27, Jedediah Strong Smith set out southwesterly from the Big Salt Lake in search of a new source of beaver. He took with him 15 men, a cavalcade of pack horses, a month's supply of dried buffalo meat, traps, guns, powder, lead, and the usual assortment of gifts for the Indians. There were no roads in those days—only game trails, rivers, and the ancient footpaths of the first people. The best map available was Robinson's *Map of Mexico, Louisiana, & the Missouri Territory &c.* (1814), the western portion of which represented little more than a challenging compendium of extrapolations and fanciful imaginings.

Smith and his men marched from one thin water source to the next. Across the great deserts they navigated by dead reckoning and intuition, often by the light of the moon. They chewed "slips of the Cabbage Pear," dug holes in the sand to sleep in, and not infrequently resorted to eating their mounts. For traveling without passports in Mexican territory (and suspected of spying for the U.S. government), they spent all of December and much of January under house arrest at Mission San Gabriel—within strolling distance of the pueblo of Los Angeles.

The primary condition of their release by the Mexican governor was that they head back across the deserts from whence they had come. Instead, they cut northeast, crossing the Antelope Valley and over into the San Joaquin by way of Tehachapi. There, in the cottonwoods along the lower stretches of the Kings River, they found what they'd been looking for.

During the first week of May, in an attempt to get 60 horses and 1,500 pounds of beaver back across the range in a snowstorm—without snowshoes—Smith lost five horses and came very close to losing it all. He turned around and left the bulk of his party and all his furs at an encampment in the foothills, to be retrieved, he hoped, the following year. On

In the days before Gore-Tex From In the Heart of the Sierras by J. M. Hutchings (1886)

the 20th he set out again, this time with "two men, seven horses and two mules." They made the east side in eight days, to become the first white men ever to cross the High Sierra—in either direction, and in any season. "I found the snow on the top of the mountain from four to eight feet deep," wrote Smith, "but it was so consolidated by the heat of the sun that my horses only sunk from half a foot to one foot deep."

Only two horses and a mule were lost in the crossing. The rest starved or otherwise succumbed during the long, dry trudge across the basins and ranges of what would one day be Nevada and Utah. When Smith finally dragged into the rendezvous, alone, the day before Independence Day, 1827—11 months and more than 2,000 miles later—he was riding a horse he'd borrowed that morning from a Snake Indian. His business associates, having long ago given him up for lost, loaded "a small Cannon [sic] brought up from St. Louis" and fired a salute.

Ten days later he was back on the trail. Two years later, having lost another 25 men in two separate Indian massacres, he again bargained his way out of prison (this time in Monterey), narrowly avoided extradition to Mexico City, forded countless swollen rivers, outran two grizzlies, and trapped and slogged his way through month after month of mud and sheeting rain as far north as the Columbia River, only to have his few remaining beaver pelts judged by the Hudson's Bay Company representative at Fort Vancouver "of very bad quality the worst indeed I ever saw." After all this, at age 30, he set off once again, eastward, broke as ever, and as ever full of optimism, for the summer rendezvous in Utah.

Water and Power

On a good year—the sort of year that brings a full 2 inches of precipitation to Death Valley—anywhere from 50 to 80 inches will hit the Sierra Nevada, which is nearly double what falls on Seattle or Boston. Average annual precipitation in the Los Angeles Basin, by contrast, is less than 12 inches—about the same as Tucson, Arizona—while San Francisco, with less than 22, was once upon a time, not that long ago, as parched as Odessa, Texas. More than 80 percent of annual precipitation in the Sierra comes down between November and April, in the form of snow. The most snow ever recorded in a single season was 884 inches (73.7 feet) at Tamarack Station, north of Yosemite, in 1906–7. In 1933, 5 feet of snow fell in 24 hours at Giant Forest in Sequoia National Park. A record 51.5 feet fell on Mammoth Mountain during the 1992–93 season, bringing an abrupt end to a six-year drought. In 2005–6 the bar was raised to 52.5 feet. The ski lifts ran through July 4th.

The Tuolomne River below the O'Shaughnessy Dam, Hetch Hetchy, Yosemite National Park

In the old days, in wet years, spring would come, the snow would melt, the great rivers and valleys would flood—on the west side all the way to the San Francisco Bay; on the east to Owens Lake—and by the end of summer everything but the Tule marshes and the highest alpine basins would be dry. And the groundwater recharged. Years of flood were followed by years of drought were followed by years of flood. Overall, the last two centuries are thought to have been the wettest in four thousand years.

By the early 1850s, miners had begun to tap into seasonal runoff by way of flumes and hoses, making jets of water powerful enough to reduce whole mountainsides to washed gravel. Flumes were built to transport cut logs to downstream lumber mills. By the 1860s farmers were already taking advantage of state and federal subsidies to "reclaim" seasonal swampland in the Central Valley. Dikes were built, and levees to control flooding; more and improved flumes brought greater volumes of Sierra runoff into canals and irrigation ditches, and from there into the fields. Citrus groves were planted in the bottomlands of the San Joaquin, and eventually, down the line, cotton, alfalfa, and rice. In 1898 the Mount Whitney Power and Electric Company began work on a flume to deliver water from the East Fork of the Kaweah to three 440-volt belt-driven generators at its Kaweah Power House No. 1, followed by a series of small dams above Mineral King (to regulate flow through the drier months). Farmers in the San Joaquin converted their old gas or steam-powered well pumps to electric, and as part of the deal had their homes wired for electric light.

As populations boomed, so too did the demand for water. Water to make electricity, to irrigate crops and lawns, to wash cars and dishes and driveways; water for drinking, for swimming and soaking in, for the flushing of toilets, for the making of coffee and concrete and the refining of petroleum. Enterprising ranchers acquired rights to millions of acre-feet of Sierra runoff on both sides of the range, then sold those rights to consolidated utilities like Southern California Edison, or to industrial-sized cotton and rice growers, or to the ever-thirstier cities on the coast. To mitigate periodic cycles of flood and drought, big guns like the Army Corps of Engineers and the Bureau of Reclamation, together with the California Department of Water, the Los Angeles Department of Water and Power, and the San Francisco Public Utilities Commission, over the course of a half century built the largest, most complex, most costly system of water distribution ever conceived.

Old flume on Tule River, above Springville Burke Griggs

Today 60 percent of the water used by Californians comes from the Sierra Nevada, most of it from watersheds protected by national parks and wilderness areas. There are dams on every major river and tributary in the range. There are siphons and forebays, pumping stations, storage basins, and pipelines. Eighty-five percent of San Francisco's drinking water travels 165 miles from the Hetch Hetchy reservoir in Yosemite National Park. Forty percent of Los Angeles's supply comes by way of a 223-mile aqueduct from the upper Owens River watershed. The largest single user of electrical energy in California—some of it produced by hydroelectric generators at the foot of the Sierra—is the State Water Project (SWP), which brings water from the Feather River 444 miles by aqueduct across the San Joaquin valley, then pumps it 2,000 feet up over Tehachapi Pass to Los Angeles and other coastal cities. Meanwhile, according to National Public Radio, "fully one quarter of the food America eats" is grown in the Central Valley of California, almost entirely with water from the Sierra Nevada.

On a fair year the Sierra makes its quota, sending down about 42 million acre-feet of runoff. And still, after every series of wet years, engineering notwithstanding, comes a series of dry. On April 1, 1977, during the driest season ever recorded in California—drier even than the notorious Dust Bowl of the early 1930s—a local snow survey found "only about ten inches of water on the Mammoth Pass snow pillow." By midsummer there were statewide shortages in hydroelectric power; irrigation pumps in the Central Valley were bringing up air; the land was subsiding again (had subsided by as much as 30 feet in some places since 1925). Even the City of Los Angeles began rationing its water. The following year brought one of the Sierra's top 10 wettest winters in recorded history—20 feet in back-to-back storm cycles by mid-January—and all was forgotten. That is, until the next drought hit in 1987.

That it had been done did not necessarily make it easier for those who followed. The autumn of 1833, for example, saw Joseph R. Walker and "a division of more than seventy men" trudging across the Sierra from east to west, along the old Mono Trail, "surrounded by snow and rugged peaks—the vigour of every man almost exhausted—nothing to give our poor horses, which were no longer any assistance to us in traveling, but a burthen [sic], for we had to help the most of them along as we would an old and feeble man." Not a few of these faithful beasts were butchered and eaten beside the trail. The discovery of some rather enormous trees, the biggest anyone had ever seen, and likely white man's first distant glimpse of Yosemite (from above) was all of very little consolation. Before they could finally consider themselves through the worst of it, their surviving animals had still to be lowered—one at a time, by ropes—down a sheer rock face to the valley below.

On the way back Walker pioneered a much easier, if longer, route around the southern end of the range, from the Kern River to the Mojave. A decade later, John C. Frémont and Kit Carson, heeding the advice of no one—except perhaps that they should bring snow-shoes—made the next full-scale midwinter run at the range. It was a comparatively mild season, and still it took them more than a month to punch through to the other side. To the snowdrifts and the stew pot they gave up more than half of their 67 horses and mules.

"We had tonight an extraordinary dinner," wrote Frémont in his journal on February 13, 1844, "—pea soup, mule, and dog."

"I should not mind," wrote the party's mapmaker (and former rider of said unlucky mule), "if we only had salt."

The Allure of the Shortcut: Wave I

By the mid-1840s, even the fastest-rising mountain range on the planet could not resist the westering impulse of the United States of America. The word was out. "The climate," wrote one of California's first great promoters, Lansford W. Hastings, "is that of perpetual spring, having no excess of heat or cold . . . fuel is never required for any other than culi-nary purposes." He remarked at great length about the abundance of game, the "innumer-able, and inexhaustible" fisheries, the way in which herds of domestic animals "require neither feeding nor housing," the year-round growing season, the variety of crops, the incomparable productivity of the land, and so on. "The deep, rich, alluvial soil of the Nile, in Egypt," he wrote, "does not afford a parallel."

All that could be said against the place was that it was not easy to get to, and that it was under the control of the Mexicans. Given the States' annexation of Texas in 1845 and President Polk's subsequent declaration of war against Mexico (May 1846), the latter problem seemed not much of a problem at all, and it was likely to be resolved sooner rather than later. The former problem—that of getting there—could be overcome. All that was required was some decent planning, fair leadership, the proper equipment, a certain amount of innate capability, delusions of grandeur, extraordinary physical fitness, strength of character (or complete lack of scruples), time, money, patience, the very best of luck, and, of course, a modicum of reliable information.

Hastings had made the journey out and back in '43 and '44, had witnessed the prosper-ity and potential at Johann Sutter's "New Helvetia" (now Sacramento), had dined and dis-cussed routes with John C. Frémont, and by the following year had typed up and published the voluminous *Emigrants' Guide to California and Oregon*. "[P]erhaps nobody will see him here again," wrote Sutter, "as his life will be in danger about his book, making out California a paradise, even some of the Emigrants in the Valley, threatened his life." Aside

Snow slide on Tioga Road, June 25, 1942   R. H. Anderson, courtesy NPS, YNP

from all the breathless descriptions of the country, the book also offered some eminently practical information. It was advised, for example, that the traveler leave behind feather beds and other such cumbersome luxuries, and that he provision himself with, at the very least, "a good gun," an ample supply of powder and lead, "two hundred pounds of flour, or meal; one hundred and fifty pounds of bacon; ten pounds of coffee; twenty pounds of sugar; and ten pounds of salt." For the conveyance of such stores, Hastings recommended a sturdy wagon, with tires recently reset, and a team of oxen (rather than horses or mules). "Oxen endure the fatigue and heat much better," he wrote, "[and] are not liable to be stolen by the Indians." He neglected to mention how they might taste if it came down to eating them.

Hastings's most important piece of advice, given almost in passing, was that all parties should be sure to put Independence, Missouri, well behind them by the first of May—"after which time they should never start, if it can possibly be avoided." The journey required at least 120 days, give or take a few weeks, and by now the lesson had sunk in: The Sierra Nevada should not be crossed in winter.

The Donners and Reeds had left on time, in April of 1846, as had some 2,700 other pioneers. The traffic on the road that year—some sections of the trail could now fairly be called a road—included such notables as Jim Bridger and Joseph R. Walker; a former governor of Missouri; a future founder of the Pony Express; a man who was to become known as the discoverer of Yosemite; Joan Didion's great-great-great-grandparents; a talented mapmaker who may or may not have been the bastard son of Thomas Jefferson; several journalists and best-selling authors-to-be; and, of course, Lansford W. Hastings himself.

Hastings was eager to try out a new shortcut—one he had likely gleaned from his conversations with Frémont. "The most direct route," Hastings proposed in his book, "would be to leave the Oregon route about two hundred miles east from Fort Hall; thence bearing west southwest to the Salt lake; and thence continuing down to the bay of St. Francisco." At Fort Bridger, Wyoming, he met up with a party comprised of some 75 wagons and proceeded to lead them along what would soon become known, rather infamously, as the Hastings Cutoff. It proved to be no shortcut at all.

Hastings and party encountered no end of unfortunate difficulty and delay but nevertheless made it safely to California. The Donner Party, on the other hand, having arrived at Fort Bridger two days after Hastings's departure (because of a broken axle) had a much rougher go of it. Struggling over the Wasatch range, pioneering yet another "shortcut" to the great Salt Lake, they fell another three weeks behind. By the time the motley assemblage of 87 exceedingly unlucky pioneers made the east side of the Sierra, in late October, it was snowing hard. They cut timber, built cabins, slaughtered their starving oxen, boiled the hides for sustenance, and dug in for the winter. It kept snowing.

By mid-December 15 starving men had set out to cross the range on snowshoes. The snowpack was more than 20 feet deep. Only seven made it into Sutter's Fort on January 18, having survived on the flesh of their fallen companions.

Between February and March three separate rescue parties managed to bring 40 more survivors over the mountains. The fourth and last "relief"—a salvage operation motivated at least in part by the possibility of recovering some of the Donners' reputedly considerable stash of gold and jewels—reached the first of the cabins a little past noon on April 17. What they found was "human bodies terribly mutilated" (including those of George and Tamsen Donner) and all manner of "sights from which we would have fain turned away, and which are too dreadful to put on record." Beside a pan containing what may have been

The Corps & the Sierra

Franklin Roosevelt was inaugurated President of the United States on March 4, 1933. Within five days he called an Emergency Session of the 73rd Congress and proposed the establishment of a "peace-time army" comprised of thousands of unemployed men, "to relieve the acute condition of wide-spread distress and unemployment existing in the United States, provide for the restoration of the country's depleted natural resources, and advance an orderly program of useful public works." On April 5, less than a month after taking office, with full support from both houses of Congress, Roosevelt declared the Emergency Conservation Work Act, better known as the Civilian Conservation Corps (CCC). The first enrollees were inducted on April 7. The Department of Labor handled enroll-ment, the Departments of Interior and Agriculture cooperated on planning and organization; the U.S. Army, with assistance from the Coast Guard, the Navy, the Marines, and the National Park Service, provided leadership and logistical support.

By October 1933, four hundred corpsmen (two companies) had arrived in Death Valley. Other com-panies established camps in locations across the southern Sierra, in Sequoia-Kings and Yosemite National Parks, with 10 camps in Yosemite alone. Corpsmen worked for a dollar a day through tours of six months. Of $30 per month, $25 was sent home to

CCC boys erecting new cables on Half Dome, May 1934 R. H. Anderson, courtesy NPS, YNP

families. The men kept $5. They graded hundreds of miles of roads and built campgrounds, view-points, restrooms, and picnic facilities. They made signs, built and improved trails, developed wells and springs, laid water mains, and strung telephone lines. They wore uniforms and slept in canvas-walled barracks. They removed invasive plants from Sierra meadows, brought historic apple trees back to life, fought fires, carved log benches, and built rock walls. Their handiwork is to this day in evi-dence throughout the region: in the tight switchbacks on CA 190 into the Panamint Valley, in the stonework along the Generals Highway in Sequoia, in the tunnels on the High Sierra Trail, the handrails at Moro Rock, the access stairs to Crystal Cave and the cables on Half Dome, in the trails and Ski House at Badger Pass, and in the backcountry huts at Ostrander and Pear Lakes.

With a general decline in unemployment, by the beginning of the 1940s the program's popularity had begun to wane. The bombing of Pearl Harbor in December 1941 fixed attention elsewhere, and the remaining corpsmen were among the first to go to war. In the summer of 1942 Congress passed a final appropriation of $8 million dollars for the CCC—to fund its liquidation.

young Landrum Murphy's liver reclined a well-fed but half-deranged Louis Keseburg, the party's last remaining survivor. "On his person," wrote one of the rescuers, "they discovered a brace of pistols recognized to be those of George Donner, and, while taking them from him, discovered something concealed in his waistcoat which on being opened was found to be $225 in gold."

The Allure of the Shortcut: Wave II

Gold is said to have been the first metal used by humans. Banked by Akkadian emperors, described in Egyptian hieroglyphics as early as 2100 B.C., gold—before coffee—was what got conquistadors out of their hammocks in the morning. On the morning of January 24, 1848, less than three hundred years after Coronado died bankrupt and disappointed in Mexico City, eight months after a nightmare-hounded Louis Keseburg was hauled into Sutter's Fort, one week before the signing of the Treaty of Guadalupe Hidalgo (by which California and most of the southwest was ceded to the United States), a fellow by the name of James Marshall, contractor on one of Sutter's sawmills, looked down at a newly eroded bank of Eocene gravels along the American River and saw what he knew "to be nothing else."

In its May 29 issue, the *Californian* reported—despite Sutter's best efforts to keep the whole thing under wraps—that "the whole country from San Francisco to Los Angeles, and from the sea shore to the base of the Sierra Nevadas [sic], resounds with the sordid cry of 'Gold, gold, gold!' while the field is left half-planted, the house half built, and everything neglected but the manufacture of shovels and pickaxes." On August 18, by way of the brig *J.R.S.*, the news reached Valparaiso, Chile. It made the *New York Herald* the following day. "The accounts of abundance of gold are of such an extraordinary character as would scarcely command belief," wrote President Polk in a December 5 message to Congress,

The voyage around Cape Horn took upwards of four months and cost about $300. "The greatest objections which can be urged against traveling by this route," wrote Lansford Hastings, "are the unpleasant, cheerless monotony, and the irksome confinement incident to this method of traveling." Courtesy Bancroft Library

THE " PRAIRIE SCHOONER."

In a pinch, mules made better eating than oxen. They were also favored by the Indians. From *In the Heart of the Sierras* by J. M. Hutchings (1886)

"were they not corroborated by the authentic reports of officers in the public service."

By late spring the overland trail had become a traffic jam of lumbering, ox-drawn wagon trains, thousands of vehicles long, together bearing westward as many as 35,000 "dreamers of the golden dream." Between April and November 697 ships arrived at the settlement of San Francisco, the nonnative population of which had recently been reported at "575 males, 177 females and 60 children." By the end of 1849 as many as one hundred thousand so-called Argonauts had made their way to California, by land, by sea, or by some combination, from as far away as Europe, China, and Australia.

One loose confederation of more than a hundred wagons, calling itself the "Sandwalking Company," had set out from Salt Lake City around the first of October. It being so late in the season, and with the horrors of the Donner Party still so fresh in everyone's mind, the plan had been to follow the Old Spanish Trail southwest, via the springs at Las Vegas, to the new Mormon settlement at San Bernardino—thus avoiding the Sierra Nevada entirely. A veteran of the Mormon Battalion by the name of Capt. Jefferson Hunt had agreed, at a rate of $10 to $12 per wagon, to show them the way.

The pace was not what everyone had hoped. On the road and in camp at night there was much discussion and back-and-forth concerning the relative merits and risks of yet another semimythical shortcut someone had heard about in Salt Lake City. The Williams Cutoff, as it was called, was said to be a straight shot west across the desert to Walker Pass— some 500 miles shorter than going around by San Bernardino. Five hundred miles! At 10 miles a day, they might be spared nearly two months. (Or gain two months on all the others.) Captain Hunt was skeptical, but it was the kind of thing that worked on folks' minds. America herself had, after all, been discovered in the trying-out of a possible shortcut.

Two weeks out, at a camp on Little Salt Lake, the train was overtaken by a smaller party under the direction of a Captain Smith. Smith was bound for the Williams Cutoff. He had with him a map, or a copy of a map, likely drawn from information furnished by Frémont. It seemed pretty convincing. The next morning he and his party were off with Godspeed to the goldfields—never to be heard from again. Three days later, at the place where Smith's tracks diverged from the main trail, there occurred something of a reckoning. "It was really a serious matter," wrote William Lewis Manly, of the Bennett-Arcane party. "Team after team turned to the right, while now and then one would keep straight ahead as first intended."

Hunt considered himself duty bound to lead those few who wanted to continue along the original route. He bade the rest "a pleasant journey." Three days later, at the first sign of difficulty—at a place called Poverty Point—the majority turned back to rejoin him (including, it is said, the one person who had made a copy of Smith's map). Twenty-seven wagons pushed on westward. The shortcut parties included, among others, "a 'Hawkeye'

Dust storms across Badwater, June 2007. For weeks the '49ers wandered the edge of the pan, looking for water and forage. Burke Griggs

train of Iowa people; the Georgians, under Captain Townshend"; the Arcane and Bennett families, with seven wagons; the "Reverend Mr. Brier and his family"; a German immigrant by the name of Louis Nusbaumer; and a group of young men from Illinois who had dubbed themselves the Jayhawkers.

The journey for those who had stuck with Hunt—"over barren deserts, volcanic, hillstrewn, sun-parched . . . accompanied by a constant cloud of dust from sands never before disturbed by wheels, etc."—was no easy stroll through the countryside. But their route had been traveled. The great distances between watering holes could at least be anticipated. For the Jayhawkers and their fellow travelers, marching blindly across the lowest, driest desert sinks in North America, it was a character-assaying exercise in thirst, starvation, and pain. A handful of them would die or disappear. Of their 27 vehicles they would burn or abandon all but one before escaping the desert. Collectively—although the parties generally traveled separately and fended for themselves—they would become known as the Death Valley '49ers.

It was late December before they came briefly together again at the eastern edge of the deepest, driest sink of all, somewhere in the vicinity of today's Furnace Creek Ranch & Resort. They were likely the first Americans (and German) to see the place. There were no pools, there was no gift shop, there was no golf course. If there was beauty there at all, they were not greatly inclined to its appreciation.

For weeks on end they had dragged across the dust and scrabble of the Amargosa drainage without finding palatable water, their supplies long dwindled to nothing but flour and coffee; their oxen, with no feed or forage, getting weaker by the day. There had been skirmishes with Indians, as well as snow (which had saved their lives). It was Christmas Eve when they found at Furnace Creek a tremendous freshwater spring, gushing 2,000 gallons a minute, and some meager forage for the animals. Still, the broad salt-crusted valley before them looked less promising even than the one they had just escaped. With no idea how many hundreds more miles they might still have to cover, they made camp. "The men killed an ox for our Christmas," wrote Mrs. Brier, "but its flesh was more like poisonous slime than meat . . . I had one small biscuit, but we had plenty of coffee, and I think it was that which kept us alive."

The Jayhawkers were then but a few miles away, at the dunes near what we now call Stovepipe Wells, burning their wagons to make jerky of the last of their oxen. Chalfant, researching the story in the late 1920s, came upon the diary of a Capt. Asa Haines, who had apparently made it out of Death Valley in the company of the Jayhawkers. Of the "terse entries, written in pencil," Chalfant was able to make out the following account:

East 4 mile, laid by; thence south 28 mile, no water, 10 o'clock at night.

Thence west 10 mile, no water.

Thence south 12 mile, no water.

Thence southeast 8 miles, got weak.

Thence due south 20 mile, no water.

Left wagons, packed cattle, six days wandering.

Stayed in canyon three days. Indians stole horses, all but two.

18 miles southwest, no water, one death, Fish from Iowa, starvation. William Ischam died same day in evening.

William G. Robinson and McGowan got through desert but died at foot of mountains. Frank, a Frenchman, wandered off.

Offered Brian Byron $5 for a biscuit but he refused. Old man Townshend left. Bill Rude and Dow Stephens bake flour and offer me food.

Luther Richards found water; snowed same night. One man laid down. Made coffee, went back and he was dead.

Find body of Townshend; scalped.

Joshua Trees, and the Sierra Nevada from the Mojave Desert

At a fair spring along what is now the Westside Road, at the base of the Panamint range, the Bennett-Arcane party spent nearly a month camped beneath their wagons. Meanwhile, John Rogers and William Manly, each with a knapsack full of ox meat, two spoonfuls of rice and two of tea, climbed over the range south of Telescope Peak and, following a trail marked by the bones of abandoned horses (and those of the man named Fish, from Iowa), crossed the dry pan of the Panamint Valley. They climbed the Argus Range and, on New Year's Day 1850, found themselves finally looking out at the shimmering, snow-clad Sierra Nevada. Beneath it ran the lush green strip of paradise that was the Owens River.

There, beside the river (now dry), they killed a cow, ate, and camped. From a generous Mexican family they borrowed "three horses, a mule, a sack of beans, a small sack of wheat, some good dried meat, and some coarse flour." The next day they headed back along the same rough trail, over two ranges, to recover the Bennetts. It was sometime in mid-January when they again crested the Panamints heading west, this time with the rest of their ragged party in tow—women, children, and all. "We took off our hats," wrote Manly more than 40 years later, "and then, overlooking the scene of so much trial, suffering and death, spoke the thought uppermost, saying: 'Good-bye, Death Valley!'"

Hence the name.

A Halt in the Yosemite Valley, *Albert Bierstadt* Gravure, c. 1863, courtesy NPS, YNP

The Changing of the Guard

It was one of the last human hunts of civilization, and the basest and most bru-
tal of them all.

—Hubert Howe Bancroft, *1890*

Jim Savage had come overland from Illinois in 1846. He'd lost a wife and young daughter on the road—whether to privation or Indians, to cholera or some other mishap, is not recorded. He fought with Frémont against the Mexicans and after the war drifted south to what would soon become Mariposa County. He did some prospecting, fell in with the natives, and started building up a kind of empire.

"Jim was smart as a whip, shrewd," recalled a woman years later who had known him back in Illinois. "He was vigorous and strong, had blue eyes and a magnificent physique, was tactful, likeable and interesting." He seems also to have had a remarkable ear for languages. Conversant in French and German, and probably Spanish, too, it wasn't long before he could manage himself in the dialects of the local Indians.

To the most powerful chiefs in the San Joaquin, of "the five great confederated tribes which then possessed the country from the Tuolomne to the Kern River Mountains," among them one known as José Juarez, and another, the much-feared José Rey, or "King

Joseph," of the Chowchillas, Jim Savage became something of a friend, an advisor, and a benevolent dictator. He became a chief himself—of more than one tribe. He took to wearing red shirts to impress his followers. From the foothills he led successful war parties against the enemy mountain tribes, especially the so-called Yosemites (alternately understood to mean "grizzly bears" or "those who kill"). He sealed his

230 Years in the Sierra

1775	Pedro Font sees *"una gran sierra nevada"*
1833	American fur trappers introduce malaria; twenty thousand Sierra Indians die
1848	James Marshall discovers gold in Sutter's millrace
1850	California becomes 31st state; population of Los Angeles: 1,610
1855	Thomas Ayres makes "First Picture of Yosemite Valley"
1856	The Lower Hotel, Yosemite's first permanent structure, is built
1859	Charles Leander Weed makes first photograph of Yosemite Valley; gold discovered at Bodie
1862	Abraham Lincoln signs Homestead Act, offering freehold title to 160-acre lots of undeveloped land in the West; smallpox epidemic further reduces native populations in California
1864	Lincoln grants Yosemite Valley and Mariposa Big Tree Grove to State of California to "be held for public use, resort, and recreation . . . inalienable for all time"
1869	Golden Spike driven on Transcontinental Railroad
1870	John Searles discovers Borax near Mono Lake
1873	First ascent of Mount Whitney by three fishermen from Lone Pine
1878	Timber and Stone Act allows for purchase of 160-acre lots "unfit for farming"
1882	Construction begins on Tioga Road
1890	Benjamin Harrison creates Sequoia and General Grant National Parks, and declares Yosemite National Park (under state management); Nikola Tesla develops alternating current (AC) generators for long-distance transmission of electricity
1891	4th Cavalry Regiment, U.S. Army, arrives in Yosemite
1892	Sierra Club founded; John Muir first president
1893	Harrison establishes 13-million-acre Sierra Forest Reserve
1897	Forest Management Act is enacted
1900	First motorized vehicle in Yosemite; population of greater Los Angeles: 130,000; California native population reduced by 90 percent
1905	Theodore Roosevelt creates Forest Service, Gifford Pinchot first chief; Congress withdraws 500 square miles of Yosemite from park status, including Devil's Postpile; Los Angeles voters approve bond measure to bring Owens River to Los Angeles
1906	Antiquities Act authorizes President and Congress to declare national monuments; California returns Yosemite to federal government; San Francisco Earthquake
1907	State Legislature lists mountain lion as bountied predator
1908	San Francisco secures water rights to Hetch Hetchy
1909	World's first reinforced-concrete multiple-arch dam at Hume Lake is constructed
1911	Howard Taft proclaims Devil's Postpile as a national monument
1913	Woodrow Wilson authorizes damming of Tuolomne at Hetch Hetchy; automobiles admitted to Yosemite Valley; Owens River water arrives in San Fernando Valley

position by marrying into a number of prominent native families.

To the swarms of pioneers, prospectors, and speculators who by the end of 1848, much to the chagrin of the natives, had begun to pick and dig and pan their way across the countryside, killing game and cutting forests as they went, Jim Savage was the subject of many an evening's storytelling. Some said he had five wives; others said he had more than 20.

1916	National Park Service created to "conserve the scenery and the natural and historic objects and the wild life therein and to provide for the enjoyment of the same in such manner and by such means as will leave them unimpaired for the enjoyment of future generations"
1926	Sequoia National Park expanded to include Kern Canyon and Mount Whitney
1933	Herbert Hoover proclaims Death Valley a national monument; Franklin Roosevelt creates Civilian Conservation Corps
1934	Taylor Grazing Act allows granting of permits on public land for grazing, fences, reservoirs, and other improvements; Tuolomne River water arrives in San Francisco
1938	Dave McCoy "secures permit to operate permanent rope tow on McGee Mountain . . . sells Harley-Davidson for $85 to raise funds for equipment"
1940	Roosevelt creates Kings Canyon National Wilderness Park
1941	Water from Mono Basin reaches Los Angeles
1942	Dave McCoy moves his rope tow to Mammoth Mountain
1946	Bureau of Land Management created
1950	Population of Los Angeles: 2 million
1963	California becomes most populous state in the Union
1964	Lyndon B. Johnson signs Wilderness Act
1965	Cedar Grove and Tehipite Valley added to Kings Canyon National Park
1968	Wild & Scenic Rivers Act; 600,000 acres of Sequoia-Kings Canyon designated "natural fire zone"
1969	National Environmental Policy Act (NEPA) is enacted to "encourage productive and enjoyable harmony between man and his environment"
1971	Congress passes Wild Free-Roaming Horse & Burro Act; Governor Ronald Reagan signs moratorium on hunting mountain lions
1973	Endangered Species Act is enacted
1976	Mining in the Parks Act is enacted; Homestead Act repealed
1978	Mineral King added to Sequoia National Park
1980	Yosemite General Management Plan: "The ultimate goal of the National Park Service is to remove all private vehicles from Yosemite Valley"
1983	California Supreme Court rules Mono Basin water diversion a violation of public trust
1984	Yosemite named World Heritage Site; California Wilderness Act, 89 percent of Yosemite designated wilderness; Town of Mammoth Lakes incorporated
1986	Bighorn sheep reintroduced in Lee Vining Canyon
1990	California Wildlife Protection Act is enacted
1994	Desert Protection Act is enacted: Death Valley becomes a national park; Saline Valley annexed
1996	4.2 million people visit Yosemite
2000	Bill Clinton designates Giant Sequoia National Monument; population greater Los Angeles: 16 million
2005	Dave McCoy sells controlling interest in Mammoth Mountain Ski Area to Starwood Capital for $365 million

Only when he went to San Francisco, as in the time he rolled a barrelful of gold dust across a hotel lobby, did he condescend to wear a hat and boots. Otherwise, they said, he went about in moccasins or bare feet, his thick blond hair hanging to his shoulders, his beard "halfway to his waist." "[H]is walk and action were so apparently confirmed in Indian characteristics," wrote one chronicler in 1882, "that the ordinary observer would intuitively fancy that he was himself a native and to that wild life born and bred."

There was much speculation as to how Jim Savage was able to exert such powerful influence over his newfound charges. What is certain is that by the spring of 1849 he had begun to use that influence to gather for himself a considerable amount of precious metal. "Never will I forget the impressions of the scene before us," reported one freshly arrived prospector, having chanced upon the man in Jamestown, in May: "Under a brushwood tent supported by upright poles sat James D. Savage, measuring and pouring gold dust into the candle boxes by his side. Five hundred or more naked Indians, with belts of cloth bound around their waists or suspended from their heads brought the dust to Savage, and in return for it received a bright piece of cloth or some beads."

By the end of the year he had freighted a load of supplies up from San Francisco and opened a profitable little trading post on the South Fork of the Merced (near present-day El Portal), less than 20 miles down-canyon from the yet-to-be-stumbled-upon Yosemite Valley, thus expanding his market to include the burgeoning population of white prospectors. Historian Carl Russell described Savage's rates of exchange as follows: "An ounce of gold bought a can of oysters, five pounds of flour, or a pound of bacon; a shirt required five ounces, and a pair of boots or a hat brought a full pound."

Indians not under Savage's sway—in other words, of the "those who kill" variety—made occasional visits to the post from upriver, boasting of a "deep valley in which one Indian is more than ten white men." In the spring of 1850, they raided the store. "With the Indian miners I had in my employ," Savage later explained, "[I] drove them off, and followed some of them up the Merced River into a canyon, which I supposed led to their stronghold, as the Indians then with me said it was not a safe place to go into." He retreated, packed up his wares, and established a new post at a safer location near the present-day town of Mariposa (then Agua Fria). Business was good and brisk enough that summer that he opened a branch post to the west of Mormon Bar (along today's CA 49), near the newest diggings on the Fresno River.

For the Indians, on the other hand, conditions deteriorated quickly. "It was found convenient," reported one J. Ross Browne in 1857 (cited by David Beesley in *Crow's Range*), "to take possession of their country without recompense, rob them of their wives and children, kill them in every cowardly and barbarous manner that could be devised, and when that was impracticable, drive them as far as possible out of the way." Whether they had come suddenly "to learn the value of the gold-dust they dug from the ground," as another contemporary writer put it, or just felt crowded and annoyed and up against a wall—the Indians began to weigh their options. The law, such as it was, was not on their side: One statute prevented their testifying in court; another, more recent, allowed for their enslavement. Against increasing waves of predation, murder, and trespass they were afforded about the same legal protection as bears and mountain lions.

At some point in the fall, perhaps through one of his wives, Savage got wind of a plot by the Yosemites to unite all the tribes of California, including their former enemies, thereby to drive out the whites for good, "and take from them their mules, horses, &c." Savage saw the proverbial writing on the wall. He called a series of councils and endeavored to explain

THE ATTACK.

Hostilities between Indians and white men increased as time went on. From In the Heart of the Sierras by J. M. Hutchings (1886)

to his fellow chieftains that the warpath was not, in fact, the path to continued wealth and prosperity. "[T]he white men are more numerous than the wasps and the ants," he explained. "If the Indians make war on the white men, every tribe will be exterminated; not one will be left."

Savage took his friend José Juarez, various other tribal leaders, and probably a wife or two downriver from Stockton to San Francisco in order to show them the considerable riches, technology, and population of the people they might have wished, in their wildest dreams, to drive out. (And also to put into storage some of his valuables.) With the notorious James D. Savage as their guide, the Indians drank and gambled, shopped and went to shows, witnessed the celebrations attendant to California's newfound statehood, and toured the city. The Indians are said to have been impressed by these urban tribes, with their "great high hats" and sticks for walking with, "even on a smooth road," and the way they drove poor, ragged gold-diggers out of the city with clubs.

"They are not like the tribe that dig gold in the mountains," explained José to his people, upon return to the foothills. "They will not help the gold diggers if the Indians make war against them." Savage's station on the Fresno was the first to be sacked, his employees promptly "filled with arrows." The Mariposa store was next, "plundered and burned," three men left dead or dying, and Savage's wives carried off upriver "by their own people." A trader by the name of Cassady and four other white men were reported murdered down on the San Joaquin. In Kaweah country, near Visalia, a company of five adventurers, having

The Last Grizzly

When Frémont came down to the lower Merced in 1844, he found the place downright "crowded" with big mammals: elk, deer, wild horses, and bears of one kind or another. "[A]long the rivers are frequent fresh tracks of the grizzly bear," he wrote, "which are unusually numerous in this country."

The California grizzly, or bruin, is thought to have been a unique subspecies of brown bear (*Ursus arctos horribilis*), perhaps the largest in the Lower 48. One particularly hefty specimen, shot in 1866 near a settlement later called Bear Valley (now Valley Center), is supposed to have stood taller than 8 feet and weighed 2,200 pounds. The Miwok word for "grizzly" is something like *Oo-soó-ma-te*, which for many years was confused with another word, *Yo-se-mi-te*, meaning, perhaps, "those who kill," in reference not to murderous bears but to unfriendly neighbors of the human kind. It was near Yosemite, in the spring of 1854, that James Capen "Grizzly" Adams is supposed to have captured his sidekick, his "firmest friend," Ben Franklin.

There may once have been as many as fifteen thousand grizzlies in California, ranging across the chaparral from the coastal lowlands to the foothills of the Sierra, up the Tuolomne and the Merced, the Kings and Kaweah, the Tule and the Kern. They ate mostly plants and berries (in vast quantities) but were also not averse to the occasional easy piece of meat. In the mixed conifer belts along the western slope, they shared range with their smaller cousins, the California black bear (*Ursus americanus*), today the largest carnivore in the Sierra—and the best trained at ripping off car doors to get at coolers.

The symbol on the California flag is a grizzly. The beast grazing in a green-grass meadow in the billboard advertisements for a certain financial institution is a grizzly (probably photographed in Alaska). The mascots of U.C. Berkeley and UCLA: grizzlies.

The last wild grizzly in California is generally thought to have been shot in Fresno County in 1922 (others say it was Tulare). "But there was no proof to be had," says Susan Snyder, Head of Public Service at the Bancroft Library and editor of *Bear in Mind: The California Grizzly* (Heyday, 2003), "and there were so many incongruities in the various versions of the story that it was never verified."

"Frequently seen in herds of fifteen or twenty in number," wrote Lansford Hastings in 1845, claiming that at a distance they might easily be confused with buffalo, "[t]heir flesh is much admired by the Mexicans, as food." The beast could be brought down soon enough, he explained, "with a good rifle [and] about eighteen balls to the pound." Spanish and Mexican *vaqueros* made high sport of roping them, dragging them to market, and pitting them against enraged bulls.

With the rush for gold came a great influx of men with guns—and with a widespread taste for killing bears. George Nidever, "a hunter bold was he," traveling companion of the likes of Frémont and Walker, is said to have killed more than two hundred grizzlies before the end of the 1850s. The

refused to pay a tribute demanded by some local tribesmen, found themselves suddenly "surrounded by yelling demons." Of the five, three were killed outright, another skinned alive; the last, his arm shattered by an arrow (later amputated), escaped only "by the fleetness of his horse."

On January 6, 1851, Savage guided Sheriff James Burney and a small band of volunteers up the Fresno in pursuit of his old friends, the two Josés. "No dog can follow a trail like he can," wrote one of the volunteers, of Savage. "No horse can endure half so much. He sleeps but little, can go days without food, and can run a hundred miles in a day and night over the mountains and then sit and laugh for hours over a camp-fire as fresh and lively as if he had just been taking a little walk for exercise." In a matter of days they had surprised sev-

The California grizzly From *In the Heart of the Sierras* by J. M. Hutchings (1886)

advent of the repeater rifle, by the end of the Civil War, put the process into overdrive. The last known grizzly in Yosemite was shot in 1887. Its pelt resides in Berkeley, at the University of California. One big male grizzly named Monarch, captured at the request of William Randolph Hearst in 1889, died in a concrete pit in San Francisco's Golden Gate Park in 1911. Monarch is said to have been the model for the new 1911 version of the state flag. His skin, stuffed and mounted, is today displayed at the California Academy of Sciences. His bones were last seen in a cardboard box at Berkeley's Museum of Vertebrate Zoology.

In 1924, the same year the last wild California gray wolf was supposed to have been captured, up in Lassen County, there were various unconfirmed sightings of a female grizzly and cub in what is now Sequoia National Park. "Even into the 1930s there were sightings," says Snyder, "but nothing proven with a dead bear."

A year-round resident of Fish Camp recently told a tale involving hikers on a disused trail on the south side of Yosemite (off the Jackson Road) and piles of bear scat "so big they had to vault over it." What was scaring off all the little bears? she wondered. This same woman also told of having seen a wolf one winter night not long ago—"the longest, leggiest coyote I ever saw"—beneath the street-light in front of her house on CA 41. There were no other witnesses.

eral hundred Indians at their *rancheria,* had torched the wigwams, and in the ensuing chaos shot dead King Joseph and 23 of his men.

Savage was thereafter appointed head of a rough band of volunteer Indian fighters, assembled by proclamation of the governor and comprised of "two hundred able-bodied men," known as the Mariposa Battalion. "This battalion was a body of hardy resolute pioneers," wrote one of its more prominent members, Dr. Lafayette Bunnell. "Many of them had seen service, and had fought their way against the Indians across the plains; some had served in the war with Mexico and been under military discipline." By mid-March they had succeeded in convincing the majority of the foothill tribes to sign agreements with the U.S. Indian Commissioners, thus consigning themselves to reservations on the lower Fresno and Kings rivers.

Tenaya Lake, June 2007

The so-called Yosemites—a ragtag band of Eastern Monos, Paiutes, and Ahwahneechee, with a recalcitrant figure by the name of Tenaya as their chief—remained at large. And so, late in the day on March 19, in rain turning to snow, Savage, with two companies, began a long march over the hill from Mariposa to what is now Wawona. The snow on the ridge was "fully four feet deep." At the edge of a meadow where today, in summer, there is a lovely golf course, they surprised and captured an encampment of Savage's former employees and in-laws. By the time the storm let up a few days later, Tenaya and 72 of his tribesmen were under guard and on their way to the Fresno. Savage and some of his men pressed on, along a thin trail where now runs the Wawona Road, to see about this valley they had heard so much about.

Ralph Waldo Emerson wrote of Yosemite that it was "the only spot that I have ever found that came up to the brag." It was magic hour on March 25, 1851—perfect timing—when the party came into full view of the 3,300-foot-tall granite face now known as El Capitan, or simply El Cap. Dr. Bunnell, for one, forgot whatever rancor he had previously been harboring toward the natives. "None but those who have visited this most wonderful valley," he wrote later, "can even imagine the feelings with which I looked upon the view that was there presented . . . and as I looked, a peculiar exalted sensation seemed to fill my whole being, and I found my eyes in tears with emotion."

Around the campfire that night, at the base of Bridalveil Fall, conversation turned to the naming of the valley—"the grandest that had ever yet been looked upon." A number of suggestions were put forward, most having some association with either God or the Devil. It was Bunnell, by his own account, who suggested that the place be named Yo-sem-i-ty, "as it was suggestive, euphonious, and certainly *American; that* by so doing, the name of the tribe of Indians which we met leaving their homes in this valley, perhaps never to return, would be perpetuated."

Tenaya and some of his people, having eluded their escort before reaching the Fresno, did in fact manage, for the time being, to skip back to the valley they knew as Ahwahnee ("mouth of the bear" or "gaping mouth," or simply "mouth"). Savage spent the rest of the season working with the commissioners, trying to secure half-decent terms for the defeated tribes. A second expedition, in May, led by one of Savage's captains, resulted in the shooting in the back of Tenaya's youngest son ("while trying to escape") and the subsequent recapture of Tenaya himself—on the shores of the lake that would thereafter bear his name.

The battalion was decommissioned on July 1.

After much pleading and cajoling and promising to be good, Tenaya was allowed, with some of his people, to return once again to his valley. But the following spring he was up to his old tricks, attacking a group of prospectors, killing two. In June, a detachment of regular infantry, under a Lt. Tredwell Moore, chased the old chief and some of his men across Tuolomne Meadows as far as Bloody Canyon, where, failing to make their quarry, they found instead some "promising" ore deposits.

As might have been expected, there was a vociferous number of white folks in the foothills—squatters, traders, miners—who felt that the federal government, with Savage as consultant, had overstepped its bounds in giving land to the Indians. Pressure was put on the legislature to have them removed from the state entirely. Savage had rebuilt his trading post and been made Indian Agent, but he found himself generally powerless to defend the treaties he'd helped to negotiate. Encroachments and general depredation continued apace. In one of various unfortunate incidents, as related in W. W. Elliott's *History of Fresno County* (1881), "one Major Harvey, first county Judge of Tulare County, either hired or incited a lot of men who rushed into one of the *rancherias* on Kings River and succeeded in killing a number of old squaws."

Savage made his displeasure known. Judge Harvey, in turn, dared Savage to pay him a visit down at the Kings River Agency. Savage found the offer impossible to resist, and on the morning of August 16, 1852, rode, with witnesses, into the yard in front of Bill Campbell's store. The magistrate, an ex-employee of Savage, appointed to the position by Harvey (and by whom Harvey was promptly acquitted), later testified as follows:

> *After they had got through their breakfast, Savage tied up his hair, rolled up his sleeves, took his six-shooter out of its scabbard and placed it in front of him under the waistband of his pantaloons. He then walked into Campbell's store and asked Major Harvey if he could not induce him to call him a gentleman. Harvey told him that he had made up his mind and had expressed his opinion in regard to that, and did not think he would alter it. He knocked Harvey down and stamped upon him a little. They were separated by some gentlemen in the house, and Harvey got up. Savage says, "To what conclusion have you come in regard to my gentlemancy?" Harvey replies, "I think you are a damned scoundrel." Savage knocked Harvey down again. They were again separated by*

gentlemen present. As Harvey straightened himself onto his feet, he presented a six-shooter and shot Major Savage through the heart. Savage fell without saying anything. It was supposed that Harvey shot him twice after he was dead, every ball taking effect in his heart.

"The night he was buried," wrote another of Savage's associates, "the Indians built large fires, around which they danced, singing the while the mournful death chaunt [sic], until the hills around rang with the sound. I have never seen such profound manifestations of grief."

Tenaya spent the rest of the year hiding out on the east side with some of his Mono allies. Late in the summer of 1853—so the story goes—he stole and ate some of their horses. Or he offended them in a game. Either way, the Monos responded by stoning him to death. Tenaya's body is said to have been burned according to tradition, his charred remains carried back to the valley to be mourned over for two weeks by what remained of his people. That fall, with the wily old renegade gone and nothing to fear but the weather (and perhaps the occasional grizzly), a prospector by the name of Leroy Vining led a party over Mono Pass to establish the mining camp that today bears his name.

The summer of 1855 brought an enterprising Englishman by the name of James Mason Hutchings with a pair of Indian guides and the first party of tourists to the Yosemite Valley. Among them was Thomas Ayres, landscape artist, who, from what is now known as Old Inspiration Point, off the Wawona Road, sketched "the First Picture of the Yosemite Valley."

The First Picture of the Yosemite Valley, *sketched by Thomas Ayres in 1855* From *In the Heart of the Sierras* by J. M. Hutchings (1886)

Sketched by Thos. Ayres, June 20, 1855—first ever taken.

GENERAL VIEW OF THE YO SEMITE VALLEY.

[From open-eta-noo-ah, on the old Indian Trail.]

Three other parties made their way into the valley that season, including Galen Clark, who would become the valley's first official custodian; the Mann brothers, who the following year would begin construction on the toll trail now known as the Wawona Road; and yet another writer, a preacher, a painter, and a magazine editor.

"At the close of 1855," wrote Sierra climbing pioneer and historian Francis Farquhar, "the total tourist travel to Yosemite had reached forty-two. Fifty years later the annual number reached 10,000; a century later 1,000,000; and in the year 1961 a million and a half visitors came to Yosemite." The high-water mark came in 1996, with 4.2 million visitors. By 2006 total visitation had declined to just 3,242,644—down nearly 25 percent from a decade earlier.

Some blamed video games and the Internet; others pointed to high gas prices and a $20 entrance fee (it was $5 in 1996). While Park Service officials scratched their heads and enjoyed a brief reprieve from trying to sort out contentious and long-standing issues of traffic and parking, they went for a hike up Half Dome with FOX News to prove the park was still safe and enjoyable.

2

INTO THE HILLS

Approaches, Traverses, Methods of Travel

Good and substantial wagons should always be selected, and however firm and staunch they may appear, they should, invariably, be particularly examined, and repaired, before leaving the States.

—Lansford W. Hastings, The Emigrants' Guide to Oregon and California, 1845

When young Samuel Langhorne Clemens set out overland to see the far West, in 1861, the route consisted mainly of a "hard, level road," pounded out by more than a decade of heavy wagon trains bound for California. From St. Louis it was six days by steamboat up the Missouri, followed by 20 more alternately inside and on top of a six-horse stage, "swinging and swaying" across the landscape. Every 10 miles the driver stopped to change horses. Passengers were allowed no more than 25 pounds of baggage each: "no stovepipe hats nor patent-leather boots, nor anything else to make life calm and peaceful." The future Mark Twain and his companions shared the coach with great stacks of mail, "the heft of it for the Injuns," explained the driver, "which is powerful troublesome 'thout they get plenty of truck to read."

Ten years later, lamented Twain, the same journey could have been made in the sump-tuous luxury of one of "Pullman's hotels on wheels," downing Krug by the bumper and feasting on garden vegetables and pan-seared antelope steak while out the window the Great American Desert unfurled like an exotic *tableau vivant* at 30 miles an hour. These days, one can still get from St. Louis to Reno by rail, via Chicago, in about 60 hours, give or take 10. But the menu—"braised beef, herbed cod fillets, tri-color tortellini," and so on—is not quite what it used to be.

In the spring of 1868 John Muir preferred to go "afoot" from San Francisco to Yosemite. But he could have spared his boot heels aboard one of the many paddle-wheel steamers that in those days regularly plied the San Joaquin as far upriver as Merced. Muir's onetime employer, J. M. Hutchings, in one of the first and most influential tourist guidebooks to Yosemite, *In the Heart of the Sierras* (1886), described no fewer than seven different routes into the valley, two of which could be reached by steamboat, "[a]ll of which can now be

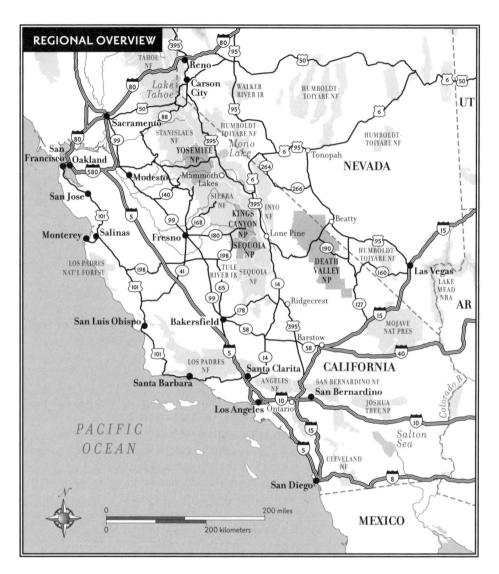

traveled by rail and coach to the door of each hotel there."

Alas, the glory days of public transportation in California have long passed. These days, for better or worse, a journey to the southern Sierra Nevada will generally involve loading up an automobile with gear and provisions, and, from the urban center of one's choice, hitting the road. From the northern fringes of Los Angeles one can strike out across the Mojave on good, fast blacktop and in three or four hours be napping in the shade of a giant sequoia or soaking one's feet in snowmelt at the south fork of the Kern. An easy half-day's drive from the Bay Bridge—across the San Joaquin and the southern end of the Mother Lode country—brings one to the gates of Yosemite. The international airports at Reno and Fresno offer daily flights from as far afield as Shanghai, Sydney, Frankfurt, Germany, and Orlando, Florida—and the usual fleet of rental vehicles for that last sinuous leg from the tarmac to the woods. Travelers making their way from Sin City can with a credit card and a driver's license procure a late-model Ferrari convertible with comprehensive collision insurance and a 3.6-liter V-8; have lunch poolside at Furnace Creek, in Death Valley; and in the evening be seated before a campfire in the folds of Mount Whitney, listening to the cooling of the engine.

BY AIR

International

Burbank/Bob Hope (BUR) (2627 N. Hollywood Way; 818-840-8840; www.bobhopeair port.com). The locals' favorite Los Angeles airport, quaint plein-air baggage carousels, easiest in and out, $2/day economy parking, easiest access from L.A. to the Sierra and points north. Alaska, American, Delta, JetBlue, Skybus (to Columbus, Ohio), Southwest, United, US Airways. All major rental car agencies.

Fresno-Yosemite (FYI) (5175 E. Clinton Way; 559-621-4500; www.flyfresno.org). Closest international airport to the Sierra Nevada: 53 miles to Kings Canyon; 63 miles to Yosemite. Alaska, Allegiant, American, Continental, Delta, ExpressJet, Hawaiian, Horizon, Mexicana, Northwest, United, US Airways. Car rental: Alamo, Avis, Budget, Dollar, Enterprise, Hertz, National.

Las Vegas/McCarran (LAS) (5757 Wayne Newton Boulevard; 702-261-5211; www.mccar ran.com). The 5th- or 6th-busiest airport in North America (10th or 11th in the world): 34

The Grand Tour de Sierra: Badwater to Bridalveil and Back

With a hard-wearing (and/or disposable) private vehicle, at least three weeks' free time (to allow for some moments outside the car), plenty of gas money, water, decent tires, a cooler full of cold beverages and picnic supplies, and an extensive archive of soundtrack music, the hardiest of modern travelers, by way of introduction to the place, may wish to undertake an epic, 3,000-mile, figure-8 circumnavigation. From Vegas, for example, one can follow the pioneers' route to Badwater; over the Panamints and Townes Pass to Owens Lake; south to Pearsonville, hubcap capital of the world; west over the Los Angeles Aqueduct to Sherman Pass; down to the Main Fork of the Kern; up over the Great Western Divide Highway to Springville, by way of the George Bush Tree; from Three Rivers to the Giant Forest to the depths of Kings Canyon, out by CA 180 to Fresno (with a side trip via the McKinley Grove of Big Trees to Mono Hot Springs and Florence Lake); then north on CA 41 to Wawona, the Yosemite Valley (another side trip to Groveland and Hetch Hetchy); thence over Tioga Pass to Mono Lake, June Lake, Mammoth Lakes, Bishop, Westgard Pass, and the Bristlecone Pine Forest, home of the oldest living things on the planet and hands down the best view of the Sierra Nevada; thence to return to Vegas via Scotty's Castle, Salsberry Pass, and Shoshone. This same route can also be tapped into, with variations, from Los Angeles, San Francisco, or Reno. It cannot be done in winter. But in spring, if timed right (and depending on the season's snowfall), you can catch the last days of the season at the Furnace Creek Inn (before May 15), see the Yosemite waterfalls in full glory, and also possibly make the opening of Tioga Pass back to the east side. Consider it a challenge.

The fastest way to the Furnace Creek Inn

airlines, 135 domestic and international destinations, 1,100 daily scheduled flights. Shopping, dining, slot machines. Booming, all-pervasive big-screen infotainment. Easy in and out. For the historic '49er approach to the Sierra: 121 speed miles to Furnace Creek; 250 miles to the Whitney Portal; 350 miles to Yosemite (in summer). All major rental car agencies.

Los Angeles (LAX) (1 World Way; 310-646-5252; www.lawa.org/lax). Fifth-busiest in the world. With 61 million passengers annually, 80 airlines, 9 terminals, and just 25,000 parking spaces for automobiles (only 140 for airplanes), the place tends to be quite the circus. Traffic on the tarmac matched only by that on the freeways. Lines to get through security often stretch beyond the terminal doors and along the curb. It's no wonder locals prefer to spend the extra few dollars to fly in and out of Burbank (or Ontario). If you're ever stuck here, make your way out through security to the fabulous Jetsons-style Encounter Restaurant (www.encounterlax.com) for blue martinis, sashimi salad, world-class plane spotting, and all the piped-in intergalactic Muzak you'll ever want to hear. To escape, slog I-405 north to I-5. Two hundred twenty miles to Lone Pine; 220 miles to Three Rivers. Approximately 40 rental car companies, all off-site.

Oakland (OAK) (1 Airport Drive; 510-563-3300; www.flyoakland.com). The friendlier, cheaper alternative to SFO, and on the side of the Bay closer to Yosemite—173 road miles from the tarmac to the Ahwahnee. Alaska, Aloha, American, ATA, Continental, Delta, JetBlue, Mexicana, Skybus (to Columbus, Ohio), Southwest, United, US Airways. Easy BART connections to San Francisco. Car rental: Avis, Budget, Dollar, Enterprise, Fox, Hertz, National, Thrifty.

Ontario (ONT) (2500 E. Terminal Way; 909-937-2700; www.lawa.org/ont). L.A.'s newest, fanciest commuter airport. Two hundred miles to Lone Pine; 251 miles to Furnace Creek. Alaska, American, ATA, Continental, Delta, ExpressJet, JetBlue, Lineas Aereas Aztecas, Southwest, United, US Airways. Car rental: Alamo, Avis, Budget, Dollar, Enterprise, Hertz, National, and Rent-4-Less.

Reno-Tahoe (RNO) (2001 E. Plumb Lane; 775-328-6400; www.renoairport.com). The airport of choice for east-side destinations from Tioga and Tuolomne Meadows to Mammoth Lakes. Easy in and out. One hundred forty mostly scenic miles to the shores of Mono Lake. Slow going through the stoplights of Carson City. Alaska, Allegiant, Aloha, American, Continental, Delta, Frontier, Horizon, Southwest, United, US Airways. Car rental: Advantage, Alamo, Avis, Budget, Dollar, Enterprise, Hertz, National, Thrifty.

Sacramento (SMF) (6900 Airport Boulevard; 916-929-5411; www.sacairports.org). One hundred fifty scheduled departures per day. One hundred fifty miles to Yosemite's Oak Flat Entrance. Air Canada, Alaska, Aloha, American, Continental, Delta, ExpressJet, Frontier, Hawaiian, Horizon, JetBlue, Mexicana, Northwest, Southwest, United, US Airways. Car rental: Alamo, Avis, Budget, Dollar, Enterprise, Hertz, National.

San José/Norman Y. Mineta (2077 Airport Boulevard; 408-277-4SKY; www.sjc.org). Silicon Valley's airport. One hundred eighty-three miles to the Ahwahnee. Thirty thousand passengers a day, slightly quieter than Oakland. Named for the former mayor, former U.S.

Climate Data

Average monthly high and low temperatures in Fahrenheit. Average precipitation in inches.

	YOSEMITE			LODGEPOLE			MAMMOTH			LONE PINE			DEATH VALLEY		
	Precip	High	Low	Precip	High	Low	Precip	High	Low	Precip	High	Low	Precip	High	Low
January	6.2	49	26	9.5	38	16	4.9	40	16	1.2	54	27	0.3	66	39
February	6.1	55	28	8.6	41	17	4.1	40	16	1	59	31	0.5	74	46
March	5.2	59	31	7.3	44	21	2.6	45	21	0.4	65	35	0.3	81	54
April	3	65	35	3.4	49	25	1.4	49	25	0.2	72	42	0.1	90	62
May	1.3	73	42	1.4	58	32	1.3	60	33	0.2	82	50	0.1	100	72
June	0.7	82	48	0.6	68	39	0.6	70	40	0.1	91	58	0.1	109	81
July	0.4	90	54	0.5	75	44	0.5	78	46	0.2	97	63	0.1	116	87
August	0.3	90	53	0.3	75	43	0.4	77	45	0.2	95	62	0.1	114	85
September	0.9	84	47	1.3	69	38	0.5	71	37	0.3	88	55	0.2	106	75
October	2.1	74	39	2	58	30	1.2	61	28	0.1	77	44	0.1	93	62
November	5.4	58	31	4.6	46	23	2.3	48	21	0.6	63	34	0.2	76	48
December	5.6	48	26	6.8	38	16	4.1	42	16	0.9	54	27	0.2	65	38
Annual	37.2			46.3			23.9			5.4			2.3		

Congressman, former Transportation Secretary under George W. Bush—the only Democrat ever to serve in the Bush cabinet—and the man who, on September 11, 2001, gave the historic order to ground all 4,546 civilian aircraft then in U.S. airspace. Alaska, American, Continental, Delta, Frontier, Hawaiian, Horizon, JetBlue, Mexicana, Northwest, Southwest, United, US Airways. Car rental: Alamo, Avis, Budget, Dollar, Enterprise, Fox, Hertz, National, Thrifty.

San Francisco (SFO) (US 101; 1-800-I-FLY-SFO; www.flysfo.com). In the 1968 movie *Bullitt*, Steve McQueen, playing the title character, chased the "real" Johnny Ross here across the runway, then shot him dead inside the terminal. Today it's the 23rd-busiest airport in the world. Traffic is frequently brutal across the Bay Bridge in the direction of the Sierra. All major airlines, plus JetBlue nonstop to Boston and JFK. Southwest is rumored to be coming back. All major car rental agencies.

Municipal/Local

Bakersfield (BFL) (3701 Wings Way; 661-391-1800; www.meadowsfield.com). Ninety-three miles to Sequoia's Ash Mountain Entrance; 60 miles to Kernville. Thirty-two flights daily to and from Las Vegas, Los Angeles, Phoenix, San Diego, and San Francisco; Friday through Sunday to Guadalajara. Delta, ExpressJet, Mexicana, United, US Airways. Separate international terminal under way. Car rental: **Avis** (661-392-4160), **Budget** (661-399-2367), **Hertz** (661-832-9005), **National** (661-393-2068).

Inyokern (IYK) (1669 Airport Road; www.inyokernairport.com). Seventy miles to Lone Pine; 83 miles to Panamint Springs. Daily flights to and from LAX on Skywest Airlines, for connections on United. Car rental: **Avis** (760-446-5556), **Dollar** (760-446-4554).

Mammoth-Yosemite (MMH) (www.ci.mammoth-lakes.ca.us/airport/awos.asp). Commercial air service into Mammoth Lakes (long anticipated by some and much dreaded by others) may or may not begin as early as fall 2008. **Horizon Air** (www.alaskair.com) has expressed its intention to fly DC-8 shuttles from LAX during ski season. Runway has been reported ready for business, but final approvals were still pending at press time. Conversations had also taken place regarding possible regular charter service by **Vision Airlines** (1-877-FLYAJET; www.flydornier.com). Also try **Mammoth Air Charter** (760-934-4279). Car rental: **U-Save** (760-934-4999), **Mammoth Car Rentals** (760-934-8111), **Enterprise** (760-924-1094).

Modesto (MOD) (617 Airport Way; 209-526-3108; www.modairport.com). Daily service to and from LAX and SFO on Skywest Airlines, for connections on United. Car rental: **Avis** (209-527-7223), **Hertz** (209-522-3236).

Visalia (VIS) (9501 Airport Drive; 559-713 4201; www.flyvisalia.com). Thirty-six miles west of Sequoia. Daily flights to and from Las Vegas on America West Express. Car rental: **Enterprise** (559-651-5888).

Winter Travel in the Sierra

It was snowing hard when Stacy Stotko and her daughter Brittany set out from Bishop for their home in Crowley, 35 miles away. It was New Year's Day, 2006. They were trying to find their way to Lower Rock Creek Road, an alternative to US 395, but they became disoriented in the blowing snow. Then they got stuck. Three days later, "January 4 at approximately 7:45 AM," according to the Mono County Search & Rescue log, "the vehicle was located by search aircraft in Inyo County in the Pine Creek drainage at about the 7,500 foot level, partially buried in fresh snow." Stacy was in the car—alive. Her daughter, she explained, had set out the previous morning for help. "On January 5 Brittany was located approximately one half mile from the vehicle and had apparently succumbed to hypothermia. She had left the vehicle wearing light clothing and had waded through 2–3 feet of fresh snow."

Lesson: The Sierra Nevada is no place to get caught unprepared. Check road conditions before setting out, and stay abreast of weather forecasts (see chapter 8). Carry winter clothing, including hats, gloves, and boots, and carry chains for your tires. Know that there are times—i.e. when a big wet winter storm cycle comes crashing in from the North Pacific—when it is most prudent to find some-place warm and stay put.

Badger Pass Ski Lodge, Yosemite National Park, March 6, 1969 Norman G. Messinger, courtesy NPS, YNP

Seasonal Closures

Tioga Pass (9,943 feet) closes for the winter with the first major snowfall (generally by mid-November)—followed promptly by the closures of Sherman, Sonora, and Ebbett's passes. The east and west sides of the range become essentially cut off from each other until snow can be cleared in late spring. In winter the only way to get from Lee Vining to the Yosemite Valley (in summer an easy hour's jaunt), other than on skis or snowshoes, is by way of an epic 6- to 10-hour journey around the High Sierra: to the south via Walker Pass (5,250 feet) and Bakersfield; or north by CA 88 over Carson Pass (8,650 feet) to Jackson and Gold Country. Walker Pass will the best option in iffy weather (and for those making their way from Lone Pine and points south). In anything truly inclement, one may have to press north all the way to Carson City (to US 50) or to Reno (I-80). When Walker shuts down—more likely due to rockfall in the lower Kern Canyon than snow or ice—the next option is Tehachapi (3,793 feet).

Winter closures in Sequoia-Kings include the Mineral King Road, the Moro Rock/Crescent Meadow Road, the Crystal Cave Road (and the cave itself), Panoramic Point, Redwood Mountain Road, and the Kings Canyon Scenic Highway (CA 180) from Hume Lake Junction to Cedar Grove. The Generals Highway and CA 180 to Grant Grove are plowed and open all season, weather permitting.

All major roads into Yosemite from the west side are plowed in winter. Glacier Point Road is closed beyond the Badger Pass Ski Area and maintained, conditions permitting, for cross-country skiing.

Road Conditions

Caltrans: www.dot.ca.gov; 1-800-427-ROAD
Yosemite: www.nps.gov/yose/planyourvisit/conditions.htm; 209-372-0200
Sequoia-Kings: www.nps.gov/archive/seki/winterrd.htm; 559-565-3341

A Note on Chains

Buy them at lower elevations (where they tend to be cheaper), and buy them before the storm. Steel chains are more durable and easier to work with, while cable chains are smoother-driving, slightly cheaper, and more likely to break. Either way, make sure they fit on your tires. Know whether your vehicle is front- or rear-wheel drive and install the chains accordingly (on the wheels that do the driving). Practice putting them on before you get to the snow, and carry them at all times. Chains (or snow tires) are often required by law—i.e. when conditions get hairy—even for vehicles with four-wheel drive. P.S. When the roads are dry, you can take them off.

BY RAIL

In 1927, according to that year's edition of *Rider's California*, the town of Stockton boasted three transcontinental railway terminals, two steamboat lines, and two different motor-stage companies serving Yosemite. There were three separate rail spurs from Stockton to Merced (one for each company), whence in three hours and 40 minutes the traveler could make the final 78 miles to El Portal aboard the Yosemite Valley Railroad (YVRR). On the east side of the range, the Southern Pacific Railway continued to operate trains on a narrow-gauge spur as far as the depot at Laws, north of Bishop, until April 1960, and standard cars to Lone Pine until 1981. The YVRR bridge at Bagby burned down on August 21, 1945, six days after the surrender of Japan at the end of World War II. The railway was shut down three days later. Today the only functioning train in the Southern Sierra is a reconditioned

Baggage platform, Yosemite Valley Railroad, El Portal, c. 1927 Courtesy NPS, YNP

steam-powered logging outfit called the **Yosemite Mountain Sugar Pine Railroad** (559-683-7273; www.ymsprr.com), which operates along a 4-mile tourist loop near Fish Camp, on the south side of Yosemite.

AMTRAK (1-800-USA-RAIL; www.amtrak.com). The *California Zephyr* runs on borrowed freight rails from Chicago to Emeryville, California. To access Mono Lake, Mammoth Lakes, and the Owens Valley, disembark at Reno, transfer to Inyo Mono Transit's **CREST** service, or rent a car (see below). Westbound travelers to Yosemite transfer at Sacramento to AMTRAK's **San Joaquins** line. The *San Joaquins* makes several daily runs between Bakersfield and Sacramento (with bus transfer between stations in Stockton), and also between Bakersfield and Oakland's Jack London Square. Regular shuttle connections meet trains at Merced and run as far as the Yosemite Lodge, through Mariposa, Midpines—for those interested in staying at the **Yosemite Bug** (see chapter 7)—and El Portal. Travel time between Oakland and Merced is three to four hours, delays notwithstanding. Merced to Yosemite, by bus, another three. An AMTRAK bus from Hanford station connects with the **Sequoia Shuttle Bus** (see below), which in summer departs five times daily from Visalia. Private shuttles can also be arranged between the Hanford or Fresno AMTRAK stations and Sequoia National Park.

Yosemite in Death Valley, May 2007

Kitchens on Wheels

"Good walkers can go anywhere in these hospitable mountains without artificial ways," wrote Muir, the consummate rambler, who seems regularly to have reached transcendence with but a crust of bread and a ration of tea from his pockets. "But most visitors have to be rolled on wheels with blankets and kitchen arrangements." The advantages are obvious: the well-stocked fridge, the ice maker, the four-burner stove, the sink with running water, the lights, the air conditioner, the screen door, the awning, the Astroturf, the relatively comfortable bed with one's own linens on it. The disadvantages become clearer as the trip wears on: the long, slow, grinding climbs; the long, slow, grinding descents (there is no visit to these ranges that does not involve a gain and subsequent loss of multiple thousands of feet in elevation); the pile-up of fellow travelers on one's rear bumper; the pervasive smell of toilet chemicals; the marriage-threatening maneuvers required to get parked and level at the end of a long day. Whatever savings there may be in food and lodging are more than made up for by the cost of fuel. Still, it's a big part of the American Dream, the same old American Dream that got James Reed of the Donner Party to build a two-story wagon for his family—the so-called pioneer palace car. Maybe everyone has to try it—once.

BY BUS OR SHUTTLE

Traveling to and/or around the Sierra by bus, especially on the east side, is an undertaking sure to enhance one's appreciation of California's pioneer heritage—and to make one hanker for a good pair of boots, a saddlebag full of hardtack, and a decent mule. Shuttle service within Yosemite and Sequoia National Parks, on the other hand, and within the town of Mammoth Lakes, has improved greatly in the last few years. There is no public transportation in Kings Canyon or Death Valley.

Crest/Inyo Mono Transit (760-872-1901; www.inyocounty.us/transit/transit.htm). One bus makes a round-trip run every other weekday, Monday through Friday—up in the morning, back in the afternoon—from Bishop to the Reno Airport ($28 one way). The other runs

Still among the most dependable means of transportation.

from Mammoth Lakes to Ridgecrest ($21)—Monday, Wednesday, and Friday—for connections with various **Kern Regional Transit** routes (1-800-323-2396; www.the-bus-stops-here.org), which in turn serve **Greyhound** connections at the Mojave McDonald's, the Lancaster Metrolink station, and Bakersfield. From Lancaster aboard **Metrolink** (1-800-371-5465; www.metrolinktrains.com), one can make downtown Los Angeles in high style. By this four-stage method it may be possible, on certain days, to leave downtown Los Angeles at 6:35 AM and arrive in Mammoth Lakes at 4:50 PM—for less than $40. It remains unclear if a similar journey can be accomplished in the opposite direction.

Greyhound (1-800-229-9424; www.greyhound.com). Experience the last crumbling vestiges of what was once America's most romantic and economical means of running away from home—and then coming back. Ten departures daily from Los Angeles to Fresno ($28; five to six hours), four from San Francisco to Merced ($30; four hours). No service to Death Valley or along the east side of the Sierra.

Mammoth Lakes Transit (www.visitmammoth.com). In summer, the trolley runs every 15 minutes from the village to Old Mammoth Road and every hour from the village to the Lakes Basin (free). The Bike Park operates a free mountain bike shuttle every half hour from the village to the mountain. In winter, the town provides free shuttle service from Old Mammoth Road to the village and the various base lodges at the ski area. From Main Lodge in summer, the mandatory shuttle to the San Joaquin River Valley and Devil's Postpile leaves approximately every 20 to 30 minutes daily ($7 round-trip).

Greyhound night coach on a test run to the Wawona Tunnel, 1932 Courtesy NPS, YNP

Sequoia Shuttle (1-877-BUS-HIKE; www.sequoiashuttle.com). Shuttles run several trips daily, from Memorial Day through Labor Day, from points in Visalia to the Giant Forest Museum in Sequoia National Park ($10 round-trip, includes park entrance fee). Advance reservations required. From the Giant Forest Museum, free shuttles run every 15 minutes to Moro Rock and Crescent Meadow, and to the Sherman Tree, Lodgepole Visitors Center, and the Wuksachi Lodge.

Sequoia Sightseeing Tours (559-561-4189; www.sequoiatours.com). Backcountry denizen Paul Bischoff and his wife, Becky, offer regular full-day van tours, year-round, of the major points of interest along the Generals Highway in Sequoia National Park. Pick-up and drop-off anywhere in Three Rivers. Private tours and custom hiker/backpacker/skier shuttle service by arrangement, as well as transportation to and from the Hanford AMTRAK station. Paul is also a backcountry instructor for the **Sequoia Field Institute** (see chapter 6).

Yosemite Area Regional Transportation System (YARTS) (1-877-98-YARTS; www.yarts.com). Serves CA 140 from various points in Merced (including AMTRAK and the Merced Airport), through Mariposa, Midpines, and El Portal to destinations in the Yosemite Valley. Twice daily from Merced ($25 round-trip), six times from Mariposa ($12 round-trip). Also once daily from the Mammoth Mountain Inn to the Yosemite Visitors Center and back ($30 round-trip). June through September only. Cost includes park entry fee.

Yosemite Shuttle (209-372-0200; www.nps.gov/yose/planyourvisit/bus.htm). Yosemite is the sort of place where you can park your car for days on end and forget about it. Free hybrid buses run every 10 to 20 minutes, from 7 AM to 10 PM in summer, covering all major valley and village stops from Camp 4 to the Day Use Parking Lot, Happy Isles, and Mirror Lake Junction. Another route, with buses running every half hour, serves the west valley, El Cap, and the Four Mile Trail. A free shuttle is available between Wawona and the Mariposa Grove, and in Tuolomne Meadows between Tioga Pass and Olmsted Point. In winter (December through March) a free shuttle runs daily from valley hotels to Badger Pass Ski Area. Note: Park shuttles are popular tools for hikers interested in point-to-point rather than out-and-back treks.

Pets

Dogs are tolerated in the national parks with certain restrictions. They're not allowed off-leash, on trails, off the pavement (except in campsites), and in any lodging facilities run by Park Service concessionaires. You can't leave them unattended in your vehicle, in your motor home, or tied up at your campsite while you go for a hike, to the visitors center, or to the restroom. Leashes have to be less than 6 feet long. Interactions between dogs and wildlife tend to be less than congenial, so you might consider leaving them at home (see chapter 8 for local kennel information). Some establishments outside the parks, like the Tenaya Lodge, Chateau du Sureau, or the Buckeye Tree Lodge, are more accommodating. Dogs are allowed on and off trails anywhere in the national forests (when duly controlled and picked up after by their owners), except in designated wilderness areas, where they are not allowed at all.

Leashed in Sequoia National Park Burke Griggs

BY CAR

The first summer of the 20th century brought the first steam-powered "locomobile" chugging into Yosemite beneath the weight of one Oliver Lippincott, a 300-pound photographer from Los Angeles, and his driver/mechanic, Ed Russell. The contraption and much of the fuel it consumed had been shipped to Fresno by Southern Pacific Rail. Lippincott made a series of photographs of himself and his "horseless carriage": beneath the Wawona Tunnel Tree, at Mirror Lake, out on the famous overhanging rock at Glacier Point. "We hung on with tooth and nail while the camera was adjusted," he remarked afterward. "No picture was ever so long in being taken." The following summer he sold copies of the photographs from a tent in Yosemite Valley. These days, the Sierra Nevada offers the automobile enthusiast some of the craziest, hairiest, best-engineered, most dramatic, and least congested roads in North America. The lazy drive up and back along the Merced River in

Pave It and Paint It Green, *Yosemite National Park, mid-1960s* © Rondal Partridge, www.rondalpartridge.com

Yosemite Valley is among the most scenic stretches of parkway in the world—especially in a convertible, in spring or autumn, when the crowds are elsewhere.

Automobiles were not officially allowed into the park until 1913. John Muir, in his capacity as president of the Sierra Club, had been present at a National Parks Conference the previous fall, at which the new machines had become a topic of heated debate. "All signs indicate automobile victory," he reported in a letter to Howard Palmer, Secretary of the American Alpine Club, "and doubtless, under certain precautionary restrictions, these useful, progressive, blunt-nosed mechanical beetles will hereafter be allowed to puff their way into all the parks and mingle their gas-breath with the breath of the pines and water-falls, and, from the mountaineer's standpoint, with but little harm or good."

How much harm they may have done in the intervening century is, on the one hand, obvious, and on the other a matter of some considerable debate—and the subject of at least one major ongoing legal skirmish between the Park Service and various environmental groups. By 1980 ever-increasing automobile traffic—reportedly about a million vehicles on approximately 30 miles of roadway annually—was, according to the Park Service's General Management Plan, signed and finalized that year, "the single greatest threat to enjoyment of the natural and scenic qualities of Yosemite." The plan was not equivocal: "The ultimate goal of the National Park Service is to remove all private vehicles from Yosemite Valley."

"The problem at Yosemite is not too many visitors," said Interior Secretary Bruce Babbitt 20 years later in November 2000, delivering a 20-pound, six-volume, $441.7-million "final" Yosemite Valley plan—a plan that did not, incidentally, involve removing a single vehicle. "The problem is too damn many cars." (On a handful of occasions in the mid-1990s—at all-time peak visitation levels—the park was declared at capacity and the gates closed. "When the theater's full," said Ansel Adams, "they don't sell lap-space." Otherwise the notion of banning cars from the park, despite some successes in that direction at Zion and the Grand Canyon, has proven too ambitious or too controversial to implement at Yosemite.) Park Service officials are today emphatic that ongoing efforts to reduce traffic congestion in Yosemite do not include reducing the number of cars allowed into the park.

The fact remains, as former Sierra Club president David Brower has pointed out: "Rarely does the number of cars in the valley exceed the capacity of the roads and parking." For the time being—and for the foreseeable future—the car seems likely to be America's conveyance of choice. And so for now visitors are "invited" to station their vehicles at their place of accommodation, or at the Day-Use Parking Lot, thereafter to seek alternative methods of transport, by hybrid shuttle, beach cruiser, longboard, or on foot, to points around the valley and beyond.

Car Rental

A variety of fairly durable late-model vehicles can be hired from major companies at each of the airports listed above. Most offer "unlimited" mileage (always be sure to check the fine print for limitations) and competitive, deep-discounted weekly rates. Specialty vehicles (i.e. convertibles, sports cars, or SUVs), children's car seats, ski racks, and snow chains may be arranged with considerable advance notice (up to a month for smaller locations). Deposits are not generally required on car rental reservations. Significant drop-off and per-mile charges apply for one-way rentals. Pickup in Nevada and drop-off in California, or vice-versa, is not generally an option. Most credit card companies offer insurance coverage for rental cars; check yours to see if you can opt out of extra collision insurance charges.
Alamo (1-800-GO-ALAMO; www.alamo.com). BUR, FYI, LAS, LAX, ONT, RNO, SFO, SMF, SJC.

Avis (1-800-331-1212; www.avis.com). BUR, FYI, LAS, LAX, OAK, ONT, RNO, SFO, SMF, SJC.

Budget (1-800-527-0700; www.budget.com). BUR, FYI, LAS, LAX, OAK, ONT, RNO, SFO, SMF, SJC.

Dollar (1-800-800-3665; www.dollar.com). BUR, FYI, LAS, LAX, OAK, ONT, RNO, SFO, SMF, SJC.

Enterprise (1-800-261-7331; www.enterprise.com). BUR, FYI, LAS, LAX, OAK, ONT, RNO, SFO, SMF, SJC. Enterprise is the only major car rental agency with locations in the Eastern Sierra: at Mammoth (Mammoth Airport; 760-924-1094), Bishop (163 N. Main Street; 760-873-3704), and Ridgecrest/Inyokern (437 N. China Lake Boulevard; 760-384-2816). To arrange for a convertible or SUV at these locations, call at least a month in advance.

Fox (1-800-225-4369; www.foxrentacar.com). LAX, OAK, SFO, SJC.

Hertz (1-800-654-3131; www.hertz.com). BUR, FYI, LAS, LAX, OAK, ONT, RNO, SFO, SMF, SJC.

National (1-800-CAR-RENT; www.nationalcar.com). BUR, FYI, LAS, LAX, OAK, ONT, RNO, SFO, SMF, SJC.

Rent-4-Less (www.rentfourless.com). BUR, LAX, ONT, SFO. Also rents motor homes.

Thrifty (1-800-THRIFTY; www.thrifty.com). BUR, LAS, LAX, OAK, RNO, SFO, SJC.

Distances & Driving Times

Approximate distances are listed in miles for the shortest possible paved route between two locations. When summer routes are shorter than the corresponding winter detour, the former is listed first. *Note:* Given the radical topography of the region and the great variety of roads, the shortest route cannot always be counted on to be the fastest.

Driving times are impossible to estimate with any degree of accuracy. One might, for example, manage an average 60 miles an hour (or more) on US 395 between Mojave and Lee Vining, give or take a stop light or two in Bishop, and the same on CA 99 from Bakersfield to Fresno, depending on the volume of traffic, while on the Mineral King Road or the Generals Highway or up the Old Priest Grade from Chinese Camp behind a smoking diesel, one might not clear 20 miles in one long hour. On the expensively engineered Tioga Road there is a temptation to go faster than one should. Potential hazards include but are not limited to abrupt, unsignaled turnouts; cyclists; bear crossing; deer crossing; squirrel crossing; wilderness-dazed backpacker crossing; precipitous cliffs; and, of course, park rangers with radar guns.

YOSEMITE / SIERRA MILEAGE CHART

NOTE: FOR ENTRIES LISTED WITH TWO MILEAGES, THE FIRST IS FOR SUMMER, THE SECOND FOR WINTER

	Bakersfield	Fresno	Furnace Creek	Las Vegas	Lone Pine	Los Angeles	Mammoth	Reno	Sacramento	San Bernardino	San Diego	San Francisco	San Jose	Sequoia-Kings	Yosemite
Bakersfield		111	247	285	168	112	268	407	277	175	236	284	241	115	169
Fresno	111		357	396	278	215	189, 365	299	164	278	339	185	151	57	60
Furnace Creek	247	357		121	107	288	207	373	435	244	350	459, 532	452, 491	361	240, 415
Las Vegas	285	396	121		231	271	308	448	562	226	332	571	530	399	353, 453
Lone Pine	168	278	107	231		209	100	259	329	191	297	352, 453	345, 412	282	133
Los Angeles	112	215	288	271	209		309	477	387	63	124	383	340	223	305
Mammoth	268	189, 365	207	308	100	309		167	236	291	397	259, 328	252, 316	264, 382	41
Reno	407	299	373	448	259	477	167		132	451	556	219	247	355	150
Sacramento	277	164	435	562	329	387	236	132		450	511	91	124	225	140
San Bernardino	175	278	244	226	191	63	291	451	450		109	446	403	280	368
San Diego	236	339	350	332	297	124	397	556	511	109		507	464	343	429
San Francisco	284	185	459, 532	571	352, 453	383	259, 328	219	91	446	507		44	242	163
San Jose	241	151	452, 491	530	345, 412	340	252, 316	247	124	403	464	44		208	156
Sequoia-Kings	115	57	361	399	282	223	264, 382	355	225	280	343	242	208		113
Yosemite	169	60	240, 415	353, 453	133	305	41	150	140	368	429	163	156	113	

The Southern Sierra comprises one of the two largest contiguous roadless areas in the Lower 48, most of which is accessible only on foot or by pack animal.

From Las Vegas & Points East

There are several perfectly reasonable ways to get from Vegas to Death Valley: north by US 95 to junctions at Lathrop Wells (NV 373 south to Death Valley Junction), Beatty (NV 374 to Furnace Creek and Stovepipe Wells), and Scotty's Junction (NV 267 via Grapevine Canyon to Scotty's Castle)—the latter affording, as W. A. Chalfant once put it, "the unusual experience . . . of driving into the mountains on a downhill slope most of the way." The most direct route— and on many levels the most interesting—follows the Blue Diamond Highway (NV 160) west from southeast Las Vegas, past Red Rock Canyon to Pahrump (gateway to the Brothel Art Museum, self-proclaimed "oldest tourist attraction in southern Nevada"), thence due west across Ash Meadows Road and the Amargosa Valley to Death Valley Junction.

In summer, the shortest route to Yosemite is by US 95 northeast to Tonopah, west on US 6 to Benton, and finally CA 120 across to US 395. The trip to Mammoth Lakes is shorter (by about 30 miles) taking NV 266 east from US 95 through Oasis and over Westgard Pass (7,271 feet) to Big Pine, but not necessarily any quicker than through Benton and across Long Valley on the Benton Crossing Road (open all winter to provide emergency escape in case of earthquake or volcanic eruption).

From Vegas to Sequoia, or to Yosemite in winter, the fastest route is most likely the least direct: south on I-15 to Barstow, east on CA 58 to Tehachapi and Bakersfield, and then north on CA 99.

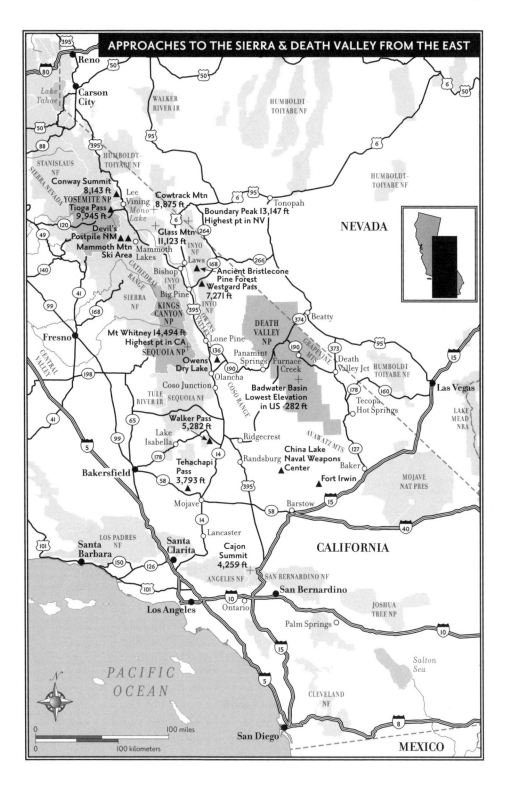

APPROACHES TO THE SIERRA & DEATH VALLEY FROM THE EAST

Reno
Lake Tahoe
Carson City
WALKER RIVER IR
HUMBOLDT-TOIYABE NF
HUMBOLDT-TOIYABE NF

STANISLAUS NF
HUMBOLDT-TOIYABE NF
SIERRA NEVADA
Conway Summit 8,143 ft
YOSEMITE NP
Tioga Pass 9,945 ft
Lee Vining
Mono Lake
Cowtrack Mtn 8,875 ft
Boundary Peak 13,147 ft Highest pt in NV
Tonopah

NEVADA

Devil's Postpile NM
Mammoth Mtn Ski Area
Mammoth Lakes
Glass Mtn 11,123 ft
INYO NF
Laws
Bishop
INYO NF
Big Pine
Ancient Bristlecone Pine Forest
Westgard Pass 7,271 ft
INYO NF

CATHEDRAL RANGE
SIERRA NF
KINGS CANYON NP
Mt Whitney 14,494 ft Highest pt in CA
SEQUOIA NP
Fresno
CENTRAL VALLEY

OWENS RIVER
Lone Pine
Owens Dry Lake
Panamint Springs
DEATH VALLEY NP
Beatty
GRAPEVINE MTS
Furnace Creek
Death Valley Jct
HUMBOLDT-TOIYABE NF
Las Vegas

Olancha
Coso Junction
TULE RIVER IR
SEQUOIA NF
COSO RANGE
Badwater Basin Lowest Elevation in US -282 ft
Tecopa Hot Springs
LAKE MEAD NRA

Walker Pass 5,282 ft
Lake Isabella
Ridgecrest
AVAWATZ MTS
China Lake Naval Weapons Center
Randsburg
Baker
Fort Irwin
MOJAVE NAT PRES

Tehachapi Pass 3,793 ft
Bakersfield
Mojave
Barstow

LOS PADRES NF
Santa Barbara
Santa Clarita
Lancaster
Cajon Summit 4,259 ft
CALIFORNIA

ANGELES NF
SAN BERNARDINO NF
San Bernardino
JOSHUA TREE NP

Los Angeles
Ontario
Palm Springs

PACIFIC OCEAN

Salton Sea

CLEVELAND NF

0   100 miles
0   100 kilometers

San Diego
MEXICO

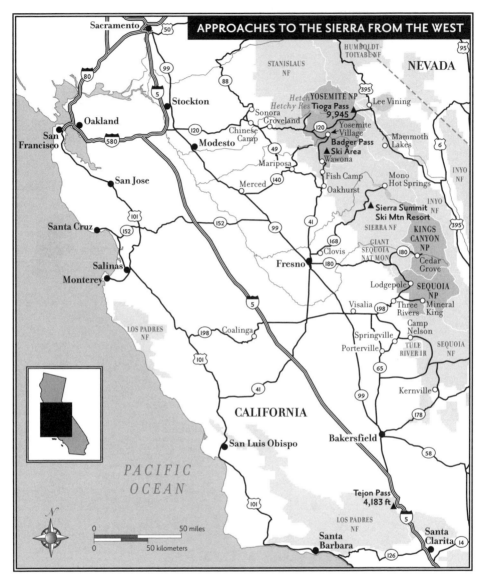

APPROACHES TO THE SIERRA FROM THE WEST

From Reno

Take US 395 south through Carson City, Minden, and Gardnerville. At Topaz Lake, on the California-Nevada line, things start to get scenic, up the West Walker River to Sonora Junction, over Devil's Gate (7,519 feet) to Bridgeport, over Conway Summit (8,143 feet) to Mono Lake, Tioga, and the high Eastern Sierra.

From Greater Los Angeles & Points South

The two main routes from downtown Los Angeles to Furnace Creek—up CA 14 and US 395 through Olancha or by I-15 via Baker to CA 127—are roughly equidistant. The former offers considerably less traffic, a glimpse of the airplane graveyard at Mojave, views of the southern promontory of the Sierra and Inyo mountains, and a heady crossing of the Panamint range. The latter affords a snapshot of "the World's Largest Thermometer" at Baker and a sense of the historic '49er approach from the east. A third and considerably more desolate route approaches from the south, from Ridgecrest through Trona and up the salt flats of the Panamint Valley. (See chapter 3 for descriptions of the various access routes into the valley.) Consider approaching by one route and leaving by another.

CA 14 and US 395 are the major arteries for access from points south to the Eastern Sierra, Mammoth and Mono lakes, and the Tuolomne Meadows region of Yosemite National Park (in summer). For fastest access to Sequoia National Park, take I-5 north to CA 99 to Visalia and CA 198. CA 65 north from Bakersfield, through Porterville, is considerably more scenic—through the oil fields and fruit orchards—but also more time consuming. The fastest route to Yosemite follows CA 41 due north from Fresno, through Oakhurst and Wawona.

From San Francisco/Oakland

The fastest route from the Bay Area to Yosemite—and to the Eastern Sierra and Death Valley, in the summer—follows I-580 to I-205, with a slight jog on I-5, to Manteca and, finally, CA 120 to Big Oak Flat and Groveland. For a thrilling demonstration of gravity, try the Old Priest Grade. To Sequoia-Kings, the most direct route is by CA 180 due east from Fresno to the Big Stump Entrance. In winter, with Tioga closed, the only way to Mammoth Lakes is by CA 88 through Markleeville, weather permitting, or Minden, Nevada. A winter journey from the Bay Area to Death Valley is best achieved by way of Bakersfield and either CA 178 over Walker Pass or, when conditions are nasty, by CA 58 over Tehachapi to Mojave.

From San Jose/Monterey

From the South Bay, Salinas, or Monterey, the most direct shot across the valley follows CA 152 over Pacheco Pass to the CA 99 corridor. CA 140 to Mariposa, El Portal, and Yosemite can be reached by way of an excellent cutoff north of Chowchilla, through Plainsburg and Planada. To get to Kings Canyon, take CA 99 south to Fresno and CA 180 east from there.

WHERE THE ROADS END

"The glaciers are the pass-makers and it is by them that the courses of all mountaineers are predestined."

—John Muir, "The Passes of the Sierra," Scribner's, March 1879

There are thousands of miles of trails into and across the southern Sierra Nevada, ranging from ancient native footpaths, sometimes mere traces through meadow grass, to highly engineered stock trails with dynamite-blasted granite staircases, bridges, and tunnels. The most popular thoroughfares include: the **Pacific Crest National Scenic Trail**, a section of which, on its way from Mexico to Canada, traverses the range from south to north, from its unheralded crossing of CA 58 beneath Tehachapi Pass, along the west flank of Mount Whitney, across the north end of Kings Canyon to its busiest miles in the vicinity of Tuolomne Meadows, thence to another mostly unheralded crossing of Sonora Pass to the

Access & Amenity Fees

Access to public lands within the Inyo, Sierra, and Sequoia National Forests, including the southern unit of the Sequoia National Monument, is free, as is access to all lands managed by the Bureau of Land Management (such as the Alabama Hills). Amenity fees are generally assessed for use of developed campgrounds, picnic areas, high-use trailheads, and boat launches. Primitive camping, where allowed, is generally free. Campfire and wilderness permits are free. Entrance fees to the national parks (Death Valley, Sequoia-Kings, and Yosemite) run $20 per vehicle (for seven days) or $10 per person on foot, bicycle, motorcycle, or bus, payable at entrance kiosks or park visitors centers. Annual Access Passes can be purchased at a rate of $40 for Death Valley and Yosemite, $30 for Sequoia-Kings, and $50 for all national parks. Children under 16 are admitted free. Depending on your plans, the best bet may be the new interagency **America the Beautiful–National Parks and Federal Recreational Lands Pass,** which at a cost of $80 provides the passholder and the occupants of his or her vehicle (not to exceed four adults) unlimited access to all federal lands and recreation sites for one year. Participating agencies include the National Park Service, the Forest Service, Fish and Wildlife Service, Bureau of Land Management, and Bureau of Reclamation. For U.S. citizens or permanent residents age 62 or older, a lifetime Senior Pass is available at a one-time cost of $10; a free Access Pass is available for those with documented permanent disabilities. These passes can be obtained at all park entrances and visitors centers, on the Internet at http://store.usgs.gov/pass, or by calling 1-888-ASK-USGS.

Tioga Entrance, Yosemite National Park Burke Griggs

Spring tracks on Skier's Alta, Sequoia National Park

north; the **John Muir Trail**, which runs from the floor of Yosemite Valley to the crest of Mount Whitney; the **High Sierra Trail**, westward from Crescent Meadow in Sequoia National Park, also to the summit of Whitney; and the **Mount Whitney Trail** itself, from Whitney Portal, on the east side, to the summit. Traffic on the Mount Whitney Trail is significant enough during the high summer season (May 1 to November 1) that a quota has been established, with trail permits issued every February by lottery (www.fs.fed.us/r5/inyo/recreation/wild/whitneylottery.shtml). Wilderness permits are required for overnight travel into all USFS or National Park lands in the Sierra and can be obtained from the nearest ranger station or visitors center. In winter these trails become the solitary domain of backcountry skiers, snowboarders, snowshoers, and pine martens.

For at least 180 years people have been making their way into the High Sierra by horse and mule. Despite ongoing and highly contentious legal battles between a vociferous minority of hikers, the Forest Service, the Park Service, and the Backcountry Horsemen of America, pack animals are still a common sight on certain backcountry trails—and a unique way to explore the country. See the "Recreation" section in each regional chapter for detailed information on local pack outfits and services.

Mountain bikes, trail bikes, ATVs, and snowmobiles are, with certain restrictions, allowed on existing trails and roads throughout national forest and BLM lands, except within the bounds of designated wilderness areas. Within Sequoia and Yosemite National Parks, such wheeled and/or motorized vehicles are not allowed beyond the pavement. In the remote canyons of Death Valley, on the other hand, hundreds of miles of old, suspension-brutalizing mining roads remain open to off-highway and four-wheel-drive enthusiasts, from Ballarat to Badwater, from the Ubehebe Crater to the Saline Valley.

3

DEATH VALLEY

Across the Great Sink

The fascination of the desert is stronger in Death Valley than at any other place.

—the prospector Dismukes, in Zane Grey's Wanderer of the Wasteland, 1923

Mr. Grey, lion hunter, big-game fisherman, and millionaire author of *Riders of the Purple Sage* and other pulp Westerns (books and movies), stepped off the Tonopah and Tidewater Railroad in March 1919. "It was sunset when we arrived," he wrote, "—a weird, strange sunset in drooping curtains of transparent cloud, lighting up dark mountain ranges, some peaks of which were clear-cut and black against the sky, and others veiled in trailing storms, and still others white with snow." Death Valley Junction was in those days not the desolate coming together of highways that it is now, but a bustling freight hub, where the mainline T & T met the narrow-gauge Death Valley Railroad (DVRR), the latter bearing heavy tonnage of rough borax from the mines at Ryan, 21 miles to the west. Aside from the depot, there was a "dingy little store," a borax processing mill, and a sprawling collection of workers' tents and shacks. Where the hotel now stands was Tubbs' Saloon and Whorehouse. Grey spent his evening at the store, fraternizing with the locals: "I heard prospectors talk about float, which meant gold on the surface, and about high grade ores, zinc, copper, silver, lead, manganese, and about how borax was mined thirty years ago, and hauled out of Death Valley by teams of twenty mules."

It seems likely there were Mexican miners (and perhaps Mormons, too) working the region by the early 1840s, but tales of riches to be found in Death Valley got their true wings with that first fateful crossing in 1849–50. "[T]wo or three of the party went to a range of hills a mile or two off the line of travel in search of water," wrote P. A. Chalfant, prospector and fellow '49er (and W. A. Chalfant's father), in 1872. "They came back and reported that they had found no water, but a mountain of something they believed to be silver." Water being the more important element at that particular moment, they pressed on. Another version has Captain Townsend, of the Georgians, at some later date taking a piece of ore carried out of Death Valley to a gunsmith, to have a new sight made for his rifle—and the ore turning out to be pure silver. In the fall of 1850, "while prospecting around Rough and Ready, Nevada County," Chalfant interviewed a Dr. McCormick, who

had recently returned to Death Valley and come back with convincing samples. "He described the mountain as being in many places literally seamed with strings or wires of silver," wrote Chalfant, ". . . that in many places the rock fairly glistened with silver."

The first problem: "it was situated in the midst of a most horrible desert some three hundred miles in the wilderness, the nearest water being 25 or 30 miles distant, and that of such a degree of badness that it was wholly unfit for use when packed so far." The second: No one thereafter was ever able to locate the place.

"It was a valley where nature had been prodigal of her treasures," wrote Grey in 1923, "and terrible in her hold upon them."

Another '49er by the name of Charles Breyfogle, who had once upon a time had a bit of luck in the Sierra foothills, was out looking for the "lost Gunsight lode" when, one warm summer morning in 1864, probably somewhere in the Amargosa Valley, at Ash Meadows or at the edge of the Funeral Range, he awoke to find his horses and supplies stolen, and—according to at least one account—the heads of his traveling companions bashed in by Indians. Days later, delirious, blistering with sunburn, and clutching a piece of rock he

Prospector's cabin, Harrisburg Flats, Death Valley National Park Burke Griggs

had broken from a ledge somewhere, he was himself picked up by Indians. Whether these people made him a slave for the entertainment of their children or tied him up to keep him from drowning himself in a spring, whether he was saved by Mormon emigrants or given a horse and set on his way, "the crazy Dutchman from Reese River" made it back to Austin, Nevada, with a nugget of gold impressive enough to drive thousands of so-called single-blanket jackass prospectors, for many decades to come, into the desert. (Prospectors these days are more likely to drive dirt bikes or ATVs than mules, and they have been known to supplement their shovel work with a certain amount of traffic in rare gems and fossils, and by the cultivation of marijuana in abandoned mineshafts.)

A silver strike in Surprise Canyon in 1874 brought the hasty construction of Panamint City, with its brief population of two thousand—considered "the toughest, rawest, most hard-boiled little hellhole that ever passed for a civilized town." The place was abandoned in 1875 and destroyed the following year by flash flood. The town of Ballarat in 1898 had a population of five hundred people and boasted "seven saloons, three hotels, a Wells Fargo station, post office, school, a jail and morgue, but not one church." The nearby Radcliffe Mine is said to have produced 15,000 tons of gold ore before it played out in 1903. A series of strikes in 1904–6—gold, silver, copper, and lead—brought fleeting settlement to places called Chloride City, Greenwater (where drinking water was sold for $15 a barrel), Harrisburg, Leadfield, Rhyolite, and Skidoo. Rhyolite peaked at ten thousand citizens, a

Original 20-mule-team wagons, Harmony Borax Works

three-story bank building, stores, bars, hotels, churches, a school, a hospital, and an ice cream parlor. Electricity came in 1907. In 1911 the biggest mill closed its doors. In 1916 the electricity was shut off—for good.

Other short-lived ventures in the region include one attempt at harvesting saltpeter (potassium nitrate) for fertilizer and gunpowder, and another at collecting sulphur for making matches. An elaborate monorail was built to haul Epsom salts (magnesium) over the Panamint range, but the operation was suspended after only a few loads.

One night in the late 1870s, also near Ash Meadows, a prospector stopped off at the dirt-floor cabin of one Aaron Winters and his Mexican wife, Rosie. The man spoke of the money being made by those who had discovered borax in Nevada. He described the look of the stuff and related the process by which it could be identified. After he had gone, the couple made a journey to procure the necessary chemicals and supplies, then made their way to a place in Death Valley where Winters had once seen loads of something "answering to the description." Winters managed to sell his claim to onetime San Francisco vigilante William Tell Coleman for $20,000.

By 1883 Coleman's Harmony Borax Works was in full swing, with 40 men scraping "cottonball" (ulexite) from the playa near Furnace Creek and an array of cooling vats producing up to 3 tons a day of rough-processed borax. Borax, according to the U.S. Geological Survey, is "a common ingredient of soaps, cleansers, herbicides, soldering fluxes, gasoline antiknock compounds, pharmaceuticals, water softeners, food preservatives, and fire retardants . . . [and] in the manufacture of glass, pyrex, and porcelain enamels used on kitchen appliances, sinks, bathtubs, stoves, and other products." Borax is used as a pesticide and a wood preservative. Ulexite, specifically, is today a fundamental component of fiber optics. For six years the stuff was hauled out of Death Valley by the celebrated (and later trademarked) 20-mule teams—later 18 mules with a pair of horses as wheel animals—165 miles over the Panamints, at 16 to 18 miles a day, with 46,000 pounds of borax and 1,200 gallons of water (for the long days and nights between springs), to the nearest railroad at Mojave. The Greenland Ranch, today known as Furnace Creek Ranch, was developed in the early 1880s to provide alfalfa for the teams, and fresh meat, shade, and accommodations for the workers.

Six years later Coleman was broke, forced to sell his extensive holdings to the Pacific Coast Borax Company. The ulexite operation at Harmony was abandoned in favor of colemanite mines in the Greenwater Mountains east of Furnace Creek. By the time Zane Grey arrived at Death Valley Junction, the famous mule teams had long since been replaced, first by a rather inept steam tractor, then by the railroads. The processing mill was "getting out twenty-five hundred sacks a day." A passenger could then board a train at the Santa Fe Depot in downtown Los Angeles (now an acclaimed school for architecture), transfer at Ludlow to the Tonopah and Tidewater, and in the space of about 16 hours, with Pullman service most of the way, step off the narrow gauge within hiking distance of the Greenland Ranch.

Grey and his traveling companion, a game and courteous Norwegian by the name of Nielsen, both ready, after a full day on the T & T and a night in Death Valley Junction, to be "lost to the works of man," opted to forego the DVRR and instead cover the last leg to Furnace Creek by mule. Near sunset they rounded a curve and caught their first glimpse of the great sink. While Nielsen continued down the canyon to set up camp—there were no tourist accommodations in those days—Grey lingered over a grand baroque spectacle of storm clouds and dying light. "When the sun had set," he wrote, "and all that upheaved and furrowed world of rock had received a mantle of gray, and a slumberous sulphurous ruddy haze slowly darkened to purple and black, then I realized more fully that I was looking down into Death Valley."

Perhaps because of Grey's less-than-flattering description of working conditions at Death Valley Junction (first in *Harper's Bazaar,* then in his travel memoir, *Tales of Lonely Trails,* published in 1922), and likely because of a sudden increase in tourism to the region (by just the sort of people who were likely to be reading Zane Grey's gauzy descriptions of the desert), the Pacific Coast Borax Company, by then a subsidiary of British mining giant Borax Consolidated, Ltd., took it upon itself, in 1923, to buy the land beneath Tubbs' Saloon and Whorehouse and build something more permanent. W. A. Chalfant, the son, described what was built as a "town under one roof": "Imagine a one-story adobe building occupying three sides of a square, and about eight hundred feet in length. The long roof sheltered offices, store, recreation places, barber shop, hospital and accompaniments, and other places, even to a handsome little theater." Two years later an enormous raw borax deposit was discovered in the Mojave desert, significantly closer to major freight lines, and the whole operation—the mines at Ryan, the mill at Death Valley Junction—shut down.

In an effort to make good on some of its investments, the company renovated rooms at the Junction to accommodate tourists, turned the defunct barracks at Ryan into the Death Valley View Hotel, and allocated $30,000 to start construction of a first-class resort, to be called the Furnace Creek Inn. The first guests arrived on February 1, 1927, by way of a gaso-

When to Go

Death Valley is famous for being one of the lowest, hottest, driest spots on the planet. Less than 2 inches of rain fall here every year. Some years (1929, 1953) there is no rain at all. Other years (1942, 1976, 1984, 1988, 2004) it falls all at once, causing violent flash floods and debris slides across alluvial fans (such as that at Furnace Creek), washing out roads and buildings and scenic overlooks, floating cars, and filling vast, once-dry lakes. The asphalt on CA 190 gives out every time. Precipitation is most likely to occur in January, February, and March, and when it does occur, afterward the wildflowers explode (mid-February to mid-April). The hottest month is July, with an average high temperature of 115 degrees Fahrenheit.

The highest ambient temperature ever recorded in the United States was 134 degrees, on July 10, 1913, at the Greenland Ranch (now Furnace Creek Ranch). For nine years this was the world record, until September 13, 1922, when a temperature of 57.7 degrees Celcius (135.9 degrees Fahrenheit) was recorded in Al'Aziziyah, Libya. (For some perspective, 140 is the temperature at which bedbugs, dust mites, and most bacteria will die; it is the minimum temperature to which hamburger must be heated in

Hot crows, Stovepipe Wells, June 2007

fast food restaurants; and it's the temperature at which coffee begins to present a significant burn hazard to human skin.) The record still stands. Some contend that if a recording station were installed at the low point at Badwater (-282 feet) instead of at Furnace Creek (-214 feet), Death Valley would take back the cup.

When silent-film director Erich Von Stroheim took his cast and crew into Death Valley in August and September of 1923, as reported at the time by the *Inyo Independent*, "[t]he temperature was 130 degrees by a properly shaded thermometer, and the heat radiation from the scorching, sun-baked sand of the desert made the trousers of the men so hot as far up as their knees that many were compelled to wrap bandages around their calves to keep the cloth from touching the skin."

The first people, the Timbisha Shoshone, before they got air-conditioning, used to head for the high country in summer. Now they mostly go to Lone Pine. The early caretakers of the Greenland Ranch are said to have spent summer nights sleeping in irrigation ditches. "It's not hot until it hits 120," said a park employee of five summers recently, one mild 112-degree afternoon in May. The most pleasant time to visit, flash floods notwithstanding, is midwinter, when there is snow on the Panamints, the nights are cool at Furnace Creek, and the days sunny and clear with temperatures in the high 60s and low 70s. The park tends to be busiest in March and April, then again in November. For those interested in experiencing the true extremes of the place—or saving money on this year's European vacation—consider joining the automotive industry's car testers and the fleets of European tourists in the 24-hour-a-day scorch of July and August in Death Valley.

Daily Death Valley weather report: www.dvnha.org/morning_report/Morning.pdf or call 760-786-3200, option (1) and (3).

Zane Grey at Zabriskie Point, 1919   From *Tales of Lonely Trails* by Zane Grey (1922)

line-powered narrow-gauge passenger car on the old DVRR line. The room rate of $10 per night included private bath and three meals. Much of the staff came from the Old Faithful Lodge in Yellowstone National Park during its off-season from November to April. By the end of 1933 Death Valley had been designated a national monument, and two companies of Civilian Conservation Corpsmen had arrived to upgrade roads and build facilities. The DVRR was dismantled and shipped to Carlsbad, New Mexico, for service in a potash mining operation. The old trestle timber was used to build a kitchen and lounge for the inn.

Charles Manson was arrested in Death Valley National Monument in 1969. Eight years later, George Lucas used the place as a stand-in for Luke Skywalker's home planet, Tatooine. Bill Clinton declared it a national park in 1994—the largest in the Lower 48—and in the same moment expanded its boundaries to include the northern end of the Panamint Range and Saline Valley. Ninety-five percent of the park's 3.3 million acres is designated wilderness.

THE LAY OF THE LAND: APPROACHES & LOGISTICS

Perhaps the most historic way to arrive in Death Valley would be to come in from the east, across the Amargosa, with oxen and enormous freight wagons bearing pianos and Louis XVI armoires. Or to come down Grapevine Canyon with a hand-drawn map on a cloth bar napkin depicting watering holes, most labeled with a skull and crossbones. Today, however, there are four well-asphalted routes into the valley from points east. From Vegas, CA 190 is the most direct (via the Blue Diamond Highway, then State Line Road from the north end of Pahrump, Nevada), following both the original emigrants' route into Furnace Creek and the old railway bed of the DVRR (still visible on the south side of the highway from Death Valley Junction).

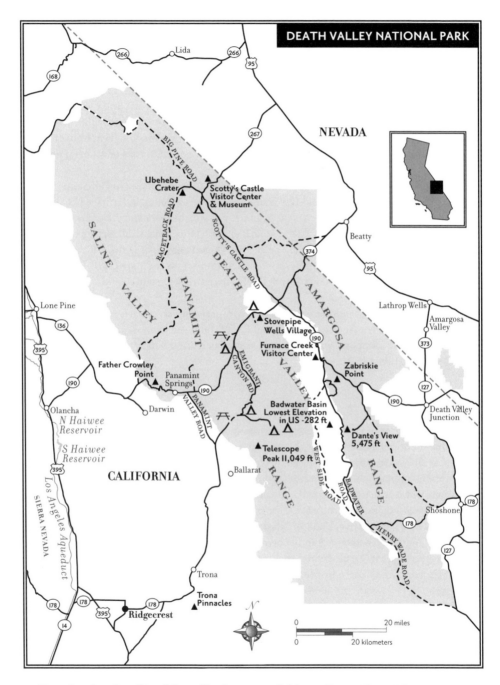

DEATH VALLEY NATIONAL PARK

From Los Angeles, CA 178 from Shoshone over Salsberry Pass is the quickest way into the park—but proves not as speedy to Furnace Creek as CA 190. For a hint of the way it used to be, try the well-graded gravel on the Greenwater Valley Road from CA 178 north to Ryan, or, from the north, try the fabulously underused Big Pine Road from CA 168 (Westgard Pass) to the Grapevine entrance, both manageable in a passenger car except during or immediately after any kind of inclement weather.

Note: The Park Service generally recommends high-clearance vehicles for travel off-pavement in Death Valley. Always check with a ranger for conditions. Bring plenty of water and know the capacity of your equipment.

The most common (and dramatic) access route from the east is by CA 190 from Olancha or Lone Pine via Father Crowley Point, Panamint Springs, Towne Pass, and Eichbaum's old toll road to Stovepipe Wells. From Los Angeles or San Bernardino, a slightly more direct route follows the Panamint Valley north from Trona to CA 190. The Emigrant Canyon Road is a worthwhile, if slower, alternative, with a significant mountain pass and a brief pot-holed section in the heart of Wildrose Canyon.

The nearest full-sized grocery store to Death Valley (Albertson's) is in Pahrump, Nevada. There is expensive gas and free water available year-round at Furnace Creek, Stovepipe Wells, and Panamint Springs. As of press time, there was no gas at Scotty's Castledue to "equipment failure." Gas is sold at slightly more reasonable prices in Lone Pine, Olancha, Ridgecrest, Shoshone, and Beatty. There is no gas at Death Valley Junction (try Mom's Convenience Store, 7 miles to the north and across the state line). There is a mechanic of some kind on general duty at the Furnace Creek Chevron—and a AAA tow truck.

Listings within each section are organized from east to west, whenever possible, beginning with listings in the Amargosa Basin and Range, followed by those to the east of Death Valley, Death Valley proper, Panamint, and Saline. Recreation listings, toward the end of the chapter, are listed alphabetically.

LODGING

Coming from the east, there are simple accommodations at Tecopa Hot Springs, and at Shoshone there is a motel with access to another warm springs pool. There are motels and motel-casinos at Pahrump and Beatty, Nevada. The only accommodations worth much consideration outside the park (in the Amargosa Basin) are Marta Becket's famed **Amargosa Hotel**—the location for David Lynch's *Lost Highway Hotel,* in the haunted old Pacific Coast Borax headquarters at Death Valley Junction (www.amargosaoperahouse.com; 760-852-4441; inexpensive)—and the **Ranch House Inn,** an eclectic two-room cottage-style B&B (and furnished tepee) in the heart of the oasis at China Ranch (www.ranchhouse inn.com; 760-852-4360; moderate, includes breakfast). The nearest accommodations west of the park are at Cerro Gordo or in Lone Pine (see chapter 4), or to the south in Ridgecrest.

Within park boundaries, lodging is available at Furnace Creek, Stovepipe Wells, and Panamint Springs. Spring is the busiest season, especially during those weeks immediately following a splashy photo spread of desert wildflowers in the travel section of the *LA Times.* Accommodations at Furnace Creek will frequently sell out on Friday and Saturday nights. Stovepipe Wells sells out less frequently, but it does happen. One weekend the park is sure to fill to capacity—steer clear or book many months in advance—is during the Death Valley '49er Encampment in November. Otherwise, with fewer than a million visitors each year, most just passing through, Death Valley is still a place where silence and wind reign supreme.

Lodging Price Code

Cost of lodging is based on an average per-room, double-occupancy rate at peak season (November to May). Tax and gratuities are not included. Rates are significantly reduced during the summer and early fall.

Inexpensive	Up to $75
Moderate	$75 to $125
Expensive	$125 to $200
Very Expensive	Over $200

✪ Furnace Creek Inn

www.furnacecreekresort.com
CA 190, Death Valley
Elevation: -179 feet
Open: Mid-October to mid-May
760-786-2345; 1-888-29-PARKS
(1-888-297-2757)
Innkeeper: Xanterra Parks & Resorts
Price: Very Expensive
Pets: No
Wheelchair Access: Yes
Internet Access: No

Built from 1927 to 1935 by British mining conglomerate Borax Consolidated, in the wake of pulling its mining business out of Death Valley, the Furnace Creek Inn today ranks among the greatest—and most civilized—of the handful of great historic national parks lodges still in operation in the United States. The architecture and decor are a remarkable hodgepodge of Mission, Southwest, and art deco styles, with red Granada-tile roofs, sea green trim, porticos, painted brick, and abundant local stonework. Recent interior renovations have combined the latest in luxury bedding (plus televisions, hair dryers, and coffeemakers) with appropriately ponderous retro furnishings. The original charm of the place may suffer ever so slightly from an institutional proliferation of the Xanterra logo—on staff uniforms, on shrink-wrapped plastic cups in the bathrooms, shampoo bottles, and so on. But the real draw here is the *situation:* Where in 1926

The pool at Furnace Creek Inn

there were rocks and sand and borax, there is now a mature North African–style oasis of deglet nour date palms, spring-fed runnels and ponds, and shaded garden paths— favored on balmy evenings by coyotes and crickets—and a close-cropped lawn on which one thinks at any moment someone might begin a game of croquet. The pool is chlorine-free and perfectly delicious, fed by the same natural 83-degree spring water that Mrs. Reverend Brier used to make her lifesaving coffee on Christmas Eve, 1849. A short list of many famous guests over the years includes Bette Davis, John Barrymore, Ronald Reagan, Peter Fonda, Dennis Hopper, and Anthony Quinn. Clark Gable and Carole Lombard had their honeymoon here in 1939.

Furnace Creek Ranch's pool Burke Griggs

Furnace Creek Ranch

www.furnacecreekresort.com
CA 190, Death Valley
Elevation: -214 feet
Open: Year-round
760-786-2345; 1-888-29-PARKS
Innkeeper: Xanterra Parks & Resorts
Price: Moderate to Expensive
Pets: No
Wheelchair Access: Yes
Internet Access: No

When the Furnace Creek Inn is closed for the season, or the budget so dictates, or the family's in tow, this is the place to stay. The property first opened to guests in 1933 as a rustic alternative to Furnace Creek Inn, after 50 years as a working stock ranch for mining operations throughout the region. The constructed pond (now a central feature of the golf course) has been serving migratory waterfowl since 1881. Accommodations range from small, upgraded Depression-era cabin units to spacious midcentury parkside motel rooms with sliding glass doors onto the lawn and pool area, all within a short salt-cedar-shaded stroll of the stables, golf course, tennis courts, horseshoe pitches, restaurants, museum, general store, and saloon. The pool is a more utilitarian, family-friendly, slightly cooler downstream version of the one at Furnace Creek Inn— fed by the same confluence of springs.

Stovepipe Wells Village

www.stovepipewells.com
CA. 190, Death Valley
Elevation: Sea level
Open: Year-round
760-786-2387
Innkeepers: Xanterra Parks & Resorts
Price: Moderate
Pets: Yes
Wheelchair Access: Yes
Internet Access: No

Somewhere near here the Jayhawkers burned their wagons to smoke the meat of their last remaining oxen. Three quarters of a century later, in 1926, a year before Borax built the Furnace Creek Inn, an electrical engineer and veteran of Rhyolite by the name of H. W. "Bob" Eichbaum got permission from Inyo County to build the first maintained road into Death Valley from the west, to charge a toll for travel thereon, and also to be the sole concessionaire. At the end of his road, across the dunes from the original Stovepipe Well, he built 20 modified tent houses, a restaurant, a pool, tennis courts, a landing strip, and a generator-powered Hollywood-style beacon to give pioneering motorists hope through the dark desert night. He called it Bungalette City. The tennis courts are gone now. The landscaping—to this day not much changed since the wagon burning, or since the end of the last little ice age—may be explained by a lack of free-flowing spring-water. The pool, open until midnight, is filled with heated and chlorinated well water, showers feature extraordinary pressure, and drinking water is produced by reverse osmosis (or bottled elsewhere and sold in vending machines). Air-conditioning; Turner Classic Movies on the TV.

Panamint Springs Resort
www.deathvalley.com
CA 190, Panamint Valley

Elevation: 1,940 feet
Open: Year-round
775-482-7680
Innkeepers: The Cassells
Price: Moderate
Pets: Yes, for a small fee
Wheelchair Access: Yes
Internet Access: Free wireless

Panamint Springs had long gone to seed by March 2006, when the Cassell family—evidently not of quite the same depth of resources as the Xanterra Corporation—took a significant leap, purchased the historic in-holding, and began its slow rescue. At press time, plumbing was being replaced and interior renovations (of the "sweat-equity" variety) had begun on several units, the late-'70s-vintage veneer furnishings, ancient floral bedspreads, sea-green indoor/outdoor carpeting, holes in sheetrock, and so on, giving way to . . . well, we'll have to see. Hopefully most of the original exterior details will stay—the old

Rooms with a view, Panamint Springs Resort Burke Griggs

Xanterra?

It begins, perhaps, with an ambitious Englishman by the name of Frederick Henry Harvey, who in 1876, at the age of 41, opened the first of a highly successful series of traveler's eateries on the Atchison, Topeka & Santa Fe Railway. By the time old Fred died in 1901, the Fred Harvey Company was operating 47 restaurants, 15 hotels, and 30 dining cars, with trademark postcards and cheap Southwestern-themed curios at most locations selling even better than the hotcakes. For the spread of decent food, and for the courteous young "Harvey Girls" who served it, Will Rogers is said to have dubbed Harvey "the civilizer of the West." His descendants expanded the empire to include food service and hospitality in such glamorous locations as the Albuquerque airport, the Illinois Tollway, and, beginning in 1956, the U.S. Borax and Chemical Company's tourist properties in Death Valley.

To look at it from another angle, it begins even earlier, with a German fellow by the name of Heinrich Hackfeld, who, in 1849, opted not to go to California but to Hawaii. By the time Archduke Ferdinand was shot dead in the streets of Sarajevo in June 1914, H. Hackfeld & Co. controlled about 60,000 acres of Hawaiian real estate, a significant portion of Hawaii's sugar trade, and a major dry goods chain named for Hackfeld's nephew B. F. Ehlers. Four years later, at the height of the War to End All Wars, the U.S. government seized the company's assets—as it did those of many who had German names or relatives still in Germany—and sold them to a group of more overtly patriotic investors. The company's name was changed to American Factors, Inc. (later shortened to Amfac, Inc.), the dry goods business to Liberty House. In 1968 Amfac—which by then had begun to diversify into the parks and resorts business—bought the Fred Harvey Company.

Twenty years later, Amfac, after acquiring its rival, TW Recreational Services, sold itself for $920 million to a company called JMB Realty, subsidiary of an entity called the Northbrook Corporation. In 2002, the Amfac brand was changed to Xanterra, which, according to company literature, is a willful derivation of Coleridge's mythical Xanadu ("an idyllic and beautiful paradise") and the Latin word *terra*, the composite therefore supposed to mean "beautiful places on earth." Xanterra is today the officially contracted steward (along with the good old, chronically underfunded National Park Service) of such national treasures as Zion, Yellowstone, the Grand Canyon, Rocky Mountain National Park, the Everglades, Mount Rushmore, and Death Valley, with plausible claims to being the largest park management company in the United States. And also the "greenest": ask about the company's latest contributions to the environment.

Xanterra owns the buildings at the Furnace Creek Ranch, Inn, and Resort (and golf course), and the property beneath them, and runs the places in cooperation with—but without any special restriction from—the Park Service. Stovepipe Wells and Scotty's Castle, on the other hand, are owned by the U.S. government and only operated by Xanterra. Park Service restrictions and pricing controls apply, and account for differences in cost and service.

wooden windows, the sun-bleached shake roofs, the desert-pink cinderblock—that together with the setting give the place a dreamy heat-induced hint of Old Mexico. The patriarch even has dreams of a beach-entry horizon pool with a swim-up bar and a grand sunset view across the dunes. In the meantime, the Cassells are a friendly and hospitable bunch, generous with their air-conditioning, their stuffed jackalope head, and their spectacular front porch—worth stopping in to visit, even if only for a burger, a cold micro-brew, a landscape-defying mango-berry smoothie, or directions up the wash to nearby Darwin Falls.

DEATH VALLEY CAMPING

	Elevation	Season	Reservations Accepted	Fee	Sites	Water	Agency
Furnace Creek*	-196	Year-round	Yes	Yes	136	Yes	NPS
Sunset	-196	Oct–Apr	No	Yes	1,000	Yes	NPS
Texas Spring	0	Oct–Apr	No	Yes	92	Yes	NPS
Mesquite Spring	1,800	Year-round	No	Yes	30	Yes	NPS
Stovepipe Wells	0	Oct–Apr	No	Yes	200	Yes	NPS
Emigrant (tents only)	2,100	Year-round	No	No	10	Yes	NPS
Wildrose	4,100	Year-round	No	No	30	Apr–Nov	NPS
Thorndike**	7,400	Mar–Nov	No	No	6	No	NPS
Mahogany Flat**	8,200	Mar–Nov	No	No	13	No	NPS
Panamint Springs‡	2,000	Year-round	Yes	Yes	67	Yes	NPS

* Reservations can be made online at www.recreation.gov or by calling 1-877-444-6777.   ** High clearance/four-wheel drive recommended.
‡ Private concession: 775-482-7680.

CAMPING

Camping on the desert is an experience not to be missed, especially after the sun goes down and the stars come out. Nights on the valley floor can be cool in winter, unbearable in summer. Wildrose, Thorndike, and Mahogany Flat (in the Panamint Range) offer pleasant alternatives to the summer heat at lower elevations. There's not much to recommend the parking-lot-style campgrounds at Furnace Creek, Sunset, Stovepipe Wells, and Panamint Springs—except perhaps their proximity to concessions (and/or swimming pools). If you have a sturdy vehicle, the right equipment, and plenty of water, more secluded sites can be found along various backcountry roads, and at the informal campgrounds at Eureka Dunes and at the popular Saline Valley Warm Springs. Bring your own shade and avoid mine shafts. No campfires are allowed in undeveloped sites. Consult a ranger for up-to-date conditions and restrictions.

DINING

Keeping in mind the location—and the fact that in the last century and a half countless people (and beasts of burden) have starved to death in this place—there is surprisingly decent, if still limited, fare to be had in Death Valley, and in the neighboring Amargosa Basin.

Dining Price Code

Based on the cost of one dinner, including entrée and appetizer (or entrée and dessert) and a beverage. Tax and gratuities not included.

Inexpensive	Up to $15
Moderate	$15 to $30
Expensive	$30 to $45
Very Expensive	Over $45

Pastel's Bistro (Tecopa Hot Springs, Noonday Road; 760-852-4307; moderate). An oasis of classical music and good food, home cooked by chef John Muccio, a Bronx/Jersey native and 20-year veteran of

Mama Joe's in Vegas. The only place to eat in Tecopa and a worthwhile stop on the road from Baker. Salad Niçoise, pasta in pink sauce, ice cream waffle sandwiches.

C'est Si Bon Café (CA 127, Shoshone; 760-852-4307; inexpensive). Crêpes, smoothies, espresso, homemade minestrone soup, crustless quiche, folk art, and Internet. Open Wednesday through Sunday 8–4 or when the sign's out front.

Furnace Creek Inn Dining Room (Furnace Creek Inn; 760-786-2345; www.furnace creekresort.com; expensive). In the spring of 1927 a dinner menu at the newly opened Furnace Creek Inn included such dry-country delicacies as pickled creosote buds, tarantula bullion, gila monster à la king, and braised burro tongue, all of which could be washed down with a choice of scorpion cocktail, arsenic spring water, or hot borax tea. Today the most exotic thing on the menu may be the rattlesnake empanadas, made on the premises with nopalitos, cumin, garlic, red chile, lime, and imperceptible tidbits of serpent imported from Nevada or Texas. The date bread, with its accompanying selection of butters, is justly famous. But be sure to leave room for the duck. For breakfast, with the heat rising over the playa beyond, imagine fresh-iced melon and corn cakes with chile hollandaise. It's hard to eat anywhere

else in Death Valley—unless you have no choice. Open mid-October to mid-May. Reservations recommended. No shorts or T-shirts.

Wrangler Buffet & Steakhouse (Furnace Creek Ranch; 760-786-2345; www.furnace creekresort.com; moderate to expensive). This bustling family-style supper house, with brass rails and comfortable booths done in airline-style upholstery, serves steak, ribs, chicken, and more. There's also a fine shrimp scampi, as if to remind a person why such an option abides. The lamb burger on rosemary focaccia with goat cheese, sun-dried tomatoes, and romaine is served with a steak knife, and the jalapeño poppers sell out fast. Progressive wine list; full bar. The copious buffets for breakfast and lunch are set to upbeat Muzac versions of great Western film scores. Open year-round (except at certain mysterious times of the year, when things are quiet and only the Forty-Niner Café is open). No reservations accepted. Gratuity included during summer (to help the Europeans).

Forty-Niner Café (Furnace Creek Ranch; 760-786-2345; inexpensive). Date shakes, pie, hamburgers, soups, salads, eggs, pancakes, biscuits and gravy, and more, and a towering club sandwich with real sliced turkey and thumb-sized freedom fries. Diner-style, but with access to a full bar. Open daily, October to May, and in summer, too (except during certain mysterious weeks when things are quiet and only the Wrangler is open).

Toll Road Restaurant (Stovepipe Wells; 760-786-2604; inexpensive). A standard cafeteria done up in vague mine-shaft accoutrements, with service reminiscent of a coffee shop in an old downtown Vegas casino. Highlights include breast of chicken smothered in barbecue sauce and topped with a bacon strip and melted cheddar

---

Scorpion Cocktail

2 parts white rum
2 parts brandy
1 part lemon juice, freshly squeezed
1 part orange juice, freshly squeezed

Combine ingredients and shake with cracked ice. Strain into a frosted goblet. Garnish with a slice of orange and a maraschino cherry. Makes 1 cocktail.

cheese (with soup or salad, baked potato, fries, or rice). The menu expands slightly in winter. The breakfast buffet—crumbled egg-substance, melon cubes, etc.—evokes something recently reconstituted from ancient stores on the planet Tatooine. If you have water and fortitude enough to keep walking, keep walking. Open all three meals daily.

TAVERNS, SALOONS & ROADHOUSES

J & R Crowbar Café & Saloon (CA 127, Shoshone; 760-852-4335). Established in 1920, built in the late '30s, and added onto in the '50s, J & R features a welded-steel railroad rail for a bar footstep. Burgers, steaks, enchiladas, and breakfast.

Corkscrew Saloon (Furnace Creek Ranch). The best place for a cold draft beer or an ice-rimmed martini is the lounge or the terrace at the Furnace Creek Inn, but when the inn's closed—or too far up the hill, or when you can't be bothered to scrape the borax out from under your fingernails—the Corkscrew'll do. Sporting events on television, pool table, acres of functional oak veneer. Note the old mule-team yokes on the wall and the inexplicable 6-foot two-man log saw—more than 100 miles from the nearest big tree.

Badwater Saloon (Stovepipe Wells). The only watering hole within reasonable walking distance. There's not much to recommend the place: It has a terrific name but doesn't live up to it. Closes early if no one's drinking.

Panamint Springs (CA 190; 775-482-7680). Fine burgers with avocado (in season), a notable selection of microbrews, friendly folks, the most extensive amateur and professional photography collection of the northern Mojave on display anywhere in the world. Best front porch in the Greater Death Valley region.

BOOKS, MAPS & INFORMATION

Shoshone Museum (CA 127, Shoshone; 760-852-4414; www.deathvalleychamber.org). Originally built in 1906 as a union hall in the mining camp of Greenwater, the building was moved here in the 1920s, first to serve as a gas station, then as a rock shop, now as a kind of homegrown museum run by the Death Valley Chamber of Commerce. Artifacts and photographs of early mining and exploration, some very old and mysterious local pachyderm bones (thought to be a mastodon of one kind or another), a good selection of local history and geology books and reports, plus the local cemetery guide. Open 10–4; closed Wednesday.

Beatty Information Center (US 95, Beatty, Nevada; 775-553-2200). Basic exhibits on natural and cultural history of the region. Books, maps, and materials stocked by the Death Valley Natural History Association. Open 8–6 daily, year-round.

Furnace Creek Visitor Center (North of Furnace Creek Ranch; 760-786-3244; www.nps.gov/deva). Here lies the mother lode of Death Valley information. Fabulous 1960s-vintage dioramas, orientation programs, lectures, racks of helpful brochures and handouts, and a team of tireless, knowledgeable, map-wielding rangers. Terrific selection of books, maps, collectibles, and kids' stuff (and Sparkletts brand drinking water) stocked by the nonprofit **Death Valley Natural History Association** (760-786-2243; www.dvnha.org). Open daily 8–5. Don't miss the natural spring water tap and drinking fountain out front by the restrooms.

Scotty's Castle Bookstore & Visitors Center (Grapevine Canyon, NV 267; 760-786-2392). Exhibits on the history of the place, the Staininger Ranch, the Johnsons, Death Valley Scotty, and so on. The bookstore is run by the Death Valley Natural History Association. Tour tickets are on sale here. Open daily 8:30–5.

Eastern Sierra Interagency Visitors Center (US 395 and CA 136, Lone Pine; 760-876-6222). Death Valley National Park is one of the cooperating agencies, so a full range of their printed materials is available here. Plus there is a selection of books, maps, and more stocked by the Eastern Sierra Interpretive Association. Open daily 8–5; extended hours in summer.

Old Guest House Museum (13193 Main Street, Trona; 760-372-5222; www1.iwvisp.com/svhs). Run by the Searles Valley Historical Society, the museum includes photos and artifacts from the old days, including John Searles's coat. Open most mornings (except Sunday) or by appointment. Also run by the society are the Trona Railway Museum and the History House (83001 Panamint Street; open by appointment only). Free admission.

Maturango Museum & Death Valley Tourist Center (100 E. Las Flores Avenue, Ridgecrest; across from Home Depot; 760-375-6900; www.maturango.org). Exhibits, maps, books, videos, and information about the Upper Mojave desert and neighboring Death Valley. Free admission to store and lobby; exhibit hall is $4 for adults. Open daily 10–5; closed on major holidays.

SHOPPING

Sundries & Souvenirs

Amargosa Hotel Gift Shop (Death Valley Junction; 760-852-4441; www.amargosaopera house.com). Peacock feathers, coffee mugs, cold sodas, ice cream, and books. Largest selection of Marta Becket performance videos in the world.

Furnace Creek Inn Gift Shop (Furnace Creek Inn). Southwest-themed gifts, apparel, accessories, Arizona-style Native American jewelry, and souvenir terry-cloth bathrobes. Open only in winter.

Nugget Gift Shop (Stovepipe Wells). Jewelry, crafts, trinkets, dream catchers, and curios. Open only in winter.

Sporting Goods & Equipment

Furnace Creek Golf Pro Shop (Furnace Creek Ranch; 760-786-3373). Balls, clubs, shoes, fashions, gifts, and more from "the world's lowest golf course."

Shot in Death Valley: A Short List

Greed (1923). Directed by Erich Von Stroheim; starring Gibson Gowland and Jean Hersholt. Skidoo, Stovepipe Wells dunes, Devil's Golf Course, and so on. Equipment and crew were hauled into the valley by mule. The film, considered a masterpiece at a running length of 10 hours, was never released theatrically.

Wanderer of the Wasteland (1923–24). Directed by Irvin Willat. Based on the novel by Zane Grey. Filmed in Technicolor; the last known print was found decomposed in the 1970s.

Twenty Mule Team (1940). Directed by Richard Thorpe; starring Wallace Beery and Leo Carrillo. Golden Canyon.

Yellow Sky (1948). Directed by William Wellman; starring Gregory Peck, Anne Baxter, and Richard Widmark. Near Furnace Creek.

Three Godfathers (1948). Directed by John Ford; starring John Wayne. Near Furnace Creek.

The Gunfighter (1950). Directed by Henry King; starring Gregory Peck. Opening titles only.

Spartacus (1960). Directed by Stanley Kubrick; starring Kirk Douglas, Laurence Olivier, Jean Simmons, and Tony Curtis. Ryan and Zabriskie Point.

One Eyed Jacks (1961). Directed by Marlon Brando; starring Marlon Brando and Karl Malden.

The Professionals (1966). Directed by Richard Brooks; starring Burt Lancaster, Lee Marvin, and Jack Palance. Sand dunes, Stovepipe Wells, and Desolation Canyon.

Zabriskie Point (1970). Directed by Michelangelo Antonioni; starring Mark Frechette and Daria Halprin. Cowritten by Sam Shepard. (Harrison Ford was considered for the lead, worked two days as an extra, and was eventually cut from the movie.)

Star Wars (1977). Directed by George Lucas; starring Mark Hamill, Carrie Fisher, and Harrison Ford. Between Stovepipe Wells and Death Valley Junction, Zabriskie Point, Ubehebe Crater, and Badwater.

Star Wars: Episode IV–Return of the Jedi (1983). Directed by George Lucas; starring Mark Hamill, Carrie Fisher, and Harrison Ford.

The Hitcher (1986). Directed by Robert Harmon; starring Rutger Hauer, C. Thomas Howell, and Jennifer Jason Leigh. Shoshone and Death Valley Junction.

The Doors (1991). Directed by Oliver Stone; starring Val Kilmer, Meg Ryan, Frank Whaley, and Kevin Dillon.

Lost Highway (1997). Directed by David Lynch; starring Bill Pullman, Patricia Arquette, et al. Baker, Barstow, Death Valley Junction.

Kill Bill, Vol. 2 (2004). Directed by Quentin Tarantino; starring Uma Thurman, Lucy Liu, et al. Zabriskie Point.

General Stores

Charles Brown Company Market (CA 127, Shoshone). Charlie Brown, state senator for 24 years, used to run the place when he wasn't in Sacramento. Now he's in the cemetery out back. Canned goods, crackers, liquor, last gas before the park, Lotto tickets, cheap souvenirs.

Furnace Creek Ranch General Store (760-786-2578). Minor groceries, snacks, shrink-wrapped sandwiches, beer, liquor, ice, margarita and Bloody Mary mix, books, curios, postcards, hats, and sunscreen. Road-soundtrack selections on CD by Marty Robbins and Frank Corrales. Multistage purified Niagara brand well water from Irvine, California.

Scotty's Castle Gift Shop (760-786-2325). Curios, postcards, trinkets, snack bar, books, cold drinks. Open daily 8:30–5:30.

Stovepipe Wells General Store (760-786-2387). Curios, T-shirts, basic lunch and snack supplies, ice, a selection of books, cheap hats and shades, Fred Harvey Signature socks, beer, liquor, wine, gas. Note the photo panel of Bungalette City in 1926.

The Outpost (Ballarat; no phone). More a point of interest (see below) than a place to stock up on essential goods and equipment. Still, if you're out this far and find yourself in need of something, this is all there is. Cold sodas and beers; motor oil; T-shirts; running water; black-powder gun trials (when there's powder). Stories, information, and shade.

POINTS OF INTEREST

Amargosa Basin & Range

Amargosa Hotel & Opera House (Death Valley Junction; 760-852-4441; www.amargosa operahouse.com). By 1930, when W. A. Chalfant came through, he found the once-bustling Borax headquarters "fallen into the doldrums." And thus Marta Becket, artist, musician, and Broadway dancer, found it in the spring of 1967 when she and her husband, after a week's camping in Death Valley, stopped here to have a tire repaired on their trailer. She found herself looking through a crack in the door of the old theater. It was in shambles, but it was a theater. "Peering through the tiny hole," she says, "I had the distinct feeling that I was looking at the other half of myself." Forty years later, into her 80s, she was giving nightly performances (in season), not merely to the screech of peacocks and to the colorful audience she once painted for herself, but to a sold-out house. Old prospectors had come down from the hills; longtime Furnace Creek employees, uncertain tourists and retirees, French backpackers, and urban hipsters alike had made the trek to the Junction for an evening of Marta's singing and storytelling. (In 2007 she was doing what she called "The Sitting Down Show," having hurt her back falling from a chair while hanging a curtain.) The season ended with a lengthy standing ovation, chocolate cake, and rum punch. She was working on a new show for 2008, she said, but wasn't yet promising anything. "I have a lot to do," she said. An off-season visit is worthwhile for the murals and broken sidewalks alone. Whether you decide to stay the night may depend on the depth of your appreciation for the work of David Lynch.

Ash Meadows National Wildlife Refuge (775-372-5435; www.fws.gov/desertcomplex/ashmeadows). Twenty-three thousand acres of original, undeveloped desert oasis, Ash Meadows is a wildly popular stopover for migratory waterfowl and the native habitat of 24 unique plant and animal species—"a greater concentration of endemic life than any other local area in the United States" according to the U.S. Fish and Wildlife Service. No fishing, swimming, or camping. Seasonal hunting permitted in designated areas. Refuge office open weekdays 8–4, depending on staff.

Devil's Hole. Across the northeast boundary of Ash Meadows NWR lies a tiny, isolated, rarely visited annex of Death Valley National Park. There is an overlook—an easy .25-mile hike from the dirt road—where through chain-link fence and razor wire one can look down into the hole in the bedrock where the world's entire population of Devil's Hole pupfish lives. The fish themselves are not visible from the overlook, and they are only about an inch long, but they are personally responsible for the tens of thousands of acres of undeveloped landscape you will have driven across to get to within a quarter mile of this spot. On a good year there have been as many five hundred of the little Nemos going about their business down there in the 86-degree saltwater, for which the place was once called the Miner's Bathtub—all that's left of what was once (ten thousand years ago) a vast lake. On a bad year, like 2006, there were 36. The Park Service and other agencies send in divers at least twice a year to do a count. Divers have been down 300 feet into the aquifer without finding its bottom, and at least two divers have gone in and not come out. The fish go as deep as 80 feet, but they do their spawning (and eating) near the surface, on a shallow shelf at one end of the hole. If the water level goes down a few feet, enough to expose the shelf, the species goes extinct. This is why in 1976 the Supreme Court put an unprecedented kibosh on any further pumping of groundwater—for agriculture or subdivisions or anything—anywhere near this place. Will the pupfish stop Las Vegas? Or will Las Vegas stop the pupfish? We'll see. Biologists are keeping a few hundred extra pups in refugee tanks at Ash Meadows and at Hoover Dam just in case.

Pupfish, Devil's Hole, Death Valley National Park

Goldwell Open Air Museum (702-870-9946; www.goldwellmuseum.org). Big sculptures in the desert and big views. Free. Open 24/7; visitors center and gift shop open sometimes.

Rhyolite. The ruins of what was once called, presumably by speculators in local real estate, "the Queen City of Death Valley." In its heyday (1905–7) it boasted a population of ten thousand—roughly that of contemporary Sonoma or Mammoth lakes on an average weekend; twice the size of Bishop or Aspen, Colorado; 10 times the size of nearby Beatty, Nevada. Most of the structures are on Bureau of Land Management (public) land. It's 4 paved miles from Beatty and 35 miles from the Furnace Creek Visitor Center.

China Ranch Date Farm (Tecopa; 760-852-4415; www.chinaranch.com). Follow the signs from the Old Spanish Trail (where the other '49ers passed), down the dirt road, through a narrow wash, and into a remarkable hidden oasis. Kit Carson and Alexis Godey of the Frémont party of 1843 shot and killed two Indians here who may have been involved in carrying off two women and several horses from a nearby settlement at Resting Springs. A

Chinese ex-Borax employee "named either Quon Sing or Ah Foo" developed a productive farm here until he was driven off at gunpoint by another fellow by the name of Morrison. The date grove was planted in the 1920s and today produces some 26,000 pounds of fruit per season. Date samplers, shakes, bread, preserves, tchochkis, and a nursery of succulents and palm trees to go. It's a delightful, otherworldly place for a picnic. Open daily 9–5. Ranch House suite and tepee available for overnight guests.

Dante's View (5,475 feet). On the gate of hell, Dante paused briefly over the following inscription: *Lasciate ogne speranza, voi ch'intrate* ("Abandon all hope, you who enter here")—and then went in. One tires quickly, in these days of speed and chemically conditioned air, of all the glib-seeming references to the underworld in Death Valley. Coming from the east, let this be your first. Here is the perfect vantage from which to appreciate the scale of the place, with the sink at Badwater 5,757 feet below, and the crest of Telescope Peak, across the basin, 5,575 feet above. The difference in elevation between the two—11,331 feet—represents the greatest topographic relief in the continental United States. Stroll out beyond the parking lot, along the ridge, to where the road on the valley floor becomes visible. Appreciate also the temperature, often more than 30 degrees cooler than at Furnace Creek. Consider hiking north of the parking lot to the summit of Mount Perry (5,739 feet).

Zabriskie Point. Oft-photographed erosional badlands named for an early executive of the Pacific Coast Borax Company, and made up of sediments from a long-gone lake. Justly popular place to take in a sunrise or sunset.

Furnace Creek Area

Borax Museum (Furnace Creek Ranch). Housed in the oldest remaining structure from the early days of the Greenland Ranch—by one account the first Borax Company office, built in 1881 and moved to its present location in 1954—this museum is jam-packed with a fascinating collection of rocks, minerals, arrowheads, old photos, excerpts of journals by early visitors, and more. It also boasts a yard full of mining implements, railroad detritus, stagecoaches, wagons, and other early means of transportation. Open 9-ish to 2-ish most days. Free admission.

Death Valley Dates (Furnace Creek Ranch). Fifteen hundred trees, mostly deglet nour from Algeria, were planted here on 33 acres in the late 1920s, first from seed, then from cuttings. It never panned out as a commercial date farm but today provides a delightful place for an evening stroll with the coyotes and roadrunners, or, when the weather's mild, an afternoon picnic. Bring your own bocce. Barbecue facilities can be reserved at the Ranch front desk or by calling 760-786-2345.

Death Valley Dates

Homeland of the Timbisha Shoshone

When Zane Grey came through in 1919, he found "half a dozen families living in squalid tents . . . a ragged unpicturesque group." They collected firewood and did chores for the Greenland Ranch, when there was such to be done. Grey found their poverty depressing. He had never in his life, in all his travels, seen so many flies. He found these people resolutely less "Indian," less frugal and simple, than the Paiute and Navajo he had met. "With all that they were trying to live like Indians," he wrote, "[t]hese children of the open wore white men's apparel and ate white men's food; and they even had a cookstove and a sewing machine in their tent." Later they would do day labor for Borax Consolidated, making bricks for the Furnace Creek Inn.

The Timbisha ("red rock") or Panamint Shoshone are descendents of the same Western Shoshone who in 1863 signed a treaty of "peace and friendship" with the people and government of the United States, by which the latter would be allowed to travel through, build upon, develop, and use the country however they saw fit, and the former would receive "as a full compensation and equivalent for the loss of game and the rights and privileges hereby conceded" 20 annual payments of $5,000—in provisions and clothing. Furthermore, according to Article 6: "whenever the President of the United States shall deem it expedient for them [the Shoshone] to abandon the roaming life which they now lead, and become herdsmen or agriculturalists, he is hereby authorized to make such reservations for their use as he may deem necessary . . . and they do also hereby agree to remove their camps to such reservations as he may indicate, and to reside and remain therein."

Timbisha Shoshone Village. June 2007 Burke Griggs

In 1936 the Bureau of Indian Affairs and the Park Service drew up "a permanent residence area" of about 40 acres, south of Furnace Creek, and built nine adobe structures. The CCC built a laundry, a community center, and a trading post. In the 1960s, under what today's Park Service calls "a less progressive administration," buildings that seemed vacant were "washed away with high-powered fire hoses." The tribe received official recognition by the Secretary of the Interior in the early 1980s—and an allotment of mobile homes. The President of the United States in 2000 (Bill Clinton) signed the Timbisha Homeland Act, setting aside five separate parcels of land in California and Nevada, totaling 7,754 acres (a portion of which likely shares groundwater with the proposed Yucca Mountain nuclear waste repository). The tribe now has the right to negotiate a Class III gaming compact with the governor of either state (or both) for gaming on any of its land—except that within Death Valley. Its members can now enter the national park without paying entrance fees.

They Shoot Wild Burros, Don't They?

Coronado, on his trip to Kansas in the 1540s, brought with him fifteen hundred animals, including horses and burros—some of which managed to stay behind with the native peoples, or to found or join feral populations. Spanish missionaries in California rode burros and horses, and so did the fur trappers, cowboys and Indians, and '49ers. Burros and horses are together required to make mules, to this day the most effective means of transportation, after the helicopter, in the High Sierra. From 1849 to the early 1920s, the burro was the prospector's ride of choice. As mines played out and cars took over the business of getting people from one place to another, burros were left to fend for themselves, which they did quite successfully all across the southwest, except for their being frequently shot by government agencies or the public, or rounded up and sold to dog food canneries.

In 1971, in what became the Wild Free-Roaming Horse and Burro Act, Congress found and declared "that wild free-roaming horses and burros are living symbols of the historic and pioneer spirit of the West; that they contribute to the diversity of life forms within the Nation and enrich the lives of

A wild burro gather on public lands. BLM photo

Wild Horse and Burro Corrals (adjacent to the Furnace Creek airport). Thousands of wild burros, and a few wild horses, have passed through here on their way out of the park.

South of Furnace Creek

West Side Road. Easy graded-dirt road follows the west edge of the Badwater Playa; past the spot where the Bennett and Arcane families spent a month beneath their wagons (where later pioneers briefly tried alfalfa farming); past the grave site of Shorty Harris,

the American people; that these horses and burros are fast disappearing from the American scene," and that they should therefore, on public lands, "be protected from capture, branding, harassment, or death." The tricky part, from the Park Service's point of view, was that wild horses and burros, like salt cedar, Washington palms, and other exotic species, were showing a capacity to out-compete the locals. In Death Valley they were trampling native plants and eating fodder that might otherwise have gone to native bighorn sheep, and they were multiplying. (The U.S. Geological Survey estimates that wild horse populations, "largely unchecked by natural predators," increase by 18 to 25 percent each year.)

The law was modified in 1976, and again in 1978, to allow for the removal or destruction of "excess animals"—at the discretion of the Secretary of the Interior—"in order to preserve and maintain a thriving natural ecological balance and multiple-use relationship in that area." One caveat: They were no longer to be used for commercial dog food. Some reports have Park Service staff or contractors shooting wild burros as recently as 1994. By 1998, according to the Bureau of Land Management, the total wild horse population in the United States, from a peak of about 58,000 head in 1977, had been reduced—by helicopter roundups, adoption programs, and "direct lethal means"—to 39,470. The total wild burro population had been reduced from 14,000 to 5,025. Still, in June 1999, various public land agencies, including Death Valley National Park, signed a strategic agreement that "recognized the overpopulation of wild burros on the desert" and outlined a policy for stepping up their removal.

In 2003 there were still an estimated five hundred wild burros in Death Valley National Park, "primarily in the areas of Saline Valley, Butte Valley, and Wild Rose"—with small herds assumed to be migrating in and out of the park from adjacent BLM lands and the China Lake Naval Weapons Reserve. There may have been as many as a dozen wild horses. The plan was still to get rid of them all—"to achieve a zero population"—as much as possible by removal and adoption, then by lethal means if necessary, but by 2007 adoptions had lagged significantly, and lethal means had not been employed. There were field trials under way to see if a specific wildlife contraception agent might be used on wild burros—as it had in urban areas on squirrels and pigeons.

founder of Harrisburg and Rhyolite, whose grave reads SINGLE-BLANKET JACKASS PROSPECTOR; and past the remains of the valley's first and first-failed borax works—to reconnect with CA 178 just north of Ashford Mill.

Devil's Golf Course. Several thousand years ago there was a lake here, 30 feet deep. Then the water evaporated, leaving a crust of salt (95 percent table salt) up to 5 feet deep. The pinnacles are diminutive, well-worn versions of those at Trona and Mono Lake. Imagine having to cross here, as the '49ers did, without a road.

Site of Bennett-Arcane Long Camp, West Side Road
Burke Griggs

Crossing the Devil's Golf Course, 1926   Courtesy Bancroft Library

Badwater. The lowest place in North America. A sign affixed to the side of the mountain, 274 feet above, to the east, indicates the level of the sea. A boardwalk has been constructed for one's strolling pleasure (to protect shoes from mud and mud from shoes). A short hike out across the tracked-up salt is a worthwhile adventure—especially when it's hot and dry. Bring good water.

Ashford Mill. Henry, Harold, and Louis Ashford sold their undeveloped interests in some dirt up the Black Mountains to a Hungarian count for $60,000 in 1914. The count, in turn, sold the claims for $105,000 to the McCausland brothers, who in turn built a state-of-the-art 40- or 50-ton mill that in the years since has produced mostly wildflowers.

North of Furnace Creek
Salt Creek. Home to another unique (endemic) species of pupfish, best spotted during high water in spring. Boardwalk covers a ?-mile loop to and from the parking lot. The water is not good for drinking.

Harmony Borax Works. Stabilized, oft-photographed ruins of Death Valley's first borax works. Original 20-mule-team wagons.

Stovepipe Well. Look east from the well—marked as it is today by the CCC—and see the century-old wagon tracks coming down the alluvial fan from Ryan. The original stovepipe is said to have once been displayed prominently at Eichbaum's resort. Note the eloquent grave of Val Nolan, victim of the elements. No water available.

Midsummer promenade, Salt Creek

Scotty's Castle. One of the West's original million-dollar off-the-grid vacation homes, named for its sometime caretaker and inspiration, the compulsive liar, swindler, and circus cowboy Walter Scott. Tours of the place were offered as early as the 1930s. A modicum of political maneuvering took place when, Death Valley having been declared a national monument, it was suddenly discovered that the "castle" had been built on the wrong land. The place has been mostly painstakingly preserved as it was in the 1930s—except for the updating of the original swamp-cooling system. The pipe organ alone is worth the visit. Fifty-minute-long living history tours begin hourly, every day, from 9 to 5. Crowded during peak season. Underground Mystery tours of the original cooling and water-heating systems are available by special request during summer and fall. Lower Grapevine Ranch tours offered in winter.

Ubehebe Crater. Two or three millennia ago, about the time the General Sherman tree began to sprout in what would eventually become Sequoia National Park (see chapter 6), magma rose nearly to the surface here, flashing groundwater to steam and blowing off a sizeable chunk of the earth. Climb down into it if you want. Bring water.

Eureka Dunes. The biggest sand dunes in California, Eureka is home to rare species and was oft-photographed by the likes of Ansel Adams. Off-limits to sand boarding and horseback riding.

The Racetrack. One of the last great unexplained mysteries of the physical world. The Park Service officially recommends a high-clearance vehicle; check with a ranger to see if that might include a rental car.

Night sky, the Racetrack, Death Valley Dan Duriscoe, NPS photo

Panamint & Saline

Emigrant Canyon Road. This paved road climbs up the backside of the Tucki Mountains to connect with decent graded-gravel side roads (the Park Service calls for high clearance) to the onetime town site of **Skidoo** and to **Aguereberry Point.** Of Skidoo (population 700), where in 1907 the unfortunate barkeep Hootch Simpson was hanged twice (the second time to accommodate the press), not much remains other than the original desolation of the site and an interpretive sign. Water was piped here from a spring on Telescope Peak, at a distance of 23 miles and a cost of $250,000. Various structures and vehicles at Pete Aguereberry's camp of 40 years testify to the life and labors of another era. Aguereberry Point (6,433 feet) affords a vantage opposite Dante's View. In summer temperatures are 20 to 30 degrees cooler than in the valley below. In winter they dip below freezing.

Wildrose Charcoal Kilns. Some of the best-preserved charcoal kilns in the West, The Wildrose kilns were Swiss engineered and built by Chinese labor in 1876. Used to convert nearby pinyon trees to charcoal for the smelting of lead and silver ore 30 miles to the west, they were operated for three years, abandoned in 1879, restored in 1933 by the CCC, and restored again in 1971 by a crew of Navajo stonemasons. Note the similarity in masonry with structures in Chaco Canyon, New Mexico.

Trona Pinnacles National Natural Landmark (www.blm.gov/ca/st/en /fo/ridgecrest/ trona.html). More than five hundred tufa (calcium carbonate) spires, some up to 140 feet tall, generally considered one of the best examples of tufa formations in North America. Like the tufa formations at Mono Lake but more of them, and bigger—and without the water. Recognizable as the location for the original *Planet of the Apes.*

Trona (population 1,885). The Jayhawkers passed through here on their way out of Death Valley, only to find the water unpalatable. In 1862 John Searles discovered borax on the surface of the dry lake that would come to bear his name. Here was the terminus of the great, brief Epsom Salts Monorail from Death Valley.

Telescope Peak (11,049 feet). A good trail leads upward from Mahogany Flat (8,133 feet) and climbs its way through juniper and pinyon to the summit. The vertical drop from here to the Badwater Basin is twice the depth of Grand Canyon. There are views of Death Valley, the Panamint Basin, and the Argus, Slate, and Amargosa ranges—"not to be compared with

Wildrose Charcoal Kilns Burke Griggs

any tawdry scene that needs the colors of vegetation to make it attractive," wrote John R. Spears in 1891. Alpine temperatures.

Ballarat (population "more or less"). Named for a sister mining camp in Australia, this particular Ballarat is an abiding feature of a fast-disappearing American outback, conjuring images of *Road Warrior* and countless dystopian Westerns. It's the home of Seldom Seen Slim's grave and Tex Watson's Power Wagon. Once a bustling supply town of four hundred permanent citizens in 1898, it now has population of two: Rocky Novak, prospector and mayor (he's been running the place since '04), and his father, George. The **Out Post General**

Rocky Novak, mayor of Ballarat, June 2007
Burke Griggs

Store and historical museum is a last stop for cold drinks, hose clamps, and directions before heading up Goler Wash to look for wild burros and the last hideout of Charles Manson.

U.S. Naval Museum Of Armament & Technology (760-939-3530; www.chinalake museum.org). Old bombs, planes, missiles, and ordnance. Open to the public 10–4 Monday through Saturday; closed Sunday and holidays. Call for information on how to get a guest pass to the base.

Last Chance Canyon Petroglyphs. Said to be the largest concentration of Indian petro-glyphs in North America, spanning 100 miles and many thousands of years of human history, Last Chance is on the National Register of Historic Places and is protected by no lesser institution than the U.S. Navy. U.S. citizenship is required for access. Contact the **Friends of Last Chance Canyon** (760-377-4976; www.tflcc.org) or the **Navy Public Affairs Office** (760-939-1683; www.nawcwd.navy.mil/pao/pages/petroglyphs.htm) for information.

BLM Wild Horse & Burro Adoption Facility (Randsburg Wash Road, off CA 178, Ridgecrest; 760-384-5765; www.wildhorseandburro.blm.gov). This preparation center for wild horses and burros gathered from public lands in the region is open 7:30–4 Monday through Friday (closed federal holidays). Adoptions by appointment only.

Road to China Lake Weapons Reserve, Darwin

Father Crowley Point. This gaping vista down Rainbow Canyon to the Panamint Dunes 4,000 feet below is worth getting out of the car for. It was named for John J. Crowley, "the Desert Padre," parish priest of Death Valley and Mount Whitney from 1919 to 1940, one of the first great promoters of tourism in the Eastern Sierra.

Darwin (population 54). In 1876, Darwin boasted a thousand citizens, two hundred frame houses, a raucous main street, and a pair of busy smelters. Today the place is inhabited by ghosts, cats, vintage aluminum trailers, a handful of artists, and a registered sex offender.

Saline Valley. One of the most isolated valleys in North America, Saline is higher than Death Valley by a thousand feet but has similar topography. It's a haven for wild burros, rock hounds, nudists, and other contemporary misfits. Annexed by the National Park Service in 1994, it's frequently used by the U.S. military for million-dollar low-altitude upside-down flight training. The roads in are long, rough, tire-shredding gravel washboards, not to be attempted frivolously or in wet conditions. Note the remains of 19th-century borax operations at the edge of the salt marsh, and the historic aerial salt tram over the Inyo Range to the west. The warm springs (alas, no longer any kind of secret) where Charles Manson and Family are said to have spent much time are today a congenial oasis of fan palms, concrete tubs, lending library, and shaded lawn, spotlessly maintained by local residents—inheritors of an earlier counterculture settlement—in a kind of working truce with the Park Service. No gas; no services; no ice; no firewood; no disrespect. Camping is still free, and clothing is still optional. Pack it in, pack it out.

RECREATION

Biking
Bicycles are allowed on all of the same park roads as vehicles. Road biking is popular—and spectacular—fall through spring, with epic out-and-back rides in all four directions from Furnace Creek. Mountain biking is confined to dirt roads and jeep trails. Nearest parts and services are in Las Vegas and in Bishop.

Bird-Watching
Desert salt marshes, springs, and oases are magnets for migratory waterfowl and havens for hundreds of endemic and nonnative species. Hoist your binoculars at the **China Ranch Date Farm** (www.chinaranch.com/birds.html), **Ash Meadows National Wildlife Refuge** (www.npwrc.usgs.gov/resource/birds/chekbird/r1/ashmead.htm), **Saratoga Springs**, or at the wildlife viewing platform off the **Furnace Creek Golf Course.**

Golf
Furnace Creek Golf Course (760-786-3373). This, the lowest all-grass course on the planet (-214 feet), is a certified member of the Audubon Cooperative Sanctuary Program for Golf Courses. It first opened in 1930, with ranch sheep keeping the greens trimmed, and expanded to 18 holes in 1968. Redesigned by Perry Dye in 1997. Par 70. Various golf and lodging packages available. In summer the "Extreme Golf 6-Pack" includes nine holes

White-faced ibis on northbound migration, Furnace Creek Golf Course

of golf, club rental, cart, and bottled water for $25. For the least extreme experience, tee off at 6 AM, before breakfast.

Hiking
Given the openness of the terrain and the sparse vegetation, opportunities for cross-country strolls are essentially limitless. Summertime "hikes" in the valley will most likely be limited to brief forays from the car to a given point of interest and back—in the shade of a broad-brimmed hat. In winter, day hikes of varying degrees of difficulty abound in side canyons up and down the basin. Popular, easy jaunts include the Golden Canyon Trail, Titus Canyon, and the Gower Gulch Loop. For something slightly more strenuous, try the Keane Wonder Mine Trail or Fall Canyon. Then climb Telescope Peak. Consult a ranger for suggestions and conditions.

Horseback Riding
The horses at the **Furnace Creek Stables** (760-786-3339; www.furnacecreekstables.com) spend their summers working the cool of the High Sierra and their winters (September –May) giving one- and two-hour trail rides on and around Furnace Creek Ranch. Wagon and carriage rides are also available. The horses are not allowed in developed camp-grounds or on most valley trails, and are discouraged in steep canyons and ranges.

Tennis
The are two courts at Furnace Creek Ranch and four at the inn. Racquets are available at the front desk. Bring low-altitude balls.

Dawn, Furnace Creek Golf Course

Off-Highway Driving

Of the 696 miles of maintained road in the park, only 243 are classified by the Park Service "as standard vehicle roads, or paved or unpaved that require no more ground clearance than a standard sedan." Those with four-wheel drive, high clearance, and sufficiently beefy suspension will want to test their skills (and the strength of their tires) on the other 442 miles open to vehicle travel. In order of ascending difficulty, start with popular Titus Canyon or Darwin Falls, then try Goler Wash, from Ballarat to the West Side Road (past Manson's last hideout), then finally Steel Pass, from the dunes at Saline to the much bigger dunes at Eureka. In all cases, six-ply tires will be appreciated. The miles of washboarded gravel on the Racetrack and Saline Valley roads are generally passable but not very pleasant in a regular passenger car—except, that is, when there's snow on South Pass and/or flooding in the canyons, when all unpaved roads become quagmires or paths for debris slides. The erstwhile "road" to Panamint City, up Surprise Canyon, remains off-limits to motorized vehicles.

Ranger & Interpretive Programs

A host of programs and tours is scheduled from October to May. Consult the visitors center.

ANNUAL EVENTS

January
Furnace Creek Invitational Golf Tournament (www.furnacecreekresort.com).

February
Bald Eagles (Ash Meadows).

Death Valley History Conference (www.dvnha.org).

March
Spring Death Valley Century and Double Century (www.adventurecorps.com).

Spring waterfowl migration begins.

April
Pupfish breeding season begins.

Wildflower Show (Maturango Museum, Ridgecrest; 760-375-6900; www.maturango.org).

May
Spring songbird migration peaks.

July
Hottest temperatures.

Badwater Ultra-Marathon (310-570-2613; www.badwater.com). Run 135 miles nonstop from Badwater to Whitney Portal.

Peak century plant boom.

August
Fall bird migration begins.

October
Fall Death Valley Century and Double Century (www.adventurecorps.com).

Fall Kick-Off Golf Tournament (Furnace Creek; www.furnacecreekresort.com).

Furnace Creek 508 (310-570-2613; www.the508.com). Ultramarathon bicycle race; 10 mountain passes; 35,000 feet of elevation gain.

Gem-O-Rama (Trona; call Jim or Bonnie Fairchild: 760-372-5356).

November
Death Valley '49ers Encampment (www.deathvalley49ers.org). Art, photography, mining, minerals, lapidary and craft shows; stringed-instrument, needlework, woodcarving, and horseshoe competitions; cowboy poetry, gold panning, four-wheel-drive tours, videos, oratories, wagon trains, and more.

Shoshone Old West Days (760-852-4524; www.deathvalleychamber.org).

December
Ash Meadows Christmas Bird Count (www.nevadaaudubon.org).

Ancient Bristlecone Pine, White Mountains
Burke Griggs

4

THE OWENS VALLEY & EASTERN SIERRA

True West

> This section of US 395 penetrates a land of contrasts—cool crests and burning lowlands, fertile agricultural regions and untamed deserts. It is a land where Indians made a last stand against the invading white man, where bandits sought refuge from early vigilante retribution; a land of fortunes—past and present—in gold, silver, tungsten, marble, soda, and borax; and a land esteemed by sportsmen because of scores of lakes and streams abounding with trout and forests alive with game.
>
> —WPA Guide to California, 1939

Sometime between church and noon on Sunday, November 16, 1924, a posse of displeased citizens began to show up at the Alabama Spillway, a few miles from Lone Pine, on the Los Angeles Aqueduct. Their contention was that the water had been stolen from the valley—and should be returned. By all accounts they had left their guns at home. A lone security guard in the employ of the City of Los Angeles stepped aside as some of the men worked to open the gates above the spillway, diverting the main flow of the Owens River away from Los Angeles, back into its original bed.

The sheriff showed up, took names. A local judge issued a restraining order, then cancelled it, citing his own lack of authority in the matter. The press came. Food was delivered. Tom Mix, on location nearby, sent over some musicians to entertain the gathering crowds.

"Los Angeles men came and were courteously received," wrote W. A. Chalfant, then editor of the *Inyo Register*. "Their declarations were similar to that of a British commander in an early Revolutionary skirmish: 'Disperse, ye rebels,' and were no more effective."

The sheriff asked the governor to send in the National Guard. The governor declined. For four long days the residents of the valley controlled the river—and Los Angeles, which had by then secured for itself more water than it knew what to do with, made do without. For four days.

Alabama Spillway, Owens Valley, June 2007 Burke Griggs

The local Indians had been diverting water from the Owens since long before Joseph R. Walker first came through in 1834. They used it to irrigate fields of native hyacinth and nutgrass. John Frémont officially surveyed the valley in 1845, along with Walker, Kit Carson, Richard Owens, and the topographer Edward Kern. The names Kern, Carson, and Walker having already been liberally distributed in other watersheds, the glory here fell to Mr. Owens. Ranchers started bringing in cattle and sheep in the late 1850s to satisfy hungry mining camps at Virginia City, Aurora, and Mono Lake. The Indians did their best to resist encroachment, to make life difficult for the settlers, but by 1863 found themselves rather forcefully persuaded to sign a treaty—allowing for their removal from the valley. In the wake of their departure—998 people marched by the U.S. Army from Independence to Fort Tejon—there was, as one correspondent put it, a "general scramble for land in Owens Valley." "Prospectors and families are flocking in," wrote another. "Large numbers of beef cattle are being driven across the mountains."

Indian troubles continued for a few years thereafter. Lawlessness abounded to a degree that would later inspire countless Hollywood Westerns (many to be shot on location in the Owens Valley). But by the mid-1870s—with 400 bars of rough-grade silver bullion daily coming down out of Cerro Gordo; with 4,800 citizens and 1,600 mules in that camp alone; and with new bonanzas every year (at Bodie and Mammoth, Lundy and Tioga), bringing successive waves of prospectors and settlers—farms, ranches, and orchards flourished up and down the valley. By 1878 large-scale irrigation was under way. Before long, local farmers would be pulling permits on eight separate dam sites for storage and control of the Owens River.

Meanwhile, down south, a fellow by the name of Fred Eaton—22 years old in 1878 and superintendent of the Los Angeles City Water Company since he was 19—hired a fellow by the name of William Mulholland, then 23, as a ditch digger. Eaton went on to serve briefly as mayor of Los Angeles from 1898 to 1900. During his tenure he created the Los Angeles Department of Water and Power and put Mulholland at its head. Around the time Eaton left office, the city's population broke the 100,000 mark. By 1903 there were 175,000 people, with hundreds more arriving daily. By July 1904 the city was consuming more water—by more than 4 million gallons a day—than was being delivered by its own river.

That summer, while on an extended camping trip to Yosemite and Mono Lake (with a side trip to Bishop for supplies), in the company of one Joseph B. Lippincott, of the U.S. Bureau of Reclamation, Fred Eaton, now no longer a servant of the public, was thinking very seriously about the water in the Owens River—and about how Los Angeles might be able to use it. Lippincott and the boys from Reclamation had already begun surveying the Owens as a possible federal irrigation project and had set aside half a million acres for such a purpose. The project counted on the enthusiastic support of local farmers; there was no disagreement anywhere in those days that 37 million acre-feet of annual Sierra runoff ought to be "saved"—one way or another—from the salty waste of Owens Lake. The only question was where the water would be used and who might benefit.

In the spring of 1905, according to a report made that summer by the Inyo County land office (to the Secretary of the Interior), "Eaton began to secure options on land and water rights in the Owens Valley to the value of about a million dollars." Whether the sellers were under the false impression that the lands were shortly to be condemned by the Reclamation Service, and/or that the water was to be used to develop other lands in the Owens Valley, and/or were simply happy to have the cash, is now rather impossible to ascertain. The report went on:

> In June or July most of these options were taken up and the said purchaser now owns all the patented land covered by the government reservoir site in Long Valley, and also riparian and other rights along the river for about fifty miles. The well known friendship between him and Lippincott and his having represented the supervising engineer for the Government made it easier for these rights to be secured, as the people were generously inclined toward the project and believed Eaton to be the agent of the Reclamation Service. Mr. Eaton's own statements were that he had bought these lands for a cattle ranch.

The people of the City of Los Angeles by a margin of 10 to 1 approved two bond measures: one for the purchase of most of Eaton's newly acquired rights in the Owens Valley; the other for the construction of a $25 million gravity-fed aqueduct to be built by Mulholland's water department. Reclamation handed its surveys over to Mulholland and stepped aside in favor of the city. In May 1907 President Teddy Roosevelt pitched in, securing a right-of-way for the city and "protecting the purity of the aqueduct supply" by withdrawing from settlement another 220,000 acres of the Owens Valley. Thus "great areas on which the only trees were those that settlers had planted" came to be called the Inyo National Forest. "[I]t is a hundred or a thousand fold more important to the state," said Roosevelt of the water in the Owens River, "and more valuable to the people as a whole if used by the city than if used by the people of the Owens Valley."

Construction on the aqueduct began in the fall of 1908. "Included in this work," read the water department's complete report, "were 215 miles of road, 230 miles of pipe line, 218 miles of power transmission line and 377 miles of telegraph and telephone line." It was a project in scale second only to the Panama Canal. On a given day there were as many as 3,900 laborers on the line, mostly Eastern Europeans and Mexicans, mostly working for $2.25 a day, minus a dollar a month for "medical, hospital and surgical service when needed, except for venereal disease, intemperance, vicious habits, injuries received in fights, or chronic diseases acquired before employment." The Southern Pacific Railroad built a branch line from Mojave to Owenyo, near Lone Pine, to carry men and materials, including a thousand barrels of Portland cement a day. Six million pounds of blasting powder were used to bore 43 miles of tunnel. Steel pipe large enough to drive wagons through was shipped around Cape Horn from the East Coast (the canal was finished a year after the aqueduct).

On November 15, 1913, ahead of schedule and under budget, the Owens River reached the San Fernando Valley. Thirty thousand people were there to meet it. Hundreds dipped cups and drank straight from the flow; hundreds more drank from bottles provided by the San Fernando Valley Chamber of Commerce. "There it is," said Mulholland to the mayor. "Take it."

"Do you have any idea what this land would be worth with a steady water supply?" remarked Jake Gittes (Jack Nicholson) in Roman Polanski's *Chinatown* (1974). "About thirty million dollars more than they paid for it." And sure enough, a number of the city's most prominent citizens, including Harrison Gray Otis, publisher of the *Los Angeles Times*, and Mulholland himself, made quick fortunes in newly irrigated San Fernando Valley real estate. The Owens, meanwhile, with its once-promising agricultural future, began a steady return to sagebrush and creosote.

In the five years it had taken to build the aqueduct, the population of Los Angeles had more than doubled—to 485,000. Between 1920 and 1930 the city climbed from 10th to 5th largest in the nation, with a population of well over a million. The population of all Inyo County during the same time period dropped from 7,031 to 6,555—down yet again from the 7,500 it had been given at the 1880 census. Los Angeles had begun drilling wells on its land in the Owens Valley as early as 1918, supplementing the flow of the river by pumping groundwater into the aqueduct. Farmers still trying to irrigate at Aberdeen began to find the levels in their own wells subsiding. By 1924, after several years of less-than-average snowfall in the Sierra, Owens Lake—once plied by a pair of steamships—was as dry as the playa at Badwater, in Death Valley.

"Ten years ago this was a wonderful valley with one-quarter of a million acres of fruit

Guard house, Nine-Mile Canyon Siphon, Los Angeles Aqueduct

and alfalfa," said famous Hollywood cowboy Will Rogers in 1932, "now this is a valley of desolation."

Dynamite was brought into play. The city men used it to clear what they saw as pirate dams and ditchworks. Locals used it to blast holes in the aqueduct. The city offered $10,000 for information leading to the arrest of local saboteurs, but no such information was forthcoming. It had been one more long, dry summer when the good people of the Owens Valley seized the Alabama Gates. Mulholland's response—so the story goes—was that he "half-regretted the demise of so many of the valley's orchard trees, because now there were no longer enough trees to hang all the troublemakers who live there."

The troublemakers dispersed on Wednesday and went home of their own accord, having achieved much favorable publicity worldwide, and received pledges of good faith on the part of the city toward some kind of equitable settlement. The city, in turn, resolved to buy up the rest of the valley. By 1933—after several more incidents with local dynamite, and a brief period of armed guards searching cars on the highway—the city of Los Angeles had, by some chicanery but also by paying premium rates in the midst of a depression, come to own 95 percent of all the agricultural land in the valley, and 85 percent of its commercial and residential real estate. (Much of the latter was eventually leased or sold back to merchants and residents, sans water rights.)

Eaton and Mulholland had a dramatic falling out over the million dollars Eaton wanted to charge the city for rights to a potential storage reservoir in Long Valley (between Bishop and Mammoth), the construction of which was delayed into the 1940s. Meanwhile, in the spring of 1928, the alternate dam Mulholland built in the Santa Clarita Valley—the St. Francis dam—collapsed, killing 450 people and burying the town of Santa Paula in 20 feet of mud. Mulholland had inspected the dam that very morning and declared it safe. The

Abandoned saltworks at Cartago, Owens Gorge Transmission Line, Los Angeles Department of Water and Power (230,000 volts) Burke Griggs

disaster set the record for the worst American civil engineering failure of the 20th century and ended Mulholland's career in disgrace. Mulholland assumed full responsibility, resigned, said he "envied those who were killed," and lived for another seven years. His onetime friend Fred Eaton died a year earlier, in 1934, bankrupt and mostly forgotten. From his heirs the city was finally able to purchase the reservoir site in Long Valley.

The drying-up of Owens Lake, as early as the 1920s, was a boon to surface mining industries. U.S. Borax is still busily working to extract an estimated 70 million tons of trona from the playa. (Trona is a "double salt" used in the making of glass and as a feed additive for livestock.) In 1987 the EPA declared the southern Owens Valley in violation of National Ambient Air Quality Standards. The lake bed was eventually singled out as the "largest source of fugitive dust in the United States"—second in the world only to the Sahara desert. In 1998 the Great Basin Air Pollution Control District pushed the City of Los Angeles to begin mitigation efforts—shallow flooding, planting salt grasses on the playa, spreading gravel, and so on. Other methods, possibly less costly and more effective, were suggested and discarded. By March 2006 the city had spent $304 million of a projected $475 million and had achieved little more, by some accounts, than a general increase in the population of mosquitoes. As one city council staffer is said to have put it: "It's tough to grow grass in the desert."

On the other hand, as Chalfant wrote in 1933, "Nature has written here, in bold strokes, studies more fascinating than the little affairs of humanity." Indeed, there is no topography in North America of so rugged and dramatic aspect. The Owens is one of the deepest valleys on the planet, with its floor on average below 4,000 feet, bordered on either side by mountains more than 14,000. Consider, for example, the Tetons in Wyoming: The total

Owens Basin and Inyo Mountains, Whitney Portal Road

rise from Moose Junction (6,500 feet) to the summit of the Grand Teton (13,770 feet) is 7,270 feet; from Lone Pine to the crest of Whitney is 10,795 feet. To put it another way, if you were to stack Yosemite's El Capitan—the largest granite monolith on earth (3,600 feet)—on top of the Grand Teton, you would achieve the approximate vertical scale of the Eastern Sierra at Mount Whitney. And while the Teton Range is 40 miles long, the high crest of the Sierra stretches more than 150 miles.

Still, as remarkable as the topography itself is the way in which, thanks to the "little affairs of humanity"—specifically the enterprising spirit (and great thirst) of Los Angeles—the Owens Valley has remained essentially unmarred by patterns of urban and suburban development so common in other valleys across the American West. "[T]he pollution and the destruction of habitats caused by such development," writes Greg James, director of the Inyo County Water Department, "have been avoided in the Owens Valley." In other words, instead of strip malls and suburban tract homes, the view here comprises vast—and increasingly rare—landscapes of sagebrush and creosote, granite boulders and snow-capped mountains.

The 2000 census found 1.8 people per square mile in Inyo County, putting it on a par with some of the emptiest terrain in Idaho and Alaska. Of the county's 10,000 square miles, 94 percent—an area larger than the state of Vermont—is owned by the government: the Park Service, the Forest Service, the Bureau of Land Management, the U.S. Navy, the State of California, the County of Inyo. Four percent is owned by the City of Los Angeles (Department of Water & Power, or simply DWP), less than 2 percent by private interests. The remaining one third of one percent remains in the hands of federally recognized Indian tribes. Fewer than 19 square miles are today under irrigation (or 1/5 of a percent), compared to 117 square miles in 1920. The county of Imperial, by way of contrast, which is

Last of the Duanes (1930), starring George O'Brien and Myrna Loy. Mt. Whitney, right of center.
Courtesy Museum of Lone Pine Film History

half the size of Inyo, receives about the same amount of annual rainfall and drains a significantly smaller watershed, has nearly 20 percent of its surface area under irrigation—and more than one hundred golf courses. In the 10,000 square miles of Inyo County—from the summit of Mount Whitney to the Amargosa Basin—there are three golf courses: one at Furnace Creek, one at Lone Pine, and one at Bishop.

The scenery here—mostly wild as it was when Joe Walker first rode through in 1834—has provided the backdrop for hundreds of movies, television shows, and commercials. It has stood in for the Himalyas, for the Andes, for the High Atlas mountains of North Africa, for distant planets, for the future, for the American West as it once was, or might have been—or in this case still is. Ten thousand Japanese American citizens were interned here, for its supposed isolation, during World War II.

"Every cañon commends itself for some particular pleasantness," wrote author Mary Austin in Land of Little Rain (1904), "this for pines, another for trout, one for pure bleak beauty of granite buttresses, one for its far-flung irised falls; and as I say, though some are easier going, leads each to the cloud shouldering citadel."

THE LAY OF THE LAND: APPROACHES & LOGISTICS

"You may come into the borders of it from the south by a stage journey that has the effect of involving a great lapse of time," wrote Mary Austin, "or from the north by rail, dropping out of the overland route at Reno." The Owens Valley can still be approached from the west by way of the ancient passes of the Sierra—on foot or by pack animal. Perhaps the best way to experience the full effect of the eastern scarp is to approach it from the east, as some of the '49ers did, coming over Townes Pass from Death Valley, or by Westgard into Big Pine. But the great majority of travelers in this part of the country come from the south, up US 395 from San Bernardino, Orange County, or San Diego; or up CA 14, as Eaton and Mulholland once used to do, along the aqueduct from Los Angeles, to join US 395 at Indian Wells.

The southernmost and lowest pass over the Sierra foothills is Tehachapi (CA 58), a major and historic shipping and transportation corridor, open year-round between Barstow and Bakersfield and thus between the southern cities and the Central Valley. It is historic in that the majority of automobile traffic from Los Angeles to the central and northern cities now crosses at a higher pass in the Sierra Madre to the west (at Tejon, otherwise known as the Grapevine). The railroad crosses at Tehachapi. Here, north of CA 58, across from the windmill farms, the Pacific Crest Trail leaves the Mojave basin and enters the high desert in earnest. The cement works here provided the bulk of materials for the Owens Valley–Los Angeles aqueduct project.

Walker Pass (CA 178) is next, then Sherman (CR J41), the latter being the first true pass into the High Sierra (closed from the first substantial snow to late spring), offering a crossing of the South Fork of the Kern, paved access to various wilderness areas, and a roundabout passage to the big trees. From Sherman Pass to Tioga Pass, 180 miles to the north, there is no road crossing the Sierra.

The entrance to the Owens Valley proper is at Little Lake. US 395 is the main artery, the only paved road south to north across the basin. Along it there are five main settlements: Olancha, Lone Pine, Independence, Big Pine, and Bishop, each with its own access spurs into the canyons of the Sierra. Lone Pine and Bishop provide the majority of services.

LODGING

True destination lodging is scarce in these parts. There are a number of half-abandoned scary-movie motels at regular intervals along CA 14 before its junction with US 395 (many in the business of renting dry acreage to cell phone service providers). There is something of a B&B, open only on weekends, in the former ghost town of Randsburg. There are motels in Ridgecrest catering mostly to those coming in or out of the China Lake Naval Weapons Station. Every town on US 395, from Olancha to Bishop, has at least two motels, some of which are remarkable examples of past booms in travel and tourism, first in the late 1920s and early '30s, then again in the post-war era. Many of these seem to have been neglected since the day they opened.

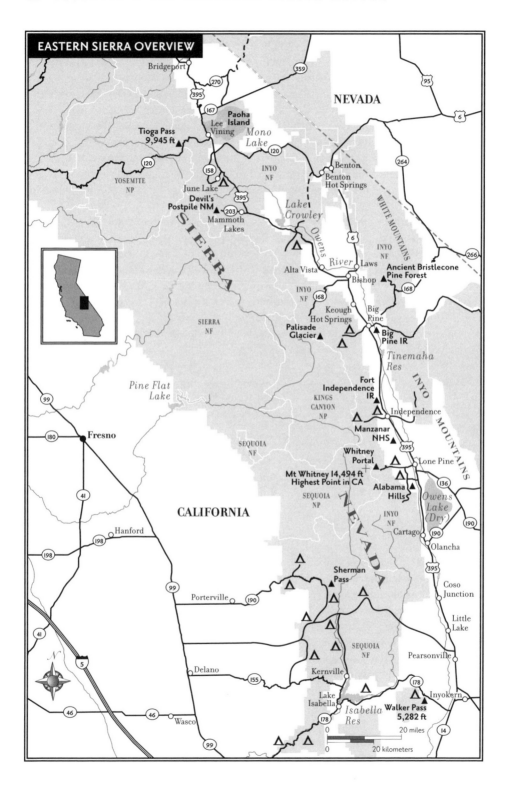

EASTERN SIERRA OVERVIEW

Lodging Price Code

Cost of lodging is based on an average per-room, double-occupancy rate at peak season (May to November). Tax and gratuities are not included. Rates are often reduced outside of fishing season.

Inexpensive	Up to $75
Moderate	$75 to $125
Expensive	$125 to $200
Very Expensive	Over $200

The **Winnedumah Hotel** in Independence is one of the oldest continuously operated lodgings on the road, along with the **Dow Hotel** in Lone Pine. Both are still a good bet today (see full descriptions below). Accommodations at **Cerro Gordo** date back to the 1860s (see below). Lone Pine also boasts several AAA-rated lodgings and two late-model franchise motels, of which the **Comfort Inn** (1920 South Main Street; 760-876-8700; www.choicehotels.com; moderate to expensive) is probably the best equipped. Bishop has more than 20 motels, many of recognizable brand name. Best bets for a quiet night's sleep in Bishop are the **Best Western Creekside Inn** (725 North Main Street; 760-872-3044; www.bishopcreekside.com; expensive) and the **La Quinta Inn** (651 North Main Street; 760-873-6380; www.lq.com; moderate). For B&B aficionados and those who appreciate the feeling of staying in someone else's home, try the ranch-style **Joseph House Inn** (376 West Yaney Street, Bishop; 760-872-3389; www.josephhouseinn.com; expensive) or the more traditional-Victorian **Chalfant House**, childhood home of local historian and newspaperman W. A. Chalfant (213 Academy Street, Bishop; 760-872-1790; moderate to expensive). Lone Pine sells out completely the first weekend in October (during the film festival); Bishop fills to capacity over Memorial Day weekend (during Mule Days). For old-school knotty-pine cabins at higher elevations, try **Glacier Lodge** (Big Pine Creek Road, above Big Pine; 760-938-2837; www.sonic.net/~kwofford/glacier-lodge; moderate) or **Parcher's Resort** (5001 South Lake Road, Bishop; www.parchersresort.net; 760-873-4177; moderate). North of Bishop on US 6, near the head of the Chalfant Valley, lies the locals' favorite hot springs getaway, the **Old House at Benton** (see below).

Cerro Gordo

www.cerrogordo.us
From Keeler, 7.5 miles and 5,500 feet of elevation up Yellow Grade Road
Elevation: 8,400 feet
Open: Memorial Day to first freeze
760-876-5030
Innkeeper: Michael Patterson
Price: Moderate
Pets: Well behaved, on leash
Wheelchair Access: No
Internet Access: No

A handful of Mexican prospectors from Lone Pine found "color" here as early as 1865, but it wasn't until 1868 that the camp began to see serious action. As much as $17 million worth of ore was shipped down the grade by freight wagon to Swansea and Keeler, thence across the Owens Lake by steamship to Cartago, thence to the nascent Port of Los Angeles. Mortimer Belshaw and Victor Beaudry headed up the syndicate that built the road, the water system, an array of silver and lead smelters, and the American Hotel (1871), where by previous arrangement with the current owner visitors can enjoy a home-cooked meal and a micro-brewed root beer. Accommodations include the two-bedroom, one-bath Belshaw House (c. 1868)—with private kitchen, indoor plumbing, a Franklin stove, and barely fathomable front-porch views across the Owens Playa to the Sierra—and the six-room Bunkhouse (1904), ideal for groups up to 12. No phone.

Mount Williamson (14,370 feet), as seen from Independence

work in surprising shades of turquoise. On opening night of the Film Festival (October) the lobby spills over with meticulously costumed bad men, buckaroos, and corseted ladies of, alas, questionable repute. The ghosts hang out where the real value is: in the old hotel. Rooms are available with private or shared bath. Upstairs front rooms offer grand Ansel Adams–style views of Lone Pine Peak and Mount Whitney above the Pizza Factory.

Dow Villa Hotel & Motel

www.dowvillamotel.com
310 South Main Street (US 395)
Elevation: 3,730 feet
Open: Year-round
760-876-5521; 1-800-824-9317
Innkeepers: Lynne Bunn and Jeanne Willey
Price: Inexpensive to Moderate
Pets: Allowed in motel section; some restrictions
Wheelchair Access: Yes
Internet Access: Free wireless

Walter Dow built the hotel in 1923 to house the movie companies working the Alabama Hills. Among the luminaries who have camped out in these rooms are Tom Mix, William Boyd (Hopalong Cassidy), Gene Autry, Roy Rogers, Errol Flynn, and, of course, John Wayne. The Duke first slept here in 1935. In 1978, while doing a commercial for Great Western Bank (his last appearance on film), he stayed in room 20 in the newer motel, now featuring wet bar and flat-screen TV. The motel annex dates to 1958. Later restoration has brought carpets in homage to some abstract tropical broadleaf plant, silver-green on a field of royal purple, vinyl wall coverings, and trim

Winnedumah Hotel

www.winnedumah.com
US 395, across from the courthouse
Elevation: 3,925 feet
Open: Year-round
760-878-2040
Innkeepers: Frank and Celia Montoya
Price: Moderate (includes breakfast)
Pets: At innkeepers' whim
Wheelchair Access: Yes
Internet Access: Wireless

In 1927 Dow built the Winnedumah to catch the overflow from his hotel in Lone Pine, for those occasions when it seemed that all of Hollywood had descended upon the Owens Valley. The Winnedumah, named for an 80-foot granite monolith in the Inyo mountains to the east of town (see the Legend of Winnedumah sidebar later in this chapter), has thankfully suffered less intrusive renovation than its sibling in Lone Pine. The stucco facade and portico remains much as it was when it was first built—as the Dow's once was before it was

Camping in the Inyo Range, March 2007

treated to a set dressing of weathered barn wood. Many of the original details—bathroom tiles, the hearth in the lobby—remain unchanged. There is no better place to stay on the way up or down the old Kearsarge trail, or after a lamb couscous and a good bottle of red at the Still Life Café. Rooms available with or without private bath. Rooms at the back offer partial views of the Sierra. The new owners promise healthier breakfasts.

✪ The Old House at Benton Hot Springs
www.historicbentonhotsprings.com
CA 120, between Benton and US 395
Elevation: 5,626 feet
Open: Year-round
760-933-2287
Innkeepers: Bill and Diane Bramlette
Price: Moderate (includes breakfast and hot springs access)
Pets: Yes
Wheelchair Access: Yes
Internet Access: No

For centuries travelers of all stripes have been drawn out of their way, across windswept wastes of sagebrush and piñon, for the simple pleasure of a good soak in the hot springs at Benton. The water is without doubt some of the most pleasant in the world. A village was established here in 1852, as a stopover between the booming settlements at Bodie and Aurora and points south—and as a destination in its own right. When gold was discovered in the surrounding hills in 1862, followed by silver, the place had its own boom, which lasted until 1889, brief and violent Indian skirmishes notwithstanding. All that's left of those days is a handful of weathered structures, some holes in the hillsides, assorted rusted implements, a graveyard—and, of course, the water. The town site and much of the surrounding ranchland has for four generations been owned by the Bramlettes, who have recently put a conservation easement on 900 acres and today run a quaint ranch-style inn with spring-water-heated saltillo tile floors and locally salvaged Victorian furnishings. The road to Mammoth is plowed all winter long. Private tubs are available for day use, with advance reservations, and for overnight camping. BYOB. Nearest food (other than breakfast) is the small, Indian-run café at the gas station in Benton.

CAMPING

There are numerous developed campgrounds along the base of the range—west of US 395—managed by various agencies: Inyo County, the Bureau of Land Management, the U.S. Forest Service, the Los Angeles Department of Water and Power (LADWP), and the Fort Independence Indian Tribe. There is top-notch car camping at Kennedy Meadows (with a handful of sites, first come first served, along the South Fork of the Kern). The highest-elevation sites are at Cottonwood Pass, above Lone Pine, and across the valley in the White Mountains. In general, the forest service campgrounds are the highest in elevation, offering the greatest access to streams, lakes, and high-country wilderness—and in the summertime the most coveted. Only on the busiest weekends in summer are campgrounds full to capacity. Leashed and attended pets are allowed at all campgrounds. Dispersed camping is allowed, with certain restrictions, anywhere on BLM and national forest land. Best spots include the Alabama Hills, the Inyo Mountains (i.e., up Mazourka Canyon Road), and the Sherman Pass area above Kennedy Meadows. Campfire permits are required outside developed campgrounds, available at any district ranger station. A handful of private campgrounds from Lone Pine to Bishop are geared mostly toward users of recreational vehicles.

DINING OVERVIEW

With few and notable exceptions, dining in this region is in the great American ground-beef-grain-and-potato tradition. But there are exceptions. For squid ink pasta, oysters from the Sea of Cortez, dry Muscat, and sweet potato gnocchi, press on to Mammoth. "And here is a hint if you would attempt the stateliest approaches," wrote Mary Austin, "travel light, and as much as possible live off the land. Mulligatawny soup and tinned lobster will not bring you the favor of the woodlanders."

Dining Price Code

Based on the cost of one dinner, including entrée and appetizer (or entrée and dessert) and a beverage. Tax and gratuities are not included. Recommendations are made based on value rather than cost.

Inexpensive	Up to $15
Moderate	$15 to $30
Expensive	$30 to $45
Very Expensive	Over $45

WALKER PASS TO SHERMAN PASS

Joseph R. Walker likely drank at Indian Wells in 1834, having just discovered the low southern pass that would later bear his name. The Death Valley '49ers filled their canteens here more than once in the winter of 1850. "A more god-forsaken, cheerless place I have seldom seen," wrote William Brewer, Chief Botanist of the Whitney Survey, having passed through in 1864, "a spring of water—nothing else." Contemporary boosters have determined it to be "the sunniest spot in the U.S." Today, the water is used chiefly in the making of an award-winning beer, distributed at certain locations throughout Southern California. The steakhouse at the **Indian Wells Brewing Company** (2565 N. CA 14,

EASTERN SIERRA CAMPING

Sherman Pass	Elevation	Season	Reservations Accepted	Fee	Sites	Water	Agency
Long Valley	5,200	Year-round	No	No	13	No	BLM
Chimney Creek	5,900	Year-round	No	No	36	No	BLM
Kennedy Meadows	5,800	Year-round	No	Yes	38	Yes	USFS
Horse Meadow	7,600	Jun-Nov	No	Yes	41	Well	USFS
Troy Meadow	7,800	Jun-Nov	No	Yes	73	Well	USFS
Fish Creek	7,400	Jun-Nov	No	Yes	40	Well	USFS
Little Lake to Lone Pine							
Fossil Falls	3,300	Year-round	No	Yes	12	Yes	BLM
Diaz Lake	3,700	Year-round	Yes*	Yes	200	Piped	DWP**
Portagee Joe	3,800	Year-round	No	Yes	15	Piped	DWP
Tuttle Creek	5,120	Mar-Nov	No	Yes	85	No	BLM
Lone Pine	6,000	Apr-Oct	Yes	Yes	43	Yes	USFS
Whitney Portal	8,000	May-Oct	Yes	Yes	43	Yes	USFS
Cottonwood Pass (walk-in)	10,000	May-Oct	No	Yes	18	Yes	USFS
Cottonwood Lakes (walk-in)	10,000	May-Oct	No	Yes	12	Yes	USFS
Horseshoe Meadow (Eq.)	10,000	May-Oct	No	Yes	10	Yes	USFS
Golden Trout	10,000	May-Oct	No	Yes	18	Piped	USFS
Independence							
Independence Creek	3,800	Year-round	No	Yes	25	Creek	DWP
Lower Grays Meadow	6,000	Mar-Oct	Yes	Yes	52	Piped	USFS
Upper Grays Meadow	6,200	Mar-Oct	Yes	Yes	35	Piped	USFS
Onion Valley	9,200	Jun-Oct	Yes	Yes	29	Piped	USFS
Oak Creek	5,000	Year-round	Yes	No	22	Piped	USFS
Fort Independence	3,975	Year-round	No	Yes	25	Piped	Tribal
Goodale Creek	4,000	Mar-Oct	No	Yes	46	No	BLM
Taboose Creek	3,900	Year-round	No	Yes	56	Creek	DWP
Tinemaha Creek	4,400	Year-round	No	Yes	55	Limited	DWP
Big Pine							
Big Pine Creek	7,700	May-Oct	Yes	Yes	30	Yes	USFS
First Falls (walk-in)	8,300	May-Oct	No	No	5	No	USFS
Sage Flat	7,400	Apr-Oct	No	Yes	28	Yes	USFS
Upper Sage Flat	7,600	Apr-Oct	Yes	Yes	21	Yes	USFS
Palisade Glacier (group)	7,600	Apr-Oct	Yes	Yes	1	Yes	USFS
Clyde Glacier (group)	7,600	Apr-Oct	Yes	Yes	1	Yes	USFS
Baker Creek	4,000	Year-round	No	Yes	70	Yes	DWP
Glacier View	3,900	Year-round	No	Yes	40	Yes	DWP
White Mountains/Bristlecone Forest							
Grandview	8,600	May-Oct	No	No	26	No	USFS
Ferguson (group)	7,200	May-Oct	Yes‡	Yes	1	No	USFS
Nelson (group)	7,200	May-Oct	Yes‡	Yes	1	No	USFS
Noren (group)	7,200	May-Oct	Yes‡	Yes	1	No	USFS
Bishop							
Millpond Recreation Area	4,400	Year-round	No	Yes	100	Yes	DWP
Horton Creek	4,975	May-Nov	No	Yes	53	No	BLM
Pleasant Valley Pit	4,500	Nov-May	No	Yes	75	No	BLM
Big Trees	7,500	Apr-Sep	No	Yes	9	Yes	USFS
Bishop Park	8,400	May-Oct	No	Yes	21	Yes	USFS
Bitterbrush	7,350	May-Oct	No	Yes	16	Yes	USFS
Forks	7,800	Apr-Oct	No	Yes	9	Yes	USFS
Four Jeffrey	8,100	Apr-Oct	Yes	Yes	106	Yes	USFS
Intake 2 (walk-in)	8,200	Apr-Oct	No	Yes	5	Yes	USFS
Intake 2 (upper)	8,200	Year-round	No	Yes	8	Yes	USFS
Mountain Glen	8,200	May-Oct	No	Yes	5	No	USFS
North Lake	9,500	Jun-Oct	No	Yes	11	Yes	USFS
Sabrina	9,000	May-Oct	No	Yes	18	Yes	USFS
Willow	9,000	May-Oct	No	Yes	7	No	USFS
Bishop Park (group)	8,200	May-Oct	Yes	Yes	1	Yes	USFS
Table Mountain (group)	8,500	May-Oct	Yes	Yes	1	Yes	USFS

Note: Reservations at USFS campgrounds, unless otherwise specified, can be made online at www.recreation.gov or by calling 1-877-444-6777.
* For reservations at Diaz Lake, call 760-876-5656.   ‡ For group reservations at the Bristlecone Forest, call 760-873-2503.
** Los Angeles Department of Water and Power

Inyokern; 760-377-5989; www.mojave-red.com) is the only place to eat along this stretch of highway, the sort of place where the choice is rice pilaf or baked potato, where garnish is a desiccated orange slice and a sprig of parsley, a place recommendable more for the view and for the tall, cold Mojave Reds than for the steaks.

Points of Interest

Pearsonville (760-377-5446; www1.iwvisp.com/hubcaps). Gas, water, fast food, and Lucy Pearson's renowned hubcap collection.

Power Lines. Of the two parallel sets of towers and cables that run the length of the Owens Valley—sometimes next to, sometimes crossing over US 395—both are managed by the Los Angeles Department of Water and Power (DWP), and both ship electricity southbound to the city. One set was completed in 1951 from DWP's three generating stations in the Owens Gorge, north of Bishop. The other—the Pacific DC Intertie, completed in 1970 from stations on the Columbia River in Washington State—"carries a million volts for 846 miles," according to the Center for Land Use Interpretation, and is "the world's longest distance and highest voltage transmission line." The latter provides just under half of DWP's total supply of electricity.

Nine Mile Canyon (CR J41). A small sign on US 395, just north of Pearsonville, points the way to Kennedy Meadows. This road—the Sherman Pass Road—represents the quickest route into the Sierra Nevada from points south. At the mouth of the canyon note the Owens River being siphoned toward the San Fernando Valley (this is not all of it; some passes unseen beneath the road, by way of a second, underground aqueduct built in the 1970s). The land and waterworks are owned and maintained by the City of Los Angeles. The river's flow can be observed through vents in the pipeline. Note the radical change in ecosystems from an elevation of 2,500 feet at US 395 (at the northern edge of the Mojave desert) to the lip of the Kern Plateau at more than 6,000 feet. In winter the road is closed beyond Kennedy Meadows (6,500 feet). In summer it continues over Sherman Pass (9,200 feet), thence to wind 6,000 feet back down to the Main Fork of the Kern River.

Joshua Trees. So named by early Mormon pioneers traveling the Old Spanish Trail to San Bernardino, these trees were made world famous in 1987 by Grammy-award-winning Irish rock band U2. Frémont called them "the most repulsive tree in the vegetable kingdom," which seems also to be the general opinion of developers in contemporary Lancaster, Palmdale, and the greater Antelope Valley. In fact, they are not trees but rather a kind of fibrous bush, a unique species of yucca (*Yucca brevifolia*) that grows only on certain plateaus and higher-altitude fringes of the Mojave desert, between 2,000 and 6,000 feet. The oldest are thought to be a thousand years old. "Tormented, thin forests of it stalk drearily in the high mesas," wrote Mary Austin in 1903, "particularly in that triangular slip that fans out eastward from the meeting of the Sierras and coastwise hills where the first swings across the southern end of the San Joaquin." Good stands can still be seen on the eastern slope of Walker Pass (CA 178); across the uplift of Nine Mile Canyon (CR J41); along the base of the Coso Range, east of Haiwee Reservoir; and along the southern promontory of the Inyos (between Death and Saline valleys).

California's Highest Peaks

There is disagreement as to whether California can boast 13 true summits over 14,000 feet, or 15, or more. Of the four needles to the south of Mount Whitney, for example, each is higher than 14,000 feet, but none is considered a separate summit worthy of listing as a "fourteener." Starlight and Polemonium are sometimes listed as separate peaks, sometimes as subpeaks of the North Palisade. There is no disagreement that all of California's highest points—with the exception of Mount Shasta—are in the Eastern Sierra.

	Peak	Elevation	Range	Nearest town
1	Mount Whitney	14,494	Sierra Nevada	Lone Pine
2	Mount Williamson	14,370	Sierra Nevada	Independence
3	White Mountain	14,246	White Mountains	Bishop/Big Pine
4	North Palisade	14,242	Sierra Nevada	Big Pine
5	Starlight Peak	14,180	Sierra Nevada	Big Pine
6	Mount Shasta	14,162	Cascades	Mount Shasta City
7	Mount Sill	14,153	Sierra Nevada	Big Pine
8	Mount Russell	14,088	Sierra Nevada	Lone Pine
9	Polemonium	14,080	Sierra Nevada	Big Pine
10	Split Mountain	14,042	Sierra Nevada	Big Pine
11	Mount Langley	14,022	Sierra Nevada	Lone Pine
12	Mount Tyndall	14,019	Sierra Nevada	Independence
13	Middle Palisade	14,012	Sierra Nevada	Big Pine
14	Mount Muir	14,012	Sierra Nevada	Lone Pine
15	Thunderbolt Peak	14,003	Sierra Nevada	Big Pine

Kennedy Meadows General Store (1445 Kennedy Meadows Road; 559-850-2314). Generally manned by Ed McFarland, this is the last place for supplies of any kind. Through-hikers on the Pacific Crest Trail have caches of food mailed here general delivery. Most try to make it up here (out of the Mojave) by the first few weeks of spring—after the last snow in the high country, but before things get heated up below. Ice, propane canisters, cold beer, Gatorade, marshmallows, basic fishing tackle. Decent burgers. Local history. No gas. Note the extensive arrowhead collection. Open daily 9–5.

Bald Mountain Lookout (9,430 feet). The highest lookout in the Southern Sierra, it was rebuilt entirely of steel in 1954. All the materials were hauled in by mule. Today's access is via a short, easy hike from the west side of the Sherman Pass crest. Big views of Kennedy Meadows and the Domeland Wilderness. Picnic table.

Red Hill Cinder Cone, Owens Basin

LITTLE LAKE TO OWENS LAKE

The Eastern Sierra Scenic Byway begins just south of Little Lake, once called Little Owens Lake, where at some point during the Pleistocene era (more than 20,000 years ago) a great flow of lava sealed off the Owens Valley from its outlet to the Mojave. In the 1940s and '50s there was a thriving hotel, store, garage, and post office at Little Lake, serving sportsmen and motorists on their way to the Eastern Sierra. All that's left today is the lake.

Dining
The Ranch House Café (US 395, Olancha; 760-764-2363; inexpensive). This charming old roadhouse, just north of the junction with CA 190 to Death Valley, in the shade of hundred-year-old cottonwoods, is the only place to eat before Lone Pine. Basic truck-stop comfort food. Pie and coffee. Open daily for breakfast, lunch, and dinner.

Points of Interest
Fossil Falls (3 miles north of Little Lake). This small canyon was carved into volcanic basalt by an ancient incarnation of the Owens River, extinct many thousands of years before the first brick was laid at the Pueblo of Los Angeles. Popular climbing spot. Abundant obsidian flakes. Campground.

Red Hill Cinder Cone (3 miles north of Olancha). Assembled by volcanic eruption some 10,000 to 14,000 years ago, Red Hill may have seen action as recently as the 1600s. Pumice and lava rock from Red Hill have been used in the making of cinder blocks, especially for sound-barrier walls along Los Angeles freeways. Borrow pit on the south flank provides cinders for Caltrans road maintenance.

Wild Burro Rescue (Falls Creek Road, Olancha; 760-764-2136; www.wildburrorescue.org). In the year 2000, on the site of an old 1930s hunting club, Diane Chontos established a shoestring refuge for wild burros captured in Death Valley. Today there are more than two hundred burros—and a pack of rescued people and domestic animals, too—living here on 140 dry acres. Visitors and volunteers welcome.

Cartago (3 miles north of Olancha). As the great historian, photographer, and water attorney Burke Griggs reminds us, Carthage was defeated by Rome (c. 146 B.C.), thereafter to suffer the salting of its farmland. So the story goes. Once upon a time, at this Cartago, the steamers *Bessie Brady* and *Mollie Stevens* unloaded the silver bullion that helped build the Port of Los Angeles. When Los Angeles salted the lake, as it were, the American Potash Company established a surface mining operation here, of which nothing now remains but ruins and a gleaming pile of soda.

Crystal Geyser Bottling Plant (1-800-4-GEYSER; www.crystalgeyserasw.com). Here at the base of Olancha Peak, in a 100,000-square-foot modular warehouse on the edge of the Owens Lake playa, one of the best-selling drinking waters in Southern California is pumped out of the ground, bottled, and hauled away on trucks. The company has also submitted plans to build a tea bottling plant up the hill along the old railroad grade. Meanwhile, Anheuser Busch is reported to be pumping water from a ranch next door. "Olancha is the water capital of California," said an Inyo County Supervisor to *High Country News* in 1996. The Crystal Geyser plant—"for insurance liability reasons and also for security"—is not open to the public.

Bartlett Glass Plant. Between the highway and the northwestern edge of the Owens Lake playa lie the silos and midcentury-modern ruins of the Pittsburgh Plate Glass Company's chemical plant, disused since the 1960s, now privately owned.

EAST OF OWENS LAKE

Once upon a time—from prehistory into the 1890s—this was the busier side of the valley. There were fewer rivers to cross and much richer mineral deposits. Now it is home to various ruins, rusted equipment, and mostly abandoned settlements.

Points of Interest

Keeler. The southern terminus of what was once the longest narrow-gauge railway in the West, the Carson & Colorado, from 1883. The long, slow decline began with the construction of a standard gauge road from Mojave to Owenyo, up the west side of the lake, in

Keeler municipal pool, June 2007 Burke Griggs

Climbing Mount Whitney

The tallest peak in the range was given its name in 1864 by members of Josiah D. Whitney's Geological Survey, nine years before anyone managed to make the summit. Its height was then estimated to be greater than 15,000 feet above sea level. Clarence King, of that early survey, climbed a peak he thought was Whitney in 1871, only to discover two years later that he'd been on the wrong summit (today known as Mount Langley). By the time he'd heard the bad news, made his way back across the country from the East Coast, engaged an outfit from Visalia, and made the true summit, on

Lone Pine Peak (12,944 feet) dominates the town of the same name; Whitney is on the right and farther back, above the Shell sign, with the needles on its left flank. Burke Griggs

1910. Mining operations came and went until the 1950s. Today it is the site of frequent alkali dust storms and is home to a few dozen ghosts and other reclusive characters.

Swansea. The Embarkation point for Cerro Gordo bullion in the 1870s, before the business was taken over by Keeler. A sporadically maintained road to the east, into the hills, provides four-wheel-drive access to Cerro Gordo, via the Swansea-Keeler petroglyphs (made between 300 B.C. and A.D.1200—including ancient equinox markers and possible

September 19, 1873, he'd been beaten to the punch. The first party was comprised of three fishermen from Lone Pine, who had erected a monument on the summit a month earlier and declared their mountain to be called "Fisherman's Peak." A slightly more scientific expedition, organized by Mortimer Belshaw of Cerro Gordo, made the top in early September and with a barometer measured its elevation at 14,898 feet. John Muir, hardy fellow, showed up a month after King. Alone he rode a horse south from Independence to Cottonwood Pass, left his horse in a meadow so as to climb what he thought was the highest peak, only to find himself, as King before him, standing atop Mount Langley. But Muir, unlike King, saw the higher peak 5 or 6 miles to the north. He ran down, moved his horse, and by sunset was at the base of Whitney. He pressed on. "By midnight I was among the summit needles," he wrote. "There I had to dance all night to keep from freezing." He failed to make the top. He retrieved his horse, returned to Independence, "ate and slept all next day," then, not to be deterred, "set out afoot for the summit by direct course up the east side." He was standing at the fishermen's monument at 8 AM on the 21st of October, the first to climb Whitney from the east.

The good people of Lone Pine, who suffered no love for Josiah Whitney after his absurd pronouncements on their earthquake the year before, made a valiant attempt to make official the name "Fisherman's Peak"—even to the extent of introducing a bill in the State Legislature. But the mapmakers, natural partisans of Whitney, won out. The Wheeler Survey in 1875 penciled Whitney in at 14,471. The first women to stand at that elevation did so in 1878. Loaded mules made the summit in 1881, and in 1883 a portion of the east side of the range—from Sheep Mountain to Williamson to the Alabama Hills—was set aside as the Mount Whitney Military Reservation, "ostensibly for military, in reality for scientific purposes." The trail was improved and a stone hut built on the summit during the summer of 1909. In 1926 the summit became the eastern boundary of the newly expanded Sequoia National Park.

The official elevation has changed a number of times over the years, from 14,522 (1881) to 14,515 (1903) to 14,502 (1905) to 14,496 (1928). "You're looking at the pride of the Sierras, brother— Mount Whitney," says the gas station attendant to Humphrey Bogart in *High Sierra* (1941), "14,501 feet above sea level." In the 1955 remake, *I Died a Thousand Times*, the guy says to Jack Palance: "You're looking at the High Sierras, mister. Mount Whitney's in there . . . 14,496 feet." AAA puts it down as 14,494, and the Park Service has it at 14,491. The Forest Service—the agency that issues the permits necessary to climb the thing—calls it 14,496, or 14,495. To keep the crowds down, all trails in the Mount Whitney zone are subject to strict quotas. Permits for the highly popular Mount Whitney Trail are issued first by mail-in lottery in February, thereafter on a certain Wednesday of each month, on a rotating basis, thereafter whenever space is available. A variety of other, longer routes can get you there with considerably less traffic. For more information check www.fs.fed.us/r5/inyo/recreation /wild/mtwhitney.shtml, or call the permit office at the Eastern Sierra Interagency Visitors Center at 760-873-2483.

evidence of early Arabic and Celtic traders) and the remains of the Saline Valley Salt Tram, completed in 1913, which operated in fits and starts as late as 1936.

Dolomite Marble Mine. A pure white marble has been quarried here, at a site once called the Mountain of Marble, since the late 1800s. Deposits are said to extend for 6 miles at a thickness of at least 500 feet. The first two stories of the historic Mills Building in San Francisco (220 Montgomery) were built of this marble in 1891 and went on to survive the 1906 earthquake.

Lone Pine

In 1904 Mary Austin wrote of the pueblo Lone Pine as it once was: "At Las Uvas they keep all the good customs brought out of Old Mexico or bred in the lotus-eating land; drink, and are merry and look out for something to eat afterward; have children, nine or ten to a family, have cock fights, keep the siesta, smoke cigarettes and wait for the sun to go down." Today the place is run by a breed that takes itself a bit more seriously. Still, it's a classic Western Main Street town in the lee of the highest crest of the Sierra, hub of contemporary tourist activity in the Owens Valley: motels, bars, restaurants, fast food, gas, basic shopping—a perfect base from which to explore the surrounding country. Sold out first weekend in October for the film festival.

Dining

Bonanza Family Restaurant (104 North Main Street; 760-876-4768; inexpensive). Naugahyde booths, counter service. The best chiles rellenos on the east side, home-fried tortilla chips, a mean enchilada with ranchera sauce, an array of respectable burritos, and a fresh salsa bar. Burgers and chicken-fried steak if you must. Beer and wine.

Margie's Merry Go Round (212 South Main Street; 760-876-4115; expensive). Steaks and seafood in an intimate carousel-shaped dining room. Dinner only, seven days a week. Outdoor dining in summer. Beer and wine. Beneath the best neon sign in town.

Alabama Hills Café & Bakery (111 Post Street; 760-876-4675; inexpensive). The old Rutabaga's, now newly renovated with counter service and booths. Bagels, breads, doughnuts, apple crisp, sandwiches to go. Breakfast served all day: a veggie scramble, a spicy sirloin skillet, peach pancakes, an egg sandwich made to order on fresh,

thick-sliced bread. Open 5:30 AM to 2 PM every day but Tuesday.

Totem Café (131 South Main Street; 760-876-1120; moderate). Knotty-pine decor, antique skis, snowshoes, bows and arrows, and a bear trap. Steaks, ribs, and fried chicken are served family-style. Entrées are served with a whole apple. Open every day.

Taverns, Saloons & Roadhouses

Jake's Saloon (119 North Main Street; 760-876-5765). A favorite watering hole of bikers, dragsters, dust-mitigation contractors, German tourists, deputy sheriffs, film crews, clampers, and cowboys (real and ersatz). "We were in Vegas one year, going up to Lake Tahoe, shooting through Death Valley," says the Englishman in the black hat, the one with the authentic 19th-century Peacemaker on his hip, "got here about five in the evening, it was getting dark, found somewhere to stay. Came in here for a couple of drinks, saw the saloon doors and thought: fantastic." Shuffleboard, pool table. Live music on the weekends. Brawls are infrequent but not unheard of. Beer and wine only; the hard stuff is served across the street at the Double L.

Food & Beverage Purveyors

COFFEE, TEA, ETC.
Espresso Parlor (123 North Main Street; 760-876-9110). Coffee, pastries, muffins, Internet.

GROCERIES
Joseph's Bi-Rite (119 South Main Street; 760-876-4378). Grocery shopping the way it used to be (since 1895). Deli counter, beer and wine, ice, charcoal, firewood, High Sierra pickled peppers, and local honey.

Evacuees of Japanese ancestry waiting to board buses from Lone Pine Station to the War Relocation Authority center at Manzanar, April 1942 Clem Albers, courtesy Bancroft Library

Books, Maps & Information

Eastern Sierra Interagency Visitors Center (USy 395 and CA 136, 1 mile south of Lone Pine; 760-876-6222). One-stop shop for regional information, sponsored by the full gamut of federal, state, and local agencies. Books, maps, displays, restrooms, wilderness permits. Open daily 8–5.

Beverly & Jim Rogers Museum Of Lone Pine Film History (US 395, south of McDonald's; 760-876-9103; www.lonepinefilmhistorymuseum.org). This mind-boggling collection of artifacts from the hundreds of movies and television shows filmed in and around Lone Pine includes original costumes, guns, spurs, saddles, props, set pieces, and more. Highlights include the typewriter used to create the script of *Gunga Din,* the 1938 Plymouth Coupe in which Bogart drove to his demise in *High Sierra,* and Mary Austin and Zane Grey first editions. The gift shop sells western-themed books, apparel, and more, and an array of Film Festival memorabilia.

Lone Pine Chamber Of Commerce, Film Commission & Tourist Information Center (120 South Main Street; 760-876-4444, 1-877-253-8981; www.lonepinechamber.org). Books, maps, brochures, local and regional information. Ask for the free publication *Motor Touring in the Eastern Sierra.*

Manzanar Interpretive Center (US 395; 760-878-2194; www.nps.gov/manz). The center features exhibits, photos (including some by Dorothea Lange and Ansel Adams), artifacts, and audiovisual presentations covering local history from 1885, with a focus on World War II relocation and internment, including a large-scale model of the camp, crafted by former residents. Bookstore, theater, temporary exhibit gallery. Open every day except Christmas.

Shopping

Sporting Gear & equipment
Elevation (125 North Main Street; 760-876-4560; www.sierraelevation.com). Poor Jon Turner, white-water enthusiast, fell in love, and for the sake of a woman found himself high and dry, running a top-notch climbing and mountaineering boutique in Lone Pine— where the only white water for miles around runs inside a steel pipe on its way to Los Angeles. Stop by and tell him you feel bad for him, and pick up the latest fashions in Gore-Tex, down, and fleece. Crampons, Ursacks, and BearVaults for rent.

Lone Pine Sporting Goods (220 South Main Street; 760-876-5365). Of the hook and gun variety. Fish and game licenses. Open daily in summer.

Sundries & Souvenirs
Lone Pine Rocks & Gifts (235 South Main Street; 760-876-1010). Local rocks and minerals, gifts, and books.

Totem Trading Post (131 South Main Street; 760-876-1120). Western apparel, hats, and knickknacks. Note the signatures on the walls, some recognizable.

General Stores
Lee's Frontier Chevron (1900 South Main Street; 760-876-5844). Lee used to drive a truck, so he knows about long hours: "Got to where 50, 60 miles would go by I wouldn't even remember." Standing at a cash register, he figures, there's less danger of a collision. Lee also knows what a body needs when it's on the road: free coffee, three choices of breakfast burrito, liquor, wine, beer, ice, bait, gas, and guns and ammo.

Whitney Portal Store (Whitney Portal; 760-876-0030; www.whitneyportalstore.com). Earlene, Doug, and Doug Jr. have been supplying the hordes on the Whitney Trail for 20 seasons. It's the last stop for bear canister rentals, hiking poles, hats, water bottles, trail food, and postcards. Grill food, breakfast, lunch, and dinner are served. Don't miss the world-famous big pancakes, made with Krusteaz, vanilla, and cinnamon, and served family-style. Open May through October.

Points of Interest
Alabama Hills. So named by Confederate sympathizers in Lone Pine during the Civil War. The *Alabama* was a cruiser that had destroyed or captured as many as 60 northern vessels by 1864, when it was finally sunk off the coast of France by the *U.S.S. Kearsarge*. Union sympathizers in Independence gave the name Kearsarge to a number of local features, including the main trail over the Sierra to the Kings River. The boulders and wild rock formations are immediately recognizable as the backdrop of hundreds of movies, TV shows, and commercials. Stop by the Lone Pine Film History Museum for a self-guided driving-

Shot in the Owens Valley: A Short List

The Round-Up (1920). Directed by George Melford; starring Fatty Arbuckle and Wallace Beery.

The Virginian (1923). Directed by Tom Forman; starring Kenneth Harlan and Florence Vidor.

Greed (1923). Directed by Erich Von Stroheim; starring Gibson Gowland and Jean Hersholt.

Riders of the Purple Sage (1925). Directed by Lynn Reynolds; starring Tom Mix.

Blue Steel (1934). Directed by Robert Bradbury; starring John Wayne and Gabby Hayes.

Hop-Along Cassidy (1935). Directed by Howard Bretherton; starring William Boyd.

The Charge of the Light Brigade (1936). Directed by Michael Curtiz; starring Errol Flynn and Olivia de Havilland.

The Lone Ranger (1938). Directed by John English and William Witney; starring Chief Thundercloud and Silver King the Horse.

Where the Buffalo Roam (1938). Directed by Albert Herman; starring Tex Ritter.

Gunga Din (1939). Directed by George Stevens; starring Cary Grant and Douglas Fairbanks Jr.

High Sierra (1941). Directed by Raoul Walsh; screenplay by John Huston; starring Ida Lupino and Humphrey Bogart.

The Ox-Bow Incident (1943). Directed by William Wellman; starring Henry Fonda, Dana Andrews, and Anthony Quinn.

Tycoon (1947). Directed by Richard Wallace; starring John Wayne.

Yellow Sky (1948). Directed by William Wellman; starring Gregory Peck, Anne Baxter, and Richard Widmark.

The Lone Ranger (TV series, 1949–57). Starring Clayton Moore and Jay Silverheels.

The Gene Autry Show (TV series, 1950–56). Starring Gene Autry.

Rawhide (1951). Directed by Henry Hathaway; starring Tyrone Power and Susan Hayward.

The Long, Long Trailer (1954). Directed by Vincente Minnelli; starring Lucille Ball and Desi Arnaz.

Bad Day at Black Rock (1955). Directed by John Sturges; starring Spencer Tracy, Walter Brennan, Ernest Borgnine, and Lee Marvin.

North to Alaska (1960). Directed by Henry Hathaway; starring John Wayne and Stewart Granger.

How the West Was Won (1962). Directed by John Ford, Henry Hathaway, and George Marshall; starring Henry Fonda, Gregory Peck, Debbie Reynolds, Jimmy Stewart, et al.

The Great Race (1965). Directed by Blake Edwards; starring Jack Lemmon, Tony Curtis, and Natalie Wood.

Nevada Smith (1966). Directed by Henry Hathaway; starring Steve McQueen.

Joe Kidd (1972). Directed by John Sturges; written by Elmore Leonard; starring Clint Eastwood and Robert Duvall.

Star Trek V: The Final Frontier (1989). Directed by William Shatner; starring William Shatner, Leonard Nimoy, George Takei, et al.

Tremors (1990). Directed by Ron Underwood; starring Kevin Bacon and Fred Ward.

Kalifornia (1993). Directed by Dominic Sena; starring Brad Pitt, Juliette Lewis, and David Duchovny.

Maverick (1994). Directed by Richard Donner; starring Mel Gibson, Jodi Foster, and James Garner.

Star Trek: Generations (1994). Directed by David Carson; starring Patrick Stewart, et al.

G.I. Jane (1997). Directed by Ridley Scott; starring Demi Moore and Viggo Mortensen.

The Postman (1997). Directed by Kevin Costner; starring Kevin Costner.

Gone in 60 Seconds (2000). Directed by Dominic Sena; starring Nicolas Cage, Giovanni Ribisi, and Angelina Jolie.

Gladiator (2000). Directed by Ridley Scott; starring Russell Crowe and Joaquin Phoenix.

Iron Man (2008). Directed by Jon Favreau; starring Robert Downey Jr., Gwyneth Paltrow, Jeff Bridges, et al.

tour brochure, or for Dave Holland's *On Location in Lone Pine,* then head for the hills. Also a popular rock climbing and bouldering spot. An easy loop can be made (in a passenger car) by following Movie Road north to Moffat Ranch Road, then back down to US 395 just north of the notorious Alabama Gates.

Whitney Portal. The paved road west from downtown Lone Pine, built in the 1930s, climbs past the Alabama Hills, up a series of dramatic switchbacks to the Whitney Portal Store, campground, picnic area, and the main Mount Whitney Trailhead at 8,360 feet. Busy in summer.

Horseshoe Meadows/Cottonwood Lakes Road. Another exciting set of switchbacks with high exposure from the southern end of the Alabama Hills to the Cottonwood and New Army Pass trailhead at 10,040 feet. Likely the third-highest paved road in California (after Rock Creek and Saddlebag Lake roads—see chapter 5), it roughly follows the trail John Muir rode on his first attempt at Mount Whitney in 1873. Closed in winter.

Manzanar National Historic Site. (US 395; 760-878-2194; www.nps.gov/manz). This site was named after the Spanish word for "apple orchard." The Owens Valley Piute were relocated away from here in 1863 (by the U.S. Army). In 1942 the U.S. Army leased the land from the City of Los Angeles for the relocation and internment of Japanese Americans from all over the West Coast (including 12-year-old Larry Shinoda, who would go on to design the 1963 Corvette Sting Ray). Site open every day dawn to dusk.

1872 Earthquake Grave. On the north side of town, a short trail leads up the highway embankment to a mass grave with a view.

The Legend of Winnedumah

Once upon a time, the Paiutes, who lived in the great valley of Wauco-ba (the Owens), were at war with their neighbors, the Diggers, from the other side of Pahbatoya (the Sierra). The Paiutes's war chief in those days was Tinemaha; Winnedumah, his brother, was a well-respected medicine man. One day, in a surprise attack, the Diggers came down out of the Sierra in great hordes. A battle raged through days and nights. "Never was there such a battle before, nor afterwards, between these primitive foes," wrote one Dan Rose in a 1927 issue of *Touring Topics.* "Hundreds fell in the first clash of arms. Locked in deadly embrace, they crashed each other's skulls with their stone tomahawks, neither giving way." Thousands were left dead or dying across the valley. The Paiutes, as bravely as they fought, were finally driven in retreat to the heights of the Inyo range. Winnedumah reached the crest "sorely pressed, exhausted and alone," his medicine having proved of little effect. His brother was dead. He took one last look across his beloved valley—the Digger warriors now nearly upon him— raised his arms to the sky, and invoked the Great Spirit. The sky cracked open; there was thunder and lightning; the earth shook; and in the great "convulsion of nature" Winnedumah was transformed into a pillar of granite. The Diggers freaked out, of course, and made their way as fast as they could back across the Sierra, never again to trouble the Paiutes. To this day, there atop the Inyos, a long scramble up and eastward from Mazourka Road, pierced only by the bolts of climbers past, stands Winnedumah, "ever faithful."

1872 Earthquake Grave Burke Griggs

Lone Pine Station. Located northeast of town along the old railroad grade. At the turn of the 20th century it was owned by Quaker farmers, supposedly among the first to sell their land to Fred Eaton. Here, in 1910, at what was then called Owenyo, the Carson & Colorado narrow gauge met the Southern Pacific standard rail from Mojave. Materials for the Los Angeles aqueduct were shipped through the depot here, as were thousands of Japanese Americans on their way to Manzanar during World War II.

INDEPENDENCE

County seat for the least populated county in the state of California, Independence was founded as a U.S. Army camp during the early period of white settlement, Indian trouble, and general violence between 1862 and 1877. Today it boasts a population of about five hundred, an authentic French Colonial bistro, a decent historic hotel, a gas station, a general store, a museum, and a courthouse.

Dining
✪ **Still Life Café** (135 South Edwards; 760-878-2555; moderate to expensive). Hours are capricious. Generally open Wednesday through Sunday for lunch and dinner, but call ahead.

General Stores
Mairs Market (149 South Edwards Street; 760-878-2169). All the last-minute basics: charcoal, firewood, marshmallows, graham crackers, beer, wine, ice, ice cream, canned goods, limited meat and produce, fresh-made sandwiches.

Points of Interest

Inyo County Courthouse (168 North Edwards Street; 760-878-0366; www.inyocounty.us). Designed by W. H. Weeks and built in 1922 in the Greek Revival style, this courthouse was the fourth in a line of previous courthouses that were lost to earthquake and fire. Here Charles Manson and Family were jailed for possession of stolen vehicles in 1969—before Manson's indictment in the Tate-LaBianca murders.

Mary Austin House (253 Market Street). "[I]f ever you come beyond the borders as far as the town that lies in a hill dimple at the foot of Kearsarge," wrote Mary Austin in 1904, "never leave it until you have knocked at the door of the brown house under the willow-tree at the end of the village street, and there you shall have such news of the land, of its trails and what is astir in them, as one lover of it can give to another." Soon after the publication of *Land of Little Rain*, her most enduring work, she moved to Carmel to hang out with Jack London and George Sterling. Then she moved to New Mexico, where she would eventually collaborate with Ansel Adams on a book about the Taos Pueblo. The house is not open to the public.

Eastern California Museum (155 North Grant Street; 760-878-0258; www.countyofinyo.org/ecmuseum). Established in 1928 as a means of preserving the varied history and material culture of the Owens Valley, this museum features a variety of artifacts, from Shoshone and Paiute baskets and a collection of 1880s buildings to a yard full of rusting equipment from the construction of the L.A. Aqueduct. The east wing houses temporary and traveling exhibits. No fee. Closed Tuesday.

Mount Whitney Fish Hatchery (Oak Creek Road, 2 miles north of Independence; 760-878-2272). M. J. Connell, State Fish and Game Commissioner in 1915, wanted a hatchery "that would match the mountains, would last forever, and would be a showplace for all time." And so, the following year, of 3,500 tons of local granite, this faux Tudor-style chateau was built. The landscaping is supposed to have been designed by a gardener from Golden Gate Park in San Francisco. Open to the public daily.

BIG PINE

Gateway to the bristlecone pines and the palisades, Big Pine was so named long before the giant sequoia—the so-called Teddy Roosevelt Tree—was planted on the north end of town, in 1923, to commemorate the opening of Westgard Pass to automobile traffic. Gas, motels, basic road food, and an Indian reservation are here.

General Stores

Carroll's Market (136 South Main Street; 760-938-2718). Basic groceries, meats, produce, deli, ice, fishing licenses and tackle, ATM. Open daily.

Points of Interest

Owens Valley Radio Observatory (4 miles north on Leighton Lane, off CA 168, east of Big Pine; 760-938-2075; www.ovro.caltech.edu). At Owens, the largest university-operated radio observatory in the world, studies include the sun and the origins of the universe.

Owens Valley Radio Observatory Burke Griggs

Public tours are supposedly offered on the first Monday of every month, excluding holidays, organized by the Big Pine Chamber of Commerce (760-938-2114).

Ancient Bristlecone Pine Forest (760-873-2400;
www.fs.fed.us/r5/inyo/recreation/bristlecone/index.shtml). What is likely the fourth-highest paved road in the state ends at the Schulman Grove (10,010 feet) and from there continues, unpaved, to the Patriarch Grove at more than 11,000 feet. From there the track continues past a locked gate—closed to vehicle traffic—to the top of White Mountain Peak, at 14,242 feet. The bristlecone pines are the planet's oldest living things. The oldest living individual, at more than 4,700 years old, is called Methusaleh, after the longest-lived person in the Bible. The tree's exact location is, for it's protection, a fairly well-guarded secret. An older specimen by the name of Prometheus (4,844 years old) was cut down by a graduate student in 1964. The visitors center is open daily, June through September. Road closed in winter.

White Mountain Research Station (at the end of White Mountain Road; 760-873-4344; www.wmrs.edu). Established in 1951 as a joint venture between the University of California at Berkeley and the Office of Naval Research, White Mountain's facilities and use permits were transferred by the Navy to U.C. in the 1970s. Facilities include an observatory on the Barcroft Plateau (12,500 feet) and a lab on the summit of White Mountain (14,250 feet). The latter facility is probably as close to Antarctica as a researcher can come without leaving the continental United States. Ground has been broken here on the sexiest of topics: hypoxia, ventilation, hibernation, polarization of cosmic background radiation, holocene paleoecology in bristlecone pines—and climate change. Open house for the public on the first Sunday in August. Check Web site for scheduled lectures.

Tule Elk

Tule elk in paddock, Yosemite Valley, pre-1932   Courtesy NPS, YNP

In 1844 John Frémont found the western slope of the Sierra "crowded with bands of elk and wild horses." "It is very common to see herds of five or six hundred elk," wrote Lansford Hastings the same year, "ranging from vale to vale, amid the oats, clover and flax, with which the plains and valleys everywhere abound." There were hundreds of thousands of Tule or dwarf elk (*Cervus elaphus nannodes*) in California before the first great influx of population in the early 1850s. By the late 1860s they were nearly gone. "[A]t its smallest, wrote naturalist Allan Schoenherr, "the population may have numbered fewer than ten." One forward-thinking (and/or nostalgic) rancher in Kern County established a private refuge for the handful that remained. In 1873 the State Legislature moved to protect them, and by 1914 there were too many for the refuge to sustain. The Department of Fish and Game began various attempts at introducing them elsewhere, but the only group of transplants that managed to thrive were those that had been introduced to the Yosemite Valley. By 1933 the elk had come to be considered a problem in Yosemite, and all 26 of them were transferred to the Owens Valley (where they were not native). The following year these were joined by 28 from the Kern County refuge. Today the herd is kept at a number not exceeding 490. They range the length of the valley and can often be seen, especially early in the morning and at dusk, grazing on irrigated alfalfa along US 395 south of Big Pine.

Palisade Glacier. "A more absurd theory was never advanced," wrote the state's chief geologist, Professor Josiah Whitney, in 1868, "than that by which it was sought to ascribe to glaciers the sawing out of these vertical walls." For the rest of his life Whitney clung to the idea that were no glaciers in the Sierra Nevada. John Muir, "ignorant sheepherder," proved him wrong. The Palisade glacier is the largest remaining in the Sierra Nevada, the southernmost in the United States, dating back to the Little Ice Age, some 700 years ago. It is thought to have been in retreat since the 1850s. These are tough times for glaciers—catch this one before it's gone. Visible from US 395 north of Big Pine, plastered to a wall of granite needles, several over 14,000 feet high, the glacier itself can be reached by way of an 18-mile round-trip hike from Glacier Lodge in Big Pine Canyon.

BISHOP

Main population and supply center for the Eastern Sierra, Bishop is the only incorporated settlement in Inyo County, named for Samuel A. Bishop, who brought cattle here in the 1860s, much to the chagrin of the locals. Today it's an internationally renowned climbing mecca and uncontested mule capital of the world. Here you'll find motels, restaurants, hardware stores, banks, fast food, Indian food, bagels, gas, Von's, Kmart, and an Indian casino. Sold out Memorial Day weekend for Mule Days.

Dining

Astorga's Mexican Grill (1347 Rocking W Drive, in the Rite Aid shopping center; 760-873-7748; inexpensive). Hands down the best taqueria on the east side of the Sierra.

Whiskey Creek (524 North Main Street; 760-873-7174; www.whiskeycrk.com; inexpensive to moderate). The low-altitude, oak-and-brass sibling of the one in Mammoth, featuring the same great locally crafted beers and a slightly more expansive menu. Sandwiches, burgers, steaks, salads, and more are served in the dining room, in the bar, or, when the weather's warm, on the patio. Climbers' favorite happy hour from 5 to 6 on weekdays: half price on all food items except for desserts.

Imperial Gourmet (785 North Main Street; 760-872-1144; moderate). Because sometimes a body needs fried wontons, a decent plate of chow mein, crisp Chinese broccoli, and a fortune cookie. Delivery to local motels is available. Open daily; Sunday all-you-can-eat champagne brunch 11–2:30. No personal checks.

India Palace (787 North Main Street; 760-873-4634; moderate). The only Indian food between Los Angeles and Carson City. Transplanted urban dwellers have been known to drive down the hill from Mammoth for a taste of the Vindaloo. All-you-can-eat lunch buffet; dinner from 5 PM. Closed Tuesday.

The Village Café (965 North See Vee Lane; 760-872-3101; inexpensive). Best breakfast in town.

Yamatani (635 North Main Street; 760-872-4801; moderate to expensive). With the same owners as Shogun in Mammoth, Yamatani serves teriyaki, tempura, miso, sushi, sake, and more. The specialty rolls are the best. It's not quite Nobu, but then Bishop is not quite Malibu. Family-friendly. Full bar. Closed Wednesday.

Taverns, Saloons & Roadhouses

Rusty's Saloon (112 North Main Street; 760-873-9066). Classic Western saloon turned dive bar. Neon beer lights, pretzels, Elvira pinball machine, sporting events on TV, two pool tables, a mosaic in antique coins and poker chips. Check out the historic ECV photos on the way to the back room. Bring your own food.

Food & Beverage Purveyors

COFFEE, TEA, ETC.

Looney Bean (399 North Main Street; 760-872-2326). A friendlier local knockoff of the famous Seattle franchise with the green logo. Beans are roasted in Mammoth. Baked items. Free wireless Internet.

Black Sheep Espresso Bar (at Spellbinder Books, 124 South Main Street; 760-871-4142; www.blacksheepcoffeeroasters.com). Back-room hangout of local sculptors, would-be politicians, and other aficionados of the well-crafted macchiato.

SANDWICHES & SUCH

Erick Schat's Bakkerÿ (763 North Main Street; 760-873-7156; www.erickschatsbakery.com). Legend has it the Schat family fired up its first bakery in the Utrecht in 1893 (probably without the umlaut). A contingent of the clan made its way to North America in the 1950s, there to gain control of an old Austrian bakery in Bishop, already known for its authentic Basque-style sheepherder bread. Breads bearing the family name today show up in supermarkets across California, and the gingerbread-style outlet on Main Street in Bishop (built in 1979) is on any given day the busiest place in town. Pastries; doughnuts; sticky buns; machine-squeezed orange juice; turkey sandwiches assembled before your eyes from real roasted turkeys by a fleet of Mexican women; an array of gifty jams, jellies, and jerkies for the road; and, of course, racks and racks of bread, fresh from the oven.

Great Basin Bakery (275D South Main Street, behind Pegasus Gallery; 760-873-9828). The Eastern Sierra's source for blue-ribbon breads, bagels, and pastries, Great Basin is where early-rising locals go for frosted cinnamon rolls, lemon scones, local artisan French roast, and the best wild, line-caught, King salmon lox bagels in 300 miles. Try a sandwich, a bacon-and-egg Pino pie, or a slice of homemade cheesecake. Daily bread specials include Asiago sourdough and kalamata olive. Open 6 AM to 2 PM Monday through Saturday and 6:30 AM to noon on Sunday.

Raymond's Deli (150 North Main Street; 760-873-7275). The locals' rock 'n' roll alternative to Schat's, favored by Caltrans employees, dirtbag climbers, and teenagers on the lam from Bishop High. Concrete floors, vintage vinyl upholstery, AC/DC on the jukebox at 8 AM (and breakfast burritos). World-famous sandwiches include the Italian Stallion, the Don't "B" Chicken, the Gut Buster, and the Soy, You Like Tofu? Open for breakfast, lunch, and dinner.

MEATS

The Meat House (150 South Main; 760-873-4990). Real-deal old-school butcher shop. Call ahead for specialty cuts and family packages. Cheapest sandwiches in town, premade.

Meadow Farms Country Smokehouse (2345 North Sierra Highway; 760-873-5311; www.smokedmeats.com). Ham, bacon, sausage; a variety of top-quality beef, turkey, elk, buffalo, and salmon jerky; plus all manner of gifty condiments, preserves, and pickled items. Not cheap, but the real deal. Stop in for generous free samples.

GROCERIES

Joseph's Bi-Rite Market (211 North Main Street; 760-873-6388). When the polish and gloss and selection offered by the "Safeway family of companies" is just too much—or when you prefer your money to stay in Bishop.

Vons (1190 North Main Street; 760-872-9811; www.vons.com). The works: deli, bakery, pharmacy, Starbucks, floral, liquor, produce. Cheaper, wider selection, and on busy weekends less crowded than the Vons in Mammoth. Open daily from 6 AM to 1 AM.

Books, Maps & Information

AAA (187 West Pine Street; 760-872-8241; www.aaa-calif.com). Travel books, maps, Mexican insurance.

Bishop Area Chamber Of Commerce And Visitors Bureau (690 North Main Street; 760-873-8405; 1-888-395-3952; www.bishopvisitor.com). Books, maps, brochures, general information. Ask for the free publication *Motor Touring in the Eastern Sierra.*

White Mountain Ranger Station (798 North Main Street; 760-873-2500; www.fs.fed.us/r5/inyo/). Books, maps, postcards, Inyo National Forest information, wilderness permits. Open daily May to November and Monday through Friday the rest of the year.

Spellbinder Books (124 South Main Street; 760-873-4511; http://bishop.booksense.com). Best selection in the Eastern Sierra: local interest, plus classic and new-release fiction and non-fiction.

Shopping

CLOTHING & FASHION

The Toggery (115 North Main Street; 760-872-3211). For all your classic High Sierra and Western fashion needs: boots, hats, belts, moccasins, Pendleton blankets, Carhartt, and Levi's.

SPORTING GEAR & EQUIPMENT

Aerohead Cycles (312 North Warren Street; 760-873-4151). The only professional bike shop in the Owens Valley. From custom beach cruisers to road bikes to full-suspension downhill combat vehicles, these guys will do what it takes to get you rolling again.

Allen Outdoor Products, Sierra Saddlery & Feed (600 South Main Street; 760-873-5903; www.allenoutdoor.com). If a person were going to ride off into the sunset for an extended period of time Jedediah Smith style, this would be the place to gear up. Full range of backcountry clothing, gear, and accessories of the cast iron, wool, and leather variety, as well as cots, tents, range tepees, stoves, lanterns, chuck boxes, and snowshoes for rent. Look for the red horse and the fleet of U-Haul trailers.

Sage to Summit (148 Willow Street; 760-872-1756; www.sagetosummit.com). The only dedicated running store in the Eastern Sierra. The latest in shoes, clothing, accessories, and beta for moving fast on local trails. Open 10–6 Tuesday through Saturday.

Wilson's Eastside Sports (206 North Main Street; 760-873-7520; www.eastside sports.com). Gear and clothing for the self-propelled. Full range of backpacking, camping, snowshoeing, and ski touring rentals.

GALLERIES

Mountain Light Gallery (106 South Main Street; 760-873-7700; www.mountain light.com). It is often said that what Ansel Adams made of this landscape in silver salts and gelatin, Galen Rowell followed in color. Rowell was never the obsessive technician that Adams was. He was above all a consummate and highly accomplished mountaineer— with more than one hundred technical first ascents in the Sierra Nevada alone—who also carried with him a 35 mm camera and knew how to use it. "Photography," he wrote, "was a means of visual expression to communicate what I had seen to people who weren't there." At 1:23 AM on August 11, 2002, "on a dark moonless night" (according to the NTSB report), Rowell and his wife, Barbara, also a photographer, were killed when a routine charter flight from Oakland collided with the Owens Valley, less than 2 miles from the runway at the Bishop airport. "I've known all along that more of what I am seeking in the wilds is right here in my home state of California," he had written just the year before. "I couldn't say it with authority until I had all those journeys to Tibet, Nepal, Pakistan, China, South America, Antarctica, and Alaska behind me." The gallery features prints, books, posters, calendars, Rowell signature graduated neutral density filters, workshops, and guest pho-tographer exhibitions. Open daily.

Vern Clevenger Gallery (905 North Main Street, next to Starbucks; 760-873-7803; www.vernclevenger.com). Classic landscape photography of the Sierra Nevada and beyond by another world-class rock climber. Prints, posters, cards, professional lab service, and seasonal photography workshops. (See photo, opposite)

PHOTOGRAPHY SUPPLIES

Phillips Camera House (186 North Main Street; 760-872-4211). Film, CF cards, filters, batteries, lens cleaners, tripods, standard processing.

Points of Interest

Laws Railroad Museum & Historical Site (North on US to Silver Canyon Road; 760-873-5950; www.lawsmuseum.org). Eleven acres of exhibits include the original 1883 Laws Depot, Post Office, and Agent's House, much as they were when the last train ran in 1960. Other buildings have been added to re-create the village of Laws as it once was when the Carson & Colorado was in full swing. Nonrailroad artifacts on display include antique cameras, photos, saddles, brands, wagons, old stoves, guns, bathtubs, telephones, and medical and printing equipment. It's also home to Death Valley No. 5, the gasoline-driven rail car once used to haul tourists from Death Valley Junction to the Furnace Creek Inn. Nice place for a picnic on a windless day in winter. No fee. Open 10–4 daily year-round.

Fish Slough Road (www.bishopvisitor.com/images/maps/motor_touring/Routes/map13-

Parcher's Lane winter aspen, Bishop Creek Drainage Vern Clevenger

14-15.pdf). Head north from Bishop on US 6. At 1.3 miles, continue straight on Five Bridges Road. After another 2.3 miles, turn right on Fish Slough Road. Go 6.4 miles to the interpretive kiosk at the **Owens Valley Native Fish Sanctuary**, home to the last remaining population of Owens pupfish, declared extinct in 1948, rediscovered in the 1960s, and still hanging on today despite predation by bigger, badder nonnative bass. On the right-hand side of the road, 4.6 miles later, behind a fence, note the **Chidago Canyon Petroglyphs**, etchings in volcanic rock dating from many thousands of years ago, to slightly less artful inscriptions from the late 20th century.

RECREATION

Bird-Watching

Countless creeks reservoirs, marshes, and springs—from the Owens Gorge and tablelands north of Bishop to Little Lake—provide world-class birding. More than 320 known species frequent the valley floor. Check the **Eastern Sierra Audubon Society's** Web site, www.esaudubon.org, for hot spots. The *Eastern Sierra Birding Trail Map* is available online (www.easternsierrabirdingtrail.org) and through most local businesses and bookstores.

Boating

Leisurely tubing and kayaking are possible on certain remnant and newly established sections of the Owens. For an afternoon float on a High Sierra lake, bring your own craft or hire one at the following locations:

Lake Sabrina Boat Landing (Lake Sabrina, Bishop; 760-873-7425). Fishing and pontoon boat rentals. April to October.

South Lake Boat Landing (South Lake, Bishop; 760-873-4177; www.parchersresort.com). Fishing and pontoon boat rentals, bait and tackle. June to October.

Fishing

The lower Owens Valley boasts the earliest trout opener in the state, so you can get in there early and angle for rainbow, brook, cutthroat, golden, and brown. As the season progresses, work your way up toward the Sierra along one of more than a dozen intensively stocked creeks. When the snow melts, hit the hatches in the upper lakes basins. For the latest reports, maps, notes, news, and insider tips, check **Michael Sommermeyer**'s Web site, www.easternsierrafishing.com. For more Eastern Sierra guide-service listings, see chapter 5.

Brock's Flyfishing Specialists (100 North Main Street, Bishop; 760-872-3581; www.brocksflyfish.com). Rods, reels, flies, wader and tube rentals. Classes, seminars, full-service guide trips.

Pat Yaeger's Eastern Sierra Guide Service (760-872-7770; www.jaeger-flyfishing.com).

Golf

Bishop Country Club (1200 US 395 South; 760-873-5828; www.bishopcountryclub.com). Built in 1963. Eighteen holes, par 71. Pro shop, club and cart rentals, restaurant and bar. Open year-round.

Mount Whitney Golf Club (2559 South Main Street; 760-876-5795). Built in 1959. Nine holes, medium length. Par 36. Open year-round. Bargain greens fees and rentals.

Hang Gliding & Paragliding

"Flying here can be categorized as extreme," notes champion pilot and multiple world-record holder **Kari Castle** (760-872-2087; www.karicastle.com), who also offers tandem

Mount Whitney Golf Club, Lone Pine Peak Burke Griggs

flights, flying clinics, local guiding, and instruction. "It's known for big air and world record flights—but also for turbulence." The biggest-air enthusiasts around have been known to launch themselves into the atmosphere from Walt's Point, at 9,000 feet, on the Horseshoe Meadows Road.

Hiking
Every major tributary canyon offers a trail into the Sierra wilderness. Each goes up first before it goes down. The most popular trailheads are Whitney Portal (Mount Whitney Trail), Onion Valley (Kearsarge Pass), Big Pine Creek (Palisades), and in the lakes basin at the head of Bishop Creek. Passes less traveled include Haiwee, Olancha, Shepherd, Baxter, Sawmill, and Taboose. Wilderness permits are required for overnight travel (available free at local ranger stations).

Horseback Riding
A range of outfitters provides day trips, dunnage, spot trips, and full custom service from nearly every trailhead in the Eastern Sierra.

Bishop Pack Outfitters (Aspendell; 760-873-4785). Mike and Tess Anne Morgan offer full service to Sabrina Basin, Lamarck, Horton, Humphreys Basin, French Canyon, and Piute Pass, from the North Fork of Bishop Creek.

Cottonwood Pack Station (Horseshoe Meadows; 760-878-2015). Dennis Winchester offers full service into Cottonwood Lakes, South Fork, Rock Creek, and Whitney Zone.

Frontier Pack Station (1012 East Line Street, Bishop; 760-873-7971; www.frontierpack train.com). Scheduled and custom trips into Ansel Adams Wilderness and Yosemite high country, from stables at June Lake, are offered by Kent and Dave Dohnel.

Glacier Pack Train (Big Pine; 760-938-2538). M. A. Stewart offers full service to Big Pine Lakes/Palisade Glacier area, Taboose Pass, John Muir Wilderness, and Sequoia/Kings Canyon National Parks.

Mount Whitney Pack Trains (Bishop; 760-872-8331). Full service into Sequoia-Kings, Golden Trout, and South Sierra Wildernesses, from Sawmill, Shepherd, Taboose, and Olancha Pass trailheads.

Pine Creek Pack Station (Pine Creek; 760-387-2797, 1-800-962-0775). Brian and Danica Berner offer full service to Horton Lakes, Pine Lake, French Canyon, Granite Park, Lake Italy, Bear Lakes, Hilton Lakes, and Morgan Lakes.

Rainbow Pack Outfitters (600 South Main Street, Bishop; 760-873-8877; www.rainbow packoutfit.com). Run by the Allen family since 1924. The stables are at South Lake, behind Parcher's Resort. Full range of trips into Inyo National Forest and Sequoia-Kings.

Sequoia Kings Pack Trains (Independence; 760-387-2797, 1-800-962-0775). Brian and Danica Berner, who also run Pine Creek Pack Station, own this pack outfit, which is the oldest in the Sierra (since 1872). Full service into the Inyo National Forest, Sequoia-Kings, and the Pacific Crest Trail, from five trailheads.

Hunting
Lone Pine Pheasant Club (Alabama Hills; 760-876-4595).

Mountain Biking
Dirt roads abound in Inyo County, from flat gravel cruisers along the old railroad grades and the Owens River to dozens of disused jeep and horse trails west of US 395 to the foot of the Sierra. Loop rides of varying difficulty are possible to the north and west of Bishop and west of Big Pine. For serious rough climbing, try Mazourka Canyon, out of Independence, or the Swansea and Yellow Grade roads to Cerro Gordo. No vehicles of any kind, wheeled or otherwise, are allowed in wilderness areas. The best overall map to the region's back roads is the *Inyo National Forest Map*, available at most bookstores and visitors centers. Check in at **Aerohead Cycles** (760-873-4151) for detailed beta.

Motor Sports
There are hundreds of miles of dirt roads and jeep trails on public land, from the Alabama Hills to the Inyo and White Mountains. The best overall map to the region's back roads is the *Inyo National Forest Map*, available at most bookstores and visitors centers. Know the rules, stay on existing trails, and be courteous. No vehicles of any kind, wheeled or otherwise, are allowed in wilderness areas.

Bishop Motosports (156 East Pine Street, Bishop; 760-872-4717; www.snomobiles.com). Sales, rentals, service, accessories. ATVs, dirt bikes, Rhinos, Harleys, snowmobiles.

Mountaineering

Bardini Foundation (Bishop; 760-873-8036; www.bardini.org). Founded in memory of the famous Allan Bard. Treks, ski tours, peak and wall climbs, range of mountaineering courses. Guides: Tim Villanueva and Don Lauria.

Sierra Mountain Center (174 West Line Street; 760-873-8526; www.sierramountain center.com). Rock climbing, backpacking, ski touring, ice climbing, guide training, avalanche courses, Whitney ascents, and custom trips. Guides: Robert "SP" Parker, Todd Vogel, Eric Owen, Chris Simmons, Todd Calfee.

Sierra Mountaineering International (SMI) (236 North Main Street; 760-872-4929; www.sierramountaineering.com). Rock climbing, peak climbing, ice climbing, backcountry skiing, backpacking, avalanche school, map and compass classes, international expeditions. Gear rentals. Founder: Kurt Wedburg.

Ranger-Guided Tours & Activities

Check at the **Interagency Visitors Center** (760-876-6222) or the **White Mountain Ranger Station** (760-873-2500).

Road Biking

If you're looking for switchbacks and epic hill climbing, try Sherman Pass, Horseshoe Meadows Road, Whitney Portal Road, Westgard Pass, or the Bishop Creek Road. On a calm day in late fall or early spring, a tour of the Owens Lake playa makes a pleasant loop (60-plus miles). From Bishop one of the Eastern Sierra's classic century rides follows the old Sherwin Grade Road north past Lake Crowley to Benton Crossing Road, east to Benton, then south along US 6 back to Bishop. The best easy cruising lies to the west and north of Bishop, as far as Round Valley. Check in at **Aerohead Cycles** (760-873-4151) for beta.

Rock Climbing

The Eastern Sierra has in the last decade or so blossomed into one of the world's premiere rock climbing and bouldering destinations. When the big alpine routes get too frosty, move down into the Owens Valley Gorge; try the Buttermilks, the Happy Boulders, or claim a new route in the Alabama Hills. Best sources for local beta and equipment are **Elevation** in Lone Pine (125 North Main Street; 760-876-4560; www.sierraelevation.com), **Wilson's Eastside Sports** in Bishop (206 North Main Street; 760-873-7520; www.eastsidesports. com), and **Mammoth Mountaineering** in Mammoth Lakes (3189 Main Street; 760-934-4191, 1-888-395-3951; www.mammothgear.com). **The Rubber Room** (175B North Main Street, Bishop; 760-872-1363; www.rubberroomresoles.com) specializes in rock shoe resoles.

Spa, Yoga & Massage

Belle Vous Day Spa & Salon (230 West Line Street, Bishop; 760-872-3307). Full service. Hair, nails, and massage.

Bishop Yoga & Massage Center (150 Willow Street, Bishop; 760-920-3764; www.bishop yogamassage.com). Yoga, children's yoga, dance. Classes daily. Drop-ins welcome. Full massage menu.

Keogh's Hot Springs (Keogh's Hot Springs Road, 7 miles south of Bishop; 760-872-4670; www.keoughshotsprings.com). The largest hot springs pool around, built in the 1920s: 600 gallons per minute at 127 degrees. Snack bar, picnic area, gift shop, massage, camping, and rustic accommodations.

Benton Hot Springs (760-933-2287; www.historicbentonhotsprings.com). Private outdoor soaking tubs available with advance notice.

Winter Sports
Most will press on to the snow-season mecca of Mammoth Lakes (see chapter 5), but those in the mood for more solitary backcountry tours will outfit themselves with snowshoes or backcountry skis (the latter with requisite climbing skins) and head for any Eastern Sierra trailhead—from Kennedy Meadows to Pine Creek. **Wilson's Eastside Sports** (760-873-7520; www.eastsidesports.com) can provide the necessary equipment and information. See Mountaineering for local guide services.

ANNUAL EVENTS

March
Banff Mountain Film Festival (Bishop; www.banffcentre.ca).

Early Opener Trout Derby (Lone Pine; 760-876-4444; www.lonepinechamber.org).

April
Pilgrimage to Manzanar (760-878-2194; www.manzanarcommittee.org). Special programs, music, and exhibits. No admission fee.

Wild, Wild West Marathon (Lone Pine; 760-876-4444; www.lonepinechamber.org).

General trout opener (statewide; www.ca.dfg.gov).

May
Mule Days (Bishop; 760-872-4263; www.muledays.org). The world's premiere celebration of this hardest-working equine half-breed, Mule Days encompasses five days of family-friendly events and high patriotism. Barbecues, concerts, slightly off-standard rodeo, and parade. Saturday night sells out. Highlights include mutton bustin', chariot roping, and the highly competitive team pack scramble.

Eastern Sierra Gem & Mineral Show (Bishop; 760-873-3588; www.tricountyfair.com).

June
Concert in the Rocks (Alabama Hills; 760-876-9103).

Lone Pine Time Trials (Manzanar Airstrip; www.lonepinechamber.org). Nonsanctioned autocross benefit.

Mount Whitney Rally & Poker Run (try Jake's Saloon for information: 760-876-5765).

July
Badwater Ultra-Marathon (www.badwater.com). Death Valley to Whitney Portal.

Independence Day Celebration (Independence; www.independence-ca.com).

September
Eastern Sierra Tri-County Fair (Tri-County Fairgrounds, US 395, Bishop; 760-873-3588; www.tricountyfair.com). Highlights include cooking contests, carnival rides, truck pull, extreme bulls and broncos, and destruction derby.

Mount Whitney Classic (Death Valley to Whitney Portal; www.whitneyclassic.com). A hard-core cycling endurance event.

California Wild Horse and Burro Show (Bishop; http://users.qnet.com/~cawhbs). Show and competition to promote the talents of adopted horses and burros.

Millpond Music Festival (Bishop; www.inyo.org/millpond). Three days of great live music and hanging out on the lawn.

Good Ole Days (Laws; 760-873-5950; www.lawsmuseum.org). Celebration of days gone by. Costumes, games, food, and craft displays.

October
Lone Pine Film Festival (Lone Pine; 760-876-9103; www.lonepinefilmfestival.org). A celebration of the millions of reels of film shot in and around Lone Pine. Panel conversations, location tours, autograph signings, live music, barbecues, parade. Bring your six-shooter and spurs.

November
General trout season closes (statewide; www.ca.dfg.gov).

Outlaws for a weekend, Lone Pine Film Festival

MMSA

5

MAMMOTH LAKES & MONO COUNTRY

Under the Volcano

> *Were the painter, the novelist, the tourist, or the geologist, naturalist or any
> other scientist, to search the world over for a point, easy of access, that com-
> bined most wonderfully in the domains of nature all elements of the sublime,
> immense, picturesque, curious, weird and varied in forms, colors and startling
> contrasts, and extent of mountains, valley and lake scenery, he would not be
> far wrong to locate it on one of the highest granite or lava peaks near the new
> mining town of Mammoth City.*
>
> —James W. A. Wright, 1879

One version went like this: There were three young Germans, brothers, making their way
across the desert in the early rush—in 1851 probably, or '52. The rest of their party had
been massacred by Indians, but these three had somehow managed to get away, abandon-
ing their gear, blazing their own haphazard path across the sagebrush, half-starving and
delirious, to the headwaters of the Owens River. "And in a gorge in the mountains they sat
down to rest," reported Mark Twain in *Roughing It,* in 1872, giving the story considerable
legs, "when one of them noticed a curious vein of cement running along the ground."
Consensus seems to locate this occasion, to the extent that it actually happened, somewhere in the pumice-coated landscape above what is now the town of Mammoth Lakes.
"The vein was about as wide as a curbstone," wrote Twain, "and fully two thirds of it was
pure gold."

Only one of the brothers made it across the Sierra alive—"exhausted, sick, and his mind
deranged by his sufferings." But on his person were samples of a reddish cement of such
miraculous assay that every summer for more than a quarter century thereafter the peaks,
canyons, and volcanic badlands south of Mono Lake were fairly overrun with prospectors
looking for "The Lost Cement Mine." Through the 1860s there were rumors of mines
developed in secret, ores smuggled out in the black of night. Here and there a Paiute
Indian would produce a nugget of pure yellow metal from his pocket, smile, and then
refuse to divulge a source. One poor fellow by the name of Hume had his head cut off and

left beneath a pile of stones in Deadman Creek, presumably because he'd had information his partner preferred to keep to himself. Then one day in 1877, finally, up on Mineral Hill, at about 11,000 feet, with a fine view across Lake Mary at a big dormant volcano, called Pumice or Mammoth Mountain, a party of prospectors found something vaguely promising.

The first boom didn't go so well.

The rough-and-ready camps at Mammoth, Mill, and Pine City had by the summer of 1879 a combined population of 2,500 people (about one-third of today's year-round population), with a brand new 20-stamp mill, two semiweekly newspapers, and a 54-mile toll trail all the way through to Fresno Flats (Oakhurst). The price to use the trail was $15 each way, with 20 pounds of free freight, 8 cents a pound thereafter. Of actual ore there'd as yet been no real sign. Of publicity there was plenty. San Francisco mining correspondent James W. A. Wright felt he could safely report "in that grand and wonderful, almost enchanting, mountain region" the recent discovery "of more than two hundred valuable mineral ledges, chiefly silver, but nearly all with some gold."

Then it started snowing.

Those who managed to dig their way out left—strapped barrel staves to their feet and went back to Bodie or Virginia City, or sold their picks and shovels and moved to San Diego. Of those who stayed, three froze to death. By the end of the following summer, with not a grain to show for three short seasons' blasting and drilling, everyone was gone. For decades to come, Lakes District, as it had been called, would be the peaceful domain of cattle ranchers, sheepherders, bears, coyotes, Indians, bighorn sheep, and a slow trickle of summertime homesteaders from down south. Into the 1920s the keeper of one rustic lodge at Mammoth Camp was still burning firewood from enormous piles cut and stacked 40 years earlier for use at the stamp mill.

"Certain it is that if the Cement Mines exist they have remained undisturbed during all these years," wrote W. A. Chalfant in 1942, "and it is probable that somewhere in those hills of summer pleasure fortune awaits a claimant." Fortune would come, eventually—not in minerals, alas (though there are still seekers), but in a substance considerably more plentiful: snow.

William Mulholland spent some days in Mammoth during the summer of 1907, taking snapshots of the impressive snowpack that would in a few years feed his aqueduct. With the aqueduct came incidental improvements in transportation from Los Angeles to the High Sierra—overnight Pullman-car rail service to Bishop (with a change of trains in Lone Pine); then pavement from Lancaster to Mojave, and again in sections all the way up the Owens Valley. By the mid-1920s a second boom was under way, with summer cabins and rustic knotty-pine fishing resorts sprouting up every major drainage from Tom's Place to June Lake.

During the epic winter of 1935–36, a 21-year-old kid from El Segundo by the name of Dave McCoy, with a couple of buddies who happened to work as snow surveyors for the Los Angeles Department of Water and Power, started experimenting with motor-serviced downhill skiing. They made the skis themselves and improvised bindings. They found a hill and rigged a rope from the jacked-up back axle of a Model A Ford pickup truck. With one man on the gas pedal, the other two hanging on for the ride—off they went. In the spring they left behind their machine, took to the backcountry, and explored the terrain from Lake Mary to the north flank of Mammoth Mountain: terrain where one day, nearly 70 years later, McCoy would make his fortune.

A fellow by the name of Jack Northrop, a budding engineer and soon-to-be founder of

Wildasinn's Store, Mammoth Meadow, July 1907 Photo by William Mulholland; Lippincott Collection, Water Resources Center Archives–University of California, Berkeley

the company that would become aerospace giant Northrop-Grumman, installed a fixed rope tow, first in his backyard in Old Mammoth—which proved too much of a pain to get to in winter—then at McGee Creek, right on US 395 (across from Fred Eaton's old ranch, where Crowley Lake was soon to be made). Funding came from a wealthy southern California ski enthusiast by the name of Cortlandt Hill, and technical assistance from McCoy. By 1940 hundreds of skiers were making the long drive up from the city every weekend. "All along Highway 395 north of Bishop is ski country," wrote a columnist from the *Los Angeles Times.* "There is a hundred mile stretch of it that has been likened to the Tyrolean Alps. You can get out of your car and ski anywhere."

There were races on weekends, a Swiss-run ski school, cameo appearances by such stylish Hollywood celebrities as Henry Fonda and Gary Cooper, and all manner of rustic après-ski shenanigans. The place seemed poised for an unprecedented boom.

Then the war hit—and with it gasoline rationing.

McCoy worked through the 1940s surveying the snowpack for the water department. He got married, had five kids, and supplemented his meager income with odd jobs—selling cordwood, guiding fishermen on Crowley Lake. He secured a temporary "roving permit" from the Forest Service and built a portable rope tow he could drag around and set up on any given weekend, wherever the snow was best. The big snow along US 395 in the late 1930s turned out to have been anomalous. Season after season the best conditions in the Southern Sierra, and the best terrain to go with it, McCoy found on the north flank of Mammoth Mountain (above where Main Lodge now stands). Here big wet winds off the Pacific tended to funnel through a uniquely low saddle in the Sierra Crest—11,000 feet at

McGee Creek rope tow, 1930s Courtesy MMSA

San Joaquin Ridge—crashing headlong into the volcano, dumping payloads that regularly buried roads, cars, cabins, and Greyhound buses.

As the American economy boomed in the postwar years—especially in southern California—so too did the ski business. "After the war things picked up very fast," McCoy told Martin Forstenzer, author of *Mammoth: The Sierra Legend*. "We would have a hundred buses parked out here in the late '40s and '50s." Still, McCoy kept his day job. He put whatever he earned, and all his free time, into improvements—with no guarantees from the

Road into Mammoth, 1950s MMSA

Forest Service as to how long he might be able to operate. With hand tools and a small crew working mostly for the fun of it, McCoy cleared trails and built a small warming hut. He bought tanklike war-surplus vehicles from the military (Studebaker Weasels) for hauling folks from town to the base of the mountain. He put big diesel engines on his rope tows, earning an early reputation for running more people faster to the top of the slope than anywhere else in the country.

As early as 1945 the Forest Service had begun to consider the possibility of developing one or two major European-style ski resorts in the Southern Sierra. Mineral King (now in Sequoia National Park; see chapter 6) was one site that was deemed to have excellent potential. Mammoth was another. "Mammoth Mountain is impressive in its ski potentiali-ties," wrote Forest Supervisor Jim Gibson. "It seems beyond any question that proper development can make this mountain one of the top ski areas of the West." In 1952 the Forest Service paved the road to McCoy's warming hut and, expecting at least a quarter-million-dollar investment in facilities—a chairlift, a T-bar, a full-service modern lodge, and more—opened the bidding.

"I thought somebody with money was going to come in and I'd be out in the cold," McCoy told Forstenzer years later. But nobody was willing to take the risk. Even McCoy's friend Cortlandt Hill, who had financed the first rope tow at McGee Creek, thought Mineral King was a safer bet. "They said it was too far from a Metropolitan area," explained McCoy, "it was too high in altitude, it was too remote. They said it wasn't what people were accustomed to—too much snow, too windy, too rugged."

And so by default McCoy found himself holding a 25-year lease on Mammoth Mountain, with not just the go-ahead to build a full-fledged resort, but the obligation to do so. He quit his job with the water department. He pulled his crew together, scrounged materials, and built the first wing of what would eventually become the sprawling Main Lodge complex.

He procured a brand new double chairlift from a fledgling tramway company in San Francisco—on credit—and started putting in towers. He raised the price of an all-day lift ticket from $2.50 to $4. By Thanksgiving morning 1955, there were 3 feet of fresh snow, wide-open blue sky, and 250 skiers lined up for the inaugural ride up Chair 1 (now Broadway Express). The next boom was on.

"During the past couple of years," wrote Wolfgang Lert in *Ski Magazine* in 1958, "a ski area hidden away in California's Eastern Sierra Nevada has jumped into national prominence. Skiers who have visited it rave not only about the beautiful slopes and incredible snow but also about the spirit of friendliness, of fairness, of trying to do the best for the skier, which pervades the whole place." In this spirit Dave McCoy managed to run the place for another half century, weathering droughts, earthquakes, economic slumps, energy shortages, a narrowly thwarted attempt to punch a Trans-Sierra highway from Mammoth through to Fresno, buy-out offers from Disney and Universal Studios, repeated failures to secure regular commercial air service, and fears of volcanic eruption (generally thought to be unwarranted). In 2005, exactly 50 years after the opening turn of Chair 1, McCoy sold his controlling interest in the mountain to Barry Sternlicht's privately held Starwood Capital Group—for $365 million.

In the late 1950s Mammoth could boast about two hundred year-round residents. By the end of the 1960s the number had grown to one thousand—and a little village of A-frame ski cabins and faux Swiss chalets had sprung up in the woods within trudging distance of CA 203. Today there are more than 7,500 people enjoying all four seasons in the incorporated town of Mammoth Lakes. The ski area—now run by McCoy's hand-picked successor, onetime lift operator Rusty Gregory—is regularly ranked among the top 10 winter resorts in North America, for its huge size, variety of terrain, snow, scenery, ski and snowboard school, snowmaking and trail grooming, terrain parks, access to the backcountry, on-mountain services, and number of skier-days per year. In winter one can ski in the morning and in the afternoon go rock climbing in the Owens River Gorge, soak in a hot spring, or play golf in Bishop. There is ice skating and sledding and snowmobiling, and an extensive network of groomed trails dedicated only to snowshoeing and cross-country skiing. On the very best years there is downhill skiing on July 4th. When the snow melts there is lift-serviced mountain biking, with hundreds of miles of dusty trails both on the mountain and beyond; there is world-class trout fishing, rock climbing, road biking, camping, skateboarding, and hiking.

The town itself offers none of the typical main-street charm of the famous Victorian mining/ski towns of the Rocky Mountains, or of old ranch-supply towns like Steamboat Springs or Jackson Hole, or nearby Bishop. Of Mammoth's early days all that remain are a handful of old ruins above Lake Mary, a few log cabins along Mammoth Creek, and a rusted-iron Knight Wheel, hauled up from Mojave in 1879 to drive the stamp mill—now almost entirely engulfed by the latest stages of the Snowcreek development. Mammoth today bears unfortunate hallmarks of its historic association with metropolitan southern California—in the form of strip malls, outlet shopping, and a proliferation of cheap, uninspired condo developments and suburban-style tract homes (built mostly in the 1970s and '80s). But what Mammoth lacks in antique architectural charm it more than makes up for in its setting.

The forest here—unlike at Tahoe, for example, or along the west side of the range—was never clear-cut. There are trees here from the days of the last Norse settlements in Greenland—old-growth firs taller than 20-story buildings, from when the Moors were still

Chair 3 and the new two-stage gondola to the summit, 1969   Tom Johnston, Courtesy MMSA

running Spain, and the Catholic kings were still hiding out in the Pyrenees refusing to bathe. There are Jeffrey pines with trunks as thick as a man is tall. And where so many other resort towns across the West have found it impossible to resist the urge to sprawl, Mammoth— hemmed into just 4 square miles by its boundaries with the National Forest, and with the Los Angeles Department of Water and Power—has been successfully held in check.

The latest big-capital developments include a "village," opened in 2003 (built by Canadian real estate conglomerate Intrawest ULC); a number of fractional-ownership residence clubs; a series of golf-course condominiums and town houses; an open-air municipal ice-skating rink; and a brand new Westin Resort Hotel. Once-vacant lots have been filled in with multimillion-dollar Mission Revival vacation lodges. Some of the old tumble-down A-frames and shag-carpet condominium complexes have been torn down, or fixed up and brought into the 21st century. But to the country beyond—to the Ansel Adams and John Muir Wildernesses, to the thousands of alpine and subalpine lakes and meadows, to the wide-open rangeland of Long Valley, to the falls of the upper San Joaquin and the Devil's Postpile, to the Minarets—access (and big views) remain essentially unchanged from that fateful day, a century and half ago, when an unlucky German prospector happened to look down and notice a curious-looking piece of cement.

The Lay of the Land: Approaches & Logistics

Mammoth is one of the most remote mountain resort towns in North America—but it is also the closest to Los Angeles (310 mostly straight miles). Most visitors arrive by automobile from the south, coming fast across the Mojave Desert and up the Owens Valley on US 395. The way is long—five-plus hours—but the road, now mostly freeway-style four-lane blacktop, is easy, uncongested, and extraordinarily scenic. Even in the most inclement of winter weather the pavement from the south is generally dry and clear—until the last few miles of the trip (see chapter 2 for winter driving tips). Southern Californians, raised on the principles of the multiple-hour commute, will often make the journey even for a short weekend. The closest commercial airport is in Reno (167 miles), and the closest big-box shopping is in Carson City (136 miles), both by way of the more mountainous sections of US 395 to the north. Access to and from Las Vegas (308 mostly straight miles) is possible by a variety of routes, year-round. In summer, access to and from the west side of the range is by the Tioga Road, through Yosemite's East Entrance (see chapter 7), 10 miles above Lee Vining (Mono Lake) and 40 miles from downtown Mammoth. In winter, once Tioga Pass is closed, the only way in from the west side is by crossing at one of the lower-elevation northern passes (i.e., Carson or Donner) or by coming around the range from the south. This chapter is organized from south to north along US 395, from Rock Creek to Mammoth to Mono Lake.

Lodging Overview

When a young man by the name of C. Clarke Keely first visited the region with his family in July 1920—later to become a surveyor on the Los Angeles Aqueduct, and one of the early summer-homestead pioneers of Old Mammoth—the place to stay was Charlie Summers's ranch, at what had been the old Wildasinn Hotel. "The accommodations consisted of three or four little board cottages," Keely remembered years later. "Then there was what was

---

A Note on Seasons

Nearly 100 percent of annual precipitation falls between November and April, the majority of it in the form of snow. Average seasonal snowfall is more than 33 feet. The usual scenario is for a storm to hit hard and fast, dumping several feet of powder, then moving on, leaving clear skies and soon-to-be-tracked slopes in its wake. Plausible claims are made to more than three hundred days of sunshine per year. The coldest months are December and January, with average temperatures in the town of Mammoth Lakes, at 8,000 feet, between 20 to 40 degrees Fahrenheit. Very rarely does the mercury dip below zero. Summers are dry and warm—hotter on the flats in Long Valley, cooler as one travels up into the lakes basins and high country. A common adage among locals is that having come for the winter, one ends up staying for the summer. Temperatures rarely climb above the 80-degree mark. Afternoon thundershowers are rare and glorious events. When a heat wave hits—the temperature broke into the mid-90s for a few days in July 2007—there are hundreds of cold snowmelt lakes within striking distance for the rapid cooling of one's core temperature. The "shoulder seasons" of fall and spring—with visitation and room rates at their lowest—are often the most pleasant times of year in the High Sierra: the former offering crisp mornings, golden stands of Aspen, and empty trails; the latter, wildflowers and corn snow.

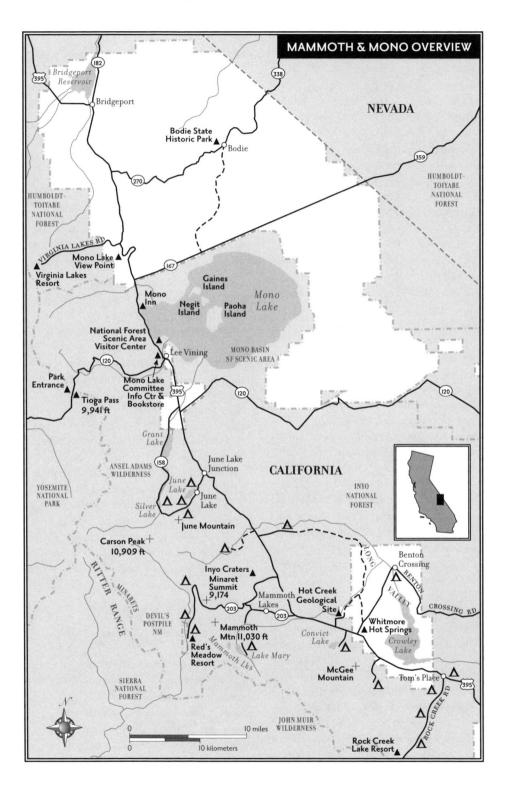

MAMMOTH & MONO OVERVIEW

NEVADA

CALIFORNIA

Bridgeport Reservoir

Bridgeport

Bodie State Historic Park

Bodie

HUMBOLDT-TOIYABE NATIONAL FOREST

HUMBOLDT-TOIYABE NATIONAL FOREST

VIRGINIA LAKES RD

Mono Lake View Point

Virginia Lakes Resort

Mono Inn

Gaines Island

Mono Lake

Negit Island

Paoha Island

National Forest Scenic Area Visitor Center

Lee Vining

MONO BASIN NF SCENIC AREA

Park Entrance

Tioga Pass 9,941 ft

Mono Lake Committee Info Ctr & Bookstore

Grant Lake

June Lake Junction

ANSEL ADAMS WILDERNESS

YOSEMITE NATIONAL PARK

June Lake

Silver Lake

June Lake

June Mountain

INYO NATIONAL FOREST

Carson Peak 10,909 ft

RITTER RANGE

MINARETS

DEVIL'S POSTPILE NM

Inyo Craters

Minaret Summit 9,174

Mammoth Lakes

Hot Creek Geological Site

Benton Crossing

LONG VALLEY

BENTON CROSSING RD

Red's Meadow Resort

Mammoth Mtn 11,030 ft

Mammoth Lks

Lake Mary

Convict Lake

Whitmore Hot Springs

Crowley Lake

SIERRA NATIONAL FOREST

McGee Mountain

Tom's Place

JOHN MUIR WILDERNESS

ROCK CREEK RD

Rock Creek Lake Resort

0   10 miles

0   10 kilometers

N

called the lodging house. It was a long, two-story building with a tub, wash basin and toilet at each far end of the corridor. The water was heated with an old boiler they had brought down from one of the mines." A host of accommodations of this sort was put up in subsequent years, throughout the 1920s and '30s, from Rock Creek to Lake George, from Reds Meadow to Virginia Lakes. In the 1950s and '60s modern A-frame cottages sprouted beside their older board-and-batten counterparts. Many of these so-called resorts still serve as rustic summertime fishing camps. Most are boarded up and inaccessible in winter, but some—as at Rock Creek, Convict Lake, and Lake Mary—have been fixed up and winterized in order to provide lodging for cross-country skiers and other snow-play enthusiasts. The town of Mammoth Lakes now offers the widest range of accommodations in the Southern Sierra—from boutique to luxury-corporate, from vintage shag to the latest three-story neo-Craftsman vacation home with golf course views, giant flat-screen TVs, and acres of polished-granite countertop. June Lake boasts the only real destination spa in the region, open year-round. In Lee Vining there are two motel-upgrades worth consideration, both conveniently located for day-trip forays to Mono Lake, Bodie, and the Yosemite High Country. For accommodations on the Tioga Road and at Tuolumne Meadows, see chapter 7.

Lodging Price Code

Cost is based on an average per-room, double-occupancy, nonholiday weekend rate at peak season. Holiday rates, especially within the town of Mammoth Lakes, can spike to as much as double the average peak season rate. Peak season here generally coincides with ski season. (In fact, the town sees more visitors overall in summer, but a significant number is absorbed by the campgrounds.) The lakeside resorts, and

the motels in Lee Vining, have their peak seasons in summer. Rates are often significantly reduced midweek and during the quiet shoulder seasons of spring and fall. Check for package deals. Tax and gratuities are not included.

Inexpensive	Up to $75
Moderate	$75 to $125
Expensive	$125 to $200
Very Expensive	Over $200

CAMPING

In developed recreation areas—Rock Creek Canyon, McGee Creek Canyon, Convict Lake, Reds Meadow, Mammoth Lakes, June Lake, Lee Vining Canyon, Lundy Canyon, and the Mono Basin Scenic Area—camping is permitted only in developed campgrounds. Only on the busiest weekends (i.e., July 4th) are campgrounds, especially those at lake and streamside locations, filled to capacity. Primitive dispersed camping is allowed on National Forest and BLM land outside these areas, especially in the Bald and Glass Mountain areas of the Long Valley Caldera. A California campfire permit—available at any ranger station or visitors center—is required for the use of any open flame (including gas stoves, lanterns, wood fires, charcoal fires, or smoking) outside of a developed campground. For up-to-date fire conditions and restrictions, call 760-873-2555. Wilderness permits are required for overnight backcountry travel in the Ansel Adams and John Muir Wilderness. Trail quotas apply in summer.

If you've always wanted to spend a weekend in a private aluminum-and-plastic lakeside guest suite but don't feel up to hauling one behind your own vehicle, **Vacation Trailer Rentals** (1-800-417-7771; www.adventureincamping.com) will rent you a late-model travel trailer and park it in the campground of your choice, anywhere from Rock Creek to Virginia Lakes.

DINING OVERVIEW

"Be sure to take a good solid lunch with you," wrote James W. A. Wright in the days of hard tack and canned beans, "for the bracing mountain air and the exertion will give you ravenous appetite." About this particular phenomenon nothing much has changed in all the intervening time. Except, that is, for the ability of Federal Express to deliver—even to the very edge of the wilderness—healthy, living crustaceans from the coast of Newfoundland, asparagus from South America, or cuts of fresh-slaughtered red deer from Australia. From oysters to elk medallions, from baked chèvre salad to lobster-claw gnocchi, from New York–style pizza to Philly cheesesteak pita wraps to Nutella and fresh-strawberry crêpes, the greatest range of well-prepared sustenance in the Southern Sierra can today be found in Mammoth (in town, on the mountain, or within a half hour's drive of the No Shooting zone). The cost undoubtedly reflects not only the quality of the food served, but also the distance most ingredients have had to travel, as well as the long, quiet off-seasons (and midweek slumps) that restaurants here find themselves forced to endure between holiday rushes. Many establishments close for a week or more in October, and again in May, depending on snow conditions and seasonal events—so that owners and staff can go to Hawaii or Aruba and get their beach fix. Nowhere in town will a person feel obliged, except by personal preference, to upgrade his or her attire from the day's sap-stained cargo shorts or Merino long underwear. *Note:* The quality of dining at some of the establishments in this region can be subject to the vicissitudes of a seasonal labor force.

Dining Price Code

Based on the cost of one dinner, including entrée and appetizer (or entrée and dessert) and a beverage. Tax and gratuities not included.

Inexpensive	Up to $15
Moderate	$15 to $30
Expensive	$30 to $45
Very Expensive	Over $45

ROCK CREEK TO CASA DIABLO

Before US 395 was rerouted from lower Rock Creek canyon to the Sherwin Grade in the late 1930s, **Tom's Place** (US 395 and Rock Creek Road; 760-935-4239; www.tomsplaceresort.com) was the place to stop—for fuel, radiator water, cold beers, lodging and après-ski camaraderie. When the timing is right, it's still a good bet for a cold beer, a milk shake, and a roadhouse-style hamburger. Upper Rock Creek Road, a serious contender for the honor of highest paved public road in California, leaves the highway here and threads its way southwest up the canyon 11 miles, past a series of small lakes and aspen groves, to its dead end at the Mosquito Flat trailhead (10,300 feet). It's a worthwhile side trip in summer, not merely for the scenery and myriad opportunities for recreation, but also for a slice of Sue King's renowned homemade pie at **Rock Creek Lakes Resort** (Upper Rock Creek Road; 1-877-935-4311; www.rockcreeklake.com; inexpensive). In winter the road is closed at East Fork, 6 miles up from Tom's Place, and groomed thereafter for cross-country skiing. North along US 395, beyond Tom's Place and Little Round Valley, the country opens up into the high sagebrush tableland of the Long Valley Caldera, with volcanic formations as old as 760,000 years and as young as 600. Most recently the valley was flooded at its south end by the City of Los Angeles to form a storage reservoir at Lake Crowley.

MAMMOTH CAMPING

Rock Creek to Convict Lake	Elevation	Season	Reservations Accepted	Fee	Sites	Water	Agency
Tuff	7,000	Apr–Oct	Yes	Yes	34	Yes	USFS
Holiday (overflow)	7,500	As needed	No	Yes	35	Yes	USFS
French Camp	7,500	Apr–Oct	Yes	Yes	86	Yes	USFS
Aspen Park (group)	8,100	May–Oct	Yes	Yes	1	Yes	USFS
Iris Meadow	8,300	May–Oct	No	Yes	14	Yes	USFS
Big Meadow	8,600	May–Oct	No	Yes	11	Yes	USFS
Palisade	8,600	May–Oct	No	Yes	5	Yes	USFS
East Fork	9,000	May–Oct	Yes	Yes	133	Yes	USFS
Pine Grove	9,300	May–Oct	No	Yes	11	Yes	USFS
Upper Pine Grove	9,400	May–Oct	No	Yes	8	Yes	USFS
Rock Creek Lake	9,600	May–Oct	No	Yes	28	Yes	USFS
Rock Creek Lake (group)	9,700	Jun–Oct	Yes	No	1	Yes	USFS
Mosquito Flat (walk-in)	10,100	May–Oct	No	Yes	10	No	USFS
Crowley Lake	7,000	Apr–Nov	No	Yes	47	No	BLM
Crowley Lake South Landing	7,129	Apr–Nov	Yes*	Yes	19	Yes	DWP**
McGee Creek	7,600	May–Oct	Yes	Yes	28	Yes	USFS
Convict Lake	7,600	Apr–Oct	Yes‡	Yes	85	Yes	USFS
Mammoth Town Area							
New Shady Rest	7,800	Apr–Oct	Yes	Yes	92	Yes	USFS
Old Shady Rest	7,800	Jun–Sep	Yes‡	Yes	46	Yes	USFS
Sherwin Creek	7,800	Apr–Sep	Yes‡	Yes	85	Yes	USFS
Pine Glen (overflow)	7,800	As needed	Yes‡	Yes	10	Yes	USFS
Pine Glen (group)	7,800	May–Sept	Yes	Yes	7	Yes	USFS
Camp High Sierra	8,100	Jun–Sep	Yes***	Yes	40	Yes	DWP
Mammoth Lakes Basin							
Twin lakes	8,600	May–Oct	Yes‡	Yes	92	Yes	USFS
Pine City	8,900	Jun–Sep	No	Yes	10	Yes	USFS
Coldwater	8,900	Jun–Sep	Yes‡	Yes	77	Yes	USFS
Lake Mary	8,900	Jun–Sep	No	Yes	46	Yes	USFS
Lake George	9,000	Jun–Sep	No	Yes	16	Yes	USFS
Reds Meadow & Devil's Postpile							
Agnew Meadows	8,400	Jun–Sep	No	Yes	21	Yes	USFS
Agnew Meadows (group)	8,400	Jun–Sep	Yes	Yes	4	Yes	USFS
Agnew Meadows Horse	8,400	Jun–Sep	No	Yes	3	Yes	USFS
Upper Soda Springs	7,700	Jun–Sep	No	Yes	28	Yes	USFS
Pumice Flat	7,700	Jun–Sep	No	Yes	17	Yes	USFS
Pumice Flat (group)	7,700	Jun–Sep	Yes	Yes	4	Yes	USFS

Lodging

Rock Creek Lodge

www.rockcreeklodge.com
Upper Rock Creek Road
Elevation: 9,373 feet
Open: Year-round
1-877-935-4170
Owner: Bobby Tanner
Price: Moderate (summer)/Very Expensive (winter)
Pets: No
Wheelchair Access: Limited
Internet Access: Wireless in main lodge

Established in 1927 and added onto over the years with varying degrees of aesthetic inspiration, Rock Creek Lodge is one of several popular rustic-cabin summer resorts in the canyon and provides a good base camp for fishing, hiking, biking, and horseback riding in the High Sierra. Its true charm emerges in winter, however, when the road is closed, the lakes drifted over, and the campgrounds and parking lots buried in snow. Arrange to have your bags hauled up the hill by snowmobile while you enjoy the reasonable 2-mile ski in. Equipment rentals available. Spend your days skate-skiing around the adjacent

MAMMOTH CAMPING CONTINUED

Reds Meadow & Devil's Postpile *continued*	ELEVATION	SEASON	RESERVATIONS ACCEPTED	FEE	SITES	WATER	AGENCY
Minaret Falls	7,600	Jun–Sep	No	Yes	27	Yes	USFS
Reds Meadow	7,600	Jun–Oct	No	Yes	52	Yes	USFS
Devil's Postpile****	7,560	Jun–Sep	No	Yes	21	Yes	NPS
Crestview (North of Mammoth Lakes)							
Big Springs	7,300	Apr–Nov	No	No	26	No	USFS
Obsidian Flat (group)	7,800	Jun–Sep	Yes	Yes	1	No	USFS
Deadman	7,800	Jun–Nov	No	No	30	No	USFS
Glass Creek	7,600	Apr–Nov	No	No	50	No	USFS
Hartley Springs	8,400	Jun–Oct	No	No	20	No	USFS
June Lake							
Oh! Ridge	7,600	Apr–Nov	Yes	Yes	144	Yes	USFS
June Lake	7,600	Apr–Nov	Yes	Yes	28	Yes	USFS
Gull Lake	7,600	Apr–Nov	No	Yes	11	Yes	USFS
Reversed Creek	7,600	May–Oct	Yes	Yes	17	Yes	USFS
Silver Lake	7,200	Apr–Nov	Yes	Yes	63	Yes	USFS
Aerie Crag (overflow)	7,200	As needed	No	Yes	10	No	USFS
Walker Canyon	8,400	May–Nov	No	No	1	No	USFS
Lee Vining Area							
Lower Lee Vining	7,300	Apr–Oct	No	Yes	54	No	USFS
Moraine	7,350	Apr–Oct	No	Yes	27	No	USFS
Boulder	7,390	Apr–Oct	No	Yes	100	No	USFS
Aspen	7,490	Apr–Oct	No	Yes	56	Yes	USFS
Big Bend	7,800	Apr–Oct	No	Yes	17	Yes	USFS
Cattleguard	7,325	Apr–Oct	No	Yes	16	No	USFS
Ellery Lake	9,500	Jun–Oct	No	Yes	21	Yes	USFS
Junction	9,600	Jun–Oct	No	Yes	13	No	USFS
Sawmill	9,800	Jun–Oct	No	Yes	12	No	USFS
Saddlebag Lake	10,000	Jun–Oct	No	Yes	20	Yes	USFS
Saddlebag Trailhead (group)	10,000	Jun–Oct	Yes	Yes	1	Yes	USFS
Tioga Lake	9,700	Jun–Oct	No	Yes	13	Yes	USFS
Lundy Canyon	7,700	Jun–Oct	No	Yes	60	No	USFS
Trumbull Lake	9,500	Jun–Oct	Yes‡	Yes	45	Yes	USFS

Note: Reservations at USFS and NPS sites, unless otherwise specified, can be made online at www.recreation.gov or by calling 1-877-444-6777. ‡ Some sites first come, first served.   * Call 760-648-1189. Seven full hookups, 12 dry camps.   ** Los Angeles Department of Water and Power *** Call 760-924-2368. Reservations available nine months in advance.   **** Located within the park.

meadow, skinning up and practicing tele-mark turns, or making extended forays upcanyon into the backcountry. The price is high but includes three excellent meals daily (see Dining) and unlimited access to the sauna. Newer modern cabins are slightly less romantic but worth the extra few dollars for the private bathroom/ shower and thermo-stat-controlled electric heat. Reservations should be made far in advance, especially on moonlit weekends, and conditions con-firmed before departure. The lodge also maintains a budget yurt-style ski hut at Mosquito Flat, at road's end.

Hot Creek Ranch

www.hotcreekranch.com
Hot Creek Hatchery Road, off US 395, past the hatchery
Elevation: 7,100 feet
Open: April to November
760-924-5637; 1-888-695-0774
Riverkeepers: Bill and Diane Nichols
Price: Expensive
Pets: No
Wheelchair Access: Limited
Internet Access: No

Zane Grey, having covered a good deal of

country, is supposed to have found this place "the most beautiful in the Eastern Sierra that I have seen yet." Padding through thick meadowgrass, the snap of sage in the air, steam rising from the creek, the first splash of dawn on the wall of mountains beyond, one cannot help but wonder at the extraordinary restraint of such a comment. A fellow by the name of Tom Poole, part Paiute, built a cabin here in the late 1800s, where his ancestors had spent their summers. And when Fred Eaton came around, Tom told him just where he could put his money. The result is one of the only pieces of private land in the valley: 300 acres with a cold, clear, spring-fed creek meandering through the heart of it—teeming with wild trout. Simple electric housekeeping cabins have kitchens and views across the meadow. No phones, no TVs. Catch and release dry-fly fishing only. It doesn't get much more old-school than this. Fly shop. Guide service available.

Dining
Rock Creek Lodge (Upper Rock Creek Road; 1-877-935-4170; www.rockcreek lodge.com; expensive). Impressive quantities of home-cooked comfort fare—marinated pork tenderloin, spinach lasagna, soup, salad, fresh-baked bread, and more—served in high family-style conviviality in the lodge dining room. Hard to imagine a better place to hole up on a cold midwinter's eve, 2 miles from the nearest plowed road. Beer and wine available for purchase, or bring your own. Meals served to overnight guests and day skiers alike. Make reservations in advance. One seating per evening: Don't be late. Sack lunches available for the trail. Open in summer, too.

The Restaurant at Convict Lake (Convict Lake Road; 760-934-3803, 1-800-992-2260; www.convictlake.com; expensive). Ten miles from the village in Mammoth Lakes—an easy 15-minute drive in clear conditions, an epic adventure in a blizzard—the restaurant at Convict Lake is a world apart. Pine-paneled cocktail lounge with leather and Craftsman-style furnishings; fish and game motifs; a touch of taxidermy; an open sheet-copper fireplace; linen tablecloths; views of the aspen trees, the lake, the surrounding granite walls. Fare is rich, saucy, French/California—a classic wild mushroom beef Wellington, duck, lamb, local farm-raised rainbow trout in toasted almonds and butter—with a list of good hefty wines to match. Outdoor seating available in summer. Open seven days a week, year-round. Dinner only. Reservations highly recommended, especially on weekends and during holidays.

Points of Interest
Lake Crowley (CA 395, 3 miles north of Tom's Place). For years, Mulholland refused to buy the ranchland here from his old pal Fred Eaton (at the rates Eaton wanted to charge). After both men were gone, the City of Los Angeles finally acquired the place and in 1941 built a storage reservoir, named for Father John J. Crowley, "the desert padre," who was among the first to promote tourism in the Owens Valley (before he was killed in 1940 in an automobile accident). Owens River water is here diverted into a pipeline with a drop of 2,300 feet to a series of power plants in the gorge below. On opening day of fishing season, despite fears of infestation by nonnative mussels, the lake's surface is obscured by thousands of anglers attached to a variety of flotation devices. The best fireworks show in the Eastern Sierra takes place here on July 4th, complete with tailgate barbecues and patriotic music.

McGee Creek (1.5 miles south along frontage road from McGee Creek Lodge). A plaque, some rusted equipment, a jeep trail, and an old cabin mark the site of the first fixed rope tow in the Eastern Sierra.

Living Volcano Country

In July 1863 William Brewer and Charles Hoffman of the Whitney Survey took a side trip south of Mono Lake ("that American Dead Sea") to explore a chain of apparently extinct volcanoes. "The rocks of these volcanoes are a gray lava pumice stone so light that it will float on water, obsidian or volcanic glass," observed Brewer in his journal. Not without difficulty in this loose and porous gravel they climbed to a height of 9,700 feet. "The scene from the top is desolate enough," he wrote, "barren volcanic mountains standing in a desert cannot form a cheering picture." Beneath much of this country—from the Lakes Basin south of Mammoth Mountain to Mono Lake—lies a vast reservoir of molten rock, or magma. One cataclysmic eruption about 760,000 years ago spewed as much as 130 cubic miles of the stuff across the landscape, causing the land to subside at what is now called the Long Valley Caldera ("Cauldron" in Spanish). Mammoth Mountain—considered a quiescent, or dormant, volcano—was formed by a series of eruptions between 220,000 and 50,000 years ago. The Mammoth Knolls, to the north of town, were made about 100,000 years ago, the Inyo Craters and Deadman Dome as recently as 550 years ago. "During the last 5,000 years," according to the United States Geological Survey, "an eruption has broken out somewhere along this chain every 250 to 700 years." The most recent occurred about 250 years ago at Paoha Island in Mono Lake. In the last two decades, a series of earthquake swarms, tree die-offs at Horseshoe Lake, and increased geothermal activity in the Long Valley Caldera has led to concern that another eruption may be on the horizon. The Mammoth Lakes Scenic Loop was paved in the 1980s to provide an alternate route to CA 395 in the event of significant volcanic activity. The Benton Crossing Road, from the green church (just south of the airport) to the town of Benton, is plowed and maintained throughout the winter for the same reason. "The probability of an eruption occurring in any given year," according to the Geological Survey, "is somewhat less than one percent per year or roughly one chance in a few hundred in any given year." Which is about the same probability given for the occurrence of a major earthquake along the California coast, or for the eruption of a more active volcano in the Cascades Range, such as Mount Shasta or Mount Rainier. "Future eruptions will occur," says the USGS, but they are likely to be "small and similar to previous eruptions during the past 5,000 years"—and far enough from population centers that their impact is likely to be more of an inconvenience (in the form of falling ash) than a threat to life or property. Whatever happens, it seems fair to say that it's bound to be interesting. "Reading these grand mountain manuscripts displayed through every vicissitude of heat and cold, calm and storm, upheaving volcanoes and down-grinding glaciers," wrote John Muir in *My First Summer in the Sierra*, "we see that everything in Nature called destruction must be creation—a change from beauty to beauty."

For more information, ballistics, eruption scenarios, and the latest conditions, check the USGS Volcano Hazards Program's Long Valley Observatory (http://lvo.wr.usgs.gov).

Convict Lake (2.5 miles south of CA 395 on Convict Lake Road). The 1939 WPA guide to California aptly describes it as "a pellucid sheet of blue, fronted by a rustic resort for fishermen and backed by the imposing height of Mount Morrison (12,245 alt)." The lake is so named because of a gun battle that occurred here in September 1871 between a group of escaped convicts from the Nevada State Penitentiary and a posse of citizens from the nearby town of Benton. Robert Morrison, merchant, of the latter group, was shot and killed, thereby giving his name to the imposing peak. Three of the convicts were eventually captured south of Round Valley; two were hanged nearby from a hastily constructed scaffold.

Long Valley homestead, slopes of McGee Mountain behind Burke Griggs

"I am prepared to meet my God," said one of the convicts, fitting the noose around his own neck, "but I don't know that there is any." **Convict Lake Resort** (7,600 feet; 1-800-992-2260; www.convictlake.com; expensive) remains essentially a resort for anglers (and their families), offering a range of older cabins with the most utilitarian of appointments (but at premium rates), several newer suburban-style houses designed to accommodate large groups, a marina, a restaurant, a general store, and horseback riding. Operates year-round.

Hot Creek State Fish Hatchery (Hot Creek Hatchery Road, just north of the airport; 760-934-2664; www.hotcreekhatcheryfoundation.org). Established in 1936 to take advantage of year-round hot-springs-fed water, the hatchery is today one of the largest in the state and said to be one of the most important broodstock and production facilities in the West. It produces nearly 13 million fertilized eggs per year, as well as millions of fingerling rainbow, brown, and Kamloops rainbow trout for stocking streams and lakes across the state. Bring quarters for fish food. Open daily 8–4.

Hot Creek Geological Site (Hot Creek Hatchery Road, 2.5 miles past hatchery). A variety of hot springs, steam vents, and low-level geysers boil up into the creek water here in a small canyon along the lower stretches of Mammoth Creek. Locations and temperatures of pools and springs vary depending on stream flow and local earthquake activity. Once a popular—if not altogether relaxing—bathing site, the waters here have been "temporarily" closed to swimming since 2006, due to increased and possibly deadly geothermal activity. Especially eerie in winter. For a slightly less challenging soak, try one of the semi-improved hot-springs tubs along Whitmore Tubs Road, or at Little Hot Creek.

Hot Creek Geological Site Chris Farrar, USGS

Casa Diablo (CA 203, south of CA 395; 760-934-4893; www.mammothpacific.com). Geothermal hotspot in the heart of the Long Valley Caldera, with source water at temperatures up to 350 degrees Fahrenheit. Once a favorite soaking spot for Indians, miners, and tourists. Geysers used to spring up here, on occasion (e.g., in 1937 and again in 1959), with water shooting up to 80 feet in the air. Geothermal drilling began in the 1960s, causing a subsequent diminishment in surface spring activity. A small utility by the name of Mammoth Pacific Geothermal now operates a series of power plants with 18 wells on 10 acres. Hot water is pumped through heat exchangers to produce a gas vapor that in turn drives a series of eight turbines, making enough electricity to power forty thousand homes—all of which energy is sold to Southern California Edison, then resold to consumers in Los Angeles (and in Mammoth Lakes). No water is lost in the process. Call to arrange a tour. Behind the power plant looms what is called a "resurgent dome," a convenient placement for radio and cell towers, and a feature that continues to rise (80 centimeters in the last three decades) with the continued rising of the magma below.

MAMMOTH LAKES

The town's main business district sprawls west and uphill along "Main Street" (CA 203)—a road built at the convenience of the state transportation authority in 1937, at some distance from the original center of affairs at Old Mammoth—and south along what is now called Old Mammoth Road. Here you will find restaurants, coffee joints, sporting goods stores, outlet shopping, gas, a full-size grocery store, a franchise drug store, a hardware store, a Bank of America, video rentals, fast food, and a variety of motels. The new "Village" is just off the upper end of Main Street to the north, along Minaret Road, in the direction of Main Lodge and Devil's Postpile National Monument. The Village offers lodging, dining, shopping, and frequent live entertainment, as well as gondola access to the mountain (in winter) and shuttle service to the Bike Park (in summer).

On midwinter weekends when conditions are good, the town is busy. On holiday weekends—Martin Luther King Day, Memorial Day, July 4th, and during Bluesapalooza in

Shot in Mammoth & Mono: A Short List

The Trail Beyond (1934). Directed by Robert N. Bradbury; starring John Wayne. Snowcreek.

The Call of the Wild (1935). Directed by William Wellman; starring Clark Gable.

The Road to Utopia (1946). Directed by Hal Walker; starring Bing Crosby and Bob Hope.

North to Alaska (1960). Directed by Henry Hathaway; starring John Wayne. Hot Creek.

Ride the High Country (1962). Directed by Sam Peckinpah; starring Randolph Scott and Joel McRea. Mammoth Lakes Basin.

Nevada Smith (1966). Directed by Henry Hathaway; starring Steve McQueen. Hot Creek, Snowcreek, Oh! Ridge.

Caprice (1967). Directed by Frank Tashlin; starring Doris Day and Richard Harris.

High Plains Drifter (1973). Directed by Clint Eastwood; starring Clint Eastwood. Mono Lake, Inyo National Forest.

The Other Side of the Mountain (1975). Directed by Larry Peerce; starring Marilyn Hassett and Beau Bridges. Based on the true story of ski racer Jill Kinmont-Boothe.

First Monday in October (1981). Directed by Ronald Neame; starring Walter Matthau and Jill Clayburgh.

Indiana Jones and the Temple of Doom (1984). Directed by Steven Spielberg; starring Harrison Ford and Kate Capshaw. Mammoth Mountain.

Perfect (1985). Directed by James Bridges; starring John Travolta and Jamie Lee Curtis.

The Golden Child (1986). Directed by Michael Ritchie; starring Eddie Murphy. Snowcreek, Mammoth Mountain.

Born on the Fourth of July (1989). Directed by Oliver Stone; starring Tom Cruise.

Revenge (1990). Directed by Tony Scott; starring Kevin Costner, Madeleine Stowe, and Anthony Quinn.

For the Boys (1991). Directed by Mark Rydell; starring Bette Midler and James Caan.

The Scorpion King (2002). Directed by Chuck Russell; starring Dwayne Johnson, aka The Rock.

XXX (2002). Directed by Rob Cohen; starring Vin Diesel, Asia Argento, and Samuel L. Jackson.

August—the town hops. Still, with some 4,700 rental units, there are always plenty of beds to go around. Until the holidays. If you want to experience what Joseph and Mary went through on that famous trip to Bethlehem, try visiting Mammoth around the same time of year without making reservations. During the last two weeks of December (and again during Presidents' Day Week, when all of Orange County is blessed with some kind of midwinter break), the valley fills to capacity: The population of Mammoth Lakes explodes from 7,500 people to as many as 35,000. The result: Freelance snow-chain installers in arctic foul-weather gear make small fortunes on the Sherwin Grade, or at the bottom of CA 203; oversized two-wheel-drive SUVs decorate the town's snow banks; the grocery store struggles to keep its shelves stocked; lines at restaurants spill out into the streets; lodging becomes impossible to come by (unless booked months in advance), even at double the usual peak-season rates, even in Bishop and June Lake; and parking, not just within striking distance of ski lifts but anywhere in town, comes at a premium. Tickets for New Year's Eve events sell out across town at prices well over $100 a head. If, as with most folks, holidays are the only time you get, make reservations as many months in advance as you can muster. Most properties will accept reservations a year in advance. Most will require a minimum stay of at least three nights, others as many as seven. The earlier you make

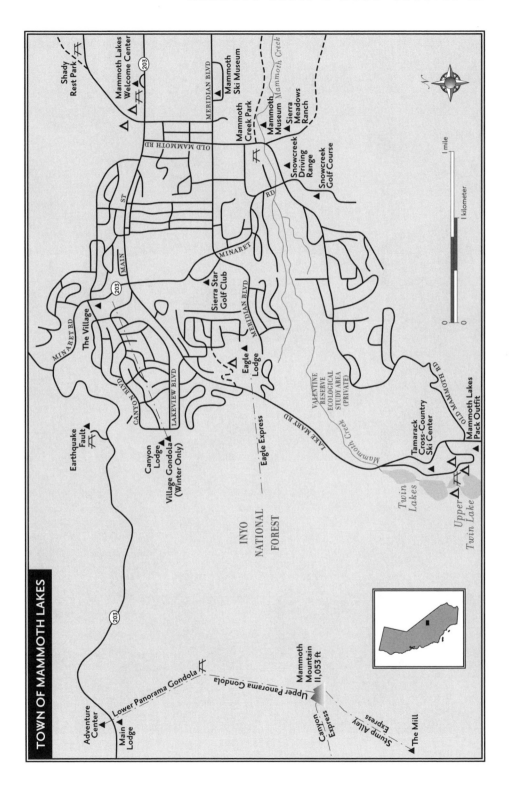

TOWN OF MAMMOTH LAKES

Shady Rest Park
Mammoth Lakes Welcome Center
Mammoth Ski Museum
MERIDIAN BLVD
Mammoth Creek Park
Mammoth Museum
Sierra Meadows Ranch
Mammoth Creek
OLD MAMMOTH RD
ST
MAIN
Snowcreek Driving Range
Snowcreek Golf Course
MINARET
MINARET RD
Sierra Star Golf Club
The Village
MERIDIAN BLVD
Eagle Lodge
CANYON BLVD
LAKEVIEW BLVD
VALENTINE RESERVE ECOLOGICAL STUDY AREA (PRIVATE)
Earthquake Fault
Canyon Lodge
Village Gondola (Winter Only)
Eagle Express
LAKE MARY RD
Mammoth Creek
Tamarack Cross-Country Ski Center
OLD MAMMOTH RD
Mammoth Lakes Pack Outfit
Twin Lakes
Upper Twin Lake
INYO NATIONAL FOREST

1 mile
1 kilometer
0

Adventure Center
Main Lodge
Lower Panorama Gondola
Upper Panorama Gondola
Mammoth Mountain 11,053 ft
Canyon Express
Stump Alley Express
The Mill

A quiet weekday morning on the mountain Brad Peatross, MMSA

plans, the more you'll have a chance to shop around.

If, on the other hand, you happen to be one of the lucky few with a more flexible calendar—or a more flexible work ethic—come up midweek, anytime after about January 2. Not only will you save loads of money, you'll find yourself sharing one of the biggest ski mountains in North America with a handful of crows and coyotes (and, depending on conditions, a few lonely, powder-glazed locals).

Lodging

Not long ago there were three types of lodgings for hire in Mammoth: rustic lakeside resort cabins; crappy, overpriced motel rooms; and cheesy, beat-up, overpriced condominium units. These options are still available, of course, for those whose aesthetic priorities stray not from the essential—or whose nostalgia (or sense of irony) happens to extend to shag and mirrors and creamsicle-colored Formica. But the fact is, times have changed. A number of luxury hotel/resort properties have recently come online, or come into their own, with several more slated for the near future. Many offer the same kinds of amenities as condos—kitchens, fireplaces, pools, and Jacuzzis—but with an entirely improved level of design and service. Also, real estate values have increased enough in recent years that many condo and vacation rental owners have found the wherewithal (and the inclination) to fix their old places up. Or at the very least to change the carpets and countertops.

HOTELS & RESORTS

The Mammoth Mountain Inn
www.mammothmountain.com
at Main Lodge
Elevation: 9,000 feet
Open: Year-round
760-934-2581; 1-800-MAMMOTH
Innkeeper: Mammoth Mountain

Price: Expensive to Very Expensive
Pets: No
Wheelchair Access: Yes
Internet Access: Wireless

There is no better place to get snowed in—with a pair of fat skis on reserve at the rental shop downstairs—than at McCoy's original A-frame ski lodge, first opened for business in 1958 and renovated in the late 1990s with all manner of neo-Craftsman detailing, varnished wood, leather, and granite. A short stroll to the gondola, a short stumble home from après-ski at the Yodler. Historic black-and-white prints from the 1950s and '60s bring back the glory days of slow center-pole chairs, long lift lines, wool trousers, and hot toddies on the sundeck. Rooms are spacious, ranging from upgraded motel-style suites to modern, fully equipped condominium units. Patios with big views of the mountain, in-house bar, restaurant and convenience store, indoor Jacuzzi, heated outdoor pool, underground parking, ski and snowboard rental, on-site child care, guest shuttle to and from town—which at 4 miles can on a busy weekend seem pleasantly distant (or if you require nightlife, an arduous commute.) In summer, these are the closest accommodations to the Adventure Center, Bike Park, and Devil's Postpile shuttle.

✪ Tamarack Lodge & Resort
www.tamaracklodge.com
at Twin Lakes, off Lake Mary Road
Elevation: 8,600 feet
Open: Year-round
760-934-2442; 1-800-MAMMOTH
Innkeeper: Mammoth Mountain
Price: Expensive to Very Expensive
Pets: Summer only (fee)
Wheelchair Access: Limited
Internet Access: Wireless in lodge

Built in 1924 as a rustic fishing retreat for vaudeville star Eddie Foy and his family,

Twin Lakes, Tamarack Resort

Tamarack is the oldest continuously operated lodge in Mammoth and remains one of the classiest of its genre anywhere in the Sierra. Skiing through a blizzard on Mammoth Pass, or on the far side of Lake Mary, one's mind tends to reconstruct the coziness of the place: its warm wood paneling; its bark-trimmed ceiling; its decor of old skis, handsaws, and brass lanterns; wool socks drying before the granite fireplace; kids in long underwear playing checkers with chess pieces; the smell of hot cider from the bar. A handful of guest cabins was added in 1927. In the 1960s the resort began to stay open year-round as a base for cross-country skiing into the world-class wonderland of the Lakes Basin. Today the Ski Center, adjacent to the lodge, maintains 19 miles of corduroy for skate-skiing, track-skiing, or snowshoeing. Rentals and lessons available. A series of tastefully appointed "deluxe" cabins has been built in the last decade, with gas fireplaces and modern kitchens, and many of the older cabins have been refurbished. Rooms also available upstairs in the lodge, with shared or private baths. Best restaurant in the Southern Sierra.

The Village at Mammoth

www.villageatmammoth.com
1111 Forest Trail
Elevation: 8,050 feet
Open: Year-round
1-800-MAMMOTH
Innkeeper: Mammoth Mountain
Price: Expensive
Pets: No
Wheelchair Access: Yes
Internet Access: Wireless

It may take a certain amount of geological time before the so-called Village—fabricated in the late 1990s using the same basic mold as at Whistler, Squaw Valley, and other latter-day mountain resorts—begins to feel organic to the landscape. At mid-week and during the off-seasons the wind populates the cobbled alleyways here with the same relentless silence as at the ruins of Pine City or Bodie. But during holidays, and on average summer weekends, thanks to rigorously optimistic entertainment programming, the place actually comes to life. People park their cars, shop, and dine and stroll about in finery—just like in the original artist's renderings. Accommodations are condo-hotel style, with a variety of individually owned units offering mostly up-to-date kitchens, gas fireplaces, TVs, and balconies—plus 24-hour reception, bell service, and daily housekeeping. Ski and snowboard rentals available for guests at McCoy Sports. Noise can be a problem on busy weekends, especially in the White Mountain Building, situated directly over a nightclub. Best bet is to book a unit on one of the upper floors of the Grand Sierra Lodge or Lincoln House, looking out toward the street rather than in toward the courtyard. Heated pool, Jacuzzi, workout rooms, free underground parking, convenient access to gondola.

The peaceful west side of the new Village

Juniper Springs Resort
www.mammothmountain.com
4000 Meridian Boulevard
Elevation: 7,953 feet
Open: Year-round
760-924-1102; 1-800-MAMMOTH
Innkeeper: Mammoth Mountain
Price: Expensive to Very Expensive
Pets: No
Wheelchair Access: Yes
Internet Access: Wireless

Built in the last days before the Village (by the same people), Juniper Springs—including the newer Sunstone and Eagle Run complexes—offers essentially the same amenities: condo-hotel units with kitchenettes/kitchens, outdoor heated pools, Jacuzzis, underground parking, in-hotel ski rental shop, and so on. What it lacks in convenience to shopping and dining, it generally makes up for in sunshine and views—and quiet. Slopeside location is a big plus in midwinter, especially with the new Chair 9 providing fast access from the east side to midmountain—but keep in mind that Eagle Express, because of its low elevation and exposure to sun, is among the last lifts to open in early season, and among the first to close in spring. Convenient access in summer to Mammoth Creek, the Lakes Basin, the town bike path, and Sierra Star golf course.

The Westin Monache Resort
www.westinmammoth.com
50 Hillside Drive
Elevation: 8,100 feet
Open: Year-round
760-934-2526
Innkeeper: Starwood Hotels & Resorts

Price: Very Expensive
Pets: Yes
Wheelchair Access: Yes
Internet Access: Wireless

Seventy-five heated steps above the Village Gondola, close enough and also just far enough away, is Mammoth's newest, tallest, most hyper-modern building, boasting 230 "upper-upscale" units—one-room studios to two-bedroom, full-kitchen deluxe suites—the best of which have private patios and views from the new Chair 9 to Long Valley. The lobby and hallways are artistically lit, detailed with varnished plywood and a variety of nods to the local environment: a scale version of basaltic columns behind the reception kiosks, twig motifs in the carpets and chandeliers. Units feel a bit cramped, for the price, but offer all the amenities Westin aficionados have come to expect: the trademarked "Heavenly Beds" (also provided for pets); high-definition TVs; deep soundproofing; 24-hour room service; kitchens/kitchenettes with granite countertops, dishwashers, and stainless-steel toasters; gas fireplaces; and windows that actually open to the mountain air. Underground parking, ski valet and rental shop, workout room, Kids Club, year-round outdoor heated pool, hot tubs, evening "unwind" rituals involving libations and light entertainment.

Condos, Town Houses & Vacation Rentals

Renting a condominium or a town house can be an economical and convenient option, especially for families or large groups. The trick is finding a nice one, in a good location, and at a decent price—with functioning appliances, heat, and the right number of sheets and towels. Units are individually owned and decorated, and therefore run the gamut of aesthetic possibilities. A host of property management/rental agencies clamors to steer you in the

right direction, with names that seem designed to muddle and confuse: **Mammoth Reservations** (1-800-223-3032; www.mammothreservations.com), **Mammoth Reservation Bureau** (1-800-462-5571; www.mammothvacations.com), **Mammoth Premiere Reservations** (1-800-336-6543; www.mammothpremiere.com), **Central Reservations of Mammoth** (1-800-321-3261; www.mammothlakes.com), **Mammoth Mountain Reservations** (1-888-204-4692; www.mammothres.com), **Mammoth Sierra Reservations** (1-800-325-8415; www.mammothsierraonline.com), and **Mammoth Property Reservations** (1-888-626-6684; www.lodginginmammoth.com). And, to spice it up, there's also **Mammoth Front Desk** (1-877-924-8490; www.mammothfrontdesk.com), **Mammoth Accommodation Center** (1-800-358-6262; www.mammothaccommodations.com), **Mammoth Five Star Lodging** (1-866-626-6684; www.fivestarlodging.com), **101 Great Escapes** (1-877-754-6688; www.101greatescapes.com), **EZ Mountain Vacations** (1-866-443-9686; www.ezmountain.com), and **Grand Havens** (1-866-464-4726; www.grandhavens.com). Each of these manages individual units for individual absentee owners in a variety of different complexes—in exchange for a significant percentage (as much as half) of the rental income. Some charge visitors a reservation fee; others do not. Some provide a decent service, with a variety of concierge-style perks (be sure to study the online pictures and location map; ask for guarantees that the specific unit you reserve will be the unit you end up with, and check your confirmation closely). Others, especially when it gets busy, will do little more than leave a key in a lockbox somewhere and a note wishing you the best of luck. The best bet is to first narrow your search to one or more of the better complexes—i.e., those with the best location (walking distance to lifts or to golf course) and/or the least deferred maintenance—and whenever possible book directly through individual owners, or through on-site management. Prices vary wildly based on location, season, size, and condition of the individual unit.

The 1849 (826 Lakeview Boulevard; 760-934-7525; 1-800-421-1849; www.1849condos.com). Possibly the apex of Mammoth's disco-era funk. One of the best (and busiest) locations in town during ski season: across the parking lot from Canyon Lodge. Views of Lincoln Mountain, heated pool, Jacuzzi, tennis (in summer), fully equipped kitchens, underground parking, video rentals, wireless Internet. Enormous units. If you're looking for contemporary upscale, this is not it. Also available through a variety of rental agencies.

The Bridges (Lake Mary Road, above Eagle Lodge; no on-site booking). Built in 1984. Ski-in/ski-out through the woods, for intermediate and advanced skiers only. Big views to the Sherwins and Long Valley. Private decks and garages. Some private spas. Some units more upscale than others. Units available through a variety of rental agencies.

Eagle Run (4000 Meridian Boulevard, above Eagle Lodge; no on-site booking). Newly built: contemporary maple cabinets, granite countertops, hardwood floors, stainless-steel appliances, and more. The only real slopeside units on the mountain. Walk to Sierra Star Golf Course. Some available through Mammoth Mountain (1-800-MAMMOTH; www.mammoth mountain.com), others through a variety of rental agencies.

Mammoth Ski & Racquet (248 Mammoth Slopes Drive, near Canyon Lodge; 760-934-7368; 1-888-762-6668; www.mammothdirect.com). Another funky vintage classic, but with good southern exposure and views. Short hike to lifts, ski back. Best access to mountain bike trails. Tennis. Pool, Jacuzzi, wireless Internet, balconies, propane fireplaces, TVs, DVD players, free telephone calls, garage parking. "Deluxe" and "premium" units have been upgraded. Units also available through a variety of rental agencies.

Snowbird Condominiums (414 Rainbow Lane, across from Canyon Lodge; 760-934-8270; 1-877-934-8270; www.1849condos.com). A smaller, quieter, slightly classier sibling to the 1849. Short walk to lifts. Outdoor Jacuzzi, free wireless Internet, fully equipped kitchens. Units also available through a variety of rental agencies.

Snowcreek Resort (1254 Old Mammoth Road; 760-934-3333; 1-800-544-6007; www.snowcreekresort.com). Mammoth's most sprawling condominium and townhouse project, and one of the oldest, begun in the 1970s by construction-worker-turned-developer Tom Dempsey on 450 acres of ranchland that once included Charlie Summers's hotel. As a location, Snowcreek is probably best suited for summertime, with its own nine-hole golf course and driving range, its convenient access to creeks and wide open meadows and the old road to the Lakes Basin. In winter, despite regular free shuttle service to the mountain, it can feel rather remote—which has its advantages and disadvantages. Phases I, II, III, and IV, set in the woods between Minaret and Old Mammoth Road, are the oldest and most dated, but they are also the best value. Phase V is a classic Orange County–style suburban subdivision on the far side of the golf course. Phase VI is the latest and most attractive—a series of town houses built by the Chadmar

Group of Santa Barbara, in a style vaguely evocative of Western barns and old mining buildings but with the latest in floors, countertops, and appliances. Units also available through a variety of rental agencies.

The Summit (3253 Meridian Boulevard, across from Eagle Lodge; 1-800-255-6266; www.summitcondominiums.com). Short hike to Eagle Lodge or to Sierra Star Golf Course. Built in the 1970s. Many units upgraded. Tennis, pools, Jacuzzis, patios, fitness center. Units also available through a variety of rental agencies.

Tallus (2610 Meridian Boulevard; www.tallus.net; no on-site booking). Built in 2005 as a gated, fractional-ownership, private residence club; also available for nightly rental. By far the most architecturally remarkable project in Mammoth: glass-and-timber towers, hand-cut stonework, detailing in red cedar and mahogany. Private terraces and hot tubs, Viking kitchens, radiant floors, digital screening rooms, and more. Full-service concierge, private on-demand four-wheel-drive shuttle service, indoor heated pool and spa, clubhouse. Units available through Grand Havens (1-866-464-4726; www.grandhavens.com).

Timber Ridge (671 John Muir Road, above Canyon Lodge; no on-site booking). Best views in Mammoth. Ski-in/ski-out, through the woods, to either Canyon or Eagle Lodge. Good access to mountain biking. Pool, indoor Jacuzzi, private garages. Chains and/or four-wheel drive required for access in winter. Some units upgraded; available through a variety of rental agencies.

The Timbers at Sierra Star (Meridian Boulevard and Sierra Star Parkway; no on-site booking). Among the most deluxe townhouse rentals in town, with all the latest features: granite countertops, hardwood and slate flooring, private spas, private two-car garages, flat screen TVs, leather furniture, Craftsman-style detailing, and more. On the 17th fairway. Shuttle bus to Eagle Lodge. Units available through a variety of rental agencies.

Val d'Isere (194 Hillside Drive, above the Village; no on-site booking). Across the street from the Grand Sierra Lodge and Village. Short walk to gondola, potential ski back, national forest access. On the uptown/downtown mountain bike trail. Many units upgraded, some with views; available through a variety of rental agencies.

Viewpoint Condominiums (3852 Viewpoint Road, off Main Street; 760-934-3132; 1-800-826-6680; www.viewpoint-condos.com). Short walk to the Village and to restaurants along Minaret. Fireplaces, fully equipped kitchens. Some units upgraded. Jacuzzi, pool, tennis court (seasonal). Outdoor parking. Excellent value.

Dining

Angel's (Corner of Main Street and Sierra; 760-934-RIBS; inexpensive to moderate). Family-friendly sandwiches, burgers, salads, chicken potpie, ribs. Ribs available to cook at home, sauces to go. More than one hundred types of beer. Open for lunch and dinner every day. No reservations accepted.

Austria Hof (Top of Canyon Boulevard; 760-934-2764; moderate to expensive). Chalet food—schnitzel, sauerbraten, bratwurst, and more—in an authentic basement rendition of Kitzbuhel in the early 1970s. Happy hour drink specials and free appetizers. Dinner only.

Base Camp Café & Coffee Bar (3325 Main Street; 760-934-3900; www.basecamp cafe.com; inexpensive). Locals' favorite for cheap breakfast specials, sandwiches, and friendly wait staff. Owned by town mayor Skip Harvey. Brown bag specials made for

On the Mountain: Access, Services & Logistics

Mammoth Mountain boasts 29 lifts—including two high-speed "six-packs," nine high-speed "quads," and two gondolas—which together accommodate 50,000 rides per hour, serving 3,100 vertical feet and more than 3,500 acres of skiable terrain. Even on the busiest days of the season there is likely to be more traffic at midmountain than at the bottom. During big storms, the top of the mountain, and all upper lifts, will close, then reopen at some highly anticipated but impossible-to-predict moment—not just when the sun comes out, but after the completion of avalanche control. There are four main access points to the mountain—Eagle Lodge, Canyon Lodge (served by the Village Gondola), the Mill (or Stump Alley), and Main Lodge. There are dining facilities at each, as well as at midstation, at the top of the mountain, and, conditions permitting, at the bottom of Chair 14. Lift tickets can be purchased at any of the four day lodges, or at the bottom of the Village Gondola. Chairs 1 and 2, out of Main Lodge and the Mill respectively, are the first to open each season and the last to close. Eagle, on the opposite side of the mountain, has the shortest season. Canyon, because of its proximity to the Village and to a majority of condominium complexes, tends to be the most congested. Mammoth's ski and snowboard school operates out of Eagle, Canyon, and Main Lodge, with full-service child care available at Main Lodge only. The only lift service in summer—for scenic rides and bike park access—is from Main Lodge. For general information and reservations, call the Mammoth Mountain Ski Area at 760-934-0745 or 1-800-MAMMOTH.

Mammoth Ski & Snow Report: 760-934-6166; 1-888-SNOWRPT; www.mammothmountain.com
Avalanche & Snowpack Information: http://patrol.mammothmountain.com
Local weather: 760-934-7669
Road Conditions: 1-800-427-ROAD
Race Department: 760-934-0642
Winter On-Mountain Naturalist Tours: 760-924-5500

MMSA

Main Lodge (8,909 feet)

The original base lodge, often the least crowded lunch spot on the mountain. Bar, food court, sundeck barbecue, coin-operated day lockers, first aid, preferred parking, ticket sales, equipment rentals, sport shop, host services. Ski and snowboard school combined with child-care backup (if your kid decides to quit ski school, you may not have to come to the rescue).

Adventure Center (Gondola building, summer only): 760-934-0706
Bike Repair (Gondola building, summer only): 760-934-2571, ext. 3269
Broadway Marketplace Food Court (third floor): 760-934-2571, ext. 3265
Lost and Found/Basket Check (second floor): 760-934-0667
Mammoth Moments Photo Service (third floor): 760-924-8395
The Mountain Shop (second floor): 760-934-0677
Performance Demo Shop (second floor): 760-934-2571, ext. 3280
Rental Shop (first floor): 760-934-2571, ext. 3270
Security (first floor): 760-934-0697
Small World Child Care (downstairs at Mammoth Mountain Inn): 760-934-0646
Ski Patrol (first floor): 760-934-2571, ext. 3276
Ski and Snowboard Repair (second floor): 760-934-2571, ext. 3280
Ski and Snowboard School (Schoolyard): 760-934-2571, ext. 3185
Ticket Office (first floor): 760-934-2571, ext. 3671
Tusks Bar (third floor): 760-934-2571, ext. 3227
Woollywood Kids (Schoolyard): 760-934-2571, ext. 3285
Yodeler Bar & Pub (across parking lot from Main Lodge): 760-934-2571, ext. 2234

Stump Alley (8,790 feet)

Small day lodge, café and bar, sundeck, ticket sales. No other services. Easy-access parking; a favorite for dog owners and RVs.

Mill Café: 760-934-2571, ext. 3675

Canyon Lodge (8,343 feet)

Once called Warming Hut II, now the busiest of all four day lodges. Find a parking spot early in the morning, pay for preferred parking, walk, or arrive by shuttle or Village Gondola. Bustling après-ski bar, food court, outdoor "beach" barbecue (classic rock on the PA), coin-operated day lockers, first aid, ticket sales, equipment rentals, sport shop, host services. Coffee, pretzel, and crêpe carts on the third floor. Adult and kids' ski and snowboard school, no child-care backup (if your kid decides to quit ski school, you have to come to the rescue).

Canyon Kids (second floor): 760-934-2571, ext. 3312 or 3398
Grizzly Bar (fourth floor): 760-934-2571, ext. 3226
Grizzly Square Food Court (fourth floor): 760-934-2571
Rental Shop (third floor): 760-934-2571, ext. 3370
Repair and Demo Center (second floor): 760-934-2571, ext. 3381
Security/Lost and Found/Basket Check (third floor): 760-934-2571, ext. 3367
Ski and Snowboard School (third floor): 760-934-2571, ext. 3389

Sports Shop (third floor): 760-934-2571, ext. 3377
Ticket Sales (third floor): 760-934-2571, ext. 3771

Eagle Lodge (7,953 feet)

Groundbreaking on the construction of a permanent Eagle Lodge is set for summer 2009. In the meantime, it all happens inside a high-tech Quonset hut dubbed "Little Eagle." Ticket sales, equipment rentals, sport shop, bar and restaurant. Adult and kids' ski and snowboard school, no child-care backup (if your kid decides to quit ski school, you have to come to the rescue).

Eagle Sports: 760-934-0725, number 4
Rental Shop: 760-934-0725, number 3
Talons Restaurant & Bar: 760-934-0725, number 1
Ticket Sales: 760-934-0725, number 2

The Mountain Center at the Village Gondola (8,100 feet)

Ticket sales, equipment rentals, and sport shop. Overnight ski storage available under the Village Gondola.

Family Center (third floor) 760-934-2571, ext. 2071
Skier Services (sport shop, rentals, repairs; first floor): 760-934-2571, ext. 3057

McCoy Station (9,630 feet)

Midstation on Panorama Gondola offers busy food-court dining, as well as European-style table service at Parallax Restaurant (reservations recommended).

Marketplace Food Court: 760-934-2571, ext. 3209
Parallax Restaurant: 760-934-2571, ext. 3118
Sports Shop: 760-934-2571, ext. 3330
Steeps Bar: 760-934-2571, ext. 3374

Top of the Sierra (11,053 feet)

At the top of Panorama Gondola; interpretive exhibits, views, café, and ski patrol.

Café: 760-934-2571, ext. 3755

Outpost 14 (9,320 feet)

Mammoth's "backside" open-air barbecue and sundeck.

Grill: 760-934-2571, ext. 3214

the trail. Open daily for breakfast, lunch, and dinner.

The Good Life Café (Old Mammoth Road, in the Mammoth Mall, behind the Chart House; 760-934-1734; inexpensive). A local favorite for healthy breakfast (and lunch). Whole wheat pancakes, overstuffed omelettes, machaca burritos, Monte Cristo sandwiches served with fries or zucchini. Kids' menu. Open every day. All-you-can-eat lunch special weekdays only. No reservations accepted. In summer, eat on the patio, in the sun, overlooking the parking lot.

✪ **Lakefront Restaurant** (at Tamarack Lodge, Twin Lakes, off Lake Mary Road; 760-934-3534; www.tamaracklodge.com/dining; expensive). Less than 3 miles out of town, tucked in the back room of Tamarack's original 1924 log lodge, with its low ceilings, old varnished paneling flickering in the candlelight, and picture windows overlooking moonlit snow-covered lakes, Lakefront is one of the world's most perfect restaurants: intimate, elegant, unpretentious, romantic, timeless. Chef Frederic Pierrel has been around long enough to weather the inevitable boom-and-bust cycle of this mining camp turned ski resort. And he's spent enough time between the wilderness and the metropole to know the value of a meticulously prepared onion soup and a good bottle of Côtes du Rhône. The lamb, vegetable Wellington, and mixed game are excellent bets, but don't think the seafood—hand-caught somewhere in the world and delivered by FedEx—won't impress. Leave room for cheeses and dessert. Dinner nightly. Reservations required. Full bar. Lunch served seasonally.

Mountainside Grill (Top of Minaret Road, at Mammoth Mountain Inn, Main Lodge; 760-934-0601; www.mammothmountain.com; expensive). If you're staying at the inn for more than one night, without a kitchen, and need a break from the pub food over at the Yodeler (or the dark, icy road into town), you'll probably end up eating here. The menu is creative—try the chipotle orange-glazed duck—but quality of food and service are variable, tied as they seem to be to the vagaries of snowpack, seasonal staffing, and overall corporate morale. Breakfast, lunch, and dinner daily. Reservations requested.

Nevados (Corner of Main Street and Minaret Road; 760-934-4466; expensive). Before the latest boom and subsequent influx of chef-driven restaurants and serious wine lists, this was one of two or three places in town to throw down some money on good, handcrafted food. Local mule-skinners still come to the low-key, locals-friendly bar to hobnob with ski patrolmen and movie producers over top-grade rye and appetizers—and the three-course prix-fixe menu is still an excellent bet for ski-town romance. Open for dinner nightly. Reservations recommended.

✪ **Petra's Bistro & Wine Bar** (6080 Minaret Road, in the Alpenhof Lodge; 760-934-3500; expensive to very expensive). Forsaking big-city lights for starry skies and deep powder, chef Kerry Mechler and friends have made this casual off-Village bistro a beacon for lovers of fine wining and dining. Start with a heaping bowl of mussels and clams in red-curry broth, accompanied by fries, garlic aioli, and a dry Portuguese Muscat; move on to the venison loin and whatever's just come of age in red from South Africa. Have your partner do the quail, then the scallops. Be sure to tour the cheeses before stepping off at a chocolate pot de crème or a simple poached pear. Menu evolves daily. Extensive selection of cruvinet-fresh wines by the glass. Eat at a table, at the bar, or on couches beside the fire. Open for dinner

Tuesday through Sunday; closed Monday. Reservations recommended.

Perry's Italian Café (3399 Main Street, by the Luxury Outlets; 760-934-6521; moderate). An old standby since 1971, Perry's is the place to take the family for heaping piles of pasta and unlimited trips to the salad bar. The pizza generally does the trick. The cioppino is a surprisingly good bet. Beer and wine. Open for lunch and dinner daily.

Restaurant Lulu (Clocktower Square, in the Village; 760-924-8781; www.restaurant lulu.com; expensive to very expensive). San Francisco Provençal transplanted in Mammoth with a successful blend of stainless steel, wood, and gallery-style lighting. Exhibition kitchen, oyster bar, wood-fired rotisserie and pizza oven. Small plates, antipasti, rotisserie specials and sides, all served family-style (à la francaise), designed to be shared. Summer: dinner nightly, brunch weekends, outdoor seating. Winter: lunch and dinner daily; brunch weekends. Half-price drinks at happy hour, year-round: martinis, mojitos, fresh-lime margaritas. Fresh-baked bread available for carryout. Reservations a good idea on busy weekends.

Roberto's (271 Old Mammoth Road; 760-934-3667; moderate). Best and biggest margaritas. Best South Bay–style rice and beans Cal-Mex: overstuffed wet burritos, mahimahi tacos, chiles rellenos, duck quesadillas, chipotle wings, saucy enchiladas. Sports bar upstairs, booth seating downstairs. No reservations accepted—the wait can be epic on busy weekends, but it can also be eased significantly with a basket of chips and a sloshing bucket of tequila and lime juice. Open daily for lunch and dinner. Take-out available.

Shogun (452 Old Mammoth Road, Sierra Center Mall; 760-934-3970; expensive). The only game in town for Japanese. The art may have moved on several light years since this place was established back in 1980, but when you start jonesing for sushi, this'll do. Best bets are the specialty rolls and the kids' menu. Good views of the Sherwins. Big, comfortable booth seating. Full bar. Tropical fish. Open for dinner nightly. No reservations accepted.

Skadi (587 Old Mammoth Road; 760-934-3902; www.restaurantskadi.com; expensive). Named for the Norse goddess of skiing, Skadi offers a surprisingly elegant ski-lodge-inspired atmosphere and big views of the Sherwins from the upper floor of a strip mall. The restaurant may have sat on its laurels for a few years while the new kids up at the Village took over, but the bar is still a favorite with locals, the wine list holds its own, and the menu still earns its umlauts. Solid bets include the venison sausage with corn pancakes, and the lingon-and-juniperberry-slathered duck. Open for dinner nightly. Reservations recommended.

Slocum's Grill (3221 Main Street; 760-934-7647; moderate). Classic steakhouse fare in an authentically weathered Victorian atmosphere. Open for dinner nightly. Hickory-smoked ribs Friday and Saturday nights, while they last. Eminently popular happy hour, 4–6, with steamed mussels and prime rib sandwiches. No reservations accepted.

The Stove (644 Old Mammoth Road; 760-934-2821; moderate). Best appreciated for its hearty, country-style breakfasts and family-friendly, knotty-pine atmosphere. Busy on weekends. Open daily for breakfast, lunch, and dinner. Beer and wine. No reservations accepted.

Whitebark Restaurant (50 Hillside Drive, at the Westin; 760-934-0400; expensive). Mammoth's newest, hippest eatery, named for the gnarled old conifers that have somehow survived for centuries at timberline along the Sierra Crest. Breakfast features cornmeal pancakes, a variety of egg scrambles, and a full-on buffet. Sushi-bar-style build-your-own salad card at lunch, plus fancy sandwiches, beef chili, miso soup, and barbecue-glazed slider burgers. Open grill and plancha at dinner. Pick your ingredient—beef, veal, pork, fish—and choose a preparation. Appetizers. Full bar. Open daily. Reservations recommended.

DELIVERY

Doorstep Dinners (760-934-DINE). Delivers from many of the above restaurants, for a small fee. Open 5–9 nightly, Thanksgiving to Easter.

Taverns, Pubs & Après Ski

The Auld Dubliner (6201 Minaret Road, at the Village; 760-924-7320; www.auld dubliner.com). Movie-set re-creation of an Irish village pub, said to have been built in Ireland (by a team of publicans based in Long Beach, California), then imported to the United States, complete with a gallery of authentic farm and kitchen artifacts, antiqued paint, and an unfortunately long-looping CD of canned jigs and reels. Full selection of traditional pub fare—fish-and-chips, shepherd's pie, boxties, and more. Guinness, Harp, Newcastle, Magners Cider, and a wide array of Irish whiskies. Rugby on the TV. Occasional live folk music on weekends. A rousing New Year's Eve. Open daily from 11 AM.

Dry Creek Bar (Top of Minaret Road, at Mammoth Mountain Inn, Main Lodge; 760-934-0601). When Main Lodge and the Yodler are slammed, and you don't feel like fighting for a beer (much less a place to take your boots off), this is the quiet choice for slopeside après ski. Big A-frame windows onto the mountain, comfortable furniture, huge sundeck, soups, sandwiches, salad bar. If you're going to pay top dollar for a Mexican coffee, you might as well do it in your socks. Also a pleasant alternative to the high-noon lunch-tray hustle across the way.

Grizzly Bar (upstairs at Canyon Lodge; 760-934-2571, ext. 3226). First stop after the slopes. Standing room only on Saturday. Don't miss the last Village Gondola at 5 PM.

Clocktower Cellar (6080 Minaret Road, basement of the Alpenhof Lodge; 760-934-2725). Hangout of choice for lift ops, snowcat drivers, and terrain-park engineers. Darts, pool, foosball, big-screen TV. Big selection of beers. No liquor.

Lakanuki (6201 Minaret Road, in the Village; 760-934-7447; www.lakanuki.com). Currently Mammoth's only real nightclub, opened by globe-trotting Kiwi, Vail-veteran Stuart Need and posse, in 2003, during the latter days of urban ski-parka fashion. South Bay tiki-style decor, with Mai Tais and Hurricanes in plastic cups, a private security force, and big-city wristbands on weekends. Locals nights, poker, karaoke, DJs, and not-infrequent lingerie parties featuring men in boxer shorts and bathrobes and lovely Hustler professionals dancing on tabletops. Decent pub food. Open every day from 11 AM.

Side Door Bistro (100 Canyon Boulevard, in the Village, across from the Gondola; 760-934-5200; www.sidedoormammoth .com). Quiet, civilized, back-room wine bar and retail wine shop. Front room is a crèperie, coffee, and panini counter, serving Mammoth's only real espresso (in a demitasse with sugar cube). Convenient, uncrowded place to meet up with friends at the end of a day's skiing. Open daily, 6 AM to midnight.

Sherwin's Folly (Sierra Meadows Ranch, Sherwin Creek Road, off Old Mammoth Road; 760-924-7222; www.sherwinsfolly .com). Sherwin's has single-handedly brought back the cozy ranch-town saloon atmosphere that Mammoth has been missing since about 1937, when the construction of CA 203 took Sherwin Creek Road off the map. Eclectic live music lineup in season, dancing, outdoor fire pits, stars, dirt parking lot, just the right amount of aura from the stables. Open weekends and for special events.

Tusks Bar (1 Minaret Road, Main Lodge, third floor; 760-934-2571, ext. 3227). Booth seating, fireplaces, view from the bar to the terrain park. Not as crowded as at Canyon. Closes at 5 PM. Start here, then move across the street to the Yodeler.

Whiskey Creek Mountain Bistro/Mammoth Brewing Company (Corner of Main Street and Minaret Road; 760-934-2555; www.mammothbrewing co.com). Home of the award-winning fleet of Mammoth beers, and the best fish tacos this side of the Mono Craters. Hands down the best happy-hour deal in town: half price on all food except desserts. Functional atmosphere. Views of the Sherwins. Big-screen TV; pool tables; live bands on weekends; Wednesday-night DJ. Full-service restaurant downstairs. Open every night.

The Yodler (Minaret Road, next to Panorama Gondola building; 760-934-0636). Legend has it that this Swiss après-ski chalet was actually built in Switzerland, sometime in the 1950s, and then transported to Mammoth. The date on the facade is 1959. Its only drawback these days, if you don't happen to be staying next door at the inn, is the long bus ride back to town—let it not be a drive—at the end of a session. Outdoor sundeck; fireside lounge; full bar. Sandwiches, burgers, and general

The Yodler Bar

pub fare. Occasional live music. Open for lunch and dinner daily. Happy hour 3–6.

Food & Beverage Purveyors

COFFEE, TEA, ETC.
Looney Bean (26 Old Mammoth Road, in the Rite Aid shopping center; 760-934-1345; www.looneybean.com). Locals' favorite java stop and office-away-from-home, tucked into the corner of a strip mall. Beans roasted on the premises. Gas fireplace. Excellent apple strudel.

Stellar Brew (3280 B Main Street, next to Napa Auto Parts; 760-924-3559). Coffee, tea, pastries, smoothies, deli sandwiches for the trail. Wireless Internet.

GROCERIES
Busy Beez General Store (6201 Minaret Road, street level at the Village; 760-924-2899). Once upon a time, before this century, there was a venerable little village store called the Pioneer Market that in its later years provided hoards of snowed-in condo dwellers with everything from milk and raisin bran to goat cheese, arugula, and candied walnuts. Now a private residence club looms quietly, semi-ominously, in its stead, and just up the street a putative general store hawks all

there is for last-minute supplies at this end of town: milk, beer, bread, wine, cereal, top-shelf liquor, pasta sauce, magazines, the *L.A. Times,* olive oil, smoked salmon, canned pumpkin, maybe a banana, maybe an onion. No goat cheese, no arugula, no candied walnuts. Open every day.

Vons (481 Old Mammoth Road; 760-934-4536). Full-service big-city grocery store, built for crowds. If possible, avoid Friday nights and the second half of December. Deli (excellent sushi, rolled fresh daily, plus sandwiches and grilled panini), bakery (the olive bread is the stuff of legends and sells out early), butcher and fish counter, pharmacy, Starbucks, flower shop (and balloons), beer, wine, liquor, produce section (with hardwood floors; arugula and avocados are available even with 15 feet of snow in the parking lot). If they don't have it, they'll be happy to order it for you. What they do have they'll offer to help you take to your car. Open daily, 5 AM–1 AM.

Sierra Sundance Earth Foods (26 Old Mammoth Road; 760-934-8122). Vitamins, Tasty-Bite Indian Cuisine, carob malt balls, yogurt pretzels, hemp granola, organic chocolate, organic produce, yerba maté, sprouted bread, and trail bars.

Sandwiches & Such

5 Boroughs Pizza (6201 Minaret Road, street level at the Village; 760-924-1045). Best pizza in town: New York style, hole-in-the-wall. Slices and whole pies. Limited seating. Lunch and dinner every day.

Hot Chicks Rotisserie (452 Old Mammoth Road; 760-934-4900). Tri-tip, pulled-pork, and chicken sandwiches; whole chickens; weekday specials. Tasty food without the attitude and fancy atmosphere. Dine in or take out. Open daily.

Nik & Willie's (76 Old Mammoth Road, next to Radio Shack; 760-934-2012). Classic pizza and sub joint. Beer on tap. Dine in or take out. Weekday specials. Discount for take-n-bake pizzas. Open daily.

Old New York Deli & Bagel Co. (6201 Minaret Road, street level at the Village; 760-934-DELI; www.oldnewyork.com). A scaled-down version of SoCal-favorite Jerry's Deli, with a full breakfast menu, matzo ball soup, heaped-up pastrami sandwiches, fresh-squeezed orange juice, and more. And bagels, of course, boiled on the premises. Prices are heaped-up, too, but when you need a real Reuben, what are you gonna do? It has the feel of a national franchise, but there are only two, both owned by the same family—the other is in Camarillo, where the prices are the same, but the smell of pine is wanting. Wireless Internet; $5 burger special; sidewalk dining in summer. Open daily from 6 AM for breakfast, lunch, and dinner.

The Pita Pit (6201 Minaret Road, street level at the Village; 760-924-PITA; www.pitapit usa.com). The Canadian invasion. Have your pita-wrapped sandwich built before your very eyes: breakfast pitas; falafel pitas; late-night Philly cheesesteak pitas. Dine in or take out. Delivery available for a fee.

Paul Schat's Bakkerÿ (3305 Main Street; 760-934-6055). Slightly grumpy kin to the

Schat's in Bishop. Rumor has it there's bad blood. Still, we get the same great sheepherder bread, the same great roast turkey sandwiches (served with pickle wedge and cookie), the same great pastries. Open every day. Long lines on weekends.

Salsa's (588 Old Mammoth Road; 760-924-0408). Mammoth's best catering-truck-style Mexican food. Tacos, tortas, burritos, horchata. Eat in or take out. Open daily for lunch and dinner.

SWEETS

Ben & Jerry's (6201 Minaret Road, pedestrian level at the Village; 760-934-9316; www.benjerry.com/mammoth). The world-famous socially conscious deep-chunk ice cream, straight from Vermont, scooped by locals.

Rocky Mountain Chocolate Factory (Two locations: 6201 Minaret Road, pedestrian level at the Village, 760-934-6962; 46043 Old Mammoth Road, next to Vons, 760-934-6269; www.rmcf.com). Colorado's favorite chocolate is right at home in the High Sierra. Boxed assortments, hot cocoa mix, fudge, caramel apples.

Books, Maps & Information

Booky Joint (Minaret Mall, 437 Old Mammoth Road; 760-934-5023; www.bookyjoint .com). Mammoth's only bookstore. Independent, locally owned, and friendly. Best-sellers, classics, children's books, magazines. Good selection of local-interest books, maps, and guides.

Mammoth Lakes Welcome Center (2500 Main Street, CA 203; 760-924-5500; www.visit mammoth.com). Newly built and jointly operated by the Inyo National Forest and the Town of Mammoth Lakes. Worthwhile first stop. Excellent selection of books, guides, recreation and topo maps, brochures, bear canisters. Bookstore run by the Eastern Sierra Interpretive Association. Doubles as a comfy reading room. Rangers on hand for latest trail and fire conditions, camping information, wilderness permits. Open daily year-round.

Shopping

CLOTHING & FASHION

Chato (6201 Minaret Road, pedestrian level at the Village; 760-934-9719). High-urban contempo designer fashion for men and women. Big names, boutique service. Diane Von Furstenburg, French Connection, Izod Lacoste. Flat-screen TV featuring runway models in clothes and accessories that could be yours. Open daily.

First Street Leather & Troppe Borse (6201 Minaret Road, street level at the Village; 760-934-8515; www.firststreetleather.com). High-quality, high-dollar leather, fur, wool, and sheepskin—for men and women. Bags, boots, belts, gloves, hats, coats, slippers, accessories. Good place to rack up airline miles. Open daily.

The Lingerie Lounge (6201 Minaret Road, pedestrian level at the Village; 760-934-6600; www.shoplingerielounge.com). Born of a high school economics project, this local mother-and-daughter boutique picks up where Bed, Bath & Beyond leaves off. All manner of slinky women's undergarments, plus camisoles, PJs, bubbles, lotions, creams, and candles. Open daily.

Mammoth Luxury Outlets (3343–3399 Main Street; www.luxuryoutlets.com). For that global shopping experience. Bass (760-934-0264), Polo Ralph Lauren (760-934-7040), Van Heusen (760-924-2038), Coach (760-934-6213). Open daily.

Munchkins (6201 Minaret Road, street level at the Village; 760-934-7337). Locally owned high-end kids' boutique since 1984, transplanted into the Village in 2003. Fashion, games, toys, stuff-your-own teddy bears. Open daily.

Panache (6201 Minaret Road, pedestrian level at the Village; 760-924-7077). Upscale après-ski leisurewear, and Beverly Hills–style one-of-a-kind fashion and accessories for the slopes. A silver bubble jacket, a set of matching faux-leopard pants and backpack, and more. Bogner, Prada, Custo. Open daily.

Tonik (6201 Minaret Road, street level at the Village; 760-924-7727). Mellow hipster boutique run by locals: high-art jeans, Dr. Seuss T-shirts, knee-length sweaters, caps, shoes, boots, full-face sunglasses. Inventory changes frequently. Sales rack. Open daily.

GALLERIES

Gallerie Barjur (6201 Minaret Road, pedestrian level at the Village; 760-924-0027; www.galleriebarjur.com). Contemporary sculpture, ceramics, glasswork, and painting. Estate and antique jewelry. Open daily.

Mammoth Gallery (6201 Minaret Road, pedestrian level at the Village; 760-934-6121; www.mammothgallery.com). Landscape, wildlife, and action photography from local masters Vern Clevenger, Jim Stimson, Christian Pondella, and Warren Magill. Vintage ski posters and historic prints, local art, and full-service custom frame shop. Open daily.

GIFTS, SUNDRIES & SOUVENIRS

Learning Express Toys (3399 Main Street; 760-924-2700; www.learningexpresstoys .com). Franchise retailer with all the latest names in brief distraction: Thomas the Tank Engine, Melissa and Doug, Rokenbok, and more.

Mammoth Memories (6201 Minaret Road, pedestrian level at the Village; 760-924-7060). Woolly logo items, posters, books, McCoy-story DVDs, and souvenirs. Open daily.

GENERAL STORES

Do It Center (26 Old Mammoth Road, next to Rite Aid; 760-924-7112; www.doitcenter .com). Hardware, tire chains, space heaters, light bulbs, Christmas tree stands, batteries, toilet plungers, propane canisters.

SPORTING GEAR & EQUIPMENT

The Alpine Approach (6201 Minaret Road, pedestrian level at the Village; 760-934-6373; www.mammothgear.com). Upscale little sister to Mammoth Mountaineering (see below), with emphasis on wearable outdoor gear: sunglasses, Arcteryx pants and jackets, delicious Icebreaker merino-wool long underwear. Open daily in season.

Brian's Bicycles and Cross Country Skis (3059 Chateau Road, off Old Mammoth Road; 760-924-8566). Boutique-sized pedal shop in summer; track and skate equipment in winter. Rentals, repairs, and personalized service by Brian himself. Open daily in season.

Footloose Sports (3043 Main Street, corner of Old Mammoth Road; 760-934-2400; www.footloosesports.com). Award-winning full-service alpine ski and bike shop since 1981. Ski, snowboard, and bike rentals; performance demos; custom boot fitting; and repairs. Less expensive than on the mountain, better selection. Helmets, snowshoes, and sleds also available. Open daily.

McCoy Sports & Wilderness Outfitters (6201 Minaret Road, pedestrian level at the Village; 760-924-7070; 760-924-REEL). High-fashion snow and sun wear, plus accessories. Ski rentals for Village guests. In summer, Mammoth's only Orvis-endorsed fly shop and guide service. Open daily.

✪ **Mammoth Mountaineering** (3189 Main Street; 760-934-4191; 1-888-395-3951; www.mammothgear.com). Best backcountry outfitter in the Southern Sierra. Full range of telemark and alpine touring gear, climbing equipment, ropes, shoes, boots, tents, bags, backpacking accessories, books, maps, and functional outdoor fashions. Friendly, knowledgeable staff; one of the best sources in town for local backcountry beta. Equipment rentals, performance demos, tuning, and repair. Open daily.

P-3 (3325 Main Street, next to Schat's bakery; 760-934-9500; www.p3mammoth.com). Picks up where traditional ski and bike shops leave off (parks, pipes, and powder). Specializing in terrain park, freestyle, and half-pipe gear; free-ride and downhill bikes; skateboards; and accompanying fashions. Open daily.

Surefoot (6201 Minaret Road, street level at the Village; 760-924-8333; www.surefoot .com). World-renowned custom boot-fitting shop, with locations from Mammoth to Aspen to London to Verbier. Open daily in season.

Wave Rave (3203 Main Street; 760-934-2471; www.waveravesnowboardshop.com). Setting and spreading trends since the late '80s. Rentals, demos, repairs, fashion.

Village Sports (8050 Minaret Road; 760-934-6370; www.skisurgeon.com). What was once the venerable Ski Surgeon has in all the latest village-making hoopla been tossed around a fair bit, and in the process taken a turn away from serious ski tuning to the trafficking of sporty fashions, logowear, and accessories. Still offers the best value rental package within clomping distance of the lifts, and a satisfaction-guaranteed overnight tune-up. Bike and cross-country ski rentals, too.

Points of Interest

Ski Museum (100 College Parkway, off Meridian Boulevard; 760-934-6592; www.mammothskimuseum.org). The Beekley International Collection of Skiing Art and Literature, the largest such collection in the world, is now housed in a handsome new space built expressly for the purpose. Permanent and rotating exhibits include vintage posters, lithographs, classic *New Yorker* covers, cartoons, pins, contemporary and historic paintings;

photographs from the 1870s of gold miners racing downhill on enormous planks, with poles between their legs; an 18th-century engraving of a Laplander on skis; an original 16th-century Italian travel book—one of the earliest illustrations of the sport to reach southern Europe. Gift shop, books, ski movies. Relics of the original Chair 1, and the old gondola. Open Thursday through Monday. Extended hours during holidays. Ski- and snow-related films shown in the brand new Pioneer Theater every Friday in season, with popcorn and drinks. Extensive research library open to the public.

Earthquake Fault (Off Minaret Road, CA 203, between the Village and Main Lodge). An impressive fissure in the underlying rock, running from the tennis courts at Mammoth Ski & Racquet, north-south across CA 203, and up the slopes of so-called Earthquake Dome. C. Clarke Keely tells of pushing an old truck up here in summertime in the early 1920s, before there was a road, to get ice for the making of ice cream. "[W]e would go down in the earthquake crack and fill big gunnysacks . . . the snow was practically solid ice and you had to pick it." There is some controversy among geologists as to whether this is actually an earthquake fault (the Paiutes have stories of a Big One having occurred here sometime back in the late 1700s) or merely a crack resulting from the cooling of lava or a monster landslide. The stairs down into the crack were closed briefly after a 6.0-magnitude tremor in 1980, then reopened. Here are some of the oldest trees in the region. Access by cross-country skis or snowshoes in winter.

Valentine Reserve (Between Juniper Springs and Old Mammoth Road; 760-935-4356; http://vesr.ucnrs.org). A 156-acre field research station and natural reserve administered by the University of California, Santa Barbara, protected from grazing and entry since the end of the 1900s. Some neighbors grumble that the forest here is overgrown to the point of being Mammoth's biggest fire hazard. Check the Web site or the *Mammoth Times* for upcoming tours and community outreach events.

Emmet Hayden's cabin, built circa 1927

Inyo Craters (Short day hike or cross-country ski from Mammoth Scenic Loop). Formed by a series of small but violent steam-blast eruptions, with mechanics similar to those that made the much older Ubehebe Crater in Death Valley. The most recent eruption in the region occurred here, about six hundred years ago, blanketing Mammoth with several inches of ash and adding to native stockpiles of obsidian for weaponry.

Mammoth Mines (Off Lake Mary Road). Sites can be found along the backside of the Sherwin Range along upper Old Mammoth and Lake Mary roads, from Mill City to the Mammoth Consolidated Mines Interpretive Site above Coldwater Campground.

Horseshoe Lake Tree Kill (North shore of Horseshoe Lake, above Lake Mary). After a "swarm" of small tremors in 1989, Forest Service rangers began noticing a localized die-off of trees above the shores of Horseshoe Lake, on the backside of Mammoth Mountain. The first and obvious thought: drought and beetle kill. Then a ranger nearly died of carbon dioxide poisoning after breathing the air in a nearby snow-covered cabin. Scientists from the U.S. Geological Survey have measured levels of carbon dioxide in the soil comparable to those at Mount St. Helens and Kilauea "during periods of low level eruptive activity." The escape of gas here is thought to be the product of movement in the magma chamber below. By 1999 there were more than 100 acres of dead trees. Camping here is strongly discouraged. In summer the beach is popular with swimmers and dogs.

Mammoth Mountain Fumarole (North side of the ski mountain, near Chair 3). A fumarole is a vent hole to the magma chamber beneath a volcano. In April 2006, in a highly publicized accident, three ski patrolmen died here of carbon dioxide exposure. Two of them were working to adjust the fence around the steamy sulfurous abyss when the snow gave way beneath them. Another saw them go and went in after. A monument was dedicated to all three at the top of the mountain on August 25, 2007—with big views from the crest of Hangman's.

Hayden Cabin/Mammoth Museum (on Mammoth Creek, off Sherwin Creek Road; 760-934-6918). Mapmaker Emmet Hayden built this cabin on the shore of Mammoth Creek in 1927. Today it is a repository for old mining equipment, artifacts, and memorabilia from the early days at Mammoth Camp. Open daily in summer; closed in winter. Equipment demonstrations held on weekends.

Knight Wheel (Old Mammoth Road, 0.5 mile west of Minaret Road). Hauled by mule teams from Mojave in 1878 to drive the Mammoth Mining Company's state-of-the-art 20-stamp mill (alas, it was never used to crush ore). The wheel was moved to its present location in 1902, where it was rigged as a Peltason water wheel to make electricity at the old Wildasinn Hotel. In the 1920s Charlie Summers used it to power, among other things, an ice cream freezer. "Lights used to fluctuate as the voltage rose and fell and sometimes it would cut out entirely due to a trout getting in the nozzle," wrote C. Clarke Keely, "and Lloyd or Charlie would have to get out there with a rod and clean it out so the water would squirt on the buckets again." Today the old wheel is surrounded by the latest phase of the Snowcreek development.

Knight Wheel, site of old Wildasinn Hotel, Snowcreek

Reds Meadow/Devil's Postpile National Monument (access by mandatory shuttle from Panorama Gondola Building, Main Lodge, Minaret Road, summer only; 760-934-2289; www.nps.gov/depo). Yosemite's boundaries once extended all the way to the west flank of Mammoth Mountain and included Reds Meadow, Devil's Postpile, and much of the upper San Joaquin drainage. "But in 1905," wrote ranger-naturalist Richard J. Hartesveldt, in 1952, "mining, water, and grazing interests succeeded in getting Congress to withdraw from park status more than 500 square miles of the western and southeastern portions." The Postpile, formed by a volcanic lava flow as recently as 100,000 years ago, is, according to Hartesveldt, "one of the best examples of columnar basalt exposed on the surface of the earth." By 1910 the whole area was scheduled to be made into yet another reservoir. John Muir and the Sierra Club, then in the process of losing the battle for Hetch Hetchy, convinced Howard Taft to avail himself of the Antiquities Act and to declare Devil's Postpile a national monument. Today the official monument is a mere mile and a quarter square, but it remains above water, surrounded by the Ansel Adams and John Muir Wildernesses. Elevation along the still-wild San Joaquin River ranges from 7,800 to 7,100 feet—lower and generally warmer than Mammoth. Because of the mandatory shuttle, this is one of the least-visited yet most easily accessed wilderness areas in the Sierra Nevada. Rainbow Falls is a very worthwhile short hike through an old burn area (2.5 miles round-trip). **Reds Meadow Resort** (760-934-2345; www.redsmeadow.com), at the last shuttle stop, has a general store with cold beer, a café, a pack outfit, mineral-spring-fed hot showers, and rustic cabins. Campers, resort guests, and people with disabilities can bring in their own vehicles. The road and all facilities are closed in winter.

Devil's Postpile, 1939 R. H. Anderson, courtesy NPS, YNP

June Lake Loop

June Lake is a sleepy fishing-resort village, of mostly middle-class Southern California heritage, whose glacier-carved setting has been compared with the Tyrol and the Italian Lakes District—for reasons that become immediately apparent upon cresting so-called Oh! Ridge. There are three natural lakes along CA 158, otherwise known as the June Lake Loop: June, Gull, and Silver. In 1916 Roy and Nancy Carson established a rustic fishing camp on the shores of this last, where today the **Silver Lake Resort** (CA 158; 760-648-7525; www.silverlakeresort.net) still offers a variety of basic cabin and guest house accommodations, a homestyle café with what some locals consider the best breakfast in the Eastern Sierra, and a general store. Below Silver Lake, to the north along Rush Creek, is Grant Lake, a storage reservoir completed in 1941 by the Los Angeles Department of Water and Power to contain the flow of the various feeder creeks into Mono Lake. The now-faded June Lake Lodge was once a popular stopover for Hollywood celebrities (Charlie Chaplin, Buster Keaton, Ingrid Bergman, Samuel Goldwyn). June Lake proper is ideal for swimming and boating in summer. Bud Hayward, in 1961, at the southwest end of Horseshoe Canyon, put in the beginnings of a ski area—later to be purchased by Dave McCoy (in 1986). Now run by the same folks who run Mammoth, the June Mountain Ski Area, when it has enough snow, is a delightfully low-key family-style place, which also happens to have direct access to some of the biggest big-mountain backcountry skiing in the continental United States. At its northern end, CA 158 rejoins CA 395 at the Mono Craters.

Lodging

Double Eagle Spa & Resort

www.doubleeagle.com
5587 CA 158, west of town and June Mountain Ski Area
Elevation: 7,500 feet
Open: Year-round
760-648-7004
Innkeepers: Ron and Connie Black
Price: Expensive (includes breakfast and spa access)
Pets: Yes (fee)
Wheelchair Access: Yes
Internet Access: Free wireless

This is not your typical rustic mountain resort. In fact, the only thing truly rustic about it is the setting: between the outrun of Devil's Slide and the curtain drop of Horsetail Falls, with Reverse Creek gurgling its way backward across the property, and Carson Peak looming 4,000 feet overhead. Accommodations range from two-bedroom knotty-pine guest cabins with fully equipped modern kitchens, decks, fireplaces, woodstoves, TV/DVD setups, and wireless Internet to luxury hotel-style rooms arranged in fourplexes around a fly-fishing pond. Extraordinary hiking, fishing, and access to lakes in summer. Cross-country, downhill, backcountry, and big-mountain skiing in winter—and ice skating on the pond. Begin and end your day with a soak, a swim, and a treatment or two at the Creekside, one of the top destination spas in the country. On-site restaurant and bar, fly shop, guiding services, and daily fitness activities.

Dining

Eagle's Landing (5587 CA 158; 760-648-7897; www.doubleeagle.com; expensive). Start the day with an epic Bodie breakfast burrito, or thick slices of Hawaiian-style French toast. The Alpers smoked-trout club makes a lunch worth coming in out of the cold for. Dinner is scaled-up chop house fare. The real attraction—in this lofty, casual, fir-paneled dining room—is the way the light slides from Carson Peak. Full bar. Box lunches available. Open daily from 7 AM.

Taverns, Saloons & Roadhouses

The Tiger Bar (Main Street, CA 158, center of June Lake Village; 760-648-7551; www.tigerbarcafe.com). Established in 1932, undoubtedly cleaned up quite a bit since then, the Tiger is an old standby for beer, bloodies, burgers, and pool.

Food Purveyors

COFFEE, TEA, ETC.

Trout Town Joe (2750 CA 158, June Lake Loop; 760-648-7010). Espresso, smoothies, baked goodies sometimes, sandwiches sometimes, local arts and crafts.

SWEETS

Cathy's Candy (2684 CA 158, June Lake Loop; 760-648-7233; www.cathyscandy.com). Imagine the delight of your traveling companions when, deep in the wilderness, you pull from your pack an assortment of Cathy Scribner's divinely inspired handmade candy— brittles, truffles, haystacks, turtles, chocolate almond toffee, peanut butter boulders, and more. Excellent for cutting high-tannin leather-cured red wine.

Shopping

GENERAL STORES

June Lake Junction (CA 395 and CA 158, June Lake Loop; 760-648-7509). Basic Shell gas mart, plus coffee bar, milk shakes, breakfast burritos, and deli sandwiches to go.

June Lake General Store (1 Main Street; 760-648-7771). Basic small town grocery, beer, liquor, ice, fishing tackle, canned goods, packaged pastries, camping supplies, hardware, charcoal, firewood.

Silver Lake General Store (Silver Lake Resort; 760-648-7525; www.silverlakeresort. net/store.htm). Basic groceries, beer, wine, ice, camping and fishing supplies, canned goods, sunblock, books, postcards, curios, and crafts.

SPORTING GEAR & EQUIPMENT

Ernie's Tackle & Ski Shop (2604 CA 158; 760-648-7756; www.erniestackleandski.com). Classic tackle and bait shop, since 1932. In winter becomes a basic ski and snowboard shop with a range of accessories and rentals.

SUNDRIES & SOUVENIRS

Sierra Wave T-Shirts & Gifts (36 CA 158; 760-648-7161; www.sierra-wave.com). Bears, mugs, curios, T-shirts, jellies, and honey.

Creekside Corner at Double Eagle (5587 CA 158; 760-648-7004; www.doubleeagle.com). Cards, candles, fancy soaps, bath salts, bathrobes, teddy bears, and spa products.

MONO LAKE & LEE VINING

This is the most remarkable lake I have ever seen. It lies in a basin at the height of 6,800 feet above the sea. Like the Dead Sea, it is without an outlet. The streams running into it all evaporate from the surface, so of course it is very salt—not common salt. There are hot springs in it, which feed it with peculiar mineral salts. It is said that it contains borax, also boracic acid, in addition to the materials generally found in saline lakes. The waters are very clear and very heavy—they have a nauseous taste. When still, it looks like oil, it is so thick, and it is not easily disturbed. Although nearly twenty miles long it is often so smooth that the opposite mountains are mirrored in it as in a glass. The water feels slippery to the touch and will wash grease from the hands, even when cold, more readily than common hot water and soap. I washed some woolens in it, and it was quicker and easier than any "suds" I ever saw. It washed our silk handkerchiefs, giving them luster as if new.

—William H. Brewer, 1863

Joseph Walker passed by here any number of times but didn't think much of the place. Lt. Tredwell Moore, U.S. Army, chasing Tenaya's band of renegade Indians out of Yosemite in 1852, saw the lake, named it for the Indians who lived there—and also found some gold flakes. Leroy Vining was among the first to come over the pass the following year. The word *Mono* is a variant of the Yokuts word *Monache,* or "people of the flies," so named because they made their primary living harvesting and eating the larvae of the alkali flies that to this day swarm and breed, by the millions, along the edge of the lake. "The Indians come from far and near to gather them," wrote Brewer. "The worms are dried in the sun, the shell rubbed off, when a yellowish kernel remains, like a small yellow grain of rice. This is oily, very nutritious . . . it does not taste bad, and if one were ignorant of its origin, it would make fine soup. Gulls, ducks, snipe, frogs, and Indians fatten on it."

Lee Vining never found much gold, but others did, and before long he was making good money milling lumber and selling it to miners in Lakeview and Aurora. Samuel Clemens spent some time in Aurora in the 1860s before he landed a reporter's gig at the *Territorial Enterprise* in Virginia City and started using the pseudonym Mark Twain. Of Mono Lake he would later write: "It is one of the strangest freaks of Nature to be found in any land." Lee Vining was over in Aurora one day, having made a lumber delivery there, got drunk at the Exchange Saloon, and sometime thereafter met his demise when his own loaded pistol went off in his pocket. "Borax" Smith made his first million near here, mining the very detergent that Brewer used to wash his hankies in Mono Lake—the stuff that would eventually make Death Valley, and Ronald Reagan (host of the popular Boraxo-brand TV series *Death Valley Days*), famous. The town of Lakeview got a post office in 1928, renaming itself Leevining (one word) after its unlucky founder, so as to avoid confusion with another Lakeview, down south, in Riverside County. In 1957 the U.S. Board on Geographic Names declared that the town should be called Lee Vining (two words).

Beginning in 1941, with the completion of Grant Lake, Crowley Lake, and a series of diversion tunnels beneath the Mono Craters, south of Lee Vining, the City of Los Angeles began siphoning the water from Mono Lake's feeder streams, and thus set about creating another Owens-style dry lake. By 1962 Mono had dropped 25 vertical feet. By 1982 it had fallen another 20—to an all-time low of 6,372 feet. Salinity levels doubled, algae photosynthesis lagged, brine shrimp had difficulty reproducing, tufa formation stopped, previously safe bird-nesting sites were suddenly accessible to coyotes, the air filled with poison dust and particulates, and so on. In 1978 an ornithologist by the name of David Gaines formed the Mono Lake Committee, took Los Angeles to court, and 16 years later—in 1994—won. The city continues to divert into its aqueducts approximately 16 percent of water that would otherwise go to the lake, but the lake is coming back. The plan is to return it to a level of 6,391 feet. By 2007 it was up 10 feet, about two-thirds of the way there.

Lodging

El Mono Motel

www.elmonomotel.com
51 CA 395, at Third Street
Elevation: 6,781 feet
Open: April through late fall
760-647-6310
Innkeepers: Kelly Miller and friends
Price: Inexpensive to Moderate
Pets: No
Wheelchair Access: Yes
Internet access: Wireless

Built in the 1920s as one of the first true motels on El Camino Sierra (later CA 395), El Mono today is the best value lodging on the east side of the Sierra Crest. It has been tastefully, artfully redone by the current owner with desert-tone paint schemes, feather comforters, and framed prints by local artists and photographers. Every room is unique. Some have two rooms and private baths. Others are small, but still more than adequate for sleeping in, with shared bathing and toilet facilities (and budget prices). Gardenside rooms offer a view of the sunflowers, but a higher degree of foot traffic by fellow guests. Upstairs, Rooms 10 and 11 share a bath but offer more privacy—plus views across the highway to the lake. The proprietors offer a wealth of insider beta on the region. Lobby doubles as a cozy coffee joint (see below).

Tioga Lodge

www.tiogalodgeatmonolake.com
54411 CA 395

Elevation: 6,400 feet
Open: May through October
760-647-6423
Innkeepers: Walter and Lou Vint
Price: Moderate to Expensive
Pets: No
Wheelchair Access: Limited
Internet Access: Wireless

An enterprising gentleman by the name of J. P. Hammond had a couple of old buildings moved over from Bodie in 1897, and another from Lundy. He installed one of the first telephones in the region, charged a toll for use of the old Indian road around Mono Lake (today CA 395), and offered travelers a popular menu of whores, poker, whiskey, and cold beer. The beer was kept in the creek that ran beneath the saloon, retrieved through a trap door in the floor. When Hammond sold to the Cunninghams in 1918, the place went fancy: rose gardens, Chinese waiters in white jackets, a dancing pavilion, a marina, a pleasure steamer named *Venita*, and a gas pump. It was all pretty well swept away in a flood in 1955, to be rescued 40 years later by the Vints, who have done a remarkable job not just of bringing the place back to life, but giving it new character. The main buildings are whitewashed board and batten with weathered-plank decks overlooking the road and the lake. Cabins are individually, sparingly decorated with wood or Saltillo-tile floors, cotton quilts, painted-clay washbasins, and windows that open to dawn over the lake. On-site dining and boat tours.

Dining

✪ **Mono Inn Roadhouse** (55620 CA 395, 4 miles north of Lee Vining; 760-647-6581; www.monoinn.com; expensive). One no longer has to eat fly larvae and wash one's woolens in cold borax brine to appreciate the beauty of Mono Lake. Consider instead a handsome Stickley table and chairs beside a grand picture window in the cozy atmosphere of a classic 1920s roadhouse—owned and run by Ansel Adams's granddaughter—with candlelight inside and outside the moon rising over what John Muir, with surprising restraint, called "a country of wonderful contrasts." Duck confit, wild boar, local heirloom tomatoes, basil, goat cheese from a farm just up the creek—everything prepared and served with clear passion by folks who spend their days (their winters, anyway) happily recreating in the great wilderness beyond these walls, and thus appreciate the necessary complement of good food at a good day's end. Ansel Adams gallery upstairs. Terrace dining available on warm evenings. Open May through October, dinner only. Closed Tuesday. Reservations recommended.

✪ **Tioga Toomey's Whoa Nelly Deli** (at the Mobil station, 22 Vista Point Road, at the junction of CA 395 and CA 120; 760-647-1088; moderate). One might wonder why chef Matt Toomey left a decent job at Mammoth's Whiskey Creek to work the sandwich counter at the gas station in Lee Vining. That is, until one sees what he's done with the place. He still makes excellent sandwiches to go, but most people—bikers, climbers, backpackers, firefighters, European tourists, truckers, geologists, park rangers, water department stooges, kids, and dogs—settle in for a full-plate meal and a bottle of something. The fish tacos and lobster taquitos, each served with black beans and some version of exotic-fruit salsa, are duly legendary, but the brick o' buffalo meat loaf and the apricot-wild-berry-glazed pork tenderloin deserve respect. Order at the counter, grab a picnic table with a view of the lake, and wait for your number to be called. Beer and wine from the cooler, glasses provided. Open daily, May to October. Hopping live music on the lawn, Thursday and Sunday through the summer.

Food Purveyors

COFFEE, ETC.
Latte Da Coffee Cafe (51 CA 395, at the El Mono Motel; 760-647-6310; www.elmono motel.com). Cozy, fair-trade, organic coffee shop, with a handful of tables and a fireplace. Local information and stories. Wireless Internet. Front porch with views across the highway to the lake.

General Stores

Mono Market (51303 CA 395; 760-647-1010). Thoroughly stocked for its convenience-store size: meat, organic produce, beer and wine, spices, tortillas, natural foods, ice cream, office supplies, chocolate, cheese, trail mix, and batteries. A variety of deli-counter foods for take-out, including quiches, sandwiches, homemade "Lizzagna," and hefty black-bean breakfast monoritos, made fresh every morning with bacon, chorizo, or vegetables. Open every day, even in winter.

Tioga Gas Mart (at the Mobil station, 22 Vista Point Road, at the junction of CA 395 and CA 120; 760-647-1088). Beer, wine, soft drinks, snack food, souvenirs, postcards, fish tacos. Open daily in summer. Closed in winter, except for gasoline.

Books, Maps & Information

Mono Basin Scenic Area Visitor Center (CA 395, 0.25 mile north of Lee Vining; 760-647-3044). Airy, fortresslike building set in 1992 on a promontory overlooking the lake. Interactive displays on the region's natural and human history. A 20-minute film, *Of Fire & Ice,* provides a good overview. Interpretive tours, lectures, rotating art exhibits, very cool large-scale model of the entire basin. Bookstore and gift shop run by the Eastern Sierra Interpretive Association (760-934-3042). Closed in winter.

Mono Lake Committee Bookstore (CA 395 and Third Street; 760-647-6595; www.mono lake.org). Home of the friendly folks who never stop working to save Mono Lake. Tourist information, T-shirts, travel mugs, gifts, gallery with rotating art exhibits, one of the best selections of local and environmental books in the Sierra. Open daily year-round, except holidays and occasional breaks.

Points of Interest

South Tufa (Mono Lake Tufa State Reserve, south of Lee Vining, off CA 120 East; 760-647-6331). Boardwalk stroll to the beach, signage showing historic subsidence of the lake and projected goals for its restoration. See the progress since Pink Floyd's *Wish You Were Here* album cover was shot here in the early 1970s. See the flies. Open every day, all year. Guided tours in summer. Bring drinking water. Lovely cross-country skiing when conditions permit.

High Sierra Brine Shrimp (54872 CA 395; 760-647-6122; www.hsbrineshrimp.com). Quantities of rare brine shrimp (*Artemia monica*) are harvested, frozen, enriched, and packaged for use as a tropical fish food here.

Old School House Museum (Hess Park, off CA 395; 760-647-6461; www.oldschoolhouse museum.com). Artifacts, implements, photos, books and maps documenting the cultural history of the Mono Basin, including the old paddle wheel from the 1930s pleasure boat *Venita.* Open Thursday through Sunday in summer only. The park is an excellent place for a picnic, supplied by the Mono Mart or Tioga Toomey.

Bodie State Historic Park (CA 270, south of Lee Vining, 13 miles east of CA 395; 760-647-6445). Waterman Body (or William Bodey) discovered small amounts of gold here in the 1860s, back in the days when spelling was an arcane form of necromancy. Not much came of the place until the Standard Company found a big vein in 1877, and before long ten thousand people were trying to make a go of it here. Timber for building was brought by Chinese-built rail from Mono Mills, on the south side of Mono Lake. There were two banks, a Chinatown (complete with opium dens), a red-light district, a school, churches, electricity (from 1893), and several dozen saloons. One hundred million dollars in gold bullion and many

Alfred Knopf and Ralph Anderson in front of the old church at Bodie R. H. Anderson, courtesy NPS, YNP

volumes of Wild West stories came out of this place. Today you can't buy so much as a bottle of water. Much of the town burned down in 1932; what remained was abandoned not long after. Designated a National Historic Landmark in 1961 and made a state park the following year, the whole area is now preserved in an interesting state of "arrested decay," which means that dust is allowed to collect on the array of valuable artifacts left behind, but buildings are kept from collapsing. No camping, no collecting.

RECREATION

Backcountry Skiing, Climbing & Mountaineering

From Rock Creek to Virginia Lakes, every side canyon offers access—by skin or by boot—to the John Muir and Ansel Adams Wildernesses. Big peaks abound. And granite crags. And couloirs for fast, steep descents. Check the **Eastern Sierra Avalanche Center** (www.esavalanche.org) for snow conditions. Chat with the folks at **Mammoth Mountaineering** (3189 Main Street; 760-934-4191; see above). Be prepared; be careful; know what you're doing; bring beacon, shovel, probe; go with a guide.

Sierra Mountain Guides (June Lake; 760-648-1122; www.sierramtnguides.com). Rock climbing, ice climbing, mountaineering, backcountry skiing. Trips and courses. Doug Nidever, Howie Schwartz, Trevor Hobbs, Neil Satterfield, Dave Miller, Scott Brown.

For Bishop-based guides offering services throughout the High Sierra, see chapter 4.

Bird-Watching

Mono Lake is said to be the birthplace of nearly every gull in California. It is a major staging area for huge populations of migratory shorebirds, such as the unique Wilson's phalarope. The many hot springs and warm-water tributaries of the Upper Owens River provide unique habitat for hundreds of species. Check the **Eastern Sierra Audubon Society**'s Web site, www.esaudubon.org, for hot spots as far north as Crowley Lake. The **Eastern Sierra Birding Trail Map** is available online (www.easternsierrabirdingtrail.org), and through most local businesses and bookstores. Also consult the Sierra Nevada Aquatic Research Lab's online list of local species at http://vesr.ucnrs.org/pages/snarlbirds.html.

Boating

Hundreds of alpine and subalpine lakes, as well as two large Los Angeles Department of Water and Power reservoirs (Crowley and Grant) provide opportunities that range from kayaking to kite boarding to puttering around some distant shore in an outboard-driven aluminum dinghy. Most marinas offer hourly, half-day, and full-day rentals throughout the summer season.

Caldera Kayaks (Mammoth Lakes; 760-934-1691; www.calderakayak.com). Variety of kayaks for use on Crowley and Mono lakes. Lessons and tours.

Crowley Lake Fish Camp Marina (off CA 395; 760-935-4301; www. crowleylakefish camp.com). Fishing boats, 15 and 30 horsepower. Tackle shop.

Convict Lake Marina (Convict Lake; 760-934-3800; www.convictlake.com/boating.html). Fishing boats, pontoon boats, canoes, and kayaks.

Gull Lake Marina (June Lake Loop; 760-648-7539). Pontoon boats, flat-bottom boats, canoes.

June Lake Marina (June Lake; 760-648-7726; www.junelakemarina.net). Valcos with Evinrudes. Bait and tackle shop.

Lake Mary Marina (Lake Mary Road, Mammoth Lakes; 760-934-5353). Fleet of fishing dinghies, some with motors, some without. Store.

Pokonobe Resort (Lake Mary, Mammoth Lakes; 760-934-2437; www.pokonobe resort.com). Pontoon boats, motorboats, rowboats, canoes, kayaks, and pedal boats. General store.

Silver Lake Resort (Silver Lake, June Lake Loop; 760-648-7525; www.silverlake resort.net). Fishing boats with outboard motors; canoes and kayaks.

Sierra Country Canoes & Kayaks (Mammoth Lakes; 760-924-8652). Canoes and kayaks available for use on June and Mono Lakes.

Twin Lakes Store (off Lake Mary Road, Mammoth Lakes; 760-934-7295). Rowboat rentals, general store.

Skate skiing at Horseshoe Lake, Tamarack Brad Peatross, MMSA

Woods Lodge (Lake George, Mammoth Lakes; 760-934-2261). Motorboat and rowboat rentals. Tackle and snack shop.

Cross-Country Skiing & Snowshoeing

The Mammoth Lakes Nordic Trail System includes 7 miles of groomed trails in and around town, with a new trail under construction that will link town with Tamarack and the Lakes Basin. The Inyo National Forest also offers a network of trails off the Mammoth Scenic Loop to the north of town. Pick up a Winter Recreation Map at the Welcome Center. Also see Rock Creek Lodge, above.

Tamarack Cross Country Ski Center (Twin Lakes; 760-934-2442; www.tamaracklodge .com). Package rentals: striding and skating skis, snowshoes. Nineteen miles of groomed trails.

Dogsledding

A French Canadian ex-bootlegger by the name of Tex Cushion ran a team of dogs here in the late 1920s, providing passenger and freight service for the tiny hamlet of Mammoth Camp. You can see what that might have been like with the help of Mammoth Dog Teams (760-934-6270; www.mammothdogteams.com). Half-hour and one-hour rides leave from Mammoth Mountain Inn, weather and trail conditions permitting. Kennel tours and overnight trips can be arranged.

Downhill Skiing & Snowboarding

Mammoth Mountain (1-800-MAMMOTH; www.mammothmountain.com). See above.

June Mountain Ski & Snowboard Resort (CA 158; 760-648-7733; 1-888-JUNEMTN; www.junemountain.com). Laid-back, uncrowded, family-style ski area. Good bet for beginner and intermediate skiers, for powder days when the top of Mammoth is shut down, and for access to the steep and deep backcountry. Sports school, rentals and demos, on-mountain dining. Mammoth lift tickets and passes valid here.

Fishing

There are countless lakes, reservoirs, rivers, spring streams, and high alpine brooks, most stocked by the **Department of Fish and Game** (760-934-2664; www.dfg.ca.gov) with hand-fed Alpers trout. Mono County fishing season runs from the last Saturday in April to November 15. From bait-trolling to traditional dry-fly casting, this part of the Eastern Sierra offers some of the best trout fishing in the world. To prevent the spread of New Zealand mudsnail, wading is discouraged. If you want the latest insider tips, there are as many local guide services as condominium rental agencies, and at least as many guides as there are productive places to fish.

Eastern Sierra Guide Service (760-872-7770; www.jaeger-flyfishing.com). Guide service.

David Moss Fly Fishing (760-937-4168; www.davidmossflyfishing.com). Guide service.

David Neal, Reel Mammoth Adventures (760-924-0483; www.reelmammothadventures .com). Guide service.

Performance Anglers (26 Old Mammoth Road; 760-924-2181; www.performance anglers.com). Shop, rentals, guide service.

Kevin Peterson's Fly Fishing Adventures (760-937-0519; www.kevinpetersonflyfishing .com). Guide service

Sierra Drifters Guide Service (760-935-4250; www.sierradrifters.com). Guide service.

The Troutfitter Flyshop (Shell Mart Center, Main Street, Mammoth; 760-924-3676; www.thetroutfitter.com). Shop, rentals, guide service.

Wilderness Outfitters (6201 Minaret Road, pedestrian level at the Village; 760-924-7070; 760-924-REEL). Orvis-endorsed shop and guide service.

Golf
Sierra Star (2001 Sierra Star Parkway; 760-924-4653; www.mammothmountain.com). California's highest-altitude 18-hole course (8,000 feet). Regulation, medium length, par 70, built in 1999, Cal Olsen design. Meadows and great narrow corridors through the woods. Club and cart rentals, lessons, midweek specials. Call or book tee times online.

Snowcreek Golf Course (Fairway Drive, off Old Mammoth Road; 760-934-6633; www.snowcreekresort.com/golf.htm). Nine holes, par 35, in the meadow where Steve McQueen's Nevada Smith tracked down his last victim. Built in 1991, Ted Robinson design. Big views, water features. Clubhouse, café (sandwiches and snacks), accessories and apparel. Lessons available. Collared shirts required. No metal spikes, no club rentals. Wide-open driving range. Sensitive to backcountry skiers in winter.

Hiking
Numerous popular hikes—from short strolls to day hikes to overnight trips—set off from trailheads in the Lakes Basin, at the end of Lake Mary Road. From Coldwater Campground try Duk Pass to Arrowhead, Skelton, and Barney Lakes (10 miles round-trip to Duk Lake), or the trail to Emerald Lake (1.5 miles round-trip), or add a few miles and make a loop around the crest to Lake George. From Horseshoe Lake hike over Mammoth Pass, then down to Reds Meadow (6 miles one way), have pie, take the shuttle or hike back. Or take the shuttle to Agnew Meadows, on the San Joaquin, and climb from there up to Shadow Lake and Lake Ediza (12 miles round-trip). Wilderness permits and bear canisters required for overnight trips. Talk it over with a ranger at the Welcome Center.

Horseback Riding
A variety of outfitters provides day trips, dunnage, spot trips, and full custom service from every major trailhead in the region.

Convict Lake Resort (Convict Lake Road; 760-934-3803; 1-800-992-2260; www. convict lake.com). Two-hour guided trips to the other side of the lake. Three times daily in summer.

Frontier Pack Station (1012 East Line Street, Bishop; 760-873-7971; www.frontierpack

train.com). Kent and Dave Dohnel. Scheduled and custom trips into Ansel Adams Wilderness and Yosemite high country, from stables at June Lake.

McGee Creek Pack Station (Mammoth Lakes; 760-935-4324). Full service into John Muir Wilderness.

Mammoth Lakes Pack Outfit (Lake Mary Road; 760-934-2434). Full service into John Muir and Ansel Adams Wildernesses. Spring and fall horse drives.

Reds Meadow/Agnew Meadows Pack Outfit (Reds Meadow; 760-934-2345; 1-800-292-7758). Full service to Yosemite, Ansel Adams Wilderness, John Muir Wilderness, and Mount Whitney.

Rock Creek Pack Station (Rock Creek; 760-872-8331). Full service to Hilton Lakes, Little Lakes Valley, Pioneer Basin, and Mono Creek.

Sierra Meadows Ranch Equestrian Center (Sherwin Creek Road, off Old Mammoth Road; 760-934-6161). Boarding and short trips into the Sherwin Range.

Virginia Lakes Pack Outfit (Bridgeport; 760-872-0271; www.virginialakes.com). Into the Hoover Wilderness and remote northern Yosemite.

Ice Skating

When conditions are just right, after weeks of freezing temperatures and no snow, hundreds of high-country lakes become natural skating rinks. A much safer bet might be the Town Ice Rink, at Sierra Park and Meridian, adjacent to the new library, a hockey-sized open-air rink with skate rentals, snacks and beverages, and a fire pit. Also try Ron's Pond at the Double Eagle Resort in June Lake.

Motor Sports

There are hundreds of miles of crisscrossing forest roads north of Mammoth and east of CA 395 open to off-highway vehicles and snowmobiles. Wilderness areas are off-limits to all vehicles.

DJ's Snowmobile Adventures (Smokey Bear Flat, CA 395, north of Mammoth; 760-935-4480; www.snowmobilemammoth.com). Five hundred acres of rolling snowmobile range from Smokey Bear Flat to Bald Mountain. Tours, rentals, guided trips.

Mammoth Mountain Snowmobile Adventures (Top of Minaret, across from Main Lodge; 760-934-9645; 1-800-MAMMOTH; www.mammothmountain.com/activities/snomo/). Tours and rentals. Reservations suggested.

Sierra Engine (58 Commerce Drive; 760-934-0347; www.sierraengine.com). Rents, sells, and services snowmobiles, snow blowers, lawn mowers, log splitters, and ATVs.

Mountain Biking

Conditions can be dusty and soft, but the terrain is nearly limitless. In general, the best

Ice skating at Twin Lakes, November 2006

riding is from 8,000 feet to timberline, in the woods. **Mammoth Mountain Bike Park** (Mammoth Mountain; 760-934-0706; www.mammothmountain.com/bike_ride) offers 90 miles of lift-accessed single track from 11,053 feet at the summit to 8,050 at the Village. Bike shuttle provided from the Village to the Gondola at Main Lodge. Downhill, free-ride, and 3,000-foot, family-friendly gradually looping descents. Bike rentals and tickets at the Mountain Center in the Village and at the Main Lodge Gondola Building. Consult the Welcome Center for maps of national forest trails and dirt roads across the Long Valley Caldera.

Road Biking

Three great rides from the Village at Mammoth: 1) Up Lake Mary Road, around Lake Mary to Horseshoe Lake, and back (approx. 12 miles); 2) down CA 203 to 395, north to Mammoth Scenic Loop, and back (approx. 14 miles); 3) down CA 203 to 395, south to the Green Church, east on Benton Crossing Road to CA 120, north to 395, and back by way of CA 395 south and Mammoth Scenic Loop (100 miles—essentially the reverse of the High Sierra Fall Century). Also try the spectacular June Lake Loop (21 miles)—start and end at the Double Eagle Resort.

Mammoth Mountain Bike Park Brad Peatross, MMSA

Rock & Ice Climbing

From the Owens Gorge to Warming Wall, from the Minarets to Lee Vining Canyon, from top-rope sport climbing to multipitch traditional ascents, there is enough good vertical here to keep a person busy through a dozen pairs of shoes.

Mammoth Mountain Adventure Center (Top of Minaret Road, Panorama Gondola Building; 1-800-MAMMOTH; www.mammothmountain.com). Good place to get hooked. Thirty-two-foot climbing wall with professional belay service for kids and adults. Zip line and junior ropes courses.

Sierra Rock Climbing School (1-877-686-7625; www.sierrarockclimbingschool.com). Private guiding, lessons, classes, and trips, plus ice climbing.

Skateboarding

Volcom Brothers Skatepark (Meridian Boulevard, near Commerce Drive; www.volcom.com). "California's best snowboard resort now boasts a world-class skatepark," wrote Muzzney in *Snowboarder Magazine* in 2006, "there are really rocks to skate—super-smooth concrete right up to boulders. There's also a giant cradle, a Burnside wall, lumps, humps, a big 'ol bowl, a love seat wall, plus zillions of different transfers and trannies, too. Its really epic; a new skate-asylum for southern California!" Tony Hawk skated here. Local hairstylist/skater Lisa McAdam calls it "cruisy." Early mornings are less crowded, for obvious reasons.

Spa, Massage & Yoga

Belladonna (3236 Main Street, at the Holiday Inn; 760-934-3344; www.belladonna spa.com). Full-service day spa and salon.

Healing Arts Center (645 Old Mammoth Road, Sherwin Plaza 2; 760-924-3223; www.mammothhealingarts.com). Massage therapy, skin and body spa, chiropractor, yoga, Pilates, Tai Chi, and more.

Mountain Mobile Massage (by appointment; 760-709-1329; www.mountainmobile massage. com). Music, table, oils, the works—brought to you. Reasonably priced.

Whitmore Pool Burke Griggs

Creekside Spa at Double Eagle Resort (5587 CA 158; 760-648-7004; www.doubleeagle.com). Full-service spa and salon: massage, shiatsu, Vichy shower body therapies, hydrotherapy, and more. Leave time to linger.

Swimming & Soaking

Most condos and hotels in Mammoth offer heated pools and

Jacuzzis, year-round. In summer, the swimming is world-class at most local lakes. The most popular swimming beaches are at Convict and June lakes. In winter, the adventurous will want to try one of the natural hot-springs tubs in Long Valley (via Hot Creek Hatchery Road or Benton Crossing; ask a local for information).

Whitmore Pool (Benton Crossing Road, just south of Mammoth Airport; 760-934-4222). Twenty-five-meter spring-fed pool, wading pool, restrooms, showers, lawn. Open mid-June through early October.

Tennis

Community Center Park Municipal Courts (Forest Trail and Minaret Road; 760-934-2712, ext. 222). Six courts, good orientation, good surfaces, good views of the Knolls. Drop in or call to reserve.

Tubing & Snowplay

Sledz (Minaret Road; 760-934-7533). Rope tow, tube rentals, groomed slopes.

ANNUAL EVENTS

January

Telebration (Stump Alley, Mammoth Mountain; 760-934-4191; www.mammoth gear.com). Free-heelers and all those who've always wanted to try come out of the woods for this daylong celebration of the knee-bend. Held during the first pleasant exhale after the holiday onslaught. Organized by Mammoth Mountaineering. Free workshops, free demos on all the latest equipment.

January Midweek Madness (1-800-MAMMOTH; www.mammothmountain.com). Post-holiday package deals on lodging.

February
Presidents' Day Week.

March
Easter Festivities & Pond Skim (1-800-MAMMOTH; www.mammothmountain.com).

April
Spring Fest (1-800-MAMMOTH; www.mammothmountain.com).

May
Spring Fest (1-800-MAMMOTH; www.mammothmountain.com).

Sierra Star Golf Course opening (760-924-4653; www.mammothmountain.com).

Average Tioga Pass opening (209-372-0200; www.nps.gov/yose/planyourvisit/ conditions.htm).

A fish fry near Mono Lake, celebrating the annual opening of Tioga Pass, 1920s Courtesy NPS, YNP

June

Ford Mammoth Motocross (Mammoth Lakes; www.mammothmotocross.com).

Mammoth Mountain Bike Park opening (1-800-MAMMOTH; www.mammoth mountain.com).

Mono Lake Bird Chatauqua (www.birdchautauqua.org). Birds, science, art, music, field trips.

July

Fourth of July Parade (Mammoth Lakes).

Fourth of July Triathlon & Freedom Mile (Mammoth Lakes; www.highsierratri.org).

Fourth of July Fireworks (Crowley Lake).

June Lake Triathlon (June Lake; www.highsierratri.org).

Jazz Jubilee (Mammoth Lakes; 760-934-2478; 1-877-MTN-JAZZ; www.mammothjazz.org). Five days, multiple tents, more than 30 bands. Jazz camp for musicians ages 13–17.

August

Bluesapalooza & Festival of Beers (Sam's Wood Site, Minaret Road; www.mammoth bluesbrewsfest.com). Two days of music and beer. Grand tasting Saturday afternoon.

Mammoth Festival of Wine, Music & Food (1-800-MAMMOTH; www.mammothmountain
.com).

September
Autumnal Equinox (September 23).

Troutstock Eastern Sierra (www.troutstock.com). Million-dollar fishing derby, kids'
activities and entertainment.

Annual Labor Day Festival of the Arts (Mammoth Lakes, Sam's Wood Site, Minaret Road).
Local craft fair in the woods.

Mammoth Mountain Wine & Jazz (www.mammothmountain.com/wineandjazz/).

High Sierra Fall Century Ride (Mammoth Lakes; www.fallcentury.org).

Mammoth Mountain Bike Park closing (1-800-MAMMOTH;
www.mammothmountain.com).

Tioga Pass Run (Lee Vining; www.monolake.org).

October
Oktoberfest (Mammoth Lakes; www.villageatmammoth.com).

Average peak fall colors.

November
Average Tioga Pass closing (209-372-0200; www.nps.gov/yose/planyourvisit/conditions.
htm).

Mammoth Mountain Ski Area opening day (1-800-MAMMOTH; www.mammoth
mountain.com).

Tamarack Cross Country Ski Center opening (Lakes Basin).

Masters Race Camp Week (Mammoth Mountain).

Mammoth Film Festival (www.mammothfilmfestival.com).

December
Volcom Peanut Butter & Rail Jam (1-800-MAMMOTH; www.mammothmountain.com).

June Mountain Ski Area opening (June Mountain).

Winter Solstice (December 21).

Christmas Bird Count.

6

Sequoia, Kings Canyon &
the Great Western Divide

Dominion of Giants

> *Such a landscape! A hundred peaks in sight over thirteen thousand feet—many very sharp—deep canyons, cliffs in every direction almost rival Yosemite, sharp ridges inaccessible to man, on which human foot has never trod—all combined to produce a view of sublimity of which is rarely equaled, one which few are privileged to behold.*

> *—William Henry Brewer, Whitney Geological Survey, 1864*

In August 1875, having just the month before walked more than 300 miles—from the Merced to the Kings River, crossing the range at Kearsarge, climbing Mount Whitney a second time, then returning to Yosemite Valley via Mono Lake and Lee Vining Canyon—a young John Muir set out once again from Clark's Station (Wawona), in the company of a mule named Brownie. His goal: to survey "the sequoia belt, making special studies of the species and visiting every grove as far as its southernmost limit."

To Muir the sequoia (*sequoiadendron gigantea*) was "the king of all the conifers," "the noblest of the noblest race." Once upon a time the earth's surface was covered with them. They were the dominant life form of the Jurassic and Cretaceous; the dinosaurs lived, reigned briefly, and died beneath them. As continents drifted apart, as mountains rose from the seas and the climate turned colder and drier, the Big Trees—most of them—went the way of the big reptiles. "No imperishableness of mountain-peak or of fragment of human work, broken pillar or sand-worn image half lifted over pathetic desert," wrote Clarence King of the ancient sequoias he had seen in 1864, on the Whitney Survey, "—none of these link the past and to-day with anything like the power of these monuments of living antiquity."

Today there are no more than 76 groves of native giant sequoias left in the world—all of them at an elevation between 5,000 and 8,000 feet on the southwestern slope of California's Sierra Nevada. They are the biggest living things on the planet. The biggest of

Once the largest grove of giant sequoias in the world, the Converse Basin was logged to a single tree.

all, the General Sherman Tree, now hulks above the Generals Highway in Sequoia National Park at a height of 275 feet, with a diameter three times that of a standard trampoline and a volume comparable to that of two late-model 747s.

Muir found isolated groves of sequoia, in generally mixed forests of sugar pine (ponderosa), white fir, and incense cedar, as far south as the Great Western Divide and the slopes of the upper Kern. Along the way—in the "wild untrampled kingdoms of the Sierra"—he was also delighted by innumerable lakes and meadows, "stupendous rocks," granite domes, cliffs, and great, wide chasms, many thousands of feet deep. The deepest of these, the canyons of the Middle and South Forks of the Kings (at their confluence a full 2,000 feet deeper than the Grand Canyon of the Colorado), Muir described with uncharacteristic understatement as "a rival to the Yosemite."

He was not so delighted to see the amount of trampling the country had already received. In one close-cropped meadow beside the Kings River, in the wake of a vast herd of sheep, he came upon a notice nailed to a tree: WE, THE UNDERSIGNED, CLAIM THIS VALLEY FOR THE PURPOSE OF RAISING STOCK. MR. THOMAS, MR. RICHARDS, HARVEY & CO.

By Muir's count there were already five commercial sawmills operating in the region, "all of which were cutting more or less of 'big-tree' lumber," to be used (because of the brittle quality of sequoia wood and the massive trees' tendency to shatter upon felling) for fence posts, grape stakes, roof shingles, and matchsticks. This at a time when the only portion of the Sierra Nevada that was in any way protected from commercial logging was the floor of Yosemite Valley. "Our forest belts are being burned and cut down and wasted like a field of unprotected grain," wrote Muir. "[U]nless protective measures be speedily invented and enforced, in a few years this noblest tree species in the world will present only a few hacked and scarred remnants."

Difficulties of transport more than anything kept most serious logging interests away from the Big Trees. But in the fall of 1885 a group of utopian socialists calling themselves the Kaweah Colony filed 40 separate claims on 10 square miles of what is today known as the Giant Forest. That spring, despite delays in the processing of their claims, the colonists began work on a wagon road to the Big Trees. Five years later, through an almost miraculous combination of activism, unholy alliances, and political subterfuge—the Southern Pacific Railroad perhaps playing a card to limit competition for its timber monopoly—legislation came before President Benjamin Harrison that by his signature, in the fall of 1890, created Sequoia and General Grant National Parks—the nation's second and third such parks, after Yellowstone. Several of the old sequoia groves, including those filed on by the Kaweah Colonists, were thus permanently withdrawn from "settlement, occupancy, or sale" and placed under the protection of the U.S. Army. The first detachment of cavalry arrived with the melting of snow in 1891. The Kaweah Colony fell apart. In 1893 Harrison proclaimed another 4 million acres set aside as the "Sierra Forest Reserve" (now the Sequoia and Sierra National Forests), encompassing the majority of sequoia groves from the Kings River south to the Tule, and the summit of Mount Whitney.

How these vast swaths of public land were to be managed, under what designation and by which agency, are questions that continue to be grappled with to this day. The general trend, with some glaring exceptions, has been toward the expansion of federally protected boundaries. In 1926 Sequoia was expanded eastward to include the upper Kern Canyon and the Sierra Crest. When in 1936 it looked as if Kings Canyon might be submerged beneath a reservoir, Ansel Adams traveled to Washington bearing photos of the place. In 1940 Franklin Roosevelt declared the Kings Canyon National Wilderness Park, combining it with the earlier Grant Grove reserve. During World War II, Sequoia and Kings Canyon National Parks were consolidated under a single management scheme (still in place today). Cedar Grove and the Tehipite Valley were added to the system in 1965; Mineral King in 1978.

As "[a]n outstanding example of significant geological processes and biological evolution," with "superlative natural phenomena, and areas of exceptional natural beauty," Sequoia and Kings Canyon National Parks were together designated an International Biosphere Reserve in 1976 and subsequently nominated for status as a World Heritage Site. In 2000, by authority of the Antiquities Act of 1906, President Bill Clinton created the Giant Sequoia National Monument, thereby prohibiting any further removal of trees from much of the public land adjacent to the parks. Timber interests have continued to challenge the designation, but prohibitions against cutting have been upheld in the federal courts as recently as 2006.

Despite more than a century of extraordinary booms in population, industry, and industrial-scale agriculture in the valley below, the country Muir explored back in 1875 remains today the wildest and least trampled part of the Sierra. Today there are no more than a handful of roads here that penetrate the range, roads carved into the sides of mountains in steep, tortuous switchbacks—some of the most dramatic and drop-dead spectacular roads in the world, engineered (mostly in the 1930s) as if expressly to test the mettle of today's oversized recreational vehicle, climbing thousands of feet to offer hundred-mile sunset glimpses across haze and smog to the coastal ranges, and beyond to the Pacific Ocean—then plunging headlong into some of the deepest canyons on the continent. Of these roads, not one crosses over the crest to the other side. Where the asphalt ends and the backcountry begins—more than 4,000 square miles of designated, unbroken, roadless wilderness—travel is still accomplished only by mule, on horseback, or at the expense of one's boot heels.

John Muir—a scene in the Kern River country Helen Luken Jones, courtesy NPS, YNP

Traditional threats by logging, mining, and grazing have for the most part been replaced by concerns over diminishing air quality (the smog in the San Joaquin Valley was recently rated on a par with Los Angeles), climate change, and the spread of invasive plant and animal species. Still, since the days of Whitney and Muir, since the spring of 1827 when Jedediah Smith first scrambled up these canyons in search of beaver, since the arrival of the ancestors of the Monaches some ten thousand years ago—the scenery has remained fundamentally unchanged.

Tourist accommodations, on the other hand, have generally improved. Today there are excellent meals to be had, and fridge-cold microbrewed beer, decent wine, a wealth of interpretive signage, soy protein bars, bad pizza, curios, books, phone cards, gasoline, and comfortable beds are available right at the edge of the wilderness.

The annual number of visitors to Sequoia-Kings Canyon National Parks, at around 1.5 million, is less than half the number of visitors to Yosemite. On your average weekend in July or August, even with the new shuttle buses in operation, one may have to circle twice to find a parking spot at the foot of the Moro Rock staircase, but that's about as bad as it gets. And even then, outside the Giant Forest, Lodgepole, and Grant Grove areas, the parks are relatively quiet. Outside the parks—other than on the busiest summer weekends, or at the opening of hunting season in the fall—the national forests have to them the peaceful air of abandonment.

In the fall and spring, when the days are still warm and the nights crisp, oncoming cars often prove infrequent enough, even inside the parks, that drivers smile and wave at each other through their windshields. In the winter, when the roads to Mineral King and the Kings River are closed and barricaded, when rain is falling hard in Three Rivers and the snow is piled higher than the restrooms at the Wolverton Ski Area, it's hard not to catch sight of, as John Muir once put it, "the clearest way into the Universe."

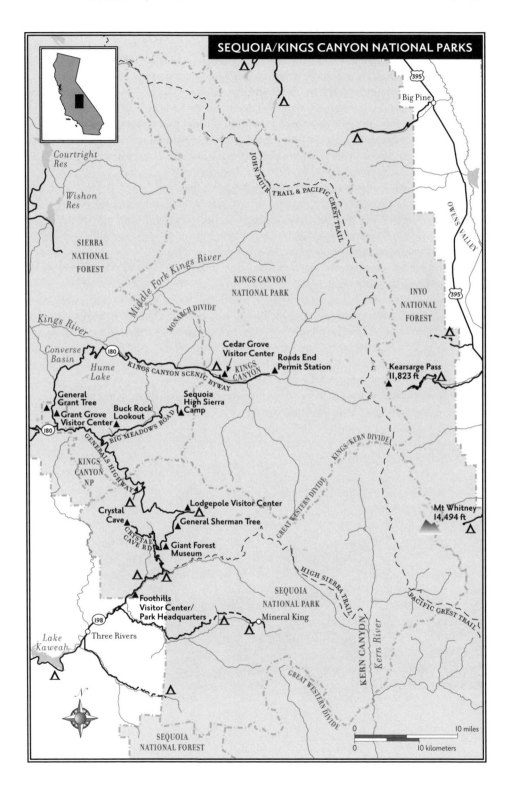

SEQUOIA/KINGS CANYON NATIONAL PARKS

Big Pine

395

JOHN MUIR TRAIL & PACIFIC CREST TRAIL

OWENS VALLEY

395

Courtright
Res

Wishon
Res

SIERRA
NATIONAL
FOREST

Middle Fork Kings River

KINGS CANYON
NATIONAL PARK

MONARCH DIVIDE

INYO
NATIONAL
FOREST

Kings River

Converse
Basin

Hume
Lake

180

KINGS CANYON SCENIC BYWAY

Cedar Grove
Visitor Center

Roads End
Permit Station

KINGS
CANYON

Kearsarge Pass
11,823 ft

General
Grant Tree

Grant Grove
Visitor Center

180

Buck Rock
Lookout

Sequoia
High Sierra
Camp

BIG MEADOWS ROAD

GENERALS HIGHWAY

KINGS
CANYON
NP

Crystal
Cave

CRYSTAL CAVE RD

Lodgepole Visitor Center

General Sherman Tree

Giant Forest
Museum

KINGS-KERN DIVIDE

GREAT WESTERN DIVIDE

Mt Whitney
14,494 ft

Foothills
Visitor Center/
Park Headquarters

SEQUOIA
NATIONAL PARK

Mineral King

HIGH SIERRA TRAIL

KERN CANYON

Kern River

PACIFIC CREST TRAIL

198

Lake
Kaweah

Three Rivers

GREAT WESTERN DIVIDE

N

SEQUOIA
NATIONAL FOREST

0   10 miles

0   10 kilometers

THE LAY OF THE LAND: APPROACHES & LOGISTICS

Travelers from Los Angeles and points south are most likely to enter the parks by CA 198, via Three Rivers, the only real gateway town to Sequoia-Kings Canyon. CA 245—connecting Visalia and points south with the northern entrance to Kings Canyon—is a lovely, forgotten little road, but it is no shortcut. For those making their way from Yosemite, San Francisco, and all other points north, the most direct route is CA 180, which shoots eastward from Fresno to the foothills, through the tough, hard-bitten agricultural towns of Minkler and Sanger, and then climbs in fairly short order to the Big Stump Entrance and the Grant Grove annex of Kings Canyon.

The only access from the east is by pack animal or on foot.

Gas is not sold within the parks' boundaries but can be purchased—at a premium—at either Stony Creek Village (on the Generals Highway) or from the antique gravity-fed pump at the Kings Canyon Lodge. The last major supply towns along these routes—for specialized outdoor equipment, cycling gear, sushi, relatively inexpensive gas, and more—are Visalia and Fresno, respectively. The farm stands at Sanger and Lemon Cove are the last chance for fresh fruit and vegetables.

This chapter is organized in six sections, according to the region's few paved roads, beginning with separate sections on Three Rivers, primary gateway town to Sequoia National Park; Mineral King Road; the Generals Highway and high-country Sequoia National Park; and CA 180, the Kings Canyon Scenic Byway, from Grant Grove to Cedar Grove. Lodging, dining, services, and points of interest along each of these roads are listed geographically within the appropriate section.

Following these are general notes on two less traveled but equally worthy scenic byways to the south and north of Sequoia/Kings Canyon. First, the Great Western Divide Highway,

Consider stocking up on luxury items before you leave civilization. Burke Griggs

also called "the Mighty 190," which meanders through the Southern Unit of the Giant Sequoia National Monument, south of Sequoia National Park, between Springville (south of Visalia, in the Central Valley) and Kernville (on the north end of Lake Isabella). Kernville can be reached from Los Angeles and points south via CA 178 from Bakersfield, or over Walker Pass from Inyokern and the Mojave

Tent cabin, Bearpaw High Sierra Camp, Sequoia National Park (11 miles from parking)

desert (see chapter 4). Second, Kaiser Pass and the "Sierra Heritage Scenic Byway" (CA 168), which climbs up into the San Joaquin drainage to the north of Kings Canyon (above Shaver and Huntington Lakes), ending at Florence and Thomas Edison reservoirs, with their unique ferryboat access to the John Muir Wilderness and the remote northern end of Kings Canyon National Park.

An overview of recreational possibilities follows at the end of the chapter.

LODGING OVERVIEW

In the spring of 1899, Visalia ranchers Ralph Hopping and John Broder partnered up to establish the first commercial accommodations in the new Sequoia National Park. For $35 a head, they provided stage and pack service up the Old Colony Mill Road, a horse to ride on for the last 4 miles to Round Meadow, a week's lodging, and three meals a day. Camp Sierra, as the enterprise was called, consisted of a collection of simple platform tents at the edge of the Giant Forest. The operation was abandoned in 1908.

Accommodations of this sort are still available at Grant Grove, as well as at Bearpaw and the Sequoia High Sierra Camps. Otherwise, lodgings within the parks range from modern, relatively upscale motel rooms to the ricketiest board-and-batten-style tourist cabins of the 1920s and '30's. There is not much to recommend lodging in Kings Canyon or along the Great Western Divide Highway—other than, of course, the scenery. Notes have been included here in case the scenery should prevail. As always, one's appreciation of the simpler amenities will improve significantly having first slept on the ground somewhere, or exhausted oneself on some dusty trail in the wilderness, or at the very least driven long hours on empty, winding mountain roads with the windows down and the iPod cranked.

For a taste of the old school, consider spending a night in a decommissioned fire lookout or Forest Service guard station. For highest adventure, try an overnight midwinter ski expedition to the Pear Lake Ski Hut. For anything approaching real luxury accommodations, the traveler will have to press on to the Yosemite region.

Lodging Price Code

Cost of lodging is based on an average per-room, double-occupancy rate at peak season (Memorial Day to Labor Day). Tax and gratuities are not included. Rates are often significantly reduced midweek and outside the summer season.

Inexpensive	Up to $75
Moderate	$75 to $125
Expensive	$125 to $200
Very Expensive	Over $200

CAMPING

Options for car camping are abundant throughout the region, ranging from the most crowded and developed sites at Lodgepole to more secluded (and primitive) dispersed-camping along Forest Service back roads, as along the Big Meadow/Horse Corral Road, where one can set up a temporary homestead nearly anywhere there is flat ground and a preexisting fire ring. Reserve upper sites along the river at Lodgepole, or look to Dorst and Stony Creek. A campfire permit is required for fires outside developed campgrounds or designated recreation sites. Permits are available free of charge from any Forest Service, California Department of Forestry and Fire Protection, or Bureau of Land Management office. Camping in the foothills is most comfortable from late fall to spring, when the high country is under snow. In summer, heat and black flies will drive all but the most intrepid to cooler altitudes. The Upper Kern River is a circus on summer weekends. Pets are allowed in all campgrounds (on a leash and attended at all times).

DINING OVERVIEW

High cuisine has only recently begun to make forays into this part of the high country. Rare is the trained and innovative chef willing to forsake the bright lights of Vegas or San Francisco for a set of propane burners on a ledge of granite at 8,000 feet above the sea. Rarer still is the one willing to stick it out for more than a couple of seasons. Water is slow to boil up here, sauces quick to cool; fixings for the delicate palate—fresh-harvested shellfish, papaya, herbs, heirloom tomatoes, and such—tend to fare imperfectly on the arduous and refrigerated journey up the hill.

That said, hunger bred from exertion is among the most powerful seasonings known to man. The food at Sequoia's High Sierra Camps, served with boxed burgundy by the light of the alpenglow, in the wake of hours-long knee-jarring descents from cold alpine lakes, has been known to open new glimpses into the sublime. But there is also decent roadside fare to be had, Mexican food at lower elevations, and in the gateway towns a host of options for respectable steak-and-potato-style fare, all of which tend to be enhanced considerably by one's having spent long hours beneath a 60-pound pack eating nothing but energy bars.

Breakfast is prepared with appropriate reverence nearly everywhere.

Be forewarned, however: the longer one dallies along the scenic byways of the sequoia belt, the more difficult it becomes to avoid the concessionaires' ubiquitous shrink-wrapped deli sandwiches and microwave pizzas. It is eminently advisable, therefore, before proceeding into the hills—here more than in any other part of the Southern Sierra—to first make a stop at one of the farm stands in the valley (i.e., between Fresno and Sanger, between Visalia and Lemon Cove, or between Porterville and Springville) and to carry in the trunk of one's vehicle a well-stocked cooler and the means to whip up, at one's convenience, a decent roadside picnic.

SIERRA/KINGS CANYON CAMPING

THREE RIVERS/FOOTHILLS	ELEVATION	SEASON	RESERVATIONS ACCEPTED	FEE	SITES	WATER	AGENCY
SOUTH FORK*	3,600	Year-round	No	Yes	10	No	NPS
BUCKEYE FLAT*	2,800	May-Sep	No	Yes	28	Yes	NPS
POTWISHA*	2,100	Year-round	No	Yes	42	Yes	NPS
MINERAL KING							
ATWELL MILL*	6,650	May-Oct	No	Yes	21	Yes	NPS
COLD SPRINGS*	7,500	May-Oct	No	Yes	40	Yes	NPS
SEQUOIA NATIONAL PARK/GENERALS HIGHWAY							
DORST*	6,800	May-Sep	Yes	Yes	204	Yes	NPS
LODGEPOLE*	6,700	Year-round	Yes	Yes	250	Yes	NPS
GIANT SEQUOIA NATIONAL FOREST/MONUMENT NORTH							
BUCK ROCK	7,600	May-Sep	No	No	5	No	USFS
BIG MEADOWS	7,600	Jun-Oct	No	No	25	Creek	USFS
ESHOM CREEK	4,800	May-Oct	No	Yes	23	Piped	USFS
STONY CREEK	6,400	May-Sep	Yes	Yes	49	Yes	USFS
UPPER STONY CREEK	6,400	May-Oct	Yes	Yes	19	Piped	USFS
FIR (GROUP)	6,400	May-Sep	Yes	Yes	‡	Yes	USFS
COVE (GROUP)	6,500	May-Sep	Yes	Yes	‡	Yes	USFS
PRINCESS	5,900	May-Sep	Yes	Yes	90	Yes	USFS
ASPEN HOLLOW (GROUP)	5,200	May-Sep	Yes	Yes	‡	Yes	USFS
LOGGER FLAT (GROUP)	5,300	May-Sep	Yes	Yes	‡	Yes	USFS
LANDSLIDE	5,800	May-Oct	No	Yes	9	Piped	USFS
TENMILE	5,800	May-Oct	No	Yes	13	Piped	USFS
HUME LAKE	5,200	May-Sep	Yes	Yes	74	Yes	USFS
GRANT GROVE/KINGS CANYON NATIONAL PARK							
AZALEA*	6,500	Year-round	No	Yes	144	Yes	NPS
CRYSTAL SPRINGS*	6,500	May-Sep	No	Yes	66	Yes	NPS
SUNSET*	6,500	May-Sep	No	Yes	119	Yes	NPS
CEDAR GROVE/KINGS CANYON NATIONAL PARK							
MORAINE*	4,600	May-Oct	No	Yes	120	Yes	NPS
SENTINEL*	4,600	May-Oct	No	Yes	83	Yes	NPS
SHEEP CREEK*	4,600	May-Oct	No	Yes	111	Yes	NPS
CANYON VIEW*	4,600	Jun-Oct	No	Yes	23	Yes	NPS
CANYON VIEW (GROUP)*	4,600	Jun-Sep	Yes	Yes	9	Yes	NPS
GREAT WESTERN DIVIDE HIGHWAY/SEQUOIA NATIONAL FOREST/MONUMENT SOUTH							
WISHON	3,900	Year-round	Yes	Yes	39	Piped	USFS
BELKNAP	5,000	Apr-Nov	Yes	Yes	15	Piped	USFS
COY FLAT	5,000	Apr-Nov	Yes	Yes	20	Piped	USFS
QUAKING ASPEN	7,000	May-Nov	Yes	Yes	32	Yes	USFS
HOLEY MEADOW (GROUP)	6,400	Jun-Oct	Yes	Yes	‡	No	USFS
REDWOOD MEADOW	6,100	Jun-Oct	Yes	Yes	15	Piped	USFS
LONG MEADOW (GROUP)	6,000	Jun-Sep	Yes	Yes	1	No	USFS
PEPPERMINT	7,100	Year-round	No	No	19	Creek	USFS
LOWER PEPPERMINT	5,300	May-Oct	No	Yes	17	Piped	USFS
LIMESTONE	3,800	Apr-Nov	No	Yes	22	Creek	USFS
LEAVIS FLAT	3,000	Year-round	Yes	Yes	9	Piped	USFS
FROG MEADOW	7,500	Jun-Oct	No	No	10	No	USFS
WHITE RIVER	4,000	May-Sep	Yes	Yes	12	Yes	USFS
UPPER KERN RIVER							
FAIRVIEW	3,500	Apr-Oct	Yes	Yes	55	Yes	USFS
GOLDLEDGE	3,200	May-Sep	Yes	Yes	37	Yes	USFS
HOSPITAL FLAT	3,000	May-Sep	Yes	Yes	40	Yes	USFS

Note: Reservations at USFS and NPS sites, unless otherwise specified, can be made online at www.recreation.gov or by calling 1-877-444-6777.
* Located within the park.　　　　　‡ Group sites accommodate from 50 to 100 people. Consult reservation agency for specifics.

Dining Price Code

The price code for restaurants is based on the cost of one dinner, including entrée and appetizer (or entrée and desert) and a beverage. Tax and gratuities are not included.

Inexpensive	Up to $15
Moderate	$15 to $30
Expensive	$30 to $45
Very Expensive	Over $45

Three Rivers

A ramble-down, artsy-funky community of foothill cabins, second homes, ranches, and motels stretching for several miles along both sides of CA 198 (Sierra Drive), Three Rivers is home to what may or may not be the world's largest wood carving—of Paul Bunyan, of course. The South, Middle, and North forks of the Kaweah River come together here before backing up into the Army Corps of Engineers's storage reservoir at Lake Kaweah. Before the 1850s some two thousand Yokut and Monache Indians are supposed to have made their living in these valleys. As of the 2000 census the population of Three Rivers was 2,248—down nearly 600 from five years earlier—of which less than 1 percent were categorized as Native American. The grizzlies are gone, but the place still teems with wildlife: ground squirrels, tree squirrels, mule deer, opossums, raccoons, bobcats, mountain lions, black bear, coyotes, foxes, rattlesnakes, red-tail hawks, wild turkeys, turkey vultures, quail, bats, and scorpions. William Shatner and Anjelica Huston are said to own ranches in the surrounding foothills.

The first white settler, Hale D. Tharp, arrived and started ranching cattle and hogs in 1856 (eventually claiming summer pastures amid the giant sequoias at Crescent Meadow). From 1866 to 1891 an ambitious colony of socialists, known as the Kaweah Co-operative Commonwealth, maintained its headquarters and post office along the North Fork—until their timber claims were denied and a national park declared where they had already built a road and a mill. In the early 1900s, in the wake of the Boer Wars, a handful of Rhodesian pioneers and British scouts are said to have built ranches here, the countryside perhaps reminding them of the Transvaal. The Hare Krishnas ran a boarding school here until the mid-1980s.

Most of the settlement of Three Rivers sits at about 800 feet in elevation. Summer temperatures frequently reach the high 90s to low 100s—a record-setting 118 degrees was recorded at Ash Mountain in July 2007—toasting the grass, testing the fortitude of radiator hoses, and generally making passers-through anxious to jump in rivers or push up into the high country. With winter rains the Kaweah booms, the hills turn back to a shocking hue of Irish green, and the town goes sleepy. The blooming of redbuds in early spring and the subsequent return of swallows to Pumpkin Hollow Bridge are spectacles worth traveling for. Basic tourist services, gas, grocery, crafts, curios, good coffee, sandwiches, home-crafted chocolate, and sit-down dining are available year-round.

Lodging

Three Rivers boasts motels, cabin resorts, and chalets of varying style and utility, franchise to funky—the best within earshot of the river. During peak season, great hordes of Sequoia-bound travelers cycle in and out of the 103 rooms at the **Comfort Inn & Suites** (40820 Sierra Drive; 1-866-875-8456; moderate), where amenities include satellite TV, wireless Internet, in-room coffeemakers, and ironing equipment, plus a daily complement of breakfast cereals and pour-it-yourself waffles. Quieter, lazier, and more in tune with its surroundings is the **Lazy J Ranch Motel** (39625 Sierra Drive; 1-800-341-8000, 209-561-4449; moderate) on the south side of town, with its spacious rooms and stand-alone brick cottages overlooking the lawn and swimming pool. Porches come equipped with plastic chairs. For more uncommon accommodations and/or better access to the river, consider the **Buckeye Tree Lodge,** the **Sequoia Village Inn,** or the **Lake Elowin Resort,** on the north end of town.

Lake Elowin Resort

www.lake-elowin.com
43840 Dineley Drive
Elevation: 850 feet
Open: Year-round
559-561-3460
Owner: Milton Melkonian
Price: Moderate to Very Expensive
Pets: No
Wheelchair Access: Coming soon
Internet Access: No

After several hours in the presence of a golden Buddha—in Thailand, in 1976—resort owner Milton Melkonian had a vision: When he got home he bought the Lake Elowin Resort. Old Herb Wilson had built the place back in the 1920s, on the site of a watering hole where his Potwisha ancestors had used to camp. Milton has worked hard to upgrade most of the cabins

Lake Elowin Resort

with knotty-pine paneling, wood floors, and modern kitchens. Peace and quiet abound to such a degree that Milt's famous friends from Hollywood and Nashville come here to get work done. The script for *Thelma and Louise* was finished in Cabin 2. The landscaping—periwinkle, pomegranate, citrus and banana, tall cedars, terraced lawns, and lily pads—all irrigated by two miner's inches of deeded flume water (by Milton's calculation, 64,000 gallons a day), is positively lush, especially in the dry heat of August. The "lake" is an artificial sandy-bottom pond, meticulously drained and aerated to keep the water just right for swimming in. A private trail leads down to the river. Barbecues, coffee percolators, and kitchen implements provided. No phones, TVs, radios, or car alarms. No smoking. Bring your own lawn chairs.

Buckeye Tree Lodge
www.buckeyetree.com
46000 Sierra Drive
Elevation: 1,300 feet
Open: Year-round
559-561-5900
Owners: Dennis and Stacie Villavicencio
Price: Moderate
Pets: Yes
Wheelchair Access: Yes
Internet Access: Free wireless (via satellite)

When Dennis Villavicencio left San Diego (and a career in securities law) to come home to Three Rivers, he thought he'd have more time to ride his bike. In 2005 he bought the Sequoia Village Inn (see below) and started fixing it up, and when the Buckeye—the old postwar motor lodge across the street—came up for sale, he couldn't help but buy that, too. The draw here is the river frontage: the spectacular jumble of boulders at the confluence of the Middle and East Forks, the swimming holes and kayaking run, the grassy lawn, the shade of native sycamores. Rooms are basic

but feature porch and patio views across the canyon. The Ash Mountain Entrance is a quarter mile up the road, and the Gateway Restaurant is next door. There's a bikeable trail from here to Mineral King, but with busy summers and an ongoing overhaul of rooms during the off season, Dennis's fleet of bikes still mostly gathers dust. "Little by little," he says. Amenities include swimming pool, barbecues, picnic tables, in-room refrigerators, and free long-distance telephone service. Larger kitchenette unit and private cottage also available.

Sequoia Village Inn
www.sequoiavillageinn.com
45971 Sierra Drive
Elevation: 1,300 feet
Open: Year-round
559-561-3652
Owners: Dennis and Stacie Villavicencio
Price: Moderate to Expensive
Pets: Yes
Wheelchair Access: Yes
Internet Access: Free wireless in some units

Across the road from the Buckeye and the Gateway sits this eclectic collection of newly renovated chalets and cottages. The local Indians used to make camp here among the oak trees. An ancient footpath still leads from here into what is now the national park. Today, a variety of lodging configurations is available for parties from 2 to 12 people. Appointments in some units include knotty-pine ceilings, bamboo floors, fireplaces, kitchens or kitchenettes, granite countertops, flat-screen TVs, VCRs, and private decks with gas barbecues. Note Stacie's folksy tile mosaics and Dennis's illustrative framed snapshots of the high country. Each room features a selection of teas, a coffeemaker, and an assortment of French roast beans and a grinder. "Rustic luxury," Dennis explains, "if there is such a thing." Lounging by the pool, with a plastic cup of wine and the alpenglow dying across the canyon, one begins to see what he means.

Dining

Serrano's (40869 Sierra Drive; 559-561-7283; inexpensive to moderate). Gulf-style Mexican food served on a pleasant patio amid the squawking of birds. Highly respectable *pollo en mole,* seafood cocktails, and stuffed red snapper. Tortillas and chips prepared fresh on the premises. Beer and wine only. Open for lunch and dinner daily.

We Three Bakery/Café (43370 Sierra Drive; 559-561-4761; inexpensive). Craig Chavez and his sisters started this highly popular eatery in 1979 as a sideline to a career in the kitchens of the California state correctional system. Today Craig's nieces run the place while he and his wife commute to real-world jobs at Avenal Prison. Robert Blakely is supposed to have eaten here the week before the murder of his wife, and no wonder—everyone eats here. The Chavez family serves the best breakfast in town, bar none. If you can commandeer a spot, sit out on the patio in the shade of the ancient oak tree. Enjoy generously stuffed omelets, quartered potatoes, locally harvested fresh fruit, and raspberry-cheese cinnamon rolls. The baked items are so delectable that local rangers have reportedly used them to bring problem bears into custody. Healthy sack lunches available for those heading up into the hills. Breakfast and lunch. Closed Tuesday.

Gateway Restaurant (45978 Sierra Drive; 559-561-4133; www.gateway-sequoia.com; expensive). Classic American fine dining of the steak/soup or salad/baked potato school. Red tablecloths, stemware, candles, and the locals' favorite tableside view of the Kaweah. Deviations into melted-cheese broccoli and gravyesque red wine sauces are delicious, and the twice-baked stuffed potato is a highlight. Safest bet may be the $12 burger and a cold Sierra Nevada. Last full-service bar before the park.

Taverns, Saloons & Roadhouses

Riverview Restaurant & Lounge (42323 Sierra Drive; 559-561-2211; inexpensive). Favorite watering hole of local artists, bikers, and park rangers on shore leave. Basic burgers, fries, and the like served on the patio overlooking the river. Live music four nights a week.

Food & Beverage Purveyors

COFFEE, ETC.

3 Rivers Cyber Café (41763 Sierra Drive; 559-561-4165; www.3riverscyber cafe.com). Computer terminals, wireless Internet, business center, and espresso bar.

Note: The once-charming riverside java room, intellectual hub, and patio briefly known as **Nectar Java & Juice** (42251 Sierra Drive), formerly known as the Cabin, with its impressive selection of trashy used paperbacks, is expected to reopen sometime in the future under new guise and new ownership. Stop in if it's open.

GROCERIES

Three Rivers Village Market (40869 Sierra Drive; 559-561-4441). The only full grocery store this side of Visalia. Decent produce, deli and meat counter, basic wine and liquor selection, beer, ice, bread, Ben & Jerry's, and charcoal.

SANDWICHES & SUCH

Anne Lang's Emporium (41651 Sierra Drive; 559-561-4937; www.threerivers .com/AnneLang.htm). Old-fashioned soda fountain, wide selection of bulk teas and coffee beans, homemade soups, salads, and sandwiches. Take lunch to go or eat on the deck over the river. Espresso, full-service flower shop, and notary.

Sierra Subs & Salads (41717 Sierra Drive;

559-561-4810). Best grilled sandwiches on the western slope. Try the Alta Peak Club, the Manzanita Melt, or the Tokopah Turkey. Fresh fruit smoothies, salads, and healthy box lunches available for picnics in the high country. Oh, and subs, too. Open for lunch and dinner daily.

Sweets

Reimer's Candies & Gifts (42375 Sierra Drive; 1-866-766-2263; www.reimerscandies .com). "Every man who finds the time long and the atmosphere difficult to bear," wrote 18th-century French epicure Brillat-Savarin, "should comfort himself with a chocolate." Properly prepared and in its darkest form, this classic Mesoamerican delicacy has been shown to be an effective antidepressant, producing some of the same effects on the brain as heroin and cannabis. It may also help combat cholesterol, high blood pressure, hypertension, coughing, diarrhea—even altitude sickness. The Aztecs found that a man could walk all day with nothing but a piece of chocolate. At Reimer's, amid high patriotism, cuckoo clocks, and nutcrackers, the stuff is as real as it gets. There's also peanut brittle, toffee, licorice, home-made ice cream—in a riverside setting all dressed up like a Bavarian teahouse. How can you not?

Books, Maps & Information

Foothills/Ash Mountain Visitor Center (47050 Generals Highway; 559-565-3135). This is Park Service headquarters for all of Sequoia–Kings Canyon. Displays and exhibits provide an introduction to the oak woodlands and wild chaparral of the Sierra Nevada Foothills, one of the most diverse—and increasingly endangered—ecosystems in North America. The bookstore, run by the venerable nonprofit **Sequoia Natural History Association** (559-565-3759; www.sequoiahistory.org), consists of a thorough selection of titles on the cultural and natural history of the Sierra. A range of guidebooks, maps, bear canister rental, and Crystal Cave tickets are also available, as well as wilderness permits. Open 8–5 in summer; 8–4:30 after mid-November.

Shopping

Galleries

Cort Gallery (41881 Sierra; 559-561-4036). Contemporary loft-style gallery space beside the river, designed by owner/architect Gary Cort. Rotating exhibits, dance and yoga classes, drum circles, lectures, and performances.

Sundries & Souvenirs

Sequoia Gifts & Souvenirs (41727 Sierra Drive; 559-561-3488; www.sequoiagifts.com). Souvenir mugs, coasters, T-shirts, chocolates, handcrafted candles, greeting cards, and a variety of bear-themed items for the halfhearted placation of relatives left at home. Shipping and office services also available.

General Stores

Kaweah General Store (40462 Sierra Drive; 559-561-3475). Features a variety of unique things, including a selection of hunting and fishing supplies, fish and game licenses, hardware, and basic groceries.

Three Rivers Mercantile (41152 Sierra Drive; 559-561-2378). Big-franchise hardware store in a metal building. Coleman-style camping equipment, bait-fishing supplies, and fish and game licenses.

Points of Interest

Three Rivers Historical Museum (42268 Sierra Drive; 559-561-2707). Look for the 17-foot-tall Paul Bunyan, carved in 1941–42—probably in Porterville—from a single 2,000-year-old giant sequoia. The "museum," run by the local chamber of commerce, houses a spare and eclectic collection of artifacts, books, and old photos. It gives a bit of flavor of the earlier days in Three Rivers. Highlights include a mountain lion pelt (with head) and a pile of news clippings on Disney's now-historic attempts to develop Mineral King.

Kaweah Colony Post Office (43795 North Fork Drive; 559-561-4745). The Kaweah Post Office was built in 1890 to handle mail for the burgeoning utopian settlement of Advance. The colony collapsed a year later. In 1910 the diminutive structure, complete with the original service window and brass P.O. boxes, was moved—probably by wagon—to its present location in the sleepy hamlet of Kaweah (population 480). In 1948 it was designated a California Historical Landmark and is now one of the smallest operating post offices in the United States.

Ash Mountain Entrance. Pay the fee and get park map and newspaper here. Up the road, appreciate the ethnic confusion (if not the artistry) manifest in the historic Sequoia National Park sign, handcarved in the 1930s by an anonymous Civilian Conservation Corps member from Arkansas. The Indian head was apparently patterned after the one on the old buffalo nickel, which figure, in turn, is supposed to have been a composite portrait of

Kaweah Colony Post Office

various Plains Indian chiefs. The word *sequoia*—the name given to the Big Tree, and then the park—is generally considered to have been a 19th-century botanist's tribute to a half-German, half-Cherokee, Appalachian silversmith by the name of Sequoyah, or George Guess (or Gist), generally known for having invented, in his workshop 3,000 miles from the nearest Big Tree, the first practical syllabary for the Cherokee language.

Hospital Rock Picnic Area. Ancestors of the Monache Indians were enjoying the shade and water here a hundred years before Columbus was born. By 1873, when a certain James Everton is said to have recovered here from a shotgun wound inflicted by a jury-rigged bear trap, the Monache were gone. Pictographs and acorn-grinding rocks remain as evidence of their tenure.

MINERAL KING

Climbing its sinuous way up along the East Fork of the Kaweah, through a full range of ecosystems (from chaparral to giant sequoia groves and broad subalpine meadows), the Mineral King Road is a genuine feat of engineering—especially considering much of it was built during a brief and failed series of mining booms in the 1870s. Don't be fooled by the sign at the junction on the north end of Three Rivers proclaiming 25 MILES TO GO. These are likely to rank among the longest 25 miles you've ever traveled on pavement—or mostly on pavement (allow up to an hour and a half from Three Rivers). The prominent peak to the east, at the head of the valley, is called Sawtooth (12,343 feet).

The current roadway was completed in 1915 to provide access to private summer cottages. Leases to these cottages, six or seven generations later, are still held by the descendants of those who built them—and cannot legally be sold or transferred outside the family. In 1926 Mineral King was declared a National Game Refuge. Forty years later, in January 1966, Walt Disney Productions signed a multiple-use contract with the U.S. Forest Service to establish a major downhill ski resort in White Chief Bowl, with fourteen ski lifts, two large hotels, and a parking garage for 2,500 vehicles. A 13-year-long legal and public-relations battle ensued, ending in 1978 with the defeat of the project and the annexation of Mineral King to Sequoia National Park. In October 2003 the collection of 66 off-grid summer cabins were promoted from Cultural Landscape District to an official listing on the National Register of Historic Places.

Note: There is no gasoline available in Mineral King. The road is open only from late spring to the first major snowfall. In winter the coveted bowls first touted by U.S. Ski Team coach Alf Engen in 1946 are accessible only to those on backcountry skis or snowshoes.

Lodging

Silver City Resort
www.silvercityresort.com
21 miles up Mineral King Road
Elevation: 7,000 feet
Open: Late May–early October
559-561-3223 (in season); 805-461-3223 (winter)
Owners: Connie and Norman Pillsbury

Price: Inexpensive to Moderate
Pets: Yes
Wheelchair Access: Yes
Internet Access: Wireless in the newer "Swiss chalets"

If you don't happen to have close ties with one of the original 66 families, your only choice for roofed accommodations in Mineral King is the Silver City Resort. Luckily, it's a great choice. For a true frontier experience, try a night or two in one of the 1930s-vintage "rustic cabins," today appointed with propane lamps, antique quilts, camp kitchens, barbecues, and cold running water. Fall asleep to the sound of the creek through knotholes in the siding. "Comfy cabins" have refrigerators, hot and cold running water, and toilets. For the latest in suburban comforts—laminate floors, composite decking, lofty ceilings, and wireless Internet, opt for the palatial new Salzburg Chalet. If you plan to stay more than one night—or if you're coming up on Tuesday or Wednesday (when the restaurant is closed)—bring groceries and cook for yourself. Children's playground, picnic tables, Ping-Pong, horsehoes, and hammocks.

Dining

Silver City Restaurant & Bakery (559-561-3223; www.silvercityresort.com; inexpensive). Copious breakfasts, burgers, salads, and tuna sandwiches served family style on red and white vinyl tablecloths and knotty pine benches (or out on the porch when the sun is warm), 8–8 Thursday through Monday. Bring your own bottle of wine. Root beer floats and the best homemade pie on the western slope of the Sierra Nevada. Dinner specials on weekends. Restaurant closed for meals on Tuesday and Wednesday; pie and coffee served seven days, all summer long.

Books, Maps & Information

Mineral King Ranger Station (559-565-3768). Books, maps, wilderness permits, first aid, and bear canister rental at 7,580 feet. Ranger Len is the go-to guy for practical information on the region: trail conditions, geology, flora and fauna, local lore. Open 8–4:30 daily, June through early September.

General Stores

Silver City General Store (559-561-3223; www.silvercityresort.com). Books, maps, souvenirs, bug spray, sunscreen, toilet paper, T-shirts, canned goods, marshmallows, marmot wire rental, and transmission oil cooler hose. No fresh food, beer, wine, liquor, or dairy products. No ice or gasoline.

Points of Interest

Atwell Mill & Skinner Grove. The old Hockett Trail, built in the 1860s as a

Cabin and sequoia stump, Atwell Mill, Mineral King Road Burke Griggs

Honeymoon Point Cabin, Mineral King Burke Griggs

resupply route from Visalia to Fort Independence and the Owens Valley, passes through here. The grove contains some of the highest old-growth sequoias in the Sierra, in elevation. Kaweah colonists leased and partially logged the area in the early 1890s, after the creation of the national park, before a series of heated exchanges with the U.S. cavalry finally persuaded them to abandon the operation. Of their efforts a steam engine and numerous big stumps remain. Lumber from this mill was used to build the flume to Mount Whitney Power Company's Kaweah Power House No. 1. **Honeymoon Point Cabin** (across the street from the stables; no phone; www.mineralking.org). The old Crowley Resort, established in 1895, once boasted, according to local historian Louise Jackson, "a hotel, store, post office, butcher shop, stable, dance hall, and more than a dozen rental cabins." The place took a big hit in the San Francisco Earthquake of 1906, rebuilt, and took its final blow by avalanche in 1969. This cabin survived and is today a humble museum maintained by the Mineral King Preservation Society.

Watermelon Snow

Patches of reddish-pink snow on lingering High Sierra snowfields, known as "watermelon snow," are made by colonies of *chlamydomas nivalis*, or "snow algae." Some say the stuff tastes like watermelon, but the Park Service says: Don't eat it.

The Generals Highway & High-Country Sequoia

In just under 16 miles, between the Ash Mountain Entrance and the Giant Forest, the Generals Highway climbs more than 6,000 feet in elevation to reach the largest sequoia groves in the world. The Mount Whitney Power Company built the first section, from Ash Mountain to Hospital Rock, in 1898 as a service road for its flume along the East Fork of the Kaweah. The flume is still visible on the opposite side of the river. The section from Hospital rock to the Giant Forest was completed in 1926, replacing the old Colony Mill Road as the main access route into the park's high country. The Civilian Conservation Corps came on board in the 1930s, adding a second lane, excavating so-called Tunnel Rock, building watering stations and native-stone guard walls, and extending the roadway—then called the Park-to-Park Highway—as far as Grant Grove. In 2006 work began on the road's first major overhaul in 70 years. The project involves resurfacing, widening certain sections, restoring historic structures, and burying utility lines. According to the Park Service, "the curves and scenery will remain." Bring folding chairs and a picnic in case of lengthy delay.

Lodging

✪ Bearpaw High Sierra Camp

www.visitsequoia.com
11.5-mile hike from Crescent Meadow on
High Sierra Trail
Elevation: 7,800 feet
Open: June–September
1-866-807-3598
Hosts: Carolyn Pistilli and Delaware North
Company
Price: Very Expensive (but includes two
meals)
Pets: No
Wheelchair Access: No
Internet Access: No

Bearpaw was originally established as a
crew camp for the construction of the High
Sierra Trail between Crescent Meadow and
the Kaweah Gap (on the way to Mount
Whitney). The trail itself, a marvel of pick-
and-dynamite engineering completed in
1931, is considered the first in the Sierra
built for strictly recreational purposes. A
handful of wood-platform tent cabins and a
canvas-sided lodge were first opened to the
public as a High Sierra Camp in 1934.
Today, with its wood-fired hot showers; its
timeless, weather-beaten front porch; its
unparalleled views of the Great Western
Divide; and its generally precarious perch
far above the headwaters of the Kaweah,
Bearpaw is in a league of its own—even
compared with its more famous cousins
in Yosemite. Towels, linens, kerosene
lamps, and down comforters are provided. Reservations fill up on a first-
come, first-served basis starting at 7 AM
on January 2 of each year, but cancellations do happen. Plan at least two nights
here—to allow a day of leisure, perusal of
the camp's vintage lending library, and
general exploration in the backcountry.
Swimming holes and glacial lakes
abound.

✪ Pear Lake Ski Hut

www.sequoiahistory.org
6 miles and 2,000 feet above Wolverton
Meadow
Elevation: 9,200 feet
Open: December–May (weather permit-
ting)
559-565-3759
Hutkeeper: Chris Miles
Price: Inexpensive
Pets: No
Wheelchair Access: No
Internet Access: No

Over the summers between 1939 and 1941,
the Civilian Conservation Corps built this
classic A-frame chalet of local timber and
granite. One of the last examples of true
rustic architecture in the parks, it is also,
according to park historian William Tweed
(et al.), "one of the most environmentally
successful alpine structures ever designed
by the NPS." In summer the building does
time as a ranger station. In winter and early
spring, surrounded as it is by thousands of
acres of snowbound terrain—gentle bowls,
glades, chutes, high ridgelines, and peaks
over 11,000 feet with big views to the Great
Western Divide—the place is paradise for
snowshoers and backcountry skiers.
Sunsets from the front porch go on forever.
Meals tend to be gourmet communal
affairs (pack creatively; bring better than

Front yard of Pear Lake Ski Hut, March 2007

freeze-dried), with impromptu live music, storytelling, and deep snores around the pellet stove. Hut sleeps 10. Check the Web site for details and equipment list. Reservations by lottery, held in November, or check the calendar for openings. Plan for at least two nights. The approach is no stroll in the park, but as hard as it is to get here, it's much harder to leave.

Wuksachi Lodge
www.visitsequoia.com
64740 Wuksachi Way (off Generals Highway)
Elevation: 7,200 feet
Open: Year-round
1-866-807-3598
Innkeeper: Delaware North Company
Price: Moderate to Very Expensive
Pets: No
Wheelchair Access: Yes
Internet Access: Dataports/wireless in lodge

As the last ramshackle cabins in the old Giant Forest Village were being hauled off and made to disappear (see Points of Interest), ground was broken on the next generation of lodging in Sequoia National Park. Opened in 1999, the Wuksachi Village—10 miles north of Giant Forest and 4 miles north of Lodgepole—consists of a series of detached motel-style buildings (walking distance from the parking lot) and a lodge of rather grand scale (also at some remove) for dining (see Dining). It's really nothing like a village, but, well, it's all there is. Rooms are modern, quiet, and spacious, done up with natural wood accents, comfortable beds, overstuffed armchairs, aluminum sliders, and a vaguely Southwestern motif that you'll recognize at other DNC properties (e.g., the Yosemite Lodge). There's an easy hiking trail from here to Lodgepole and occasional fireside activities in the evenings, but the impulse at the beginning of the day is still to get in one's car and drive—somewhere else. Maybe one day they'll build a bike path à la Yosemite, and the place won't feel quite so disconnected. The new shuttle, which drops by every 30 minutes in summer, seems a step in the right direction.

Montecito Lake Resort
(formerly the Montecito-Sequoia Lodge)
www.mslodge.com
63410 Generals Highway, Sequoia National Monument
Elevation: 7,500 feet
Open: Year-round
1-800-227-9900 (reservations);
1-800-843-8677 (front desk)
Owners: the Dally family
Price: Moderate to Expensive (package rates)
Pets: No
Wheelchair Access: Limited
Internet Access: Wireless in lodge

If you ever wish you could go back to the glory days of summer camp, or if you never went and always wish you had, here's your chance: Pack the troop into the minivan and head for Lake Homovalo. Weeklong "summer family camp" packages include three meals a day, utilitarian lodging dating back to the early 1940s, and a profusion of activities for kids *and* adults: archery, tennis, kayaking, horseback riding, hiking, mountain biking, fencing, yoga, trampoline, gymnastics, and more. Hook your toddler up with a morning in the play yard while you go waterskiing. Let the surly teen learn horse whispering while you lounge by the pool with the latest best-selling confessional memoir. Variety shows, night hikes, and, of course, campfire sing-alongs. Full bar, Starbucks coffee, and copious buffet-style meals. Mini-week summer sessions and Saturday-night-only rates also available. Winter brings cross-country skiing, sledding, dogsled rides, and ice skating. New ownership, as of January 2007, promises lots more of the same—plus a significant investment in upgrades to the physical plant.

Big Meadows Guard Station

www.fs.fed.us/r5/sequoia/recreation/rec_r
entals/big_meadows.html;
www.reserveamerica.com (reservations)
Big Meadows Road, Giant Sequoia National
Monument
Elevation: 7,600 feet
Open: June–October (weather permitting)
1-877-444-6777
Management: U.S. Forest Service
(559-338-2251)
Price: Moderate (Inexpensive for groups)
Pets: Not inside
Wheelchair Access: Limited
Internet Access: No

Built in the mid-1930s (by the CCC) to house
fire crews in the wide-open country between
Kings Canyon and the northern edge of
Sequoia National Park, the Big Meadows
Guard Station is within convenient striking
distance of all major points of interest in
both parks. It's also far enough off the beaten
path to give one the sense of having the whole
place to oneself. Bathroom, kitchen, pots,
pans, utensils, miscellaneous cleaning supplies, refrigerator, woodstove, living room
with pull-out couch, bedroom stuffed with
beds, desk. Sleeps six inside, with plenty of
room to pitch tents in the yard. A stay here
requires a bit more self-reliance than at a
concessionaire-serviced cabin—as well as all
the requisite leave-no-trace-style cleanup on
the back end—but the payoff is savoring one's
own home-cooked meal on a porch overlooking one's very own meadow. And after
breakfast in the morning, you can stroll or
ride a mountain bike on miles of dirt track.
Bring your own bedding, towels, food and
beverages, toilet paper, and firewood.

The Sequoia High Sierra Camp

www.sequoiahighsierracamp.com
Off Marvin Pass trail
Elevation: 8,500 feet
Open: June–September
1-866-654-2877

Owners: Burr and Suzanne Hughes
Price: Very Expensive (all meals included)
Pets: No
Wheelchair Access: No
Internet Access: No

This recently inaugurated "tent hotel" may
lack the historic charm of Bearpaw, but
neither is it so arduous to get to. (You can
bounce a low-slung hybrid to road's end;
the camp staff, upon request, is happy to
hump your gear the final mile from trailhead to tent-bungalow.) Nor does it require
such advance planning to get reservations
(yet). Terraced into a sloping grove of red
fir and ponderosa, with hazy sunset views
across the distant rim of Kings Canyon, the
deep sound of wilderness all around, and
the best and most elaborate food on the
west side of the Sierra (see Dining), this is
the sort of place one might feel inclined to
settle into for a few days (if only to contem-
plate the aesthetics of crown molding in a
pipe-frame tent). Hikes to Mitchell Peak,
Seville Lake, and the Silliman Crest are
among the emptiest in the parks—if you can
bring yourself to hit the trail after a thick
slab of New Orleans–style French toast. For
maximum appreciation of such luxuries as
hot showers, feather beds, and a purist's
Caesar salad, consider walking here from
Lodgepole (11 miles) or Cedar Grove (8
miles). Return shuttles can be arranged.

Dining

✪ **Bearpaw High Sierra Camp** (meals for
camp guests only). Late afternoon brings
lemonade and brownies on the porch, and
the faint wafting of bluegrass from the
solar-powered satellite radio in the
kitchen. At 5:30 the call to dinner comes in
the form of a cast-iron skillet rung with a
metal spoon. If you're hiking in, be sure to
leave the trailhead early enough that you
make camp by dinner. One recent evening's
fare included a layered asparagus salad,
white pizza, "collapsed" tomatoes, pork

View from Bearpaw High Sierra Camp

tenderloin, and organic white bean "goop" with roasted garlic and fresh rosemary—all ingredients hauled in by mule—followed by camp-crafted chocolate ice cream, boxed red wine, ceramic-filtered spring water, and the rising and fading of alpenglow on granite. Sack lunches available for a modest fee.

○ **Montecito-Sequoia Lodge** (at the Montecito Lake resort; 1-800-843-8677; www.mslodge.com; moderate). The atmosphere is pure summer camp, with banged-up eight-top tables, aluminum folding chairs, and the general mayhem of kids on vacation in the woods, but the food—buffet-style vats of veggie lasagna, chicken cordon bleu, rice pilaf, baby-green salads, mashed potatoes, and such—is some of the best and healthiest in the parks. Milk, juice, and Sierra Nevada on tap. Homemade desserts and breakfasts to last through a full day of adventure. Dining hall open to the public year-round. Call ahead for mealtimes.

Dining Room at the Wuksachi (64740 Wuksachi Way; 1-866-807-3598; www.visitsequoia.com; expensive). With its lofty post-and-beam construction, its stone fireplace, and retro mission-style furnishings, the Wuksachi aims for the grandeur of national parks lodges of bygone days, but it can't quite mask its contempo corporate-generic heritage. Alas, it's still the best

(read: only) place around to enjoy a snifter of Armagnac and check one's e-mail in view of the Silliman Crest. The staff has considerably less of that banished-to-the-gulag aspect one finds farther down the road in Kings Canyon. The cocktails are honest; the wine list perfectly respectable; the food—dubbed "Sierra Alpine" Cuisine—will bring the trail-weary traveler right back to the present, whether he/she has just skied down from Alta Peak or spent the afternoon riding the tailgate of a rented recreational vehicle. Imagine spring greens with prosciutto and feta, sweet potato chile soup, trout Piccata with baby bok choy (or, okay, filet mignon), and a tablet of triple-fudge cake in a puddle of strawberry sauce. Good acoustics help toe the line between family-friendly and civilized. Reservations recommended. Decent breakfast buffet.

○ **The Sequoia High Sierra Camp** (1-866-654-2877; www.sequoiahighsierracamp.com; meals for camp guests only). Opened in 2006 under the direction of executive chef Ryan Solein—onetime personal chef to Bruce Springsteen, Tool, Faith Hill, and Tim McGraw—this is surely one of the most remote outposts in the world to offer such eclectic and elevated fare as cauliflower and Brie soup dressed with truffle oil, osso bucco on a bed of chevre-mint risotto, and Sauternes-macerated strawberries over shortcake biscuits. Served in an impressive acropolis-style dining pavilion, on wrought-iron tables, with a campfire crackling beyond, and bats and jet trails in the sky, what you pay for here, what you make the schlep for, is the food. Here's hoping standards remain high through future seasons. Beer and wine available—or bring your own. Open June–September.

Wolverton Barbecue (Wolverton Meadows; moderate). All you can eat. Open every evening in summer. Tickets are available at Lodgepole Market or Wuksachi.

Books, Maps & Information

Beetle Rock Nature Center (across from Giant Forest Museum; 559-565-3081).
According to Hall's *Guide to Sequoia & General Grant National Parks* (1930), "the Rock was named in 1905 when a new species of beetle was there discovered by Ralph Hopping [the son], a Government entomologist." Today the center houses interactive children's exhibits from the old Walter Fry Nature Center, and it also serves as an education and conference center run by the Sequoia Natural History Museum. For sale are children's books, puppets, stuffed animals, and science kits. Open in summer.

Giant Forest Museum (559-565-4480). What was once the Giant Forest Market is now a beautifully tooled museum documenting the history of the Big Old Trees and their strange, historic interactions with man. The bookstore, run by the Sequoia Natural History Association, offers essentially the same excellent selection of books and maps as Ash Mountain and Lodgepole Visitors Centers.

Lodgepole Visitors Center (559-565-4436). A range of exhibits covers the natural and human history of the Southern Sierra. The movie *Bears of the Sierra* runs on a continuous loop in the theater. Books, maps, postcards, and souvenirs are for sale, and wilderness permits, first aid, and Crystal Cave tickets are also available. Open daily, early spring through late fall.

Shopping

GIFT SHOPS

Wuksachi Gift Shop (Wuksachi Lodge) has a small selection of books and souvenirs; Wuksachi and Sequoia logo wear; beer, wine, and soft drinks; and Native American–themed gifts. Open year-round.

GENERAL STORES

Lodgepole Market, Deli & Gift Shop (63024 Lodgepole Road, across from visitors center and post office; 559-565-3301). Built in 1975 as a means to pull the load away from the Giant Forest Village, it offers a half decent selection of beer, wine, picnic supplies, books, curios, phone cards, and outdoor equipment. Deli, pizza, and burgers across the hall. Charcoal and firewood. Ice, Laundromat, and showers. Closed in winter.

Stony Creek Village (11 miles north of Lodgepole). This basic convenience-style market and curio shop has the only modern gas pumps in the region.

Points of Interest

Giant Forest Ex-Village. "This part of the Sequoia belt seemed to me the finest," wrote John Muir, "and I then named it 'the Giant Forest.'" By the 1930s, with the completion and subsequent improvement of the Generals Highway, the grove became the hub of activity in the park. The Giant Forest Village eventually consisted of "four campgrounds, dozens of parking lots, a garbage incinerator, water and sewage systems, a gas station, corrals, and over 200 cabin, tent-top, dining, office, retail, and bath-house structures." In the 1970s,

Moro Rock: On a clear day you can see the Coast Range.
Burke Griggs

with annual park visitation numbers more than a million, the gas station, post office, and campgrounds were transferred to the Lodgepole area. Full restoration of the groves and meadows began in 1997 with the painstaking removal of all remaining facilities save the market and general store building (now the museum). Open year-round.

Moro Rock–Crescent Meadow Road. This worthwhile side road from the Giant Forest is now also serviced by a free shuttle. The original wooden stairs to the top of Moro Rock, built in 1917, were replaced with a stone stairway in 1931. Handrails were added by a CCC crew in 1933. In December 1937 an unnamed sequoia fell across the road, prompting the cutting of a tunnel through the log the following summer. Farther on is the parking lot for the High Sierra Trail, Crescent Meadow, and Hale Tharp's unique summer cabin. John Muir met Mr. Tharp here in 1875, had supper, and spent several days at this "noble den in a fallen sequoia . . . weatherproof, earthquake-proof, likely to outlast the most durable stone castle, and commanding views of garden and grove grander far than the richest king ever enjoyed." Road closed in winter.

General Sherman Tree. This is the Big One: The world's most voluminous living thing. And it's still growing, at an incredibly rapid rate—likely the fastest of any tree on the planet. Every year the thing puts on about 40 cubic feet of new wood, as much as what makes up an entire 60-foot-tall Douglas fir. Imagine the number of toothpicks. Park at the lot off the Wolverton road and enjoy a leisurely paved stroll replete with world-class people-watching opportunities down into the grove (uphill on the way back). Near the bottom, note the cross-section of the General Sherman as represented on the pavement, with a surface area equivalent to that of 25 tournament-sized billiards tables. From the base of the tree itself, continue along the 2-mile Congress Trail (easy, paved) to various other named trees. If you'd prefer to do this in solitude, try during a snowstorm, at night, in the depth of winter.

Walter Fry Nature Center. Now closed due to apparent lack of interest. Many of its hands-on exhibits have been moved to the Beetle Rock Nature Center.

Crystal Cave (559-565-3759; www.sequoiahistory.org). One summer day in 1918, Walter Fry and another off-duty park ranger were scrambling down along Cascade Creek, wrestling their fly rods through thickets of poison oak, when one or the other stumbled upon the entrance to a cavern—with more than 3 miles of chambers and passageways,

How the Rest of the World Came to Learn of the Big Trees

Captain Walker and his men might be forgiven a degree of nonchalance when in the fall of 1833 they happened to be the first Europeans to see the biggest trees in the world. Having traveled some 1,200 miles across "poor, sandy country" from the Great Salt Lake, surviving mostly on buffalo jerky and rabbit, ever imagining themselves surrounded by hostile Indians (and in their anxiety shooting and killing scores of them), having then struggled for nearly four weeks across some of the roughest terrain in the High Sierra, their horses worthless in "the cold and famished region of snow"—except, that is, for the caloric content of their flesh—these men had slightly more pressing things on their minds than the size of the local conifers. "It seemed to be the greatest cruelty," wrote Zenas Leonard, chronicler of the expedition, "to take your rifle, when your horse sinks to the ground from starvation, but still manifests a desire and willingness to follow you, to shoot him in the head and then cut him up & take such parts of their [sic] flesh as extreme hunger alone will render it possible for a human being to eat."

Leonard did make the first brief printed mention of "some trees of the Red-wood species, incredibly large—some of which would measure from 16 to 18 fathoms round the trunk at the height of a man's head from the ground." The Indians had for thousands of years been pretty well versed in the great variety of local trees. In reference to the species we now call the giant sequoia (*sequoiadendron gigantea*) the Tules are supposed to have made sounds along the lines of *Toos-pung-ish* and *Hea-mi-withic*. The Southern Miwok word *Wa-wona* has been described variously as the word for "owl," or "guardian of the big trees," or simply "big trees." It took some years, however, before European-Americans—generally preferring to discover things for themselves—began listening to the natives. Two copies of Leonard's narrative survived a printing-shop fire in Pennsylvania in 1839. News of the big trees failed to spread.

Frémont had passed without undue pause beneath "some trees extremely large" in 1846, probably on the North Fork of the Kings. A less renowned pioneer by the name of J. M. Wooster may indeed, in 1850 (as he later claimed), have carved his moniker into the flank of a giant sequoia. But it was Augustus T. Dowd, Union Water Company employee from Murphy's, who started the real publicity storm. In 1852, on his way up the North Fork of the Stanislaus after a wounded bear, Dowd found himself suddenly face to face with the biggest living thing he'd ever seen. He went back to camp and told everyone who would listen—including the press. There seems to be no record of what happened to the bear.

Within a year, Dowd's "Discovery Tree" was felled, sawed into pieces, and shipped back to New York for exhibition. It took "five men twenty-two days" to bring it down, "drilling by pump augurs through to the center from opposite sides." Its stump of it was used as a dance floor. The stump of another served time as a two-lane bowling alley. Other specimens had their bark stripped off, were marked in sections, and then were reassembled as far away as Chicago and London. Seeds were carried back eastward and planted, such that today there are individual sequoias dwarfing the local flora in Pennsylvania, Switzerland, Croatia, and New Zealand.

July 4th festivities, 1854

A COTILLION PARTY OF THIRTY-TWO PERSONS DANCING ON THE STUMP OF THE MAMMOTH TREE.

Buck Rock Lookout, Kings Canyon beyond

home to four or five unique species of invertebrate. "It is in this cave," wrote Fry, "that nature has lavishly traced her design in decorative glory." Of some two hundred such caverns in Sequoia-Kings, Crystal and Boyden are the only two open to the public. The CCC built the pathway, rails, and stairs in 1939. The trail inside the cavern was paved in 1985 to keep dust from inhibiting the formation of crystals. Bathrooms were removed from within the cave's entrance in 2000. Forty-five-minute guided tours are offered throughout the summer; tickets are available only at Lodgepole or Ash Mountain Visitors Centers. Allow an hour and a half from the Giant Forest to the cave's entrance, and wear layers and practical shoes. "Wild cave tours" are available every Saturday in summer.

✪ **Buck Rock Lookout** (559-336-9319; www.buckrock.org). A telephone line was strung from Pinehurst to a fire-lookout platform on Buck Rock in 1914. The current wooden structure, built in 1923, is one of only three 4A-style cabs in existence today. The insane hanging stairway was built in 1942. Starting in 1997, after years of neglect, Kathy Ball and the nonprofit Buck Rock Foundation brought the lookout back into service. Access is via jeep trail—a nice day hike or horseback ride—from the Big Meadows Road. On a rare clear day the 360-degree views cover the whole of the country from the Monarch Divide to the Grapevine, from the Silliman Crest to the Coast Range. Open to the public 9:30–6:30 in summer. Interpretive and environmental education programs on Friday evenings in summer.

Redwood Mountain Grove (Kings Canyon National Park). The overlook on the south side of the Generals Highway, smog permitting, provides a rare overview of this largest grove of giant sequoias on the planet, with more than 2,100 big trees in 5 square miles. To lose oneself therein, descend the poorly marked dirt road opposite Quail Flat and the Hume Lake Road to the Redwood Canyon trailhead.

How Old Are the Big Trees?

Counting rings on the largest stump he could find in 1875 (in the Converse Basin), Muir "made a little over four thousand without difficulty or doubt," thus placing the specimen's earliest years as a sapling sometime before the Amorite conquest of Ur, before the building of Stonehenge—more than a thousand years before the founding of Rome.

Sequoias do not die of old age or disease, Muir noted, but simply, finally, of toppling over. That they do not reach the towering height of their generally younger cousins, the coastal redwoods (*sequoia sempervivens*), is perhaps not so much the result of any genetic deficiency as it is of circumstance: the Big Trees poking their crowns, as they do, into prevailing winds and electrical storms at elevations up to 8,000 feet. "It is a curious fact," wrote Muir, "that all very old sequoias have lost their heads by lightning. Of all living things it is perhaps the only one able to wait long enough to make sure of being struck."

Muir's record-holding ring count has never been confirmed. Future parks' superintendent Walter Fry is supposed to have spent five days with four buddies, sometime before 1912, sawing down a big sequoia and counting 3,266 rings on its stump. "Precise cross-dating of tree rings on cut stumps has shown that sequoias can reach at least 3,266 years in age," writes Nathan Stephenson of the current U.S. Geological Survey, "making sequoia the third longest-lived, non-clonal tree species known." The only trees older are the bristlecone pine (see chapter 4) and the alerce of South America.

The world's largest living thing, the General Sherman Tree, is considered "a mere teenager" at somewhere between 2,000 and 2,500 years old. On a list of the top 10 oldest tree species in the world, the western juniper and the foxtail pine, also found within the parks, are numbers 4 and 7 respectively.

Tree rings and how they relate to history

GRANT GROVE & THE KINGS CANYON SCENIC BYWAY

*In the vast Sierra wilderness to the southward of the famous Yosemite Valley
there is a yet grander valley of the same kind.*

—John Muir, 1891

On the holy day of Epiphany in 1805, Lt. Gabriel Moraga and a small band of Spanish sol-
diers and missionaries made camp on the lower banks of a river they called *El Río de los
Santos Reyes* (The River of the Holy Kings). "The river abounds with beaver and fish," wrote
Father Pedro Muñoz in his journal. He estimated the number of natives living along the
river to be more than five thousand. "It is a location suitable for a mission," he added,
"although there would also have to be a presidio."

Twenty-two years later, with no significant resistance from the natives, Jedediah Smith
and his crew harvested hundreds of pounds of beaver pelt along the lower stretches of the
Kings and may have attempted to penetrate some distance into the canyon itself. Of the
first white men to reach the head of the canyon there is no published account. Captain

Small road, big country: Kings Canyon Scenic Byway, Tehipite and Kings canyons   Burke Griggs

Kuykendall, of the southern detachment of Savage's Mariposa Battalion, came up the Kings in 1851, in pursuit of renegade Kaweahs. One of his men, also involved in the second expedition against Tenaya, remarked to a compatriot on that journey: "The King's river country [sic], and the territory southeast of it, beats the Yosemite in terrific grandeur, but in sublime beauty you have got us."

By the time John Muir wandered through, first in 1873 and twice again in 1875, the meadows here were already well used by sheepherders and San Joaquin Valley stockmen, and the old Indian trail along Bubbs Creek, over what is now Kearsarge Pass, was already a popular thoroughfare to the east side of the range.

The General Grant Grove was set aside in 1893 as General Grant National Park. Of the neighboring Converse Basin Grove—once the largest grove of giant sequoia in the world, not so protected as the General Grant—every Big Tree was cut down and hauled off save one: the Boole Tree.

On average, the annual number of visitors to Kings Canyon comes in at just over half that of Sequoia (in 2006 the numbers were 552,766 and 954,507 respectively). In terms of total acreage, Kings Canyon is just over 10 percent larger than Sequoia. The obvious result, of course, from the point of view of the traveler entering the northern park after a day or two in the southern one, is fewer people per acre: i.e., less crowding, less traffic, more peace and quiet—especially when one strikes out beyond the Grant Grove area and into the depths of Kings Canyon proper.

The road from Hume Lake Junction to Cedar Grove, now a designated National Scenic Byway (closed in winter due to rockfall), was completed in 1939. The best time to visit the canyon floor is in early spring when the road first opens, when the grasses are green, the flowers abundant, and the black flies absent. Or in midwinter, self-propelled.

Grant Grove Village, cooler in summer, under snow in winter, is open year-round.

Lodging

There is a considerable difference in the quality of services and facilities in Kings Canyon compared to those in Sequoia. Most of the concessions in Sequoia (other than in Mineral King or at the Sequoia High Sierra Camp) are operated as part of an enormous, hugely capitalized international hospitality and entertainment conglomerate—the various Delaware North Companies—with tentacles stretching from London's new Wembley Stadium to the Boston Bruins, from the Los Angeles Airport to the Kennedy Space Center, from Niagara Falls to Yosemite. Concessions in Kings Canyon, on the other hand (and at the Stony Creek Lodge in Sequoia National Monument), are managed by a small local operator, the Sequoia–Kings Canyon Park Services Company, which has been running the concessions here as far back as anyone can remember, but which, according to a company lawyer (as quoted in the year 2000), "has not been able to operate profitably."

All of which is not to say that one should write off the possibility of decent overnight accommodations in Kings Canyon. The more discriminating visitor may prefer to bring his or her own camping and cooking equipment, but there is a particular old-school charm—and undeniable value—to the historic-rustic 1920s camp cabins at **Grant Grove Village** (1-866-522-6966; www.sequoia-kingscanyon.com; inexpensive to moderate). Many of the structures here, tobacco-brown paint and all, are designated National Historic Landmarks. Units available with or without private bathrooms; no cooking allowed. For more modern franchise-motel-style accommodations, with aluminum doors and windows, high-traffic carpeting, fireside wireless Internet access, and board games in the "lobby," try the adjacent

John Muir Lodge (1-866-522-6966; www.sequoiakingscanyon.com; expensive), built in 1998. Open year-round.

For a pair of motel-style queen beds within earshot of the rushing waters of the mighty Kings, as deep into the rugged heart of the Sierra Nevada as one can get by automobile, there is no other option than the **Cedar Grove Lodge** (1-866-522-6966; www.sequoia -kingscanyon.com; moderate to expensive). Wood-veneer furniture, cottage-cheese ceilings, well-worn carpeting. When available, the three "patio rooms" are worth the extra few dollars. Closed in winter.

Dining

The **Grant Grove Restaurant** (Grant Grove Village), vaguely reminiscent of so many roadside cafés along defunct sections of Route 66, provides decent sit-down dining, three meals a day. Breakfast is hearty and unimpeachable. The **Pizza Parlor** (Grant Grove Village) is open during the summer. For cultural more than culinary value, consider stopping in for burgers and ice cream on the way in or out of the canyon at the privately owned **Kings Canyon Lodge** on CA 180 (559-335-2405; lodging available in a pinch). Eat at the bar or outside in the shade of fruit trees. Multiple-day visits to the Cedar Grove area may be limited by the quality of dining available at the **Cedar Grove Snack Bar** (shoes and shirts required), closed in winter.

Books, Maps & Information

Grant Grove Visitor Center (Grant Grove Village; 559-565-4307). Recently renovated, with a range of bilingual exhibits on the history of Grant Grove and the natural history of Kings Canyon and the High Sierra. Excellent selection of books and maps stocked by the Sequoia Natural History Association. Wilderness permits, pay phone, first aid.

Cedar Grove Visitor Center (Cedar Grove Village; 559-565-3793). This 1932-vintage Forest Service cabin houses a tiny selection of books and maps, and a retinue of friendly rangers to answer questions. Pay phone and first aid. Closed in winter.

Road's End Permit Station (at the end of the road in Kings Canyon; no phone). Maps, trail conditions, bear canister rentals, wilderness permits. Open 7–4 in summer.

Shopping

GIFT SHOPS

Grant Grove Gift Shop (Grant Grove Village; 559-335-5500). Eclectic selection of Sequoia–Kings Canyon souvenirs, post cards, T-shirts, tchotchkes, and nature-themed gifts.

GENERAL STORES

Grant Grove Village Market (Grant Grove Village). Small purveyor of groceries, firewood, beer, wine, soft drinks, ice, limited fresh fruit and vegetables, basic picnic and camping supplies, and phone cards.

Cedar Grove Market (Cedar Grove Village). Basic convenience store, books, maps, souvenirs and postcards, ATM, and laundry facility.

Points of Interest

General Grant Tree. The second or third biggest sequoia (once thought to be the biggest), depending on one's estimation of volume, this tree was designated the Nation's Christmas Tree by President Calvin Coolidge in 1926—at the behest of Charles E. Lee, then secretary of the Sanger Chamber of Commerce. An annual "Trek to the Tree" ceremony is held here in December. President Eisenhower added to the tree's list of honorary titles in 1956, declaring it a living National Shrine to America's war dead. A paved stroll through the grove (0.3 mile) wanders its way past the Robert E. Lee tree, the Fallen Monarch, and many more of the approximately 40 named trees in the grove.

The World's Top Ten Biggest Trees (according to Wendell Flint, *To Find the Biggest Trees*, Sequoia Natural History Association, 2002)

	Tree	Location	Height (feet)	Circumference (cubic feet)	Volume
1.	General Sherman	Giant Forest	274.9	102.6	52,508
2.	Washington	Giant Forest	254.7	101.1	47,850
3.	General Grant	Grant Grove	268.1	107.5	46,608
4.	President	Giant Forest	240.9	93.0	45,148
5.	Lincoln	Giant Forest	255.8	98.3	44,471
6.	Stagg	Alder Creek	243.0	109.0	42,557
7.	Boole	Converse Basin	268.8	113.0	42,472
8.	Genesis	Mountain Home	253.0	85.3	41,897
9.	Franklin* (near Washington)	Giant Forest	223.8	94.8	41,280
10.	King Arthur*	Garfield	270.3	104.2	40,656

* unofficial name

Converse Basin, Chicago Stump & Boole Tree. Once the largest grove of sequoias in the world, the Converse Basin today provides the starkest possible contrast to the majestic Giant Forest and General Grant groves. A disused trail leads from Forest Service Road 13S03 to the so-called Chicago Stump, once the ancient General Noble Tree, which was cut down, taken apart, and shipped to Chicago for the World's Fair in 1893. "Through all the wonderful, eventful centuries since Christ's time—and long before that—God has cared for these trees," wrote Muir in 1897, "but he cannot save them from fools." Meanwhile the Sanger Lumber Company, also in 1897, one step ahead of its creditors, set about felling and dynamiting the entire grove—an estimated 191 million board feet of brittle sequoia lumber, of which only about 20 percent is said to have made it to the mill in Sanger. The Boole Tree, the world's seventh biggest living thing, was spared. Wildfires in 1929 and 1955 cleared brush and remaining log debris and gave the grove a new start.

Hume Lake. The lake was built as a millpond for the Hume-Bennett Lumber Company, successor to the Sanger Lumber Company, and to supply water for what was once the longest log-transport flume ever constructed—to a planing mill at Sanger, some 70 miles

distant. The dam itself, the first concrete multiple-arch dam in the world,
completed in 1909, is today a National
Historic Landmark. Opposite the dam
is a bustling Christian summer camp.
Anglers and swimmers will enjoy the
beaches on the east shore.

Kings Canyon Lodge (559-335-2405).
If David Lynch ever felt compelled to
make a period Western, he might consider this vintage 1930s roadhouse
saloon a prime location. Set dressing
includes a pair of stuffed coyotes and
other assorted taxidermy, an old
upright piano, a bearskin on the ceiling, an array of antlers, and a purple
velour couch for napping beside the
cold woodstove on a hot afternoon. A
must-stop for basic hamburgers, cold

Kings Canyon Lodge: Stop by for cold beer, ice cream, and taxidermy. Burke Griggs

beer, and ice cream on the way in or out of the canyon (or both), the sort of place where
"Anchor Steem" (sic) is billed as an import,
and where the proprietors prefer to nod than speak aloud. Gas available from an antique
gravity-fed pump.

Junction View & Yucca Point. Thousands of feet above the confluence of North America's
two deepest canyons, CA 180 makes its first switchbacks for the grand descent. Stop here
for impossible pictures and unfathomable views.

Boyden Caverns (1-866-762-2837; www.caverntours.com). There are more than two hundred such passageways beneath these mountains. Yet another, dubbed Ursa Minor, was
discovered as recently as the summer of 2006. Boyden is the other of only two caves in
Sequoia-Kings open for visitation by the public. Potential visitors often want to know
which is better. The approach to Crystal Cave is down first, then up. The approach to
Boyden is up first, then down. Both are paved, deliciously cool and dark on a hot afternoon, serve as impressive showcases of underground mineral formations and the human
capacity for metaphor, and must be visited by way of a 45-minute tour led by a knowledgeable (and sometimes humorous) guide. A ticket to Crystal Cave is more expensive, by six or
seven dollars, but the money goes to an educational nonprofit rather than to something
called the Sierra Nevada Recreation Corporation. Your call. Why not do both?

River Road. A brief stretch of scenic dirt road along the Kings River (3 miles). Try it on a
bicycle.

Zumwalt Meadow. On a site formerly owned by Daniel Kindle Zumwalt (1845–1904), agent
for the Southern Pacific Railroad, this meadow now features a 1-mile self-guided nature
trail and boardwalk.

THE GREAT WESTERN DIVIDE HIGHWAY

From the old one-street ranching town of Springville, an easy hour or so south of Three Rivers, CA 190 climbs its way up the Tule River Canyon. The road was once part of a now-forgotten scheme to build a trans-Sierra highway from Porterville to Lone Pine. "Because of its comparative remoteness," wrote old-school guidebook writer Russ Leadabrand of this road in 1964, back when much of it was still unpaved, "this island byway in the Sequoia National Forest high country is never heavily used." Today, the stretch of fine asphalt between Springville and the Johnsondale Bridge, to the great delight of those few cyclists, bikers, and sports car drivers who've made its acquaintance, remains one of the emptiest scenic byways in North America.

At Quaking Aspen the "Mighty 190" turns south and becomes "The Great Western Divide Highway," which in turn runs wide and fast for 20 miles through the ancient forests and granite domes of the southern unit of Giant Sequoia National Monument. The road ends abruptly at a junction with CA 155. From here one has the option to drop westward, back down to the foothills, via the historic waters at California Hot Springs, or south and east to the Kern River Canyon and Kernville (the latter route approximately 70 miles one way).

It may have been here, in this southernmost part of the range, that the last California grizzly was shot in 1922 (then again, it may have happened north of Sequoia, at Horse Corral Meadow—or in Fresno County). It was here, near Johnsondale, on June 26, 2004, that 27-year-old Shannon Parker of Santa Monica lost her eye to a malnourished two-year-old mountain lion. Within hours, the lion was tracked down and shot by federal officials.

John Ford's *Stagecoach* was shot here in the late 1930s, and in the mid-1940s John Huston's *Treasure of Sierra Madre*. Here stands the largest unlogged grove of sequoias outside the national parks—the Freeman Creek Grove—home to both the Castro Tree and the George Bush Tree.

Services along the road are as limited today as they were 40 or 50 years ago—if not more so. For overnight accommodations there are a handful of campgrounds; several old Forest Service guard cabins (available by advance arrangement); a funky, half-renovated historic river-rock lodge; a pack station; and two roadhouse motels. Dining is generally best accomplished out of the back of one's vehicle.

The most popular section of this byway, to the south along the Kern River—from the Johnsondale Bridge to Kernville, every turnout and picnic area and campground—can be overrun in midsummer, when the population of Bakersfield comes upstream to bask in its own water supply. Kernville itself, southernmost of the true gateway towns to the Sierra, is a mostly charming collection of picket-fence vacation cottages, river cabins, antiques shops, and vintage motels—most charming when approached from upriver rather than from Lake Isabella (and most charming at any other time of year than in the furnace heat of summer). Many of the town's older buildings were moved here in 1953 from the site of Old Kernville, once a popular shooting location for Hollywood Westerns, now somewhere beneath the waters of the reservoir.

Lodging

Among the least developed regions in the Sierra, this part of the Sequoia National Forest has the least to recommend by way of tourist accommodations. The **Springville Inn** (1-800-4-THE INN, 559-539-7501; www.springvilleinn.com; expensive) offers last-chance

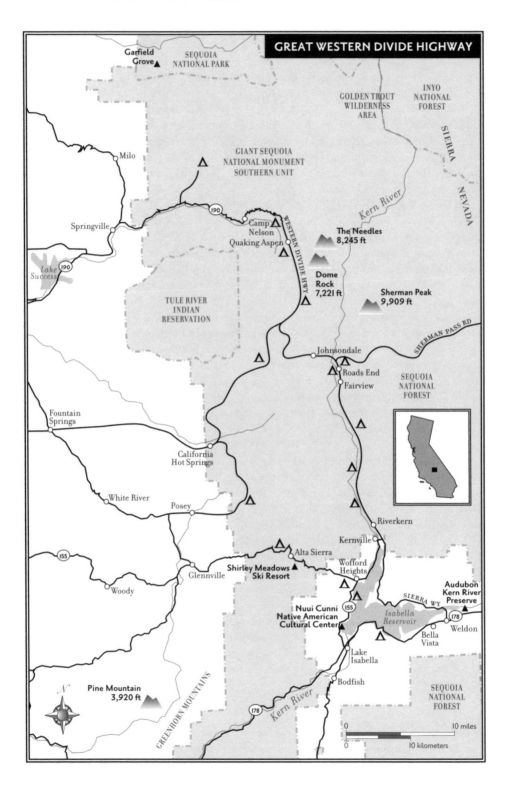

GREAT WESTERN DIVIDE HIGHWAY

Garfield Grove ▲

SEQUOIA NATIONAL PARK

GOLDEN TROUT WILDERNESS AREA

INYO NATIONAL FOREST

SIERRA NEVADA

Milo

GIANT SEQUOIA NATIONAL MONUMENT SOUTHERN UNIT

Kern River

190

Springville

Camp Nelson
Quaking Aspen

WESTERN DIVIDE HWY

The Needles 8,245 ft

Lake Success

190

Dome Rock 7,221 ft

Sherman Peak 9,909 ft

TULE RIVER INDIAN RESERVATION

SHERMAN PASS RD

Johnsondale

Roads End
Fairview

SEQUOIA NATIONAL FOREST

Fountain Springs

California Hot Springs

White River

Posey

Riverkern

Kernville

155

Alta Sierra

Shirley Meadows Ski Resort ▲

Glennville

Wofford Heights

Audubon Kern River Preserve ▲

Woody

SIERRA WY

Nuui Cunni Native American Cultural Center ▲

155

178

Isabella Reservoir

Weldon

Bella Vista

Lake Isabella

Pine Mountain 3,920 ft

GREENHORN MOUNTAINS

N

Bodfish

178

Kern River

SEQUOIA NATIONAL FOREST

0   10 miles
0   10 kilometers

B&B-style rooms—comfortable, if somewhat frilly—in a newer (1972) annex to the old Wilkinson Hotel building on Main Street. Between Springville and Kernville the only decent option is the lavishly renovated but still slightly spooky **Camp Nelson Lodge** (559-542-0904; www.campnelsonlodge.com; expensive; no alcohol allowed, but the very best in mattresses and log furnishings). In a pinch, very basic and inexpensive motel rooms can be had at the **Pierpoint Springs Resort** (559-542-2423; www.pierpointsprings.com) and at the **Ponderosa Lodge** (559-542-2579).

The most interesting—and economical—way to establish a base camp in the region is to reserve one of several housekeeping-style **Forest Service cabin or lookout rentals** (559-539-2607; www.fs.fed.us/r5/sequoia/recreation/rec_rentals; moderate). The **Quaking Aspen Cabin** in particular, next door to the idyllic Quaking Aspen Campground, stands within easy striking distance of all the major points of interest along CA 190, sleeps up to six very close friends, and offers such luxuries as electricity, hot and cold running water, a fridge, a stove, a motley collection of kitchen implements, an outdoor fire pit, and a porch for entertaining the abundance of local wildlife. Check the Web site for other options farther afield. Be sure to call ahead and clarify directions.

In Kernville, where motor-court lodgings are plentiful, the quality of a given establishment can generally be estimated by the furnishings on its front porch. Try the old cottonwood-shaded **River View Lodge,** with its upholstered wood gliders (760-376-6019; www.riverviewlodge.net; moderate), or the **Whispering Pines Lodge/B&B,** with its private cantilevered decks and poolside view of the river (760-376-3733; www.kernvalley .com/whisperingpines; moderate to very expensive; no pets).

Dining

Stagecoach Bar & Grill (at the Springville Inn; 559-539-7501; www.springvilleinn.com; moderate to expensive). The only real sit-down dining room in Springville. Steak, salmon, shrimp scampi, chicken Piccata, cheesecake, and more in an earnest high-Victorian atmosphere. Closed Monday and Tuesday.

Pierpoint Springs Resort (CA 190; 559-542-2423; www.pierpointsprings.com; inexpensive to moderate). Classic diner-style fare, vinyl tablecloths, beer, wine, cocktails, and the only free wireless Internet between Springville and Kernville. Live music some weekends.

Ewing's On The Kern (125 Buena Vista Drive, Kernville; 760-376-2411; expensive). Serving up voluminous slabs of prime rib and "the World's Coldest Beer" with the best view in town. The beer is cold because the glasses are put in the freezer wet. Recent dinner specials included tempura eggplant with chipotle dipping sauce and chicken cordon bleu. Note the authentic bear and lion skins on the wall. Note, behind the bar, the diorama of pre-reservoir Isabella Valley showing the historical progression of means of transport (mule to horse to pack train to covered wagon to stagecoach).

Marge's (10 Big Blue Road, Kernville; 760-376-8822; inexpensive). Silver-beehived Marge Harmening won't say just how long she's been collecting pigs. "Oh, a long time," she demurs. Long enough anyway that they take up a significant amount of coveted counter space—where otherwise, on an average day, four or five hungry diners might squeeze in to "pig out" on a variety of Marge's egg-skillet dishes, burgers, and grilled sandwiches. But never fear: There's also seating outside.

CA 190 follows the old Tule Flume into giant sequoia country.

Taverns, Saloons & Roadhouses

Wellsville Saloon (CA 190, Cedar Slope; 559-542-2319). Jim's fine selection of tequilas may be the perfect antidote to the curves in the road. Clear the palate with a couple of dollar tacos (ground beef). Play a round of pool; appreciate the craftsmanship in the wood floor and the organ-pipe-sized wind chimes on the deck. Press on.

Ponderosa Lodge (CA 190, Ponderosa; 559-542-2579). In summer, a favorite stop for the Harley-Davidson crowd, but still plenty friendly for spandex-clad cyclists and German tourists freshly emerged from the bowels of Rent-America RVs. Burgers and beers. Outside or in. Saturday night steak dinners. Fat tire on tap. Open Thursday–Monday. In winter, a cozy cross-country ski lodge ministering bowls of chili and hot chocolate.

Kern River Brewing Company (13415 Sierra Highway, Kernville; 760-376-BEER; www.kernriverbrewingcompany.com). Hand-drawn local brews, burgers, brats, fish-and-chips. Taco Tuesdays and live music on weekends.

Sportsman's Inn (11123 Kernville Road, Kernville; 760-376-2556). Where university-trained biologists studying owl habitat patterns in burnt-out forests might congregate to play pool and sip buckets of Red Bull with Crown Royal and peach schnapps.

General Stores

James' Store (13432 Sierra Highway, Kernville; 760-376-2424). Meat, produce, ice, bait and tackle, camping supplies, gas, liquor, and ammo.

Camp Nelson General Store (Camp Nelson; 559-542-3700). Basic grocery and hardware, video rentals, beer and wine.

Points of Interest

The Needles. Impressive granite formations offer world-class climbing and a fire lookout with a frighteningly, exhilaratingly historic set of stairs, and big views into the Kern River Canyon and Golden Trout Wilderness. The lookout was built by the CCC in 1937. Access is by a moderately steep trail (5 miles round-trip).

George Bush Tree. President George H. W. Bush, the father, signed a proclamation here on July 14, 1992, protecting all giant sequoias "in perpetuity, as unique objects of beauty and antiquity for the benefit and inspiration of all people." Efforts to cut down these trees were renewed under the son's administration. As recently as 2007 the trees were defended in the federal courts.

Trail of 100 Giants. Paved stroll through the Long Meadow Grove, past more than 125 giant sequoias. Here President Bill Clinton, in April 2000, signed his own proclamation, designating 327,769 acres of forest to be protected as the Giant Sequoia National Monument. Interpretive walks every Saturday and Sunday in summer, at 10 AM and 2 PM. For information call the Tule River Ranger District at 559-539-2607.

Kern River Valley Museum (49 Big Blue Road, Kernville; 760-376-6683; www.krvhist oricalsociety.org). Extensive homegrown museum with evocative piped-in old-time pickin' music and friendly volunteer docents. On display: arrowheads, rocks, antique mining and farm implements, photos of Old Kernville (before Lake Isabella), artifacts from the early days of Southern California Edison, Hollywood memorabilia (including one of the stagecoaches used in the John Ford/John Wayne movie), and a collection of stereoscope photos of pack trips on the Upper Kern River (1922–26).

KAISER PASS ROAD

The Sierra Heritage Scenic Byway begins at Clovis, but it isn't until some 60 miles later—above the march of vacation-home subdivisions at Shaver and Huntington reservoirs, past developments with names like Apple Ridge and Meadow Ridge and Sierra Pines, past the ski area at Sierra Summit—that it begins to earn its designation. Abruptly, at a place called Badger Flat, CA 168 changes its tenor. Here the road becomes a remarkable single-lane mountain track, built in the early 1920s as a service route over Kaiser Pass (9,200 feet),

now rough-paved, for workers on the upper waterworks of Southern California Edison's monumental Big Creek hydroelectric project—in those days the biggest such project ever undertaken. "Men, mules, plows, scrapers and donkey engines were used to remove boulders and trees," writes local historian Carole Steele. "Juniper trees were spared whenever possible." A 6-mile spur to Mono Hot Springs was completed in 1927 and nicknamed the C & N, or "Cheap & Nasty," for reasons that will be immediately apparent to all travelers thereon.

Frémont likely passed through this country sometime in the winter of 1845–46, discovering "some trees extremely large" on the way up (perhaps

Kaiser Pass and the Ansel Adams Wilderness   Burke Griggs

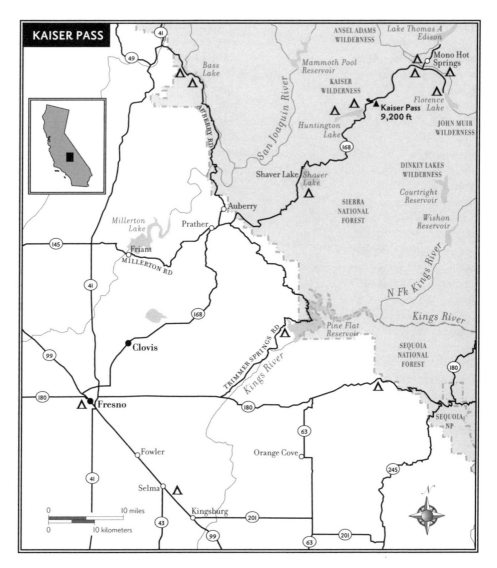

at Dinkey Creek), and from a flat granite ridge at 11,000 feet looked out at a small lake, far below, somewhere in the upper drainages of the San Joaquin. "I had grown, by occasional privation," he wrote, "to look upon water as a jewel beyond price, and this was rendered even more beautiful by its rough setting."

Today, three vast wilderness areas come together here—the Kaiser, the Ansel Adams, and the John Muir—separated only by the road itself and the limits of Edison's catchment reservoirs. In summertime, the highest of these "lakes," Florence and Thomas Edison, offer unique ferry access into the upper San Joaquin drainage and the remote northern end of Kings Canyon National Park. For a hilarious and lightly political survival guide to this road, with relevant tips on downshifting, see www.muirtrailranch.com/kprsurvival.html.

Note: There is no gas available above Huntington Lake.

Lodging

Mono Hot Springs Resort
www.monohotsprings.com
CA 168
Elevation: 6,560 feet
Open: May–November
559-325-1710
Owners: The Winslow family
Price: Inexpensive to Moderate
Pets: Yes
Wheelchair Access: Limited
Internet Access: Wireless (at the store)

A series of bathhouses has come and gone at the springs across the river, where once upon a time Mono Indians—and likely their prehistoric ancestors, too—made their annual summer camp. The soaking tubs remain. Walter Hill, a contractor and avid sportsman from Sanger, secured a permit from the Forest Service in 1939 to allow passenger cars up the road, and to build a rustic summer resort. During all the short seasons between 1939 and 1947 Walter and his wife, Polly, literally cobbled this place together from local San Joaquin river rock. The Hill kids eventually sold to the Winslows, of which family the third generation can today be seen scurrying about trying to keep the place standing (and the plumbing functioning). In late 2000, in a letter recommending that the resort structures be listed on the National Register of Historic Places, Forest Historian Thomas Nave cited "the unique use of cobblestone," "the influence of the Arts & Crafts movement," and "Walter Hill's mastery of the vernacular bungalow style." With a handful of days, a carload of kids, and a trunkful of provisions, it's hard to imagine a more timeless and idyllic spot to set up house-keeping.

✪ Muir Trail Ranch
www.muirtrailranch.com
6 miles from the far end of Florence Lake
Elevation: 7,600 feet
Open: June–September
209-966-3195
Owners: Adeline Smith and family
Price: Very Expensive
Pets: No
Wheelchair Access: No
Internet Access: No

As the story goes, Karl Smith, professional trombone player, was traipsing through the High Sierra one summer with his friend Sam Peckinpah—this must have been sometime in the 1940s—when, at some point, Sam, later to become a famous film director, fell and cut his hand. The fastest way out was via the old Diamond D Ranch. Sam got his hand fixed up proper, and Karl, after a soak in the hot springs and a good look around, set his sights on buying the place. He started by buying the boathouse and store on Florence Lake and in 1953 he and his wife, Adeline, swung a deal for the ranch itself. Log cabins, tent cabins, tiled hot springs tubs, ranch-generated hydro-electric power, limitless hiking, horseback riding, fishing, swimming, and general lounging around. A popular resupply stop for hikers on the John Muir Trail. Getting here is no small endeavor: It involves a long drive, a ferry ride, time in the saddle, or a 6-mile hike—assuming you're coming in from the nearest road. But securing a reservation is the hardest part. Book the whole ranch for a week, or try for a shorter stay in spring or fall. Bring your own liba-tions, towel, flashlight, and sleeping bag.

Dining
The River Rock Café (at Mono Hot Springs; 559-325-1710; moderate). Lunch and din-ner served alfresco on the shaded porch—most days, while supplies last. Try the corned buffalo Reuben.

Vermilion Valley Resort (West shore, Lake Thomas A. Edison; 559-259-4000; www.edis
onlake.com; moderate). Where else can you sit by a roaring campfire, in a grove of lodgepole pine, at the edge of the wilderness, talk shop with wild-eyed through-hikers on their
way from Mexico to Canada, watch baseball on a TV powered by a diesel engine, and gorge
on stuffed pork chops, barbecued tri-tip, or fresh-caught rainbow trout Piccata. Rustic
tent and trailer accommodations also available.

Books, Maps & Information

High Sierra Ranger Station (at Bolsillo Creek, east of Portal Forebay; 559-877-7173).
Good selection of books, guides, wilderness maps, and general Sierra National Forest
information. Wilderness and campfire permits available. Open daily June–August. Note
the grave marker for three Alaskan sled dogs who in the early 1920s helped run mail and
supplies to workers at Florence Lake.

General Stores

Florence Lake Store (Florence Lake; www.florence-lake.com). Books, toys, batteries,
souvenirs, trail supplies, and ferry tickets sold beneath a one-of-a-kind log cupola. Owned
and operated by the Muir Trail Ranch. No alcohol sold here.

Mono Hot Springs General Store (Mono Hot Springs; 559-325-1710). Basic staples, ice,
ice cream, beer, wine, fishing tackle, microwave burritos, aspirin, Band-Aids, books,
Adirondack chairs, and wireless Internet.

Mono Hot Springs General Store and post office   Burke Griggs

Vermilion Camp Store (Vermilion, on the west shore of Lake Thomas Edison; 559-259-4000; www.edisonlake.com). Connoisseur's selection of microbrews, graham crackers, marshmallows, white gas, and other trail supplies.

Points of Interest
Dinkey Creek (access from CA 168, before Shaver Lake). "Here is a grove of about two hundred [sequoia] trees growing upon coarse flood soil," wrote John Muir in the *San Francisco Daily Evening Bulletin* in 1875. "This little isolated grove was discovered a few years ago by a couple of bear hunters, but on account of its remoteness from traveled roads and trails is hardly known." In all the years since—more than a century and a quarter—not much has changed but the occasional distant whine of a two-stroke engine.

RECREATION

Bird-Watching
Along the South Fork of the Kern River, east of Kernville and above Lake Isabella, is California's largest lowland riparian forest, nearly 3,000 acres of which make up the Kern River Preserve. Home to 332 species, the area has been designated a National Natural Landmark and is one of Audubon's top 10 Globally Important Bird Areas. Contact the Kern Valley Audubon Society (http://kern.audubon.org) for information on spotted owls, turkey vultures, peregrine falcons, and other winged creatures throughout the southern end of the Sierra.

Boating
The motorboat and Jet Ski crowd flock to the flat waters of the **Lake Kaweah Recreation Area** (U.S. Army Corps of Engineers) and other area reservoirs, which by the end of the summer begin to show their full range of bathtub rings. Rentals and information available at the **Kaweah Marina** (559-597-2526). For white-water enthusiasts the adventures are upstream. Dropping from its various headwaters above 12,000 feet to an elevation of less than 700 at the reservoir, the Kaweah is considered one of the steepest in the country. Sections vary from moderate Class III to gnarly Class V boulder fields. Bill Pooley's **Kaweah River Page** (www.kaweahriver.org) is the one-stop resource for river runners, with detailed descriptions, flow graphs, gauge data, snowpack and weather reports, links, and a Web cam at Pumpkin Hollow Bridge. The South Fork of the Kings, from Bubbs Creek to the Park boundary, is off-limits to watercraft of any kind. Die-hard wilderness kayakers have been known to haul their boats up the Middle Fork.

Kaweah Whitewater Adventures (1-800-229-8658, 559-561-1000; www.kaweah-whitewater.com) offers half- and full-day rafting trips on the Kaweah during the season. Locally owned and operated. For commercial trips below Kings Canyon (but above Pine Flat Dam), try **Kings River Expeditions** (1-800-846-3674; www.kingsriver.com) or **Zephyr Whitewater Expeditions** (1-800-431-3636; www.zrafting.com).

On the Kern River, try **Mountain & River Adventures** (11113 Kernville Road, Kernville; 1-800-861-6553, 760-376-6553; www.mtnriver.com) for rafting, kayaking, mountain

Florence Lake Ferry to the John Muir Wilderness

biking, and rock climbing. Home base is a private campground on the Kern River. Snowshoe, cross-country ski, and sledding equipment for rent in winter. **Sierra South Mountain & Paddle Sports** (11300 Kernville Road, Kernville; 760-376-3745; www.kernriver.com) offers rafting, kayaking, and rock climbing. Day trips, overnights, lessons, and classes. New and used boats for sale; large selection of white-water equipment.

Floating of a more leisurely variety is popular on the high-country reservoirs above Kaiser Pass. **Vermilion Valley Ferry & Resort Rentals** (559-259-4000; www.edisonlake.com) has fishing boats, canoes, bizarre-looking paddleboats, and a pontoon boat for hire. Water levels are determined by Southern California Edison: Sometimes the "lake" comes right to the edge of the resort, and other times, such as when the water's needed downstream, the landscape is one of sand dunes and puddles. Guided fly- and ATV fishing trips also available. The **Florence Lake Ferry** (www.florence-lake.com)—the *Sierra Queen,* in service since 1969—makes at least five trips a day, out and back, to the other side of the lake; more on Saturday. Check the Web site or the store for schedules, rates, and water levels. Also available for hire: 15-foot aluminum fishing boats with outboard motors and bailing buckets ($65 a day).

Courses, Seminars & Guided Activities

For ranger-led walks and activities, check the bulletin boards at visitors centers, try the park hotline at 559-565-3341, or consult the latest copy of the park newspaper, *The Guide,* available at visitors centers or at park entrance kiosks. **The Big Trees Trail** and **Hazelwood Nature Trail,** both in the immediate vicinity of the Giant Forest Museum, provide excellent self-guided introductions to the history and ecology of the Big Tree groves. For a full calendar of organized educational adventures ("edventures") at extraordinarily reasonable rates, contact the **Sequoia Field Institute** (559-565-4251; www.sequoiahistory.org). Seminar topics include mammal tracking in snow, black bear management, bats, wildflowers, reforestation, and pottery. "Edventures" range from beginning cross-country skiing and kayaking to ghost tours and overnight backcountry skiing expeditions. Or hire your own private naturalist, starting at $150 for a half day.

Mountain & River Adventures (11113 Kernville Road, Kernville; 1-800-861-6553, 760-376-6553; www.mtnriver.com) offers guiding, courses, and private instruction in rafting, kayaking, mountain biking, and rock climbing in the Kern River area; **Sierra South Mountain & Paddle Sports** (11300 Kernville Road, Kernville; 760-376-3745; www.kern river.com) in rafting, kayaking, and rock climbing.

Mountain Biking

Off-pavement riding is not allowed within national park boundaries, except for along one brief section of scenic gravel along the Kings River, from Cedar Grove to Road's End. Vehicles of any kind—including those that are self-propelled—are prohibited in wilderness areas. That said, the national forests and Bureau of Land Management offer hundreds of miles of fire roads, jeep trails, and single track for the knobby-tire enthusiast.

From Three Rivers, head up to Salt Creek and the BLM's **Case Mountain Area** (www.blm.gov). Access via Skyline Drive from Three Rivers or Oak Grove Road off the road to Mineral King. For trail maps and route descriptions, check the **Central California Cyclists**' Web site (www.ccorc.com). Riding is intermediate to advanced. Hazards include mountain lions, poison oak, and occasional crossfire between DEA agents and backcountry marijuana farmers.

The northern unit of the Giant Sequoia National Monument, north of Grant Grove, from **Converse Basin** to **Horse Corral Meadow** to **Hume Lake** offers hundreds of miles of old and not-so-old fire and logging roads for two-wheeled exploration. Consult Sequoia National Forest's Hume Lake Ranger District OHV maps, available online at www.fs.fed.us/r5/sequoia. The southern unit, along the Great Western Divide Highway, has its own network of dirt roads and trails, including a smooth, whooping descent to the **George Bush Tree.**

Sierra Bicycle Works (123 E. Main, Visalia; 559-741-0700; www.sierrabicycle werks.com) provides a full range of cycle gear, service, and local beta.

The Kaiser Pass region offers some off-highway riding, but the competition is fierce with the motorized set.

Fishing

There is enough productive water in this region to keep an angler busy for a lifetime. Bait fishermen line up along the shores of Lake Kaweah to catch largemouth bass, catfish, and rainbow trout. Some of the best front-country wild-trout fly-fishing can be found along the **Middle Fork** of the Kaweah, inside Sequoia National Park. (See Swimming for river access issues.) The existence of productive holes along the **Marble Fork,** from the Lodgepole to the falls, seems plausible—as from the crowded bridge at the campground rank amateurs have been seen landing healthy brook trout. "The upper section of the Kings in the Kings Canyon National Park has smaller fish," writes fly-fishing guru Bill Sunderland, "but lots of them."

Buz Beszek's Fly Shop (110 W. Main, Visalia; 559-734-1151; www.buzsflyshop.com) is one of the oldest full-service fly shops in California, and the only one within striking distance of Sequoia National Park. Guiding available.

The forks of the Kern are home to the renowned California-native golden trout. For well-stocked high-country stillwater, try Hume Lake or the reservoirs above Kaiser Pass. Award-winning browns have been pulled from Lake Edison, and all manner of fleshy pink monsters are said to lurk beneath the surface of Florence.

Golf

Three Rivers Public Golf Course (41117 Sierra Drive; 559-561-3133). Nine holes, oak trees, ponds, deer, views up the Kaweah toward the high country. Open year-round.

Hiking

There are at least a thousand miles of trail to be accessed from the Sequoia-Kings region. Centuries-old footpaths climb through chaparral and oak woodlands from trailheads at Potwisha and Buckeye Flat, just inside the park. From the end of North Fork Drive, one can hike up the **Old Colony Mill Road,** hand-built by Kaweah Colony socialists in the 1880s, as far as the road to Crystal Cave. Beware extensive colonies of poison oak. For secluded forays to lightly visited sequoia groves, head up into the **Salt Creek** and **Case Mountain Areas** (see Mountain Biking above, and www.blm.gov), or up the South Fork to **Ladybug Waterfall** and/or the **Garfield Grove.**

Mineral King is one of the top jumping-off spots for day hikes and extended trips into

The Great Western Divide from the High Sierra Trail

the High Sierra. Trails climb out of the bowl in every direction, follow tumbling snowmelt creeks to clear alpine lakes, and onto the high ridges and peaks of the Great Western Divide, from which, on an extraordinary day, one might see east to Mount Whitney and west to the coastal range. Numerous multiday loops are possible from here. A short 1-mile nature trail begins and ends at the Cold Springs campground. For guided walks and camp-fire programs, check in at the ranger station.

Along the Generals Highway section of Sequoia, one of the most popular (and easy) trails is that which follows the clear pools of the Marble Fork from the Lodgepole camp-ground to **Tokopah Falls** (3.4 miles round-trip). Other popular day hikes include the short climb to **Little Baldy** (3.4 miles round-trip), and the **Lakes Trail** from Wolverton to Heather and Pear lakes, from which the most ambitious can make a run at the worthy sum-mit of **Alta Peak** (13.8 miles round-trip). For paths less traveled, head up into the **Jennie Lakes Wilderness** from the Big Meadows/Horse Corral Road. For custom hiker/back-packer shuttles, contact **Sequoia Tours** (559-561-4189; www.sequoiatours.com).

From Kings Canyon, access to the wide-open backcountry—for day hikes and extended trips alike—is rivaled only by Mineral King's. The main difference here is the significantly greater elevation gain between the valley floor and the surrounding ridges and peaks. In midsummer start early to avoid the heat. Day hikes include the **Don Cecil Trail**, once the main access route to the valley floor (before the completion of the road in 1939), the **Hotel Creek-Lewis Creek** loop (8 miles), and the trip out and back along the South Fork to **Mist Falls** (8 miles). A fellow by the name of Bill Finch, of the Sequoia Kings Canyon Hikers Club, has put together an exhaustive online resource for hikes in the region at www.sierra hiker.com.

All overnight trips require a wilderness permit, available at no charge from local ranger stations and visitors centers.

Horseback Riding

Even John Muir deigned to ride an animal on several of his long-distance romps in and around the Sierra. Pack outfits throughout the region offer a range of services, including half- and full-day rides, spot pack trips, hunting and fishing trips, stargazing rides, cus-tom backcountry expeditions, and annual cattle drives. See chapter 4 for outfitting service from the east side.

Cedar Grove Pack Station (latest phone disconnected) may or not be open in the near future for day rides and/or pack trips in Kings Canyon high country.

Clyde Pack Outfit (559-298-7397; www.clydepackoutfitters.com). Full service from Dinkey Creek into the Kings River and Kings Canyon National Park backcountry.

Balch Park Pack Station (559-539-2227; www.balchpark.com). Tim and Dianne Shew offer a full range of services to the Garfield-Redwood Grove of Big Trees (what John Muir called "the finest block of Big Tree Forest in the entire belt"), the Golden Trout Wilderness, the upper Kern River, and the southern end of Sequoia National Park.

Grant Grove Stables (559-335-9292). One- to two-hour rides in the Grant Grove and Sequoia Lake areas. Opens at 8 AM in summer; last ride leaves at 4 PM. Reservations recommended.

Grant Grove Stables

Golden Trout Pack Trains (above Quaking Aspen on the Great Western Divide Highway; 559-542-2816; www.goldentroutpacktrains.com). Steve and Rinda Day offer a full range of services to the Freeman Creek Grove, George Bush Tree, and into the Golden Trout Wilderness. Cabins and lodge meals available.

High Sierra Pack Station (559-285-7225; www.highsierrapackstations.com). Run by John and Jenise Cunningham and friends, High Sierra has stables at Florence and Edison Lakes. Full service into the Ansel Adams and John Muir Wildernesses, the Evolution Valley, and the northern wilds of Kings Canyon National Park.

Horse Corral Pack Station (559-565-3404; www.horsecorralpackers.com) is run by Charley and Judy Mills, the last of their kind in Sequoia National Park.

Rainbow Pack Outfitters (760-873-8877; www.rainbowpackoutfitters.com). Greg and Ruby Allen have permits to run trips from the east side into Sequoia–King Canyon National Parks.

Road Biking
Cycling in this region is generally limited to epic alpine-style hill climbing of the out-and-back variety. The Mineral King Road (50 miles out and back), for all its 600 stubble-raising switchbacks and undeniably high scenic value, offers considerably less traffic than the Generals Highway (plus homemade pie at Silver City). RVs and trailers are seriously discouraged. For a shorter, less vigorous cruise, try North Fork Drive through Kaweah to pavement's end. For a truly heroic loop, start in the cool of dawn, ride down the Kaweah to

Lemon Cove, wind your way north along the foothills on J21 to Badger, and then climb into the parks via Pinehurst and the Big Stump Entrance. Return via Lodgepole and a final, mad, RV-slaloming descent of the Generals Highway (82 miles, 6,000 feet of elevation).

An excellent loop ride can be made from Grant Grove to Hume Lake. Head north on CA 180 past the Converse Basin to Hume Lake Road. Descend to the lake, follow Tenmile Road (NF 13S09) past the Christian Camp along the south shore of the lake, and enjoy the long climb up **Tenmile Creek** to **Quail Flat**. At the top, turn right onto the Generals Highway, then right again at the "Wye" intersection with CA 180, through Wilsonia, and back to Grant Grove (20 miles total).

For a multiday stage route of Tour de France proportions, consider riding from the Central Valley to the Mojave, over the Southern Sierra—from Springville via the Great Western Divide Highway and Sherman Pass (9,200 feet) to Pearsonville. Return by way of Walker Pass and the lower Kern Canyon. Avoid the hottest and coldest seasons.

The Kaiser Pass road would make a spectacular climb (and descent) were it not for the tree roots, frost heaves, potholes, and bottlenecked toy haulers.

Rock Climbing

There is more good granite here—between the Domeland Wilderness and Bubbs Creek, between Moro Rock and Mount Whitney—than in all of Yosemite. It's just harder to get to and is not as well known. Popular areas include the **Needles** and **Merlin Dome**, off the Great Western Divide Highway, **Moro Rock** itself, **Hospital Rock**, **Little Baldy**, and the **Charlito** and **Charlotte Domes** along the Bubbs Creek trail in Kings Canyon.

Swimming

Despite the abundance of swimming holes along the lower stretches of the **Kaweah**, public access is severely limited (and remains one of the most contentious issues in local politics). Without permission from a riverfront property owner (i.e., by staying at the Buckeye Tree Lodge or the Lake Elowin Resort), the only way down to the water is at the **Slick Rock Recreation Area** and by the **Cobbleknoll Trail** on the east end of Lake Kaweah. Access within the national park is limited only by the difficulty of the terrain. Try the trailheads at **Potwisha, Buckeye Flat**, and **South Fork**. Use extreme caution during periods of high water in spring and early summer: Drowning is the number one cause of death in Sequoia-Kings.

The **Marble Fork** offers a trove a good plunges both above and below Tokopah Falls, as does the upper **Middle Fork** from Bearpaw to the Kaweah Gap. One very popular series of slides and swimming holes can be found along **Stony Creek**, about a half mile down a trail from the Stony Creek Lodge. At higher elevations the parks abound with backcountry glacial lakes and forehead-numbing snowmelt creeks.

Hume Lake is the best place to practice your triathlon starts within a short drive of Grant Grove. The best beach is on the east shore.

Swimming in the fast-running **Kings River** is tricky business—and discouraged by the Park Service. The holes get better as the valley flattens out inside the park. Tributary creeks are best in early summer, before they dry up.

To the south, the **Tule** and **Kern** rivers have abundant swimming holes but tend to be crowded during the hottest part of the summer. The South Fork of the **San Joaquin**, in the Kaiser Pass area, offers a host of decent pools for swimming in—depending on release of water from upstream dams. There are pleasant, secluded beaches on **Florence** and **Thomas Edison** reservoirs—the more pleasant and secluded the more you hike—and, of course, the ancient hillside soaking tubs at **Mono Hot Springs**.

Winter Sports

With proper equipment (and weather), the intrepid traveler can strike out across snow nearly anywhere in the Sierra's higher elevations, generally from 6,000 feet. An overview map of the most popular cross-country ski trails, from Lodgepole to Moro Rock, can be purchased at park visitors centers. The **Grant Tree Trail** loop is the only trail plowed in winter. All others are open for touring by snowshoes or cross-country skis. Rentals are available at the Grant Grove Market (559-335-5500). **Panoramic Point Road** and the many miles of logging roads in the **Converse Basin** and along the **Big Meadows/Horse Corral Road**, snow permitting, provide excellent terrain for winter touring. For extended winter travel in the backcountry, consider a free-heel or randonée ski setup with climbing skins, rather than snowshoes. Try them out before you get in too deep.

All overnight trips require a wilderness permit, available at no charge from local ranger stations and visitors centers. Beware rapidly changing weather conditions (see the Winter Travel in the Sierra sidebar in chapter 2).

Montecito Lake Resort (63410 Generals Highway; 1-800-843-8677; www.mslodge.com). Nearly 50 miles of groomed cross-country ski and snowshoe trails, three warming huts, equipment rental, and lessons. The Mountain Top Ski Shop also rents snowboards for groomed practice runs or backcountry powder. Tubing, sledding, dogsled rides, "snow biking," and ice skating.

Wolverton Ski and Recreation Area (Wolverton; 559-565-3435). The Wolverton Ski Bowl was developed here in 1921, and the last rope tows were removed in 1990. Today, 70 miles of quiet forest trails radiate from the meadow, with winter access to the General Sherman Tree and Giant Forest. Half- and full-day ski and snowshoe packages, lessons, sledding, telemark practice, and general snow play.

Wuksachi Ski Shop (Wuksachi Lodge; 1-888-252-5757). Cross-country ski and snowshoe rentals and lessons; Snow play equipment for sale.

Ponderosa Lodge Ski Shop (CA 190, Ponderosa; 559-542-2579). This small shop offers basic rentals, equipment, and local trails information.

Mountain & River Adventures (11113 Kernville Road, Kernville; 1-800-861-6553, 760-376-6553; www.mtnriver.com). Snowshoe, cross-country ski, and sledding equipment for rent in winter.

Annual Events

January
Polar Dip River Swim (Gateway Restaurant, Three Rivers).

Chimney Rock Challenge (Montecito-Sequoia Ski Resort).

February
Whiskey Flat Days (Kernville). Parade, carnival rides, frog jumping contests, gold panning, epitaph contests, and line dancing.

March
Return of swallows to Pumpkin Hollow Bridge (Three Rivers; http://kern.audubon.org).

April
Jazzaffair (Three Rivers; www.jazzaffair.info).

Kern River Festival (Kernville; www.kernfestival.org).

Lions Team Roping (Three Rivers; 559-561-2222). Good old-fashioned small-town entertainment. Former roping chairman Van Bailey calls it "a champagne event at Pepsi-Cola prices." Highlights include dummy roping, barrel racing, and a pig scramble.

Springville Sierra Rodeo (Springville; 1-866-763-3649; www.rodeo49.com). "The Biggest Little Rodeo in the West."

National Park Week (www.nps.gov/npweek). Free access to all national parks.
Kern Valley Spring Nature Festival (Kern Valley; http://kern.audubon.org).

May
Redbud Arts & Crafts Festival (Three Rivers; 559-561-4417).

July
Buck Rock Lookout Annual Open House & 4th of July Celebration (www.buckrock.org).

August
Kern Valley Hummingbird Celebration (Kern River Preserve; http://kern.audubon.org).

September
Celebration of Sequoias Festival (559-338-2251).

Kern River Valley Turkey Vulture Festival (Kern River Preserve; http://kern.audubon.org).

October

Springville Apple Festival (Springville; www.springville.ca.us; 559-539-0619).

Fat Tire Classic (Springville; www.springville.ca.us; 559-781-6234).

December

Trek to the Nation's Christmas Tree (Grant Grove; Sanger Chamber of Commerce, 559-875-4575, www.sanger.org).

7

YOSEMITE

The Incomparable Pleasure Ground

No photograph or series of photographs, no paintings ever prepare a visitor so that he is not taken by surprise . . . no description, no measurements, no comparisons are of much value.

—*Frederick Law Olmsted, 1865*

On March 28, 1864, four score and eight years after the founding of the nation, just as newly promoted Lt. Gen. Ulysses S. Grant was preparing Union troops for an all-out springtime assault on Richmond, California senator John Conness introduced a rather abstract piece of legislation in Washington. The idea was that the federal government would grant to the State of California—in those days still several hard months' travel to the west—a certain portion of the Sierra Nevada that no one in the building had ever seen (in person); that only a few hundred Californians, and Indians, had managed to get to; and that had not yet even been surveyed. The proposal in itself was not remarkable: The bulk of the nation's territory, from the Mississippi to the Pacific Ocean, had in the space of 50 years been acquired on the strength of hand-drawn maps, rough sketches, and explorers' journals (with here and there an actual painting for color). What was remarkable in this case was the idea that the place—any place—might be so granted, as was proposed, "for public use, resort and recreation . . . inalienable forever."

There were in those days, in sophisticated places like Paris and London, great urban parks for the recreational use of the citizenry. Charles I had opened Hyde Park to the public in 1637. Napoleon III had followed suit with the Bois de Boulogne in 1852. There were popular "pleasure gardens" such as Vauxhall (London), Tivoli (Copenhagen), and Prater (Vienna), with fountains and fireworks, music and merry-go-rounds. New York's Central Park had been under construction since 1857—with its looping carriage roads and bridges, its artificial lakes, its soil and trees imported from New Jersey, its courteous and helpful "park keepers"—under the visionary guidance of its superintendent and architect-in-chief, Frederick Law Olmsted. The well-designed urban park was one of the great hallmarks of modern civilization. There was as yet no such thing, anywhere in the world, as a

LEFT: *Vernal Fall from the Mist Trail*

government-protected public park in the depths of the wilderness. The idea was essentially counterintuitive.

Most of the legislators in the nation's capitol that war-torn year, and surely President Lincoln as well, would have read about or at least heard of Yosemite, if not seen it represented in pictures. In the nine years since Thomas Ayres made and published his first sketch of the place, in Hutchings's *California Magazine,* the word had spread far and wide. The first edition of T. Richardson's best-selling *Illustrated Handbook of American Travel* (1857) had called the valley's scenery "perhaps the most remarkable in the United States, and perhaps in the world." Horace Greeley, the most influential newspaperman of his day, editor of the *New York Tribune* and founder of the Republican Party, had in 1859 made the trip overland to see for himself. When he got back, despite considerable suffering in the saddle and the fact that the much touted Yosemite Falls had been stone dry (as it generally is in August), he wrote: "Of all the grandest sights I have enjoyed—Rome from the dome of St. Peter's, the Alps from the Valley of Lake Como, Mount Blanc and her glaciers from Chamouni [sic], Niagara, and the Yo Semite—I judge the last named the most unique and stupendous."

Charles Weed and R. H. Vance had managed—earlier that same season, when the waterfalls were still in fine form—to haul all manner of equipment by mule over the rough trails to make the first photographs of the place. Thomas Hill, a landscape painter from Philadelphia, said to be the last of the Hudson River School, set up a studio at Wawona in 1861. Carleton Watkins made the trek up from San Francisco with his stereoview and mammoth-plate cameras. His images of the valley—and of the Big Trees in the Mariposa Grove—were exhibited to much applause at the swank Goupil & Cie. gallery in New York. "Nothing in the way of landscapes can be more impressive," wrote the *New York Times.* Albert Bierstadt saw the show and the following summer was on his way west, easel strapped to his saddle, to make his first famous sketches of Yosemite. Where the earliest attempts to reconstruct actual giant sequoias in New York and London had generally failed to convince, Watkins's photos did the job. As Ralph Waldo Emerson put it, the images "made the tree possible."

In February 1864, Israel Ward Raymond, California representative of a New York steamship concern, shipped a set of Carleton Watkins prints across the country to John Conness, in Washington—"some views of the Yosemity Valley [sic]"—in order that the senator might have "some idea of its character." "No. 1," wrote Raymond, "is taken from a point on the Mariposa trail and gives a view of about seven miles of the Valley, and the principal part of it. You can see that its sides are abrupt precipices ranging from 2,500 feet to 5,000 feet high. Indeed there is no access to it but by trails over the debris deposited by the crumbling of the walls." Lest there be some debate, he was careful to add: "The summits are mostly bare Granite Rocks in some parts the surface is covered only by pine trees and can never be of much value."

The matter came before the 38th Congress during the third week of May. It passed the Senate after a moment or two of discussion, Conness having assured his colleagues that the lands in question were "for all public purposes worthless" and would involve "no appropriation whatsoever." There were, as it happened, more pressing issues on the docket. Union troops were having bad luck in Virginia; in Louisiana they were on the run. It was hard to say what was going on with Sherman in Georgia, other than that it was very bloody. On June 3rd Grant lost 2,000 men in 20 minutes at the Battle of Cold Harbor—a hundred miles from the Federal capitol. By June 12th he had disengaged, having lost 13,000 of his men to Lee's 2,500.

On the 29th, with not much ado, the Yosemite matter passed the House, to be signed the following day by President Lincoln. Eleven months later, in April 1865, Lee surrendered to Grant at Appomattox, and at Ford's Theater in Washington, D.C., John Wilkes Booth fired a .44-caliber slug 6 inches into Lincoln's brain, ending the possibility that the president might one day see Yosemite. John Conness was a pallbearer at the funeral. Today, there is a big tree named after Lincoln, not in Yosemite but in the Giant Forest in Sequoia. It is considered the world's fourth-largest living tree, after the Sherman, Grant, and President trees. The name "Conness" went to a prominent peak (12,590 feet) above Tuolomne Meadows, on the eastern border of what is now Yosemite National Park.

It was left to California what to do with the place. There were no specific guidelines. There were no precedents. There had been no money appropriated. The mandate was impossibly vague: "for public use, resort and recreation." Should there be funhouses, platform carousels, and gravity railroads? Should there be bandstands and nightly fireworks displays? Should there be a grand public bathhouse on the banks of the Merced? First and foremost: Should roads be built, and decent accommodations provided, such that the public could actually visit the place? What sort of accommodations? Who should do the work, provide services, manage the place? How should it all be paid for? If and when there was profit, how should it be allocated?

To study these issues and to come up with a preliminary report, the governor appointed a First Yosemite Commission of eight relevant gentlemen, including Mr. Raymond of the steamship concern; Professor Whitney, state geologist; Galen Clark, the homesteader at Wawona who in those days ran the only lodgings on the trail to Yosemite and provided guide service to the Big Trees. Frederick Law Olmsted, then ex-superintendent of Central Park (today generally considered the father of American landscape architecture), was appointed chairman. Olmsted's vision for the park in New York, and his scruples, had for the time being exceeded those of his employers, causing him in 1863 to accept a job as manager of a vast mining estate in Mariposa County, California (on 18,000 acres that John C. Frémont had purchased for $10,000 after the close of the Mexican War). In this last capacity Olmsted had found occasion to explore not only the Mariposa Grove and Yosemite Valley but also Tuolomne Meadows and some of the surrounding High Sierra. What he saw there was, as he wrote in a letter to his father, "far the noblest park or pleasure ground in the world."

Olmsted spent the summer of 1865 on location, hiking around, having discussions with scientists (Whitney, Torrey, et al.) and artists (Watkins and Hill), entertaining visiting politicians and newspapermen, hammering out not so much the specifics of how to proceed but a general philosophy. The first order of business was to commission a survey and a map, which he did, engaging Clarence King of the Whitney Survey out of his own pocket. The next step, and by far the most challenging, was to determine—and as much as possible describe—what it was about the place that made it so unique and enjoyable and *necessary* to the public. What made the scenery here so great? What was so "peculiar to this ground" that it should, by order of Congress, be treated "differently from other parts of the public domain"? And, anyway, what was so important about scenery in general, that people should go so far out of their way not just to see it, but to protect it, and/or develop it in such a way that others might see it, too—for all time?

The photographs, stereoviews, and paintings were extraordinary, and served a certain purpose. They seemed no less than glimpses of the garden in the days of Genesis. But still, for those who had been there, for those who had slept on its ground and walked among its wonders, the images failed to get at the essence of the place. Words, too, tended to fall short. "By no statement of the elements . . . can any idea of that scenery be given," wrote Olmsted in his report, "any more than a true impression can be conveyed of a human face by a measured account of its features." Naturally, as others before him, and so many after, he resorted to comparisons. "The stream is such a one as Shakespeare delighted in," he wrote, "and brings pleasing reminiscences to the traveler of the Avon or the Upper Thames." The "cabinet pictures," revealed in every side canyon, recalled "the most valued sketches of Calame in the Alps and Appenines." Yosemite Falls he declared to be "fifteen times the height of Niagara." And yet, he wrote: "There are falls of water elsewhere finer, there are more stupendous rocks, more beetling cliffs, there are deeper and more awful chasms, there may be as beautiful streams, as lovely meadows, there are larger trees."

What was it, then, about Yosemite? "I shall not attempt to describe it," Richardson would write in *Beyond the Mississippi* (1867), "the subject is too large and my capacity too small." Lafayette Bunnell, in his account of that first teary-eyed sighting in 1851, would mention "the vapory clouds . . . a weirdness to the scene . . . the conviction that it was utterly indescribable." Olmsted cited "the imperceptible humidity of the atmosphere and the soil . . . some temporary condition of the air, of clouds, of moonlight, or of sunlight through mist or smoke," lending the scenery in the valley its "indescribable softness and exquisite dreamy charm." More than a century later Ansel Adams, in his autobiography, put it this way: "It is easy to recount that I camped many times at Merced Lake, but it is difficult to explain the magic."

The bottom line, concluded Olmsted, was that people would have to experience the place for themselves, in person—if not for merely aesthetic reasons, then for their health. "It is a scientific fact," he wrote, "that the occasional contemplation of natural scenes of an impressive character, particularly if this contemplation occurs in connection with relief from ordinary cares, change of air and change of habits, is favorable to the health and vigor of men . . . that it not only gives pleasure for the time being but increases the subsequent capacity for happiness and the means of securing happiness."

Built into Olmsted's proposal was a fundamental contradiction, one that to this day provides a never-ending challenge, not merely for the Park Service in managing places like Yosemite, but for all booming populations stuck between democratic ideals and diminishing natural resources. On the one hand the place was to be preserved in as "pristine" a state as possible—"as a museum of natural science." On the other hand facilities and access were to be improved, so that not only the rich but "the whole public" might enjoy the park. A decent road was to be built in place of what was then "a very poor trail," to reduce "the expense, time and fatigue of a visit," but also for fire suppression, and to bring in timber and supplies for an increasing number of visitors, without having to cut down the valley's trees or till its meadows. Strict regulations were to be devised, and enforced, against "injury to the scenery." Traffic patterns were to be considered; roads, trails, and structures built in such a way that they "should not

> It is but sixteen years since the Yosemite was first seen by a white man, several visitors have since made a journey of several thousand miles at large cost to see it, and notwithstanding the difficulties which now interpose, hundreds resort to it annually. . . . in a century the whole number of visitors will be counted by millions. An injury to the scenery so slight that it may be unheeded by any visitor now, will be one multiplied by these millions.
> —Frederick Law Olmsted, 1865

detract from the dignity of the scene."

For the construction of a good access road into the valley, and of "30 miles more or less of double trail & foot paths," bridges, cabins, stairways, surveys, advertising, incidentals, and so on, and for two years' expenses already incurred, Olmsted proposed appropriations by the State Legislature to the tune of $37,000. After this admittedly lavish expenditure, he imagined, "the further necessary expenses for the management of the domain will be defrayed by the proceeds of rents and licenses which will be collected upon it."

. . . when after a rest from the fatigues of the journey the tourist sets out from the hotel, armed with his instrument, to register, if may be, a few of those glorious scenes about him, that those at home might enjoy them, there comes a feeling of utter helplessness at the prospect before him. It is like going out to do battle with a toy pistol.
—Samuel Douglass Dodge, "A Day in Yosemite with a Kodak," *The New England Magazine*, 1890

In August 1865, five of the eight commissioners (all those present, not including Whitney and Raymond) endorsed the proposal. Olmsted went back to New York to resume his duties as architect and superintendent of Central Park (this time with greater leeway, and terms more favorable to his ambitions for the place). He would go on to design Prospect Park in Brooklyn, and the landscapes of at least 16 other major urban parks across the country, as well as the grounds at the U.S. Capitol building and at Niagara Falls. In the 1880s he returned to California to design the campus at Stanford University, but he would never again return to Yosemite.

After Olmsted had gone, in November 1865, Whitney moved to suppress the report, fearing that the legislature would balk at the cost—and/or that such a project would cut into the already limited budget for his own ongoing Geological Survey. The document was "lost," not to resurface until 1952. Yosemite's early infrastructure was, as a result, pieced together by private interests, leaseholders, and competing concessionaires, some well meaning, some otherwise, but without any kind of master plan, and without any official precautions taken against "injury to the scenery." When a young John Muir ambled into the pleasure ground for the first time, in 1868, three years after the disappearance of the Olmsted Report, he was able to find employment first as a sheepherder, then as a foreman at J. M. Hutchings's sawmill, at the base of Yosemite Falls.

Muir was, on the one hand, a great promoter and forceful advocate for public access. "Everybody needs beauty as well as bread," he would write in his seminal narrative guide to the park, *The Yosemite*, "places to play in and pray in, where nature may heal and give strength to body and soul alike." But with equal force he would decry the people's despoilment of the cathedral. "Ax and plow, hogs and horses, have long been and are still busy in Yosemite's gardens and groves," wrote Muir in *The Century Magazine* (September, 1890). "All that is accessible and destructible is being rapidly destroyed."

On the first of October, 1890, fast upon signing Sequoia and Grant Grove National Parks into existence, President Harrison put his name to another bill giving national park status to Tuolomne Meadows and a million acres of the Yosemite High Sierra (the valley and the Mariposa Grove would remain under the management of the State of California for another decade). African-American troopers from the U.S. Army's famed Buffalo Soldier regiments rode in from the now-quiet Indian frontier to drive out Basque sheepherders. The year 1892 saw the incorporation of the Sierra Club in San Francisco, with Muir as its first president. The group's mission was twofold: on the one hand, "to explore, enjoy, and

President Theodore Roosevelt and John Muir riding in Yosemite Valley, May 1903 Courtesy NPS, YNP

render accessible the mountain regions of the Pacific Coast"; and on the other, to work for their preservation and protection. In 1903 Muir spent three days and two nights giving President Theodore Roosevelt a personal tour of the park's finer points, and of the threats thereto. "The first night we camped in a grove of giant sequoias," wrote the president, years later. "It was clear weather, and we lay in the open, the enormous cinnamon-colored trunks rising about us like the columns of a vaster and more beautiful cathedral than was ever conceived by any human architect."

Every year brought more tourists, more photographs, more stereoviews and photo-postcards, more magazine articles and guidebooks promoting the salubrious aspects of a visit to the "wilds" of Yosemite, and touting the great improvements in facilities. In 1906, at the urging of Muir and the Sierra Club, and with Roosevelt's support in Washington, the State of California agreed to give back to the federal government the original 1864 grant—the valley and the Mariposa Grove—such that the whole tract could be managed as a single national park. In 1914 civilian park rangers replaced the cavalry troops. In 1916—the same year 14-year-old Ansel Adams read Hutchings's *In the Heart of the Sierras* and made his first visit to Yosemite (later to serve for nearly three decades on the Sierra Club's board of directors)—Congress created the National Park Service. Its purpose: "to conserve the scenery and the natural and historic objects and the wildlife therein and to provide for the enjoyment of the same in such manner and by such means as will leave them unimpaired for the enjoyment of future generations."

"In God's wildness lies the hope of the world," wrote Muir, echoing Thoreau before him. There is still wildness in Yosemite, of a kind. Ninety-five percent of the park is road-

Yosemite's first rangers, the 24th Infantry, 1899 Celia Crocker Thompson, courtesy NPS, YNP

less backcountry, legally designated and for the most part unmitigated "wilderness," serviced only by pack trains and dirt trails, populated by marmots and mountain lions, ancient whitebark pines, wildflowers, granite, and colorfully costumed backpackers in varying states of blissful dishevelment. Yosemite in our time is not generally a place for solitude—in the sense of being by oneself, without other people, in the way John Muir and even Ansel Adams once experienced it—except, that is, atop certain unheralded subpeaks and nameless granite promontories; along certain disused, half-forgotten trails many miles from the valley, from the Tioga Road, from the John Muir Trail; or else midweek in midwinter, when lo, one might stand on one's skis at some untracked point along Horizon Ridge, utterly alone, looking across at the smooth black shoulder of Half Dome in the silence of new-fallen snow, there to imagine oneself briefly (for a brief eternity) beyond the reach of time.

There is wildness in the valley, too, even in midsummer, when on a busy day the population can exceed twenty-five thousand people. It is a carefree sort of half-civilized wildness—incomparable, indescribable—one that does not exclude humankind but rather indulges it. It is the wildness of blackberry thickets and creeping roses, of old apple orchards and tennis courts long untended, of squirrels and jays battling for picnic scraps, of deer grazing in parking lots, stone footbridges and impromptu float trips on plastic rafts, and

After the initial excitement we may begin to sense the need to share the living realities of this miraculous place. We may resent the intrusion of urban superficialities. We may be filled with regret that so much has happened to despoil, but we can also respond to the challenge to re-create, to protect, to re-interpret the enduring essence of Yosemite, to re-establish it as a sanctuary from the turmoil of the time.
—Ansel Adams, 1960

bicycles strewn beside a beach. It is the strange wildness of nature-paparazzi scurrying along overgrown footpaths after the quick-fading light; of boys and girls chasing bears through the canvas alleyways of Curry Village. "Yosemite Park is a place of rest," wrote Muir, "a refuge from the roar and dust and weary, nervous, wasting work of the lowlands, in which one gains the advantages of both solitude and society." The trick these days is to let the engine cool, to strike out across a meadow on foot, or to stretch out in the shade beside the lazy Merced long enough to allow the place, exactly as it is, to take hold.

THE LAY OF THE LAND: APPROACHES & LOGISTICS

There are four main roads into the park, all paved, all high-gear: the Wawona Road (CA 41), from the southwest via Oakhurst; the El Portal Road (CA 140), from the west via Mariposa and Midpines; the Oak Flat Road (CA 120), from the northwest via Groveland; and the Tioga Road (CA 120), from Lee Vining—the only road into the park from the east, open only in summer. Notes and listings in this chapter are organized geographically along these four gateway corridors. The final section is devoted to the Yosemite Valley itself. Hetch Hetchy is accessed via the Big Oak Flat Road.

There is a grocery store in Yosemite Valley, with a decent, if expensive, selection of gourmet items—wine, cheese, packaged foods, and more. Best bets for fresh produce and chain-style value shopping are Oakhurst and Mariposa (or the farmer's market in Groveland if you happen to be there on a Saturday morning in summer).

For sporting equipment before you head into the hills, stop off at **Herb Bauer** in Fresno (6264 North Blackstone Avenue; 559-435-8600; www.herbbauersportinggoods.com) or the new **REI** (7810 North Blackstone Avenue; 559-261-4168; www.rei.com). Exit CA 41 at Herndon Avenue, head west for less than half a mile, and go north on Blackstone. Last-minute items and basic equipment are available in Yosemite Valley and at Tuolomne Meadows.

LODGING OVERVIEW

It seems fair to say that everyone should, at least once in their lives, spend a night—or several—on the floor of Yosemite Valley. "If it is among the possibilities," wrote pioneer and Yosemite hotelier J. M. Hutchings in 1886, "if you would make your visit healthful, restful, and thoroughly enjoyable . . . do not attempt any very fatiguing excursion the first day after arrival, [but rather] devote it to day-dreaming and rest . . . an easy jaunt among some of the attractive scenes not very far from the hotel." There is no substitute for settling in: for lingering over the fading alpenglow, watching the moon rise over Illilouette Canyon, sipping a cocktail beside the lawn at the Ahwahnee, letting slip into oblivion memories of the car and the road home, and much later, after a good night's rest, stumbling onto the lodge porch in time for dawn to catch the crest of the falls. There are options for every budget. Plan ahead as far in advance as practicable, as beds can be hard to come by at the last minute, especially in summer. If you prefer a modicum of silence and solitude, make it midweek in midwinter. An overnight trek to one or more of the historic High Sierra Camps is also an experience not to be missed (facilities only open in summer)—especially for those who might prefer to enjoy the wilderness without the full complement of camping gear borne upon their shoulders, and to let someone else do the cooking and the dishes. That said, there are excellent reasons for spending a night or two in some of the finer

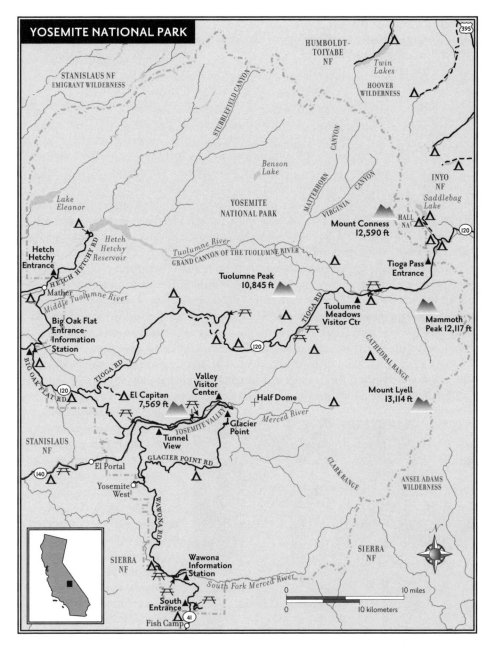

establishments along the gateway corridors: to break up the trip on the way in or out (or both); to get away from the crowds; to explore less-trampled country; to have a place for your pet to sleep; to go mountain biking or geocaching or to pursue any number of other activities not permitted within the national park; to spend less money; to find relief from the inevitable institutional character of Park Service concessions; and so on. For a memorable winter adventure, try an overnight ski trip to Glacier Point or to the historic hut at Ostrander.

Lodging Price Code

Cost of lodging is based on an average per-room, double-occupancy rate at peak season (May through September). Tax and gratuities are not included. Rates are often reduced during the winter.

Inexpensive	Up to $75
Moderate	$75 to $125
Expensive	$125 to $200
Very Expensive	Over $200

CAMPING

In the old days, a person could lay out his bedroll or pitch a tent anywhere he so desired. To a certain degree this is still possible along back roads in the Stanislaus, Sierra, and Inyo National Forests, and in the backcountry of Yosemite's High Sierra. (It is emphatically required, by terms specified on a backcountry permit, that a person camp only on ground previously used for that purpose, and at a certain distance from water sources, roads, and trails.) Permits are available at no charge from the ranger station or visitors center nearest the departure trailhead. Call 209-372-0200 for locations and hours. During peak season (May to September) some trails in Yosemite are subject to quotas for overnight travel. Permit reservations may be made in advance for a small fee (209-372-0740; www.nps.gov/archive/yose/wilderness/reserve.htm). It is illegal to sleep in one's car or RV within Yosemite National Park, except in a designated campground.

Developed campgrounds anywhere within striking distance of Yosemite routinely fill up on summer weekends, and often during the week as well. More than anywhere else in the Sierra, reservations are recommended. Of the 13 car campgrounds inside the park, seven have sites that can be reserved in advance. Reservations can be made up to five months prior, through the **National Recreation Reservation System** (1-877-444-6777; www.recreation.gov), beginning at 7 AM Pacific Time on the 15th of the month. For example, reservation requests for campsites during the third week in July will be accepted beginning at 7 AM on the 15 of March—and will likely sell out within minutes. Cancellations and no-shows do occur, with sites

Curry Village tent-cabins Burke Griggs

YOSEMITE CAMPING

WAWONA ROAD (CA 41)	ELEVATION	SEASON	RESERVATIONS ACCEPTED	FEE	SITES	WATER	AGENCY
GREYS MOUNTAIN	5,400	Jun-Oct	No	Yes	26	No	USFS
TEXAS FLAT (GROUP)	5,400	Jun-Nov	Yes	Yes	4	No	USFS
SOQUEL (OVERFLOW)	5,400	Jun-Oct	Yes	Yes	11	No	USFS
NELDER GROVE (PRIMITIVE)	5,300	May-Sep	No	No	7	No	USFS
KELTY MEADOW (EQUEST.)	5,800	Jun-Oct	Yes	Yes	11	No	USFS
FRESNO DOME	6,400	Jun-Oct	No	Yes	15	No	USFS
BIG SANDY	5,800	Jun-Oct	No	Yes	18	No	USFS
SUMMERDALE	5,000	Jun-Nov	Yes	Yes	29	Piped	USFS
SUMMIT	5,800	Jun-Oct	No	No	6	No	USFS
WAWONA*	4,000	Year-round	Yes**	Yes	93	Piped	NPS
BRIDALVEIL CREEK*	7,200	Jun-Sep	No	Yes	110	Piped	NPS
EL PORTAL ROAD (CA 140)							
McCABE FLAT	1,200	Year-round	No	Yes	14	No	BLM
RAILROAD FLAT	1,200	Year-round	No	Yes	9	No	BLM
WILLOW PLACER (WALK-IN)	1,200	Year-round	No	Yes	8	No	BLM
JERSEYDALE	4,000	May-Nov	No	No	10	Yes	USFS
DRY GULCH (WALK-IN)	1,600	Year-round	Yes	Yes	4	Yes	USFS
DIRT FLAT (WALK-IN)	1,600	Year-round	Yes	Yes	5	Yes	USFS
BIG OAK FLAT ROAD (CA 120)							
THE PINES	3,200	Year-round	No	Yes	11	Piped	USFS
THE PINES (GROUP)	3,200	May-Nov	Yes	Yes	2	Piped	USFS
LOST CLAIM	3,100	May-Sep	No	Yes	10	Well	USFS
SOUTH FORK	1,500	Apr-Oct	No	No	8	No	USFS
LUMSDEN	1,500	Year-round	No	No	10	No	USFS
LUMSDEN BRIDGE	1,500	Apr-Oct	No	No	9	No	USFS
SWEETWATER	3,000	Apr-Oct	No	Yes	12	Piped	USFS
MOORE CREEK (GROUP)	3,100	Year-round	Yes‡	No	1	No	USFS
DIMOND "O"	4,400	Apr-Oct	Yes	Yes	36	Piped	USFS
CHERRY VALLEY	4,700	Apr-Oct	No	Yes	45	Piped	USFS
HETCH HETCHY (BACKPACKERS)*	3,800	Year-round	No	Yes	19	Piped	NPS
HODGDON MEADOW*	4,900	Year-round	Yes**	Yes	105	Piped	NPS
CRANE FLAT*	6,200	May-Oct	Yes**	Yes	166	Piped	NPS
TIOGA ROAD (CA 120)***							
TUOLUMNE MEADOWS*	8,600	Jun-Oct	Half	Yes	304	Piped	NPS
PORCUPINE FLAT*	8,100	Jun-Oct	No	Yes	52	Creek	NPS
YOSEMITE CREEK*	7,659	Jun-Sep	No	Yes	40	Creek	NPS
WHITE WOLF*	8,000	May-Sep	No	Yes	74	Piped	NPS
TAMARACK FLAT*	7,569	May-Oct	No	Yes	52	Creek	NPS
YOSEMITE VALLEY							
UPPER PINES*	4,000	Year-round	Yes**	Yes	238	Piped	NPS
LOWER PINES*	4,000	Mar-Oct	Yes	Yes	60	Piped	NPS
NORTH PINES*	4,000	Apr-Oct	Yes	Yes	81	Piped	NPS
CAMP 4 (SUNNYSIDE WALK-IN)*	4,000	Year-round	No	Yes	35	Piped	NPS

Note: Reservations at USFS and NPS sites, unless otherwise specified, can be made online at www.recreation.gov or by calling 1-877-444-6777.
* Located within the park.   ** First come, first served in winter.   *** For campgrounds east of the park, see chapter 5.
‡ For reservations call the Groveland Ranger District at 209-962-7825.

reassigned on a first-come, first-served basis, starting at 8 AM, at **Campground Offices:** at the edge of the Curry Village parking area, at Wawona, at the Big Oak Flat Entrance Station, and at Tuolomne Meadows. The only other camping in the valley available on a first-come, first-served basis, in summer, with parking adjacent, is at Sunnyside (the old Camp 4), where a certain amount of walk-in square footage is rented cheap, per person, with six people to a site. "Camp 4 is the physical and spiritual home of the Yosemite Climbers," wrote Doug Robinson in 1969, ". . . and other hard to classify and vaguely undesirable visitors." A much better bet, if you can carry your gear on your back, or in a bike trailer, is the little-used backpackers' campground beneath the Royal Arches, across Tenaya Creek from the North Pines campground (wilderness permit required; parking at Curry Village). Upper Pines is available on a first-come, first-served basis in winter. Pets are not allowed at Camp 4 (Sunnyside), Tamarack, or Porcupine Flat. For further information and the latest Yosemite camping policies, call the main Campground Office at 209-372-8502.

For camping-style exposure to the elements, but without the hassle of pitching tents and blowing up air mattresses, try **Housekeeping Camp** (Southside Drive; 559-253-5635; www.yosemitepark.com; inexpensive). Best bet, if you can secure one, is a site—three concrete walls, a canvas roof, a patio, bunk beds, and a picnic table—right on the river. Linen packages are available for a nominal fee. Traditional canvas tent-cabins are available for hire at **Curry Village** (off Southside Drive, east end of the valley; 559-253-5635; www.yosemitepark.com; moderate)—which during peak season can feel reminiscent of some U.N. refugee camp—as well as at **Tuolomne Lodge, White Wolf**, and the **High Sierra** camps (see below). An interesting alternative for families visiting the Hetch Hetchy region would be to secure a cabin or tent site at historic **Camp Mather** (209-379-2284; www.campmather.com; inexpensive), owned and managed by the City of San Francisco, Recreation and Parks Department (415-831-2715; www.services.sfgov.org/rpkcamp down.htm). Summer reservations are assigned by lottery in February of each year.

DINING OVERVIEW

"Considering the sixty-five miles and more of mountainous road over which all supplies must be carried for the use of the hotels," wrote early Kodak-slinger Samuel Douglass Dodge in 1890, "and the difficulty in getting and retaining proper help, no one, as he sits down to a fairly good meal at either hotel or pays his seemingly large bill will be disposed to grumble, for he will consider that there is but one Yosemite, and that it is a long way from the beaten track." These days, of course, the track is fairly beaten (and paved) all the way to the far side of the valley. The main dining rooms at the Wawona, the Yosemite Lodge, and the Ahwahnee serve up remarkably complex fare, fresh and well prepared (especially given the volume served during the busy season), and at prices no more extravagant than one might expect (given the location). Outside the park are several excellent restaurants, at least one along each of the four routes, to remind a person what is good and desirable in civilization.

Dining Price Code
Based on the cost of one dinner, including entrée and appetizer (or entrée and desert) and a beverage. Tax and gratuities not included.

Inexpensive	Up to $15
Moderate	$15 to $30
Expensive	$30 to $45
Very Expensive	Over $45

THE WAWONA ROAD (CA 41)

The straightest shot from Los Angeles to Yosemite runs via Fresno and Oakhurst. If you're one of those who prefers to beat traffic out of the city, to throw the whole pile of gear from the last trip into the trunk and deal with provisions later, Oakhurst (population 18,000, elevation 2,300 feet) is your last best stop for cleaning out the mold in the cooler and restocking. Oakhurst is the sort of town J. M. Hutchings would have described—had it existed as such in the 1880s—as one "with all the usual accessories of business, amusement and education." There's a Vons, a Raley's, a bike shop, basic sporting-goods stores, a Hi-Tec footwear outlet, banks, thrift stores, check-cashing outlets, Mexican and Japanese restaurants, a Blockbuster Video, and a range of franchise motels that serve as overflow on busy weekends when the park is full. (Be forewarned: There are nights in July and August when even Oakhurst is sold out down to the last flimsy cubicle at the Days Inn.) If there's credit on your plastic, and you feel you deserve it, stop over for a meal, or better yet a night, and a spa treatment, and an afternoon beside the pool, at the Chateau du Sureau. Otherwise, press on. Between Oakhurst and the South Gate are 12 miles of fast pavement (fast except for on a Friday evening in summer). The woods begin around the first curve out of town. There is lodging to be recommended at Fish Camp and Wawona. From Wawona onward runs the oldest route into the valley—the way Jim Savage's bunch came in, the way most of Tenaya's people went out—and the oldest section of paved road in the park, since 1902.

Lodging

✪ Chateau du Sureau

www.chateausureau.com
48688 Victoria Lane, Oakhurst
Elevation: 2,300 feet
Open: Year-round
559-683-6860
Owner: Erna Kubin-Clanin
Price: Very Expensive
Pets: With permission
Wheelchair Access: Yes
Internet Access: Wireless

California has its share of ersatz European castles: Hearst's, Scotty's, the Disney Castle in Anaheim, Vikingsholm at Tahoe. It should come as no great surprise to find, on the way to Yosemite, on the outskirts of a raggedy supply town like Oakhurst, a gracefully proportioned hillside European-style château—completed in 1991. And yet it does. Most surprising of all, however, is the way it seems always to have been here—its ivy-clad stone tower, whitewashed walls, and terra-cotta roofs set into a hillside of coulter pines, elderberries, and manzanita—as if it had once been some nobleman's country estate and the town had only recently sprung up around it. Through the gates all notion of traffic disappears. There are fountains and koi ponds, herb gardens, rose gardens, a bocce court, a pool, a garage for one's collectible automobile. There are solicitous maids in traditional black-and-white uniforms, classical music and Campari in the salon, a music room, a chapel, a fireplace and balcony in every room, and a discreet stand-alone villa for those attempting to elude the tabloid press. "Consider any individual at any period of his life," wrote Alexis de Tocqueville, "and you will always find him preoccupied with fresh plans to increase his comfort." No more so, perhaps, than when he is on his way in or out of the wilderness. Two-course European-style breakfast is served in the sunroom or *dehors*, in the courtyard; lunch is prepared by request. Multiple-course dinners are served next door at the

Elderberry House. Television available on request. Spa *de charme*, customized excursions, limousine service, and gift boutique.

Narrow Gauge Inn

www.narrowgaugeinn.com
48571 CA 41, Fish Camp
Elevation: 4,990 feet
Open: Year-round
559-683-7720; 1-888-644-9050
Innkeeper: Martha Van Aman
Price: Moderate to Expensive
Pets: Yes ($25 fee)
Wheelchair Access: Yes
Internet Access: Wireless

Within earshot of the train depot, and a short walk up the hill, is a series of terraced motel units offering a decent value alternative to the deluxe corporate resort up the road. A variety of rooms and suites, each with some combination of wood paneling, pioneer-style, and/or Victorian furnishings; a flat-screen TV; a private or semiprivate shaded porch; a pair of Adirondack chairs; and a view into the woods across the tracks. The Mission suite features rough-pine paneling, caribou antlers, a mini-fridge, and two bathrooms. Sleeps a family of five. Jacuzzi, pool, on-site dining, and bar. Two-night minimum on weekends between Memorial Day and Labor Day. Continental breakfast included.

Tenaya Lodge

www.tenayalodge.com
1122 CA 41, Fish Camp
Elevation: 5,288 feet
Open: Year-round
1-888-514-2167
Innkeeper: Delaware North Companies
Price: Very Expensive
Pets: Yes (with $75 Canine Concierge fee)
Wheelchair Access: Yes
Internet Access: Wireless

Two short miles from the South Entrance

and the Mariposa Grove, 35 long and scenic ones to Glacier Point or the valley, and convenient to Badger Pass, Tenaya was built in the early 1990s as a Marriott resort, then purchased and treated to an extensive Native American–themed makeover by Delaware North—with granite floors, diamond-motif carpeting, antler chandeliers, chainsaw bears, Rocky Mountain elk heads, and piped-in music to keep you moving. The 244-room Tenaya Lodge is the deluxe, contemporary, corporate-retreat version of the Yosemite gateway hotel. Because of its size, and price tag, it's often the last place to fill up on a busy weekend. Rooms are enormous, deeply soundproofed, and pleasingly lit. Beds are well dressed with high-thread-count cotton and goose down; water pressure is spectacular. Full-service spa, fitness center, indoor and outdoor pools, Jacuzzi, ice skating, mountain biking, geocaching, wall climbing, horseback riding, cross-country skiing, arcade, and children's activities. Two options for on-site dining, plus a deli, coffee shop, and convenience store. Babysitting services are available. Check for activity packages and discounted winter rates.

✪ Wawona Hotel

www.yosemitepark.com
CA 41, Wawona
Elevation: 4,000 feet
Open: Year-round
559-253-5635
Innkeeper: Delaware North Companies
Price: Moderate to Expensive
Pets: No
Wheelchair Access: Yes
Internet Access: No

The second-oldest operating hotel in the West, Wawona is a handsome collection of glossy white clapboard buildings, like some grand old Victorian resort lost in the Adirondacks. It's artfully aged, thoughtfully maintained, and protected by National

Wawona Hotel, 1880s Thomas Hill

Historic designation as much from decay as from ambitious renovation. James Savage and his Mariposa Batallion camped here early in the spring of 1851, at a comfortable distance from the Indians. By 1856 the Indians had gone and Galen Clark had built a cabin on the west end of the meadow, from which he regularly served venison and trout to hungry travelers. Ulysses S. Grant stayed here in 1879, before the paint was dry on the new two-story building, followed by other such dignitaries as William Jennings Bryan, William Harrison, and the actress Lillie Langtry. The Wawona is still a welcome refuge from road and trail and crowds—with its wide wraparound verandas creeping with hops, wicker chairs that prove on close inspection to be plastic, a lawn made for strolling on, a cold swimming tank from the 1920s, a classy old-world golf course, and canvas awnings that come up in the evening to reveal the sun catching the crowns of ancient trees for which the place was named. Even the Park Service trash cans are painted white. "I do

not know a more idyllic spot," wrote J. Smeaton Chase in *Yosemite Trails* (1911), describing the confluence of mountain, meadow, and forest. "[I]f Yosemite has the greater glory, Wawona has the deeper charm." The newest building dates from 1918. Rooms are available with private bath or without. No TVs, no telephones.

Glacier Point Lodge

www.yosemitepark.com
Glacier Point
Elevation: 7,200 feet
Open: Winter, by reservation only
209-372-8444
Innkeeper: Delaware North, Yosemite Mountaineering School
Price: Expensive to Very Expensive (includes guide and all meals)
Pets: No
Wheelchair Access: No
Internet Access: No

It seems important to mention, lest the word *lodge* kindle visions of varnished

Skiers looking at Half Dome from Glacier Point, 1936 Ralph Anderson, courtesy NPS, YNP

timbers, bear rugs, and oversized stone fireplaces, that winter accommodations here are carved from what in summer is a bustling gift shop and snack bar. There was a grand hotel here once—Ansel Adams made publicity photos of it in the 1920s—but it burned down in 1969. Glacier Point is the most popular, most famous, and in summer most easily accessed and crowded vantage of Half Dome, the valley, and the High Sierra beyond. In winter it is left to those select few who are willing—or rather, thrilled—to ski out the smooth, groomed road from Badger Pass (11 miles), and then eventually to ski back (11 miles, mostly mellow uphill). If you want to be there for sunset, moonrise, meteor showers, and dawn, but don't want to haul a tent, a bivvy sack, and cooking gear, your best bet will be to sign up for a guided Glacier Point Lodge trip. All meals are provided. Sleeping is dormitory-style; bring your own bag and pillow. One- and two-night trips, equipment rentals, and midweek packages are available. Good especially as a trial run for an Ostrander trip.

✪ Ostrander Ski Hut

www.ostranderhut.com
Ostrander Lake, off Glacier Point Road
Elevation: 8,500 feet
Open: Winter
209-372-0740
Innkeepers: Howard Weamer and Fritz Bagget
Price: Inexpensive
Pets: No
Wheelchair Access: No
Internet Access: No

Hand-hewn and assembled by Civilian Conservation Corpsmen of local granite and lodgepole pine, the hut at Ostrander Lake—started and completed in less than 10 weeks during the summer of 1940, 6 miles from the nearest road, with nothing but hand tools and a block-and-tackle—is one of the best and most enduring examples of rustic park architecture in the United States. It was built expressly for ski touring. "[F]rom that center skiers could ski for days always on new terrain," wrote Badger Pass ranger Frank Givens in 1939. "The scenery is the best. Snow conditions are always good due to many different exposures." The hut is a 10-mile ski/snowshoe trek from the Badger Pass parking lot, which, depending on conditions, can take from a few hours to all day. There's nothing technical about it, but neither is it recommended for beginners on skis. Maps, current conditions, and wilderness permits are available at the Badger Pass ranger station. The two significant uphill sections on the way in—with ever-improving views of the Illilouette drainage, the Clark Range, Cloud's Rest, and Half Dome—are best tackled with climbing skins on free-heel or randonée skis (something you can make rough turns on going down). No matter how light you travel, no matter what kind of shape you're in, or how spectacular the weather, you're always glad to smell the wood smoke from Ostrander. Stove, kitchen, pots and pans, unfiltered water, solar-powered light, thousands of acres of relatively avalanche-free intermediate to advanced terrain. Sleeps 25. Bring sleeping bags, hut slippers, and the best food and beverages you can carry. Stay at least two nights to allow for exploration, lounging, and telemark practice. See the Web site for details. Reservations are by lottery in early November, or by telephone after the first of December.

Dining

Erna's Elderberry House (48688 Victoria Lane, Oakhurst; 559-683-6800; www.elderberryhouse.com; very expensive). For fans of Monty Python, the word *elderberry* (*sureau* in French) may conjure scenes somewhat inappropriate to one of the world's top-ranked restaurants. In this case it refers to a native California shrub, protected by the federal government as home to the delicate larvae of a certain threatened species of beetle. Vienna-born restaurateur Erna Kubin-Clanin made her way here via Los Angeles and the tiny hamlet of Wawona, where before the Park Service declined to renew her lease, the first incarnation of the Elderberry House had already garnered international acclaim. "All I had was my reputation," she says. Today that reputation includes the classification of her latest labor of love as one of only four *Relais Gourmands* in the western United States. Multiple-course meals are served prix-fixe in a dining room furnished with French antiques, tapestries, and oil paintings. Consider wearing different attire from what you wore on the trail.

Yosemite Forks Mountain House Restaurant (CA 41, at turnoff to Bass Lake, Oakhurst; 559-683-5191; inexpensive to moderate). An old 1940s roadhouse converted to a family-friendly, faux-woodsy diner complete with angling motifs and an elk head from the Rocky Mountains, Yosemite Forks Mountain House serves sturdy fire-grilled burgers and homemade blackberry pie. It's your best bet for road food or breakfast on the way into the park.

Sierra Restaurant (at the Tenaya Lodge; 1-888-514-2167; www.tenayalodge.com; expensive). Menu selections include pasta, seafood, filet mignon, bounteous salads, and good crunchy vegetables *juliennes*, California style, from down the road in the Central Valley. New World wine list; full bar; leather chairs; fireplace. The chipotle chocolate pudding proves a dangerous revelation. A breakfast buffet boasts two versions of scrambled eggs or eggs made to order, fat pork sausages, Freedom toast, a variety of Odwalla-squeezed juices, and a view of the pool.

Wawona Dining Room (at the Wawona Hotel; 209-375-1425; expensive). Seating is first-come, first served, leaving plenty of time on busy summer evenings to cozy up to a string of old standards on the piano, to peruse the lobby's historic photograph collection (guide available at front desk), or to lounge on the veranda with a cool gin and tonic. The menu has expanded a bit since the days when Ah You and Ah Louie ran the kitchen, when all the food was raised, caught, or shot within a few miles of the hotel. Tourist fashions have changed, but the general atmosphere—linen tablecloths, candles, Big Tree-motif lamp-shades, high-back oak chairs, and wainscoting—remains much the same. The ancho-chile espresso grilled flatiron is the best version of that ubiquitous cut anywhere in the Southern Sierra. Reservations accepted for large groups. An excellent breakfast buffet is included in the price of a room. Lunch served daily. Western-style barbecue on the lawn Saturday evenings; Sunday brunch, Easter through Thanksgiving and during the Christmas holidays.

Food Purveyors

GROCERIES, ETC.
Oakhurst Fruit Stand (40842 CA 41; 559-692-2777). Last stop for farm-fresh produce. Open every day.

Old Corral Grocery & Tackle Shop (41872 Road 222, Oakhurst; 559-683-7414). Basic supplies, hamburger meat, beer, ice, fishing licenses. Open 8–8 daily.

Raley's Superstore (40041 CA 49, Oakhurst; 559-683-8300). The local full-service chain, founded in Placerville in 1935. Meat, produce, pharmacy, deli counter, bakery and coffee bar, WiFi hotspot. Open every day.

Vons (40044 CA 49, Oakhurst; 559-642-4250). The other chain. Deli, bakery, pharmacy, Starbucks, liquor, produce, and gasoline. Open every day.

Books, Maps & Information
Yosemite Sierra Visitors Bureau (41969 CA 41, Oakhurst; 559-683-4636; www.yosemitethisyear.com). Tourist information, mini store, animal books, postcards. Open every day.

Hill's Studio & Information Center (adjacent to the Wawona Hotel; 209-375-9531). Built in 1886. Books, maps, quality souvenirs, wilderness permits, bear canister rental. Run by the Yosemite Association. Open only in summer.

Shopping

SPORTING GEAR & EQUIPMENT
Hi-Tec Boot Outlet (40343 CA 49, Oakhurst; 559-683-6688). Reasonable-quality discount footwear for the trail.

Miller's Mountain Sports (40015 CA 49, Oakhurst; 559-683-7946). Gear and clothing for camping, hiking, and backpacking. Good source for local trail conditions and information.

Yosemite Bicycle And Sport (40120 CA 41, Oakhurst, behind McDonald's; 559-641-BIKE; www.yosemitebicycle.com). The only full-service bike shop within semi-reasonable biking distance of the park (14 miles). Guide and shuttle service, rentals available.

Wawona Golf Shop (Wawona Hotel Annex; 209-372-6572). Clubs, balls, rentals, clothing, swimwear. Open spring to fall.

Badger Pass Sport Shop (Badger Pass Ski Area; 209-372-1333). Winter clothing and accessories, goggles, sunblock, snacks. Open only in winter.

GENERAL STORES

Pioneer Gift & Grocery (Wawona, adjacent Pioneer Village; 209-375-6574). Basic last-minute groceries, camping and fishing supplies. Sundries, souvenirs, pioneer-themed gifts, and books next door. Open all year.

Points of Interest

Bass Lake (County Route 274). Hunter S. Thompson described it as "not really a town, but a resort area—a string of small settlements around a narrow, picture-postcard lake." It's about the same today, 40 years later, and worth a brief side trip if you're interested in motorized water sports, warm-water fishing, hydroelectric power generation, or the various ways in which the world has changed (and not changed) since Thompson spent a memorable holiday weekend here with the Hell's Angels in 1965.

Yosemite Mountain Sugar Pine Railroad (56001 CA 41; 559-683-7273; www.ymsprr.com). Here kids and full-grown train enthusiasts can crowd aboard a converted logging train—"the logger"—for a good old-fashioned narrow-gauge chug through the woods (at contemporary prices). Snack bar, bookstore, gift shop, train museum. Runs daily from mid-March through October. Moonlight runs some Saturdays and Wednesdays. Limited schedule in winter.

Mariposa Big Tree Grove (South Entrance). Part of the original 1864 Grant, Mariposa is the most extensive of the three sequoia groves in Yosemite and is home to the famed **Grizzly Giant,** subject of more than 150 years of painting and photography. There are several dozen other named trees as well, most christened in the 1860s by the grove's original caretaker and guide, Galen Clark. "[T]here are hundreds of such beauty and stateliness," wrote Frederick Olmsted in his report, "that, to one who moves among them in the reverent mood to which they so strongly incite the mind, it will not seem strange that intelligent travellers have declared that they would rather have passed by Niagara itself than have missed visiting this grove." The Yosemite Stage and Turnpike Co. in 1881 carved open what became known as the **Wawona Tunnel Tree** such that wagons and later automobiles could pass beneath and have their pictures taken. Photographs of this tree were featured in popular magazines and children's textbooks for three generations, even after the great snows of 1969 finally did her in—a millennium or two before her time. The **California Tunnel Tree** still stands, scooped out in 1895 for the same purpose, but never to make the big time. Somewhere here Teddy Roosevelt spent the night with John Muir in 1903, on the ground, amid the "cinnamon-colored trunks." The **Mariposa Grove Museum** is open dur-

Motor stage at Wawona Tunnel Tree, 1927. The tree fell in 1969.   Courtesy NPS, YNP

ing the summer, in the upper grove, modest but well worth the climb, in a restored 1930s cabin on a site first built upon by Galen Clark himself. Hiking opportunities abound, from short strolls to longer through-trips. Take a free shuttle from Wawona and hike back (6 miles, mostly downhill).

Galen Clark's cabin in Mariposa Grove George Fiske, courtesy NPS, YNP

Tram service is available within the grove for those who prefer to ride. In winter, the place can be explored in relative solitude on snowshoes or cross-country skis.

Pioneer Village & Yosemite History Center (Wawona; 209-375-6574). This collection of original structures was moved here at one time or another from elsewhere in the park—from Crane Flat and from the valley floor—including a blacksmith shop, a Wells Fargo office, a jail, and the original Degnan's Bakery. From July to Labor Day it is open as a "living" museum, staffed by costumed volunteers. The fastest tour of the place is by historic mudwagon stage, with Burrel Maier, the only ranger/stage driver in the Park Service, at the reigns. Starts and ends at the covered bridge (the park's oldest, 1868–78).

Burrel Maier and the mudwagon, Pioneer Village, Wawona Burke Griggs

Glacier Point (terminus of Glacier Point Road). The first decent road from Chinquapin to Glacier Point was built by Clarence Washburn, by then owner of Clark's Hotel at Wawona, in 1882. Previously, the viewpoint was most commonly accessed by the so-called four-mile trail coming up from the valley (a mule trail improved in 1929 by legendary trail engineer John Conway). "Here we are on the edge of an abyss three thousand two hundred and fifty-seven feet deep," wrote Hutchings in 1886, "and although the great sweep of

Derrick Dodd's Tough [Hen] Story
(As quoted from J. M. Hutchings's *In the Heart of the Sierras*, 1886)

As a part of the usual programme, we experimented as to the time taken by different objects in reaching the bottom of the cliff. An ordinary stone tossed over remained in sight an incredibly long time, but finally vanished somewhere about the middle distance. A handkerchief with a stone tied in the corner, was visible perhaps a thousand feet deeper; but even an empty box, watched by a field-glass, could not be traced to its concussion with the Valley floor. Finally, the landlord appeared on the scene, carrying an antique hen under his arm. This, in spite of the terrified ejaculations and entreaties of the ladies, he deliberately threw over the cliff's edge. A rooster might have gone thus to his doom in stoic silence, but the sex of this unfortunate bird asserted itself the moment it started on its awful journey into space. With an ear-piercing cackle, that gradually grew fainter as it fell, the poor creature shot downward; now beating the air with ineffectual wings, and now frantically clawing at the very wind, that slanted her first this way and then that; thus the hapless fowl shot down, down, until it became a mere fluff of feathers no larger than a quail. Then it dwindled to a wren's size, disappeared, then again dotted the sight a moment as a pin's point, and then—it was gone!

After drawing a long breath all round, the women folks pitched into the hen's owner with redoubled zest. But the genial McCauley shook his head knowingly, and replied:—

"Don't be alarmed about that chicken, ladies. She's used to it. She goes over that cliff every day during the season."

And, sure enough, on our road back we met the old hen about half up the trail, calmly picking her way home!!

the northern rim of the Valley is before us, with its multitudinous crags and rents, the Half Dome, as omnipresent as ever, overshadows and eclipses every lesser object." For years—from the 1870s all the way to 1968—there was terrific entertainment to be had for those on the Point, and also for some of those thousands of feet below, in the dropping of objects to the valley floor: stones, empty boxes, chickens, campfires, and so on. Such activity is no longer legal. The road is closed from Badger Pass in winter but groomed for cross-country skiing. **Gift shop** and snack bar in summer (209-372-8610). The once-famous Overhanging Rock, where automobiles and costumed Indians and ballerinas once posed for scary photographs, now hangs in relative obscurity, strictly off-limits, beyond the railing to the west.

EL PORTAL ROAD (CA 140)

While the other routes afford famous, last-minute, jaw-dropping panoramas of Half Dome and Bridalveil, the El Portal Road, the least traveled overall but the main artery for commuting park employees and public transportation, starts the drama earlier in the journey. From Merced it climbs into the foothills normally enough, speedily enough, to the agèd southernmost gold rush town of Mariposa (2,252 feet)—last stop for half-reasonable gas, Mexican food, cheap motels, antiques shopping, and a fabled back-alley hole-in-the wall saloon. Midpines is a barely discernible collection of cabins and homesteads tucked away into the woods, and locus of the venerable Yosemite Bug (see Lodging), after which the road drops fast and hard to Briceburg, deep in the lower canyon of the Merced. From 1907 to 1945 the Yosemite Valley Railroad bore passengers along the river from Merced to El Portal. The old railroad bed is visible along much of the route through the canyon, and in places provides excellent minimal-grade mountain biking opportunities. CA 140 was once called the all-weather road into Yosemite due to its low-elevation approach, but it is frequently subjected to damage from seasonal flooding. In the big flood of 1997 the road was completely washed out in several places. In the spring of 2006 a section of the road 6 miles below El Portal was buried beneath a 300-ton rockslide. The road was closed for nearly four months, then reopened via a one-lane detour across the river and along the old railroad grade. The rockslide is visible on the opposite bank. El Portal, once the transfer point from rail to stage, is populated almost entirely by Park Service or Delaware North employees. Entrance to the park is through the so-called Arch Rock.

Lodging

✪ Yosemite Bug
www.yosemitebug.com
6979 CA 140, Midpines
Elevation: 2,250 feet
Open: Year-round
209-966-6666; 1-866-826-7108
Owners: Caroline McGrath and Douglas Shaw
Price: Inexpensive to Moderate
Pets: Yes
Wheelchair Access: Limited
Internet Access: In the lodge

Yosemite Bug is by far the best place to stay on CA 140, not only as a stopover on the way to Yosemite (25 miles up the road), but as a destination in its own right. It's carved into an oak-shaded hillside in the foothills above Mariposa; summer camp meets college meets backpacking in Europe meets Yosemite. Accommodations include ultra-budget youth-hostel-style dormitories, tent cabins that are cheaper and more comfortable than in the park, and some of the most interesting and elegantly appointed private rooms in the region. Dining is gourmet camp-style, in the most congenial setting this side of the High Sierra Camps. Full range of activities, tours and classes, live music, a wealth of regional information. Massage therapy, spa treatments, sauna, and a stainless-steel outdoor hot tub. Easy access to swimming holes, local hikes, mountain biking trails, and the Merced River Recreation Area. Public transportation–friendly, plus three chartered buses weekly to and from San Francisco. Hot in midsummer, mild in winter.

Dining

For the last real taco-cart-style Mexican food this side of the Sierra Crest, try **Sal's** in Mariposa (5038 CA 140; 209-966-7227; inexpensive). The **Happy Burger Diner** (5120 CA 140; 209-966-2719; inexpensive) is a local favorite for fast charbroiled items, salad bar, and milk shakes. If you need a break from the road, and to sit down for something more substantial, try **Savoury's** (5027 CA 140; 209-966-7677; moderate), or the more traditional western-themed surf-and-turf at the **Charles Street Dinner House** (5043 CA 140; 209-966-2366; www.charlesstreetdinnerhouse.com; expensive). Otherwise, press on. It's only 7 miles to the Bug.

Café at the Bug (6979 CA 140, Midpines; 209-966-6666; moderate). Order at the counter; eat beneath wagon-wheel chandeliers, snowboards, and a wild boar's head—or outdoors on the porch; bus your own table. No reservations, no dress code. One recent evening's menu boasted marinated grilled tri-tip, pan-fried lemon-tahini trout, and a veggie stir-fry with coconut curry over udon noodles. All good, all hearty, all excellent value. Cold draft beers and a variety of quality wines. After dinner, guests gather around laptops, play poker, or read guidebooks by the fire. Heaping breakfasts from 7 AM. Lunch made to eat there or to take out on the trail.

Food Purveyors

Coffee, Etc.
Pony Expresso (5040 CA 140, Mariposa; 209-966-5053). Coffee, smoothies, juices, icees, sandwiches, and bagels.

Mariposa Coffee Company (2945 CA 49 South, Mariposa; 209-742-7339; www.mariposa coffeeco.com). Visit the source. Stop in for a tasting, demonstration, tour, or a pound or two of beans to go. Open most days all day; Sunday after noon.

Groceries
49er Market (CA 140 and CA 49 North, 49er Shopping Center, Mariposa; 209-966-2040). Full-service market, deli, video rentals. Open daily.

High Country Health Food & Café (5176 CA 49 North, 49er Shopping Center, Mariposa; 209-966-5111). Bulk food, trail mix, herbs, juices, vitamins, snacks, sandwiches, salads, coffee, holistic camping supplies. Closed Sunday.

Pioneer Market (5034 Coakley Circle, at CA 140, Mariposa; 209-742-6100; www.pioneer supermarket.com). Locally owned full-service grocery. Bakery, deli, meat counter, produce, wine and liquor. Open daily.

Mountain View Grocery (6428 CA 140, Midpines; 209-966-2600). Convenience store, gas.

Herbs
Country Kitchen Herb Farm (5467 Clouds Rest, Mariposa; 209-742-6363). Pick your own organic herbs; self-conducted tours; theme gardens, pygmy goats, and sheep. Open every day but Sunday, spring to fall. Call ahead to make sure someone's there.

Books, Maps & Information
Mariposa County Visitors Center (5158 CA 140, Mariposa; 209-966-7081, 1-866-HALF-DOME; www.homeofyosemite.com). Books, maps, brochures, general tourism information. Open daily.

Mariposa Museum & History Center (5119 Jessie Street, Mariposa; 209-966-2924; www.mariposamuseum.com). Gold rush artifacts and implements. Bookstore and gift shop. Self-guided tour map of Mariposa. Picnic area. Open daily; weekends only in January.

Bug Store (6979 CA 140, Midpines; 209-966-6666). Fine-tuned selection of relevant books and maps. Best source on CA 140 for beta on local activities, trails, and transportation.

Shopping

LEATHER GOODS & GIFTS

Nativearth (5002 Fairgrounds Road, Mariposa; 209-966-5568, 1-888-NATIVE-2; www.nativearth.net). Custom-crafted boots, sandals, belts, bags, pouches, and accessories. Costume and period styles, repairs. Bird kits and antique-style buttons.

SPORTING GOODS & EQUIPMENT

Blue Heron Sports (5103 CA 140, Mariposa; 209-742-2300). Fishing supplies, camping gear, clothing. Fly-fishing guide service available.

SUNDRIES & SOUVENIRS

Yosemite Gifts (5023 CA 140, Mariposa; 209-966-4343). Housed in the old Capital Saloon (established in 1867). Totem poles, rocks and minerals, fossils, jewelry, trinkets, vintage books and signs.

Points of Interest

California State Mining & Mineral Museum (CA 49 South, at Mariposa County Fairgrounds, Mariposa; 209-742-7625; www.parks.ca.gov). Thirteen thousand objects related to the history and geology of California's gold rush, including the famous 13.8-pound Fricot nugget, found in the American River in 1864. Hands-on displays, tours, kids' activities, mine tunnel. Books and gifts at the museum shop. Open daily in summer; closed Tuesday in winter.

Mariposa County Courthouse (5088 Bullion Street, Mariposa; 209-966-7081). Oldest working superior courthouse west of the Mississippi, built in 1854. Open during business hours. Tours given Saturday and Sunday, May through October. Call for details.

Site of Savage's Trading Post (West of El Portal). Historical marker on the site where in 1849 James D. Savage had his first run-ins with Indians from the Yosemite.

BIG OAK FLAT ROAD (CA 120)

The earliest version of this road was punched through to the valley in 1874. Today it remains the most popular way in from the Bay Area, Sacramento, and points north—and generally it's the fastest, though it can be slow going on Friday afternoon of a busy holiday weekend, and impassable during a big snowstorm. The topography kicks in in earnest on the east side of the Moccasin Reservoir, after the junction with CA 49. The main road, along with all heavy trucks, toy haulers, and recreational vehicles, follows the sinuous "New" Priest's Grade (completed in 1915) from an elevation of 910 feet to 2,450 at the long-abandoned Priest's Station Hotel 8 miles later. The older grade, once called Moccasin Hill, or Rattlesnake Hill, climbs the same 1,540 feet in 2 miles. In earlier days travelers were obliged to walk while frothing beasts pulled empty stages. There is a spring midway up the hill where all—including fellow travelers, animals, Miwok families, ruthless highwaymen, and the like—could pause for shade and water. "It is no longer necessary to stop at the spring," wrote one local historian in 1955, who even then preferred the old grade to the new. "Any well-driven modern car in good condition can, in the cool of the day, go straight

Big Oak Flat Road and Bridalveil Fall, 1903 | . T. Boysen, courtesy NPS, YNP

up." Not far from Priest's stood the large tree that gave the flat, and subsequently the road, its name. By the time the venerable old oak burned the first time, in 1863, it had already been undermined by gold-seekers carting dirt from its base. Its charred top fell off in 1869, and what was left burned a second time in 1900. Groveland is the newer, more genteel moniker for the old mining settlement once called Garotte, after the summary hanging from another oak of a Mexican fellow who may or may not have put his hands on two hundred dollars' worth of someone else's gold. Groveland today is among the most charming of Mother Lode villages, and it's the last supply stop before Yosemite or Hetch Hetchy, boasting a brief main street, a pair of historic inns, an excellent restaurant, a nursery/coffeehouse/gallery/general store, gas, and groceries. Most of the forests here have been cut over at least once in the last century and a half. Note the difference in size of timber outside the park versus inside. Hetch Hetchy Road is open beyond Camp Mather from 8 AM to 7 PM only, gated at night. At Crane Flat, just below the Tuolomne Grove, the two loose ends of CA 120, east and west, come together for the final three-tunnel descent into the Yosemite Valley, affording along the way the same brief view over the Merced that Hutchings once described as "one of the most magnificent and comprehensive scenes to be found anywhere."

Lodging

Groveland Hotel

www.groveland.com
18767 Main Street, Groveland
Elevation: 2,800 feet
Open: Year-round
209-962-4000; 1-800-273-3314
Innkeepers: Peggy and Grover Mosley
Price: Expensive to Very Expensive
(includes breakfast)
Pets: Yes (with small fee)
Wheelchair Access: No
Internet Access: Wireless

The oldest part of the hotel was built of local adobe brick in 1849. The newer Queen Anne–style annex was added in 1914 to house bigwigs on the O'Shaughnessy dam project at Hetch Hetchy. Today, with its wraparound porches and wicker chairs, its abundant floral patterns, quilts, feather beds, and period antiques, the place fairly creaks with old-world charm. In-room coffeemakers, telephones, and wireless Internet generally seem to keep Lyle, the inn's resident ghost, at bay. Breakfast goes above and beyond the call for a B&B, with squeeze-your-own OJ and heaping, made-to-order skillet scrambles. Spa services, bathtubs, and romantic packages available. Fine dining in the evening. Historic, discreet back door to the Iron Saloon in case the romance goes awry. See the Web site for scheduled wine tasting events and summertime courtyard theater.

✪ Evergreen Lodge

www.evergreenlodge.com
33160 Evergreen Road, Groveland (on the road to Hetch Hetchy)
Elevation: 4,550 feet
Open: Year-round
209-379-2606; 1-800-93-LODGE
Owners: Lee Zimmerman, Brian Anderluh, and Dan Braun
Price: Moderate
Pets: No
Wheelchair Access: Limited
Internet Access: Wireless in recreation building

The Sierra is peppered with "rustic" cabin resorts of the kind that had their heyday in the decades of flapper skirts, touring cars, and moonshine. The majority of these has since fallen so far into disrepair—or worse, been subjected over the years to such haphazard shag-carpet-and-linoleum surface renovations—that today the word *rustic* is less evocative of the simplicity of yesteryear than it is redolent of propane leaks and general mouse-infested squalor. The Evergreen is one of a select few that has been rescued from such a fate. Originally a post office and general store, later a brothel and speakeasy servicing workers on the O'Shaughnessy Dam project, briefly left for dead in the early 1970s, the Evergreen has recently (in 2004) been expanded and brought back to even greater glory by a team of creative and socially conscious investors from San Francisco—to the tune of $10 million. Cabins are clean and spare, with tastefully retro furnishings, galvanized sconce lighting, personal satellite radio, and just the right amount of knotty-pine trim. The new recreation building, with its crackling fire, cozy armchairs, local-resource library, board games, and wireless Internet, provides one of several congenial social hubs (others being the courtyard and the Tavern). A recreation concierge is on hand from early morning until late in the evening to help you earn your end-of-the-day libations. Activities include fly-fishing, mountain biking, white-water rafting, hiking, snowshoeing, pine-needle basket weaving, Ping-Pong, geocaching, hammock-lounging, horseshoes, and massage.

Hetch Hetchy, June 2007

Hetch Hetchy: Once and Future Meadow?

Once upon a time, after the glaciers receded, before any people showed up, both Yosemite and Hetch Hetchy valleys were made into lakes, with meltwater backed up against dams of glacial moraine. Eventually the moraine eroded away, the lakes drained, and meadows and forests moved in. (The name Hetch Hetchy is said to come, for whatever reason, from the Southern Miwok word for "magpie.") In 1906 the San Andreas Fault broke open beneath San Francisco, thousands died, and a good part of the city burned to the ground. The idea was circulated that if there'd been more water, the fires might have been stopped. All eyes turned to the Sierra, and to the 459-square-mile Tuolomne River watershed.

By the end of 1913, despite a fervent campaign by John Muir, Congress had adopted the Raker Act, which gave San Francisco City Engineer Michael "The Chief" O'Shaughnessy the green light to begin

Dining

The Victorian Room Restaurant (at the Groveland Hotel; 209-962-4000; www.groveland.com; expensive). Bacon-wrapped scallops, warm spinach salad, a mixed-grill option featuring venison, quail, duck-and-foie-gras sausage. Award-winning wine list. This is where Her Majesty the Crown Princess of Thailand had dinner on her trip to Yosemite in 2007. Eat outdoors on warm summer evenings or in the intimate 150-year-old formal dining room. Reservations are recommended. Ask about picnic-basket lunches to go.

Evergreen Lodge Restaurant (at the Evergreen Lodge; 209-379-2606; www.evergreenlodge.com/dining.html; moderate to expensive). Molasses chicken wings, 10-bean soup, lamb moussaka,

building his now-notorious curved gravity dam. John Muir died the following year—according to legend, of a broken heart. Not everyone was so deeply opposed to the backing-up of the waters. William Randolph Hearst was a big fan, and William Jennings Bryan, and the nation's first Chief Forester, Gifford Pichot, and Woodrow Wilson—and a good number of locals. "The lake which will soon be created," wrote University of California Geology Professor Andrew Lawson in Ansel Hall's *Handbook of Yosemite* (1921), "will be but a restoration on a larger scale of the lake which once existed there . . . [it] will seem very natural in its mountain setting." The dam was completed in 1923. The resulting reservoir, stretching 8 miles upstream into the Grand Canyon of the Tuolomne, off-limits to boating or swimming, is now said to provide up to 85 percent of San Francisco's drinking water, at 220 million gallons a day, and clean power for 2.5 million people. For this resource the city of San Francisco pays the federal government rent, at the rate of $30,000 per year—plus another million or so to help pay for park rangers and trails and such.

As there was in the windblown aftermath of the great Owens Valley water grab on the other side of the range, there was at Hetch Hetchy an unintended consequence: silence. Where today the place might otherwise be filled with cars and tourist buses and hotels, it is instead the wildest, most rattlesnake-infested, least-visited part of Yosemite National Park.

In 1987, Ronald Reagan's interior secretary, Donald Hodel, proposed to study the feasibility of removing the dam and restoring the valley to an earlier state of affairs. "This is the worst idea I have heard since the sale of weapons to Iran," said Dianne Feinstein, then mayor of San Francisco. "There is no issue on which there is more controversy and concern than water in California." Reports were made and the idea dropped. But the wheels were turning. In 2006, in response to a flurry of proposals from academic and environmental sectors, the California Department of Water Resouces, together with the Department of Parks and Recreation, took a good hard look at the matter. There were many concerns: How would it be done? Diamond-saw cutting? Blasting? Hydraulic ramming? How long would it take the meadow to come back? Would the stains on the rocks go away? What about flood control? Where would San Francisco's water and power come from? How much would it cost? For every obstacle there seemed at least the possibility of a solution. The final recommendation was that further studies be conducted to the tune of $7 million. The Bush administration, in its 2008 budget proposal, included an item allowing for just such a study, to be paid for by the City of San Francisco.

"It's a raid on San Francisco resources," said Feinstein, then a U.S. Senator.

It seems unlikely that the reservoir will be drained anytime soon. For now, in the meantime, the sounds of nature prevail: the lapping of waves, the sawing of crickets and the rattle of snakes in the grass, and in springtime the thunder of Wapama Falls.

smoked-chicken-and-sausage lasagna, hava-bean vegetarian and buffalo burgers. Start with a martini at a picnic table in the courtyard, or something from the well-considered wine list; eat outdoors, or in the tavern, or in the original dining room from 1921; finish with a caramel bread pudding and cinnamon ice cream by a fire beneath the stars. Open daily for breakfast, lunch, and dinner. Hours vary seasonally.

Taverns, Saloons & Roadhouses

✪ **Iron Door Saloon** (Main Street, Groveland; 209-962-6244; www.iron -door-saloon.com). Serving prospectors, tourists, stagecoach drivers, dam builders, and weekend motorcycle gangs since "sometime before 1852." The grill next door serves basic pub food and a hearty spaghetti bolognese. The original iron doors, still in place, made their way here from England by way of Cape Horn and a team of mules. The stone walls are locally quarried schist. Unique collection of historic artifacts, photos, natural history displays, and bullet holes, all of which is available daily for public perusal. Children welcome. Quality live music most weekends. The sort of place you might hear a grunge version of "Whiskey River," where the bartender might be induced to get on stage and sing a round of "Mustang Sally," where a pause for a quick draft along the road might just turn into an overnight at the hotel next door (or across the street).

✪ **Tavern at the Green** (Evergreen Lodge; 209-379-2606; www.evergreenlodge.com/tav ern.html). What the Iron Door is to the 19th-century Western saloon, the Tavern is to the classic pine-paneled roadhouse of the 1920s and '30s. Ten beers on tap, an impressive selection of single-malt scotches, a cocktail menu for the kids. Pool table. Excellent live music all year long. The shame of it, from this author's point of view, is that the two best bars in the Southern Sierra, each within half an hour of the other, are both shut off from the east side of the range for six months of the year—except by a two-day trek on fast skis.

Food Purveyors

GROCERIES
Main Street Market (19000 Main Street, Groveland; 209-962-7452). The last stop for fresh produce. Basic groceries, meat counter, beer, liquor, wine.

Books, Maps & Information
Groveland Yosemite Gateway Museum (18990 CA 120, Groveland; 209-962-0300; www.grovelandmuseum.com). A variety of simple displays, including artifacts from old Priest's Station, fishing gear from the 1930s, old bottles, baskets, and animal pelts. Selection of regional books, gifts, videos and DVDs. Open daily except holidays.

Shopping

SUNDRIES & SOUVENIRS
Groveland Mercantile (18743 Main Street, Groveland; 209-962-4438). Gifts, cards, pet supplies.

GENERAL STORES
✪ **Mountain Sage** (18653 CA 120, Groveland; 209-962-4686; www.mtnsage.com). Just the sort of home-cooked roadside stopover you might expect to come upon in Vermont or the Adirondacks, or in Sonoma—set in a lovingly reclaimed Victorian farmhouse, with a nursery out back, fruit trees blooming in their pots; medicinal herbs; hammocks; organic fairtrade coffee and healthy breakfast burritos; a tasteful selection of books, music, Nepalese woolens, and backpacking necessities; and a gallery featuring a selection of owner Robb Hirsch's landscape and wildlife photography. Stop by the farmer's market Saturday mornings in summer for baked goods, juices, and locally grown organic produce. Check the schedule for frequent concerts and readings.

Evergreen General Store & Gift Shop (at the Evergreen Lodge; 209-379-2606). Espresso bar, soda fountain, sandwiches and quiche, convenience store, camping and fishing supplies, souvenirs. Open daily; hours vary according to season.

Crane Flat Store (Crane Flat, junction of CA 120 West and CA 120 East; 209-379-2349). Gas and convenience store.

Points of Interest
O'Shaughnessy Dam (Hetch Hetchy). One day it may only exist in pictures.

Tuolomne Grove of Big Trees (north of Crane Flat). Historians generally agree that these must have been the trees—"of the Red-wood species, incredibly large"—of which Joseph Walker and his men took passing note on their way across the Sierra in the winter of 1833. "My first impressions of the Big Trees were somewhat disappointing," wrote Joseph LeConte nearly 50 years later, "but . . . a sense of their immensity grew upon me." Give them a chance. Linger. They are giants. This grove is smaller, but also much quieter and less frequented, than the more famous Mariposa Grove.

TIOGA ROAD & TUOLOMNE MEADOWS (CA 120)

It is a good deal like a roller coaster, only rougher! But if your car's in good shape and you are confident of your driving skill; if you are looking for an adventurous route and breathtaking scenery, there's no better place to find them than along the Tioga Pass Road.

—Travel News Bulletin, *May 1947*

The beginnings of a road had been hammered and blasted up the east side of the range, from Mono Lake, by the late 1870s. In 1881, by the impetus of the Great Sierra Consolidated Silver Company, surveying began for the construction of a wagon road from Crane Flat to the mines at Tioga. "Priest's powder gang, following the picks and shovels, reached Lake Tenaya Thursday," wrote the Homer Mining Index on August 11, 1883, "and will skip the heavy blasting along the margin of the lake for the present and follow up to the Tuolomne River, after which one hundred blasters will be put on to finish the three-fourths of a mile along the lake. It is believed that freight wagons will reach Tioga by or before the end of the month." Meanwhile, towns with official post offices had been thrown up at Dana City and Bennetville, a tunnel punched nearly 2,000 feet into Tioga Hill. By 1884 the whole endeavor was bust—with not an ounce to show. But the road—the great Sierra Wagon Road—was established. The east side sections of Tioga Pass were upgraded from 1899 to 1907. In 1915 the U.S. government purchased the roadway for $10. That summer 190 automobiles entered the park from the east side. By 1940 all but 21 miles had been widened, realigned, and paved. By June 24, 1961, the final 21 miles, including another round of dynamiting along the granite shore of Lake Tenaya (much to the chagrin of the Sierra Club), was complete. "NPS people should have been jailed for what they destroyed at Tenaya Lake," wrote David Brower years later. Sections of the original wagon road can still be driven: from White Wolf to Yosemite Creek campground, and up the short spur along Snow Creek to the May Lake trailhead.

Tioga is said to be a Mohawk word, generally applied to a fork in a river, brought here from the East during the brief mining boom. Tuolomne (pronounced *too-all-lumee*) is considered the largest subalpine meadow in the Sierra. The word is said to be a gentle

Tioga Road and Tenaya Lake, 1935   Ralph Anderson, courtesy NPS, YNP

corruption of a local Miwok word *taa-walïmni,* or "place of the squirrels." Gas and basic supplies are available here, and at Crane Flat. After the first major snowfall of the season (October or November), the road is closed (except for travel by cross-country skis or snowshoes). The springtime opening of the road is a much anticipated event, impossible to predict. Lore has it that the Park Service does its best to get the road cleared by Memorial Day such that its award-winning pack team can make Mule Days in Bishop without having to go the long way around.

Lodging

Tioga Pass Resort (TPR)

www.tiogapassresort.com
CA 120, 1 mile east of Tioga entrance
Elevation: 9,641 feet
Open: Year-round
reservations@tiogapassresort.com (no phone)
Owners: John Landsberger, Michael Entin, and Ron Cohen
Price: Moderate to Expensive
Pets: No
Wheelchair Access: Limited
Internet Access: No

Known as Camp Tioga into the 1950s, TPR's first structures were built in 1914 by onetime trapper and prospector Albert Gardisky. Today the place offers a variety of roadside knotty-pine cabins with kitchenettes, four high-value motel rooms with private water closets and showers down the hall, and the best, most reasonable place to eat between Groveland and Lee Vining. After the pass closes and the park tourists relegate themselves to more temperate elevations, TPR kicks into backcountry-skier mode, serving up three hot meals a day, warm beds, thousands of acres of cross-country touring—as well as what Hans Ludwig, in *Powder* magazine, once called "the finest concentration of kick-ass, big-vertical skiing between Valdez and Verbier."

Tuolomne Meadows Lodge

www.yosemitepark.com
CA 120, Tuolomne Meadows
Elevation: 8,575 feet
Open: Approximately June–September
559-253-5636
Innkeepers: Delaware North Companies
Price: Moderate
Pets: No
Wheelchair Access: Limited
Internet Access: No

Tuolomne Meadows Lodge was first opened by the Desmond Park Company in 1916 to provide lodging for travelers on the newly acquired government road. The only truly significant changes since those early days have been the paving of the road in, and of the parking lot, and the electrification of the kitchen and dining room. The word *lodge* may seem a bit grandiose, unless you've been out wandering in the wilderness for a forgotten period of time. *Camp* might be more appropriate. As such, it is the stopover of choice for those heading farther afield (i.e., to the High Sierra Camps), the perfect place to begin acclimation to the altitude, and a good base for day trips and other romps across the meadows. Accommodations are canvas tent-cabins with metal-frame camp beds, wool blankets, and synthetic comforters. Bring your own sleeping bag, flashlight, and thermal clothing. The ancient woodstoves, with their accompanying ration of logs, newspaper, matches, and candles, give a hint of warmth on the front and back ends of a cold High Sierra night. Tents by the river provide the best atmosphere for sleeping— especially if your neighbors haven't hiked as hard or driven as far as you have. Dining available (see Dining).

White Wolf Lodge

www.yosemitepark.com
Off CA 120
Elevation: 8,000 feet

White Wolf Lodge

Open: Approximately late June–September
559-253-5636
Innkeepers: Delaware North Companies
Price: Inexpensive to Moderate
Pets: No
Wheelchair Access: Limited
Internet Access: No

Set in a small meadow along the Middle Fork of the Tuolomne, White Wolf was first used by ranchers for summer pasture, then by surveyors of the original wagon road. By 1930, according to a Park Service land survey, the property comprised a small resort with 12 tents, two tourist cabins, a diminutive main lodge and dining room, a power plant, and a gas station. Today there are twice as many tents, and no gas station. The quaint, cottage-style cabins and lodge appear exactly as in photographs from the 1930s. The main road has since moved several miles uphill to the south, giving the place an air of remoteness, but the old diesel generator still thunders away in the early evenings. One day maybe the concessionaire will find itself motivated to go solar. Tent accommodations are the same as at Tuolomne Meadows, and more reasonably priced. The cabins, with porches and Adirondack chairs looking across the road to the meadow, are the best bet. Dining available by reservation (see Dining).

✪ High Sierra Camps

www.yosemitepark.com
Five locations in Yosemite backcountry
Elevation: 7,150–10,300 feet
Open: Approximately late June–September
559-253-5674
Innkeepers: Delaware North Companies
Price: Very Expensive (includes two meals)
Pets: No
Wheelchair Access: No
Internet Access: No

The first of a series of backcountry camps was built at Merced Lake in 1916, at the behest of the Park Service's first director, Stephen Mather. Facilities included a row of canvas dormitory tents—for hikers and travelers on horseback—and a mess tent/lounge, staffed by a manager, a cook, and a fisherman. Basic supplies were hauled in by mule. The idea took hold in the 1920s and 1930s as one of the most popular ways to experience the more remote parts of the Yosemite high country. Today there are five such camps, each 5 to 10 miles apart along a rough loop, each offering the same basic luxuries as seven or eight decades ago: camp beds, mattresses, wool blankets, good society, and copious hot meals. Spend one night out or make an extended loop of all five. **Merced Lake** (7,150 feet), the lowest in elevation, closest to the valley, and farthest from the Tioga Road, accommodates the most visitors and is most likely to have availability; **Vogelsang** (10,300 feet) is the highest, coldest, and most reminiscent of an overnight in the high Alps. **May Lake** (9,270 feet) is the easiest to access (1 mile from the parking lot) and thus best for families and children. **Glen Aulin** (7,800 feet), the smallest camp, has a waterfall and a nearby view of Mount Conness. **Sunrise** (9,400 feet) is the newest camp (built in 1961) and probably the most beautifully situated. Reservations are highly coveted and not easy to secure, made by mail-in lottery prior to November 30th for the following season. Call for an application. Cancelled reservations are filled by telephone on a first-come, first-served basis. Chances for last-minute availability increase dramatically after Labor Day. Sleep sacks are available for purchase at each camp, but an ultra-light-weight down bag is preferable. Bring your own camp pillow, pack towel, toothbrush, lunch money, flashlight, whatever you require for a day on the trail between camps, and something to spike your lemonade with at trail's end. Pack and saddle service, and naturalist-guided trips also available.

Sunrise High Sierra Camp

Dining

Tioga Pass Resort (CA 120, 1 mile outside the park; no phone; www.tiogapassresort.com; inexpensive to moderate). Better food, better service, better value than in the park.

Tuolomne Meadows Lodge (209-372-8413; moderate). Staffed as it is by people who'd generally rather be in the backcountry (or otherwise kicking back with beers after a long day of jamming their fists into split granite), the lodge's quality of food and service is highly variable. And likely to feel overpriced. Safest bets are the simplest and cheapest: burgers, chicken, and such. The atmosphere—the real draw—is spirited and congenial, conversations tending to the high adventures of people who have traveled much, read not a little, and appreciate a good walk. Reservations are required. Box lunches available. For happy hour try the mini-fridge by the front desk, where a cold Sierra Nevada is several dollars cheaper than in the adjacent dining room.

High Sierra Camps (559-253-5674; expensive). The menu rotates in such a way that hikers on the loop will not have to eat the same meal two nights in a row. Halibut, pork, chicken, and more; vegetarian alternatives; pancakes, eggs, soufflés, and such for breakfast. Meals prepared in each case according to the inventive whimsy of the folks in the kitchen—generally to most excellent effect. There is no better, warmer, more copious fare to be had in the wide open backcountry. BYOB. Meals sometimes available, especially with advance reservations, for those not staying in camp but schlepping their own accommodations.

White Wolf (209-372-8416; moderate). Essentially the same menu as at the High Sierra Camps, without the added flavor of distance from pavement—but with the benefit of red tablecloths, candlelight, and a fire in a fireplace. On weekend nights, opt for the first seating if possible. Be patient. Have a beer or a glass of wine. Enjoy the front porch and the fading light. When you finally get to sit down, family-style, there is sure to be more grub on the table than you can possibly pack away—no matter what you've been up to—and all manner of rousing stories from the trail. Recent fare included a communal bowl of roasted pepper and corn bisque, a communal bowl of mixed greens with jalapeño-canteloupe vinaigrette, and chicken fajitas. Prix fixe. Reservations required. Come as you are.

Food Purveyors

Burgers & Such
Tuolomne Meadows Grill (Tuolomne Meadows, next door to gas station; 209-372-8426). Basic fast food: burgers, dogs, sandwiches, fries, ice cream. Breakfast is the best bet. Closed in winter.

Books, Maps & Information
Tuolomne Meadows Visitors Center (Tuolomne Meadows; 209-372-0263). Books, maps, and more by the Yosemite Association; photos; a handful of classy vintage displays illustrating aspects of glaciation, bears, butterflies, and wildflowers. Friendly rangers dispensing helpful information. Closed in winter.

Shopping

Sporting Gear & equipment

Yosemite Mountaineering School & Outdoor Shop (Tuolomne Meadows, next door to gas station; 209-372-8435; www.yosemitemountaineering.com). Climbing, backpacking, camping, and general mountaineering boutique. Trail maps and guidebooks. Equipment rentals. Basic selection of nuts, chocks, cams, carabiners, and more. Full range of courses and guided trips—rock climbing, hiking, backpacking. Closed in winter except for ski touring trips.

General Stores

Tuolomne Meadows Store & Gas Station (CA 120, Tuolomne Meadows; 209-372-8428, 209-372-1236). Souvenirs, basic convenience items, camping and fishing supplies, licenses, bear canister rental. Closed in winter.

Points of Interest

Tioga Pass Entrance Station (9,945 feet). The highest pass on the California state highway system. The station, constructed of peeled logs and granite boulders, was built in 1931.

Parsons Memorial Lodge (20–30 minute stroll from Lembert Dome parking lot or Tuolomne Visitors Center, at the northern edge of Tuolomne Meadows; 209-372-4542). An Angora goat herder by the name of "Hermit John" Lembert homesteaded property here, and the nearby Soda Springs, beginning sometime in the early 1880s. Then he lost his goats in a snowstorm in 1890 and decided to make his way down to lower elevations, where in 1896, near El Portal, he was murdered. The property was bought and sold a couple of times, picked up by the Sierra Club in 1912, and finally sold to the National Park Service in 1973, as a management headache, for $208,750. The lodge, a small fortress of local rubble stone and peeled logs, was built by the Sierra Club in 1915—possibly designed by Berkeley architect Bernard Maybeck. Interpretive services, lectures, readings, slide presentations, and a fall poetry festival organized by the Yosemite Association. Closed fall to spring.

Lake Tenaya (CA 120). Chief Tenaya was captured here on May 22, 1851. Lafayette Bunnell, feeling sorry for the old man, applied his name to the lake. Tenaya explained that the place already had a perfectly good name: *Py-we-ack,* or "Lake of the Shining Rocks." An Irishman by the name of John Murphy is said to have planted here, in August 1878, 52 brook trout from the lower Tuolomne River. Four seasons later an eastside mining newspaper would claim: "the lake is swarming with fish, some already two feet in length." Today there's a lovely swimming beach, picnic tables, and a trailhead for the shortest hike to the summit of Cloud's Rest (13 miles round-trip).

Yosemite Valley

At another turning of the road we look into the profound and haze-draped depths, and up toward the sublime and storm-defying heights, with feelings all our own, and behold Yo Semite.

—J. M. Hutchings, In the Heart of the Sierras, 1886

All roads ultimately enter the valley from the west, from downriver, merging into a fine two-lane parkway along the south bank of the Merced, at the parking area for **Bridalveil Fall** (reached by way of a pleasant, if busy, stroll along a trail and series of rustic bridges built by cavalry troops around the turn of the last century). "When carriages are introduced," wrote Olmstead in his 1865 report, "it is proposed that they shall be driven for the most part up one side and down the other of the valley, suitable resting places and turnouts for passing being provided at frequent intervals. From this trail a few paths would also need to be formed, leading to points of view which would only be accessible to persons on foot. Several small bridges would also be required." And so it is today, for the most part. From Bridalveil, views of **El Capitan** opening on our left, we wind around past the turnoff for **Sentinel Beach**, past the trailhead of the historic **Four-Mile Trail** to Glacier Point, past the popular swimming hole at the now quite-sturdy **Swinging Bridge** (glimpses of **Yosemite Falls**, in season), and past the New England–style **Yosemite Chapel** (209-372-4831). The chapel, still in service today, was built in 1879, moved to its present location in 1901, and is now all that remains of the original Yosemite Village (the rest of which was dismantled and/or moved to Pioneer Village at Wawona between the mid-1920s and 1980). **Sentinel Bridge**—shortcut to the new **Yosemite Village**, to the **Ahwahnee Hotel**, and to the **Lodge at Yosemite Falls**—was the first bridge built by the National Park Service, in 1919. Many of the other bridges throughout the valley—Pohono, Ahwahnee, Happy Isles, Stoneman—were built in the 1920s and '30s. Continuing west along Southside Drive we pass **Housekeeping Camp**, on our left, and the handsome **LeConte Memorial Lodge** on our right, before we arrive at the intersection with Northside Drive at **Stoneman Bridge**. From here, a right-hand turn takes us to the bustling hub that is **Curry Village** (dining, budget lodging, recreation center, equipment rental, pool, day-use and trailhead parking for **Happy Isles**, the **Mist Trail**, **Half Dome**, and **Mirror Lake**). Straight over the intersection takes us past the **campground reservation office** to the **Upper, Lower,** and **North Pines** campgrounds (parking available only for those with campsite reservations), and to the **Yosemite Valley Stables**. Crossing over the Merced River via Stoneman Bridge (popular put-in point for the leisurely float trip down valley), we angle back westbound on Northside Drive to the main day-use parking lot at Yosemite Village (visitors center, museum, gallery, food, shopping, activities, auto repair, post office, medical clinic—no lodging). A side road to the right, past the **Village Store**, leads to the Ahwahnee Hotel (lodging and dining, limited parking available). Continuing along Northside Drive, we reach, across from **Yosemite Falls**, the Yosemite Lodge complex (lodging, dining, shopping, activities, and equipment rental), beyond which the parkway leads us back past El Capitan to all park exits, or to **Pohono Bridge** for another loop.

From Swinging Bridge to Happy Isles to the mouth of Tenaya Canyon, along the base of the Royal Arches to the village, and beyond to Yosemite Falls, the valley is well served by 12 miles of easy-cruising, paved bicycle path—and an extensive network of walking trails,

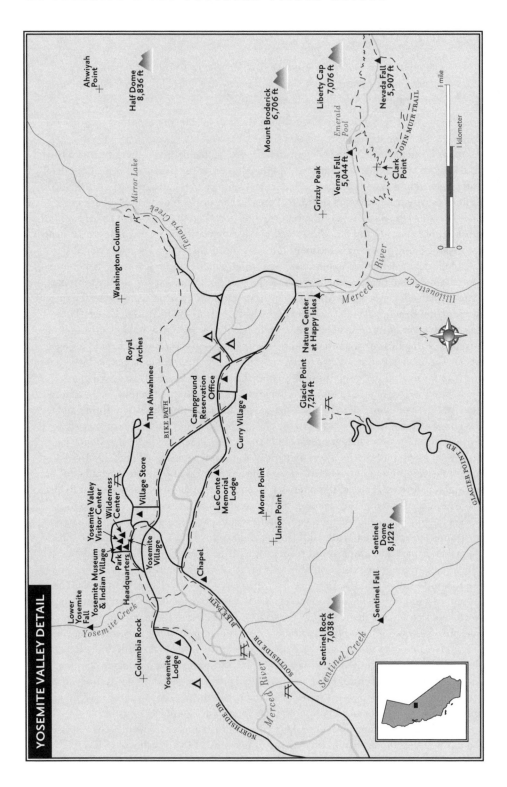

YOSEMITE VALLEY DETAIL

Ahwiyah Point

Half Dome 8,836 ft

Mount Broderick 6,706 ft

Liberty Cap 7,076 ft

Nevada Fall 5,907 ft

Emerald Pool

Vernal Fall 5,044 ft

JOHN MUIR TRAIL

Clark Point

Grizzly Peak

1 mile

1 kilometer

Mirror Lake

Tenaya Creek

Washington Column

Royal Arches

The Ahwahnee

BIKE PATH

Campground Reservation Office

Curry Village

Merced River

Illilouette Ct

Nature Center at Happy Isles

Glacier Point 7,214 ft

Village Store

Wilderness Center

Yosemite Valley Visitor Center

Yosemite Museum & Indian Village

Park Headquarters

Yosemite Village

Chapel

LeConte Memorial Lodge

Moran Point

Union Point

Sentinel Dome 8,122 ft

GLACIER POINT RD

Lower Yosemite Fall

Yosemite Creek

Columbia Rock

BIKE PATH

Yosemite Lodge

Merced River

NORTHSIDE DR

SOUTHSIDE DR

Sentinel Rock 7,038 ft

Sentinel Fall

Sentinel Creek

some of which are thousands of years old. The Yosemite Valley Shuttle runs a regular circuit, every 15–30 minutes, to all main points along the parkway. The best bet is to park your automobile as directly as possible and to strike out by alternative means.

Lodging

✪ The Ahwahnee Hotel

www.yosemitepark.com
Ahwahnee Road, east of Yosemite Village
Elevation: 4,000 feet
Open: Year-round
559-253-5635
Innkeeper: Delaware North Companies
Price: Very Expensive
Pets: No
Wheelchair Access: Yes
Internet Access: Wireless

"A large first-class hotel is very much needed," wrote Muir in 1912. Whether there is truth to the legend that Vicountess Nancy Astor, in the early 1920s, took one look at the old Sentinel Hotel, got back in the car, and headed straight back to London, the fact was this: Accommodations had failed to rise even partway to the grandeur of the surroundings. And so funds were raised, a prominent architect hired, and construction begun on what would become one of the most extraordinary lodges in North America—a grand, 99-room, rustic-deco-gothic-Craftsman palace, made of steel, concrete,

and granite—a place, as Park Service director Mather put it, days before its opening in 1927, "for people who know the delights of luxury living, and to whom the artistic and material comforts of their environment is important." The lobby and lounges downstairs, open as they are to the gawking of the public, may feel more crowded and democratic than at other outrageously priced properties elsewhere on the continent, but the rooms upstairs—the best have private, awning-shaded porches overlooking the valley—fit the bill quite nicely for those occasions when you simply must have the best there is (in Yosemite). A variety of suites and junior suites is available, including the one chosen for Queen Elizabeth II on her visit in 1983, and private cottages in the woods. Pool, tennis, afternoon tea, room service.

Ahwahnee Hotel Burke Griggs

The Lodge at Yosemite Falls

www.yosemitepark.com
Northside Drive, across from Yosemite Falls
Elevation: 4,000 feet
Open: Year-round
559-253-5635
Innkeeper: Delaware North Companies
Price: Expensive
Pets: No
Wheelchair Access: Yes
Internet Access: Wireless in lobby only

The U.S. Cavalry established a barracks and command post here in 1915, not far from where J. M. Hutchings had built his earliest homestead and hotel, at the base of Yosemite Falls—where young John Muir worked the sawmill. Hutchings's hotel is said to have been notoriously spartan, with curtains strung between bunks for privacy. The lodge, a collection of matching, stand-alone, two-story structures, constructed in high midcentury-motor-lodge style in 1956—with louvered windows and doors, and ceiling fans in lieu of air-conditioning—is still a few years away from garnering any significant architectural acclaim. Thoroughly updated by Delaware North in 2003 and '04, with waffle-weave shower curtains, 20-inch TVs, mini-fridges, irons, hairdryers, new carpets, and simple pine furnishings, the lodge provides the best balance between comfort and practicality. If not the most peaceful retreat in the Sierra, it is, at the very least, a giant step up from the tent cabins at Curry Village. Private porches offer views of the falls, in season, or of the woods and meadows opposite. Convenient access to bike path and hiking trails. A short stroll to Yosemite Village. Dining, shopping, bicycle rentals, evening programs, pool.

Dining

In the valley there is food to get you over the hump to the next activity, and there is food worth lingering over. All of it, for better or worse—every microwave burrito, every pan-seared diver scallop—is brought to you by the Delaware North Companies (DNC), a multibillion-dollar hospitality conglomerate, one of the largest privately held companies in the United States, and, since 1993, the sole concessionaire charged with putting chow into as many as twenty-five thousand mouths a day in the Yosemite Valley alone. Food services are provided in four locations: at Curry Village, Yosemite Village (see Food Purveyors), the Ahwahnee, and the Lodge at Yosemite Falls. By the quality of stuff provided at the various snack bars, ice cream stands, short-order grills, convenience stores, buffets, pizza counters, and delis, it will come as little surprise that the company got its start, as early as 1915, selling popcorn in movie theaters and hot dogs at baseball games.

Curry Village Pavilion (Curry Village; inexpensive). Respectable breakfast and dinner buffets. Open daily during the summer; weekends and holidays only from December to mid-March. The ski buffet, offered some Saturday nights in winter, features food, live entertainment, and dancing. Beer and wine available.

✪ **Ahwahnee Dining Room** (at the Ahwahnee; 209-372-1489; expensive). With its trestle-beamed cathedral ceilings, wrought-iron chandeliers, floor-to-ceiling linen drapes, and divided-light windows, the dining room is one of the grandest halls in the American West. Dinner is elegant, if not quite formal: linen, silver, wrought-iron candelabras, the original china service from 1927, collared shirts, trousers, skirts, and dresses. The food, though plated with award-winning artistry, may not always achieve the highest standard it proclaims for itself. But as the building modestly tips its hat to the great half-cleaved cliffs from which it was hewn, so does the meal leave the greater glory to the circumstances in which it is served. Reservations suggested. By daylight the best breakfast buffet in the valley, with overstuffed, made-to-order omelets; thick-slab French toast; local fruit; and fresh-squeezed orange juice. Outrageous Sunday brunch with nine buffet stations. For a light but civilized lunch, try the trout amandine and boysenberry pie.

Food Court at the Lodge (the Lodge at Yosemite Falls; 209-372-1265; inexpensive). Buffet-style: grilled items, pizza, pasta, premade salads, and desserts. Best baguette sandwiches ready-wrapped for picnics in meadows. Beer and wine available. Open daily year-round.

Mountain Room Restaurant (the Lodge at Yosemite Falls; 209-372-1281; www.yosemitepark.com; moderate to expensive). No matter how well framed the view of the falls—and well framed it is—this is not the place to be when the sun is setting in Yosemite. Afterwards, however, when the alpenglow lifts and darkness spreads across the rocks and trails and meadows, and the air takes on the scent of a thousand cookstoves grilling meat, a small army of servers in polyester waistcoats and name tags awaits your pleasure at the Mountain Room. Remarkably, given the size of the hall, the distance from the kitchen to the table, and the number of meals served on a busy summer evening, the food arrives with manifest care and skill, worth hiking out of the wilderness for. The Chef's Prix Fixe is a good bet. One recent lineup featured a generous pile of organic, Madera-raised arugula and radicchio with smoked duck breast, pears, and almonds; a solicitous shank of lamb; and a pear cobbler to help ease the impending transition out of the valley. Beer, fine wine,

cocktails. Open for dinner daily year-round. No reservations, except for parties of eight or more.

Taverns, Saloons & Roadhouses

Ahwahnee Bar (at the Ahwahnee; 209-372-1289). Live music from the Steinway most Fridays and Saturdays. Vintage cocktails, fine cheeses, smoked salmon, and chili, served indoors or at tables beside the lawn. Seating first-come, first-served. Open daily.

Curry Bar (at Curry Village Pavilion). A handful of stools at the service bar off the Pizza Deck, generally occupied by employees, resident bouldering aficionados, or big-wall climbers on shore leave. Draft beers by the pint, premixed margaritas.

Mountain Room Lounge (the Lodge at Yosemite Falls; 209-372-1035). The only place in the world where you can sip on a basil gimlet, catch a ball game on TV, roast marshmallows indoors, and watch the moon glow on Yosemite Falls. Appetizers and limited bar food available.

Food Purveyors

COFFEE, ETC.
Ice Cream & Coffee Corner (Curry Village Pavilion). Coffee, espresso, pastries, hand-dipped ice cream. The earliest coffee available each morning at Curry Village. Open seasonally.

Degnan's Café (Yosemite Village, in the A-frame between the village store and the post office; 209-372-8454). Coffee drinks, tea, smoothies; items baked once upon a time somewhere else. Computer terminals for public Internet browsing. Open year-round.

PIZZA
Pizza Deck (Curry Village; 209-372-8333). No-frills pies and chili dogs slung to the

waiting throngs through a service window, to be eaten alfresco with the squirrels and acorns. Cold beer available next door. Tacos and nachos around the corner, depending on staff availability. The whole affair is closed early fall through late spring.

Sandwiches & Such

Degnan's Deli (Yosemite Village, in the A-frame between the village store and the post office; 209-372-8454). Named for John Degnan, the Irishman who, with the help of his wife, from 1884 until they both died in the 1940s, baked fresh bread for everyone in the park. The bread is no longer fresh, nor is it baked anywhere near Yosemite, but the sandwiches are reasonably priced and made to order. An array of convenience-style items and beverages are available to round out your picnic. Open year-round. Family-style pizza restaurant upstairs in the **Loft** (209-372-8381), with better pizza than at Curry Village. Open spring through fall.

Short Order

Village Grill (Yosemite Village, next to village store). Beef, veggie, and salmon burgers; grilled chicken sandwiches; fries; milk shakes. Open spring to fall.

Snacks & Sweets

Happy Isles Snack Stand (Happy Isles Nature Center, east of Curry Village; 209-372-0287) Cold bottled water, soft drinks, and packaged ice cream designed for those coming off the Mist Trail or waiting for the shuttle. Closed in winter.

Ahwahnee Sweet Shop (at the Ahwahnee; 209-372-1271). Candy, cigars, wine, soft drinks, magazines, newspapers, and postcards. Open year-round.

Books, Maps & Information

Happy Isles Nature Center (east of Curry Village). Kids' books, games, toys, displays, and ranger-led activities.

Valley Visitors Center (Yosemite Village; 209-372-0299). Recently renovated series of displays and exhibits, organized in timeline fashion from the geological beginnings of the Sierra through its more recent natural and social history. Staff of friendly rangers on hand to provide information. Video and live programs in West Auditorium Theater. Bookstore adjacent.

Yosemite Association Bookstore (Yosemite Village, next to Valley Visitors Center; 209-379-2648; www.yosemitestore.com). The park's most complete selection.

Wilderness Center (Yosemite Village, next to Ansel Adams Gallery; 209-372-0740). Specialized collection of guidebooks and maps. Interpretive displays. Wilderness permits and bear-canister rentals. Closed in winter.

Shopping

Galleries

Ansel Adams Gallery (Yosemite Village; 209-372-4413, 1-888-361-7622; www.anseladams.com). Housed in the handsome "new" Best's Studio, built in the 1920s on the occasion of the Park Service—ordered abandonment of the old village, this is where Ansel Adams and Virginia Best were married in 1928. Fine-art prints, books, calendars, and posters—by Ansel and by a rotating selection of contemporary nature photographers. Ask about upcoming photography workshops. Open year-round.

Sporting Gear & Equipment

Village Sport Shop (Yosemite Village, next to Village Store; 209-372-1253). A general outdoor boutique featuring an array of hiking wear, boots, river sandals, hut slippers, fishing gear, camping supplies, daypacks, maps, and books. Open year-round.

Mountain Shop (Curry Village; 209-372-8396). The best selection of backpacking, camping, climbing, and mountaineering gear between Mammoth Lakes and Fresno. Clothing, footwear, "Go Climb a Rock" memorabilia, books, maps, and general information. Interesting display of vintage climbing hardware. Winter equipment rentals when weather warrants. Open year-round.

SUNDRIES & SOUVENIRS
The Nature Shop (at Yosemite Lodge; 209-372-1438). Quality, environmentally conscious gifts, clothing, jewelry, and accessories. Open year-round.

Ahwahnee Gift Shop (at the Ahwahnee; 209-372-1409; www.yosemitegifts.com/ahwah neespirit.html). Quality Ahwahnee-themed gifts and souvenirs: bathrobes, polo shirts, sweaters, china, vintner's accessories, books, journals, and holiday ornaments. Open year-round.

GENERAL STORES
Village Store (Yosemite Village; 209-372-1253). The biggest grocery store in the valley has a decent stock of gourmet backpacking and picnic items, cheeses, pâtés, olives, organic chocolate, canned and dehydrated goods, basic produce, beer, wine, ice, books, maps, magazines, clothing, gifts, and souvenirs. Open daily year-round.

Yosemite Lodge Store (Yosemite Lodge; 209-372-1297). Basic convenience items, cold beer, books, maps, curios, stuffed-bear toys, and souvenirs. Open daily year-round.

Curry Village Gift & Grocery (Curry Village; 209-372-8325). Familiar array of convenience items, beer, shrink-wrapped sandwiches and microwave food, souvenirs, postcards, and batteries.

Points of Interest
LeConte Memorial Lodge (Southside Drive; 209-372-4542; www.sierraclub.org/educa tion/leconte) Built of local granite and timber in a rustic Tudor style in 1903–4 by the Sierra Club as Yosemite's first public visitors center, LeConte was named for scientist, author, early Sierra advocate, and friend of John Muir, Joseph "Little Joe" LeConte (1823–1901). A teenaged Ansel Adams was custodian here in 1919. Features include interesting pop-up presentations and displays about conservation history in the Sierra, as well as a comprehensive library, relief maps, and a children's play area. Open Wednesday through Sunday, May to September. Closed the remainder of the year.

Mirror Lake. A seasonal lake at the mouth of Tenaya Canyon, Mirror Lake was given its latest name by Lafayette Bunnell in 1851, although he claimed to have been open to suggestion. One scholar in the 1950s found an old stereoview on which the lake was dubbed "the toilet glass of Yosemite." "The water is remarkably clear and placid," wrote John S. Hittell in one of the earliest Yosemite guidebooks (1868), "and the reflection of the Washington Column and of the South Half Dome on its surface is so nearly perfect that photographic views of them are frequently mistaken for upright views taken directly from the objects themselves. The photograph . . . is from its western shore." Capture has been attempted from this very spot by no less illustrious company than Weed, Muybridge, Watkins (for

To the Top of Half Dome—and Back

To make the top of the valley's most prominent feature (8,836 feet) is for many park visitors—as many as a thousand per day on a busy summer weekend—a kind of right of passage. It does fairly scream to be stood on top of. A Scottish pioneer by the name of George Anderson, whose attractive floorless log cabin is nowadays on display at Wawona, took it upon himself in October 1875 to hand-drill a series of eyebolts and thus string 400 feet of rope up the near-sheer granite backside of Half Dome. John Muir, in the wake of that season's first snow, was among the first to use the ropes to make the summit. The next year Anderson was charging tourists for the privilege and dreaming of making a fortune with a staircase. In 1877 he took Hutchings up, and a photographer, and had his picture taken on the same overhanging ledge where today people wait in line to achieve similar immortality—striking fearless poses nearly 5,000 feet of gauzy air above the valley floor. By 1884 the ropes, and many of the bolts, had been destroyed by snow and ice—and Anderson had died alone, and broke, in his cabin. A system of fixed cables was installed in 1919, the essence of which is still in use today (with some improvement by the CCC in the 1930s). The Park Service takes the cables down every winter and puts them back up every spring. The most popular route—15 to 17 miles round-trip, at least 4,836 feet of elevation gain, a long day's trek not to be undertaken lightly, or without adequate supplies—begins at Happy Isles and climbs to the Little Yosemite Valley by way of either the John Muir or the Mist Trail.

The cables take a bit of getting used to. They are eminently trustworthy—as long as you hang onto them. There is a pile of old gloves at the bottom, worth borrowing from, especially for the descent. Look for a break in the crowd, keep your head, keep moving, and trust your feet. Don't try it if the rock is wet, or the cables aren't there, or if there's the vaguest possibility of lightning.

Ten to 12 people die every year in Yosemite, mostly by drowning. From 1919 to 2007 not a single person had actually met his maker in an attempt at the cables on Half Dome. Then, on a typically spectacular June afternoon, on a Saturday, with a standard 45-minute wait at the bottom, hundreds of people on the rock—climbing over and under and around each other, everybody mostly cheerful and pleasant but also duly nervous (and hungry and tired), some working their way up, some down, some just taking a moment, gripping both cables with crusty mismatched gardening gloves, working to retrieve wits, to trust feet, to remember why there was this notion to stand on top of Half Dome in the first place—why not a nice, relaxed lunch at the Ahwahnee?—then, with no ado whatsoever, without so much as a scream, a 37-year-old Japanese citizen by the name of Hirofumi Nohara slipped, lost his grip, and fell. One minute he was laughing and talking, the next he was silent, outside the cables and on his way down—fast. It was other people who did the screaming. "The last I saw him," said the guy who'd been right behind him on the way up, "he was backwards in a somersault going over the ledge."

Is the Park Service planning to retire the cables on Half Dome? Not anytime soon, says Scott Gediman, public relations ranger for Yosemite. "We wouldn't build them today," he says, "but now they're historic."

There may be efforts in the future to limit the number of people on the rock at any given time. Until then, consider doing it on a weekday, or in the fall, when there's room to maneuver. Or do it at night, with a couple of friends by the light of the full moon. Bring a head lamp. Make yourselves a cup of tea on the top, watch the sun rise over the Clark Range, and be back in time for a midday beer and lamb shank at the Ahwahnee.

For more information log on to www.nps.gov/yose/planyourvisit/halfdome.htm.

George Anderson atop Half Dome, 1877 S. C. Walker

whom the reflected mountain on the left is named), Fiske, Bierstadt, and Adams. The "lake" becomes a grassy meadow by mid- to late summer and is said to be going slowly extinct from sedimentation. It was dredged for the last time in 1971. An easy stroll from the end of the road. (For some reason, rental bikes are not allowed up the hill.)

Ahwahnee Hotel (end of Ahwahnee Road). See the rustic porte cochere (a successful afterthought), the rubber-tile mosaics, the walk-in Rumsford fireplaces, the concrete rafters formed to look like wood, the original kilims and tapestries, the Howard mural in the Writing Room, and the classic old photos in the Winter Sports Room in the opposite transept. Bring your laptop; check your e-mail. Or curl up in front of the fire and spend an afternoon in the heart of the Sierra with a good novel (or a rousing guidebook). Open to the public year-round. Free tours. See concierge or call 209-372-1426 for schedule.

Yosemite Museum & Indian Village (next to Yosemite Village Visitors Center; 209-372-0282). Features displays on Miwok and Paiute history and culture, baskets, beadwork, and a reconstruction of a traditional Indian village. Gift Shop and art gallery. Cemetery guide available. Open daily.

Yosemite Cemetery (across the road from the Yosemite Museum). Galen Clark's body resides here "in the Sequoia-shaded grave which, after the tranquil fashion of those biblical patriarchs whom in simplicity of spirit he resembled, he had prepared himself years ago" (J. Smeaton Chase, 1911). J. M. Hutchings is here, and the photographer George Fiske, as well as "A Boy," a "Frenchman," and a handful of Piute and Yosemite Indians. Open year-round.

Hutchings Orchard (between Yosemite Falls and the shuttle stop). Good place to see deer grazing among the ancient, long untended apple trees that once upon a time provided good hard cider for weary travelers.

RECREATION

There are few places in the world with such a high concentration of resources for outdoor recreation—150-plus years of local dedication to the subject—combined with such superlative terrain. If what you're looking for involves one or more of the following ingredients—rock, air, sunlight, fresh water, snow, ice, dirt, and/or gravity—you've come to the right place. Here is an overview of the possibilities.

Art & Photography

When people ask Howard Weamer, photographer and longtime caretaker of the Ostrander Ski Hut, how he got his famous 1989 shot "Storm Light, Half Dome"—expecting, perhaps, to hear about aperture and shutter speed and the length of his lens—what he says is something to the effect of (this according to Fritz Bagget): "Well, I guess I was in the right place at the right time." The ongoing effort to get a moment like that on film, or on canvas, is one of Yosemite's oldest and most enduring pastimes. And what better excuse to be out in the thick of it when the light is at its best.

Art & Education Center (Yosemite Village, next to Village Store; 209-372-1442). Art supplies, paints, books, classes, and workshops. Open spring to fall, and during holidays. For the latest schedule, check the current issue of *Yosemite Today,* available at all entrance kiosks and visitors centers.

Ansel Adams Gallery (Yosemite Village; 209-372-4413; www.anseladams.com). Digital and traditional photography workshops. See Web site for schedule.

Bicycle Cruising

There are 12 miles of mostly dead-flat bike path from Swinging Bridge to within a half mile of Mirror Lake. Features include scenic bridges, beaches, meadows, boardwalks, forgotten carriage roads, and major trailheads. Old beat-up cruisers, child trailers, strollers, and wheelchairs for hire by the hour at **Curry Village Recreation Center** (209-372-4FUN), or bring your own.

Boating & Floating

Perhaps the grandest, most carefree way to take in the Yosemite Valley is Tom Sawyer–style, from the half-deflated pontoon of an undersized inflatable raft. The Merced River is generally open for floating upon, from Stoneman Bridge to Sentinel Beach, from late May to sometime in July, depending on water levels. Bring your own nonmotorized flotation equipment—raft, inner tube, kayak—or hire a four- to six-person craft from the **Curry Village Recreation Center** (209-372-4FUN). Fees include paddles, life jackets, and return shuttle. Children must be over 50 pounds. For more active adventure, consider a white-water trip below the park, on the lower Merced (April through July) or the lower Tuolomne (April through September). Class IV. Not recommended for small children.

Zephyr Whitewater Expeditions (P.O. Box 510, Columbia; 209-532-5249, 1-800-431-3636; www.zrafting.com). Half-, full-, and multiday guided trips on the Merced and the Tuolomne. The Yosemite Whitewater Special includes one day on the Merced and two or three on the Tuolomne.

American River Touring Association, Inc. (ARTA) (24000 Casa Loma Road, Groveland; 209-962-7873, 1-800-323-2782; www.arta.org). This locally based nonprofit offers one- to three-day guided trips on the Tuolomne and Merced. Newcomer specials.

O.A.R.S. (P.O. Box 67, Angels Camp; 209-736-4677, 1-800-346-6277; www.oars.com). Variety of trips on the Tuolomne and Merced. Multisport tours include mountain biking, rock climbing, and white-water rafting.

Fishing

Hutchings quotes an old adage: "It takes an Indian to catch a trout at Yo Semite." The fact is, before the mid- to late-1800s, there were no fish of any kind in the Yosemite High Sierra. The glaciers of the Little Ice Age killed them off, and after their retreat the waterfalls made a rather impenetrable barrier. Then the miners and ranchers and Basque sheepherders began to stock high country lakes and streams in order to have a ready food supply in summer. Later on, the National Park Service picked up where they'd left off. It wasn't until the late 1970s that Park Service officials began to realize that nonnative trout species (especially the hardy European browns) were having an adverse effect on native species (especially the yellow-legged frog). Since 1991 there has been no stocking of fish in the park. Nevertheless, the wily bastards still rise to the hatch in streams and lakes from Hetch Hetchy to Chilhualna Creek to the South Fork of the Merced. One interpretive park ranger came padding much like an Indian into the Merced Lake High Sierra Camp late in the summer of 2006, with a fly rod and at least six small trout in his creel for the evening fire. "Save the frogs," he said. "Catch as many as you can." For bigger fish try for the native rainbows in the lower reaches of the Merced and the Tuolumne, below the park. Guide services available through the recreation desk at the **Evergreen Lodge** (33160 Evergreen Road, off CA 120; 209-379-2606; www.evergreenlodge.com) and through **Southern Yosemite Mountain Guides** (North Fork; 1-800-231-4575; www.symg.com).

Geocaching

Geocaching is not permitted within park boundaries, except during occasional special events, such as Earth Day cleanups. For newcomers to this increasingly popular means of making one's way half blindly across the landscape, starter kits and GPS rentals are available at **Tenaya Lodge** (1122 CA 41, Fish Camp; 1-888-514-2167; www.tenayalodge.com) and at the **Evergreen** (33160 Evergreen Road, off CA 120; 209-379-2606; www.evergreen lodge.com).

Golf

Wawona Golf Course (CA 41, Wawona; 209-375-6572). An Audubon Certified Sanctuary, Wawona was built in 1918 as the first regulation course in the Sierra Nevada. Nine-hole, par 35, with alternate tee options for par 70, 18-hole format. Pro shop, cart and club rentals, lessons.

Pine Mountain Lake Golf Club (12765 Mueller Drive, off CA 120, Groveland; 209-962-8620; www.pinemountainlake.com). Eighteen holes, par 70, in the oaks and new-growth pines. Designed by Billy Bell in 1969. The public can reserve tee times up to 10 days in advance. Dress code.

Guided Bus Tours

A variety of ranger-led bus and open-air tram tours is available for nonagoraphobes, from spring through fall. The information comes to you by way of an amplifier, and someone else does the driving. Valley Floor, Big Trees, Glacier Point, Tuolumne Meadows (with hiker-shuttle option), plus a combination Grand Tour, wintertime tours, and a round or two on full-moon evenings (weather and sky permitting). Check in at any **Tour & Activity Desk**—at Curry Village Registration, at the Yosemite Lodge lobby, in front of the Village Store—dial ext. 1240 from any house phone, or call 209-372-4FUN.

Hiking

There are at least 840 miles of trails in Yosemite National Park, and some that have fallen off the modern maps and are worth rediscovering. The most popular (and easiest) strolls in the valley are those to the most famous points of interest—**Bridalveil Fall, Happy Isles, Mirror Lake,** and **Yosemite Falls.** The **Mist Trail,** not a long hike (3 miles round-trip to the top of **Vernal Fall**) but steep—is worth a few hours, not just for the extraordinary cascade, but also for the world-class people-watching along the way. The Valley Floor Loop (13 miles round-trip) is a surprisingly peaceful alternative, and it's great for families with small children—with plentiful options for bailing out early and taking the shuttle back to the hotel. From Tuolomne Meadows, the **John Muir Trail** and the trails that connect the **High Sierra Camps** are busy in summer and well rutted by stock travel. Whenever possible, consider side routes to no-name lakes. As with everywhere else in the park, things quiet down considerably after Labor Day, especially if you can get up during the week. Trailheads off the Wawona and Glacier Point Roads, and from Hetch Hetchy, tend to be the least crowded during the busy season. The best bet is to get a decent topographic map (e.g., the Tom Harrison *Yosemite High Country Trail Map*, available at local bookstores and visitors centers), pack a lunch and plenty of water, and strike out wherever your fancy leads you. When you get into the backcountry, note the century-old Ts blazed by cavalry troops into the bark of pine trees—to mark the way. In summer, use free park shuttles to your advantage: Wawona to the **Mariposa Grove** with a shuttle back (or vice versa); shuttle to the **Yosemite Creek** trailhead on the Tioga Road and hike down to the valley by way of John Conway's brilliant **Upper Yosemite Falls Trail** (or the reverse); or try Mirror Lake to **Olmsted Point** with a shuttle back. For current trail conditions check in with a ranger at the **Big Oak Flat Station** (209-379-1899), **Tuolomne Meadows** (209-372-0263), **Wawona** (209-375-9531), the **Valley Visitors Center** (209-372-0299), or the **Wilderness Center** (209-372-0740). Wilderness permits are required for overnight travel in the backcountry. For guided hiking trips contact the **Yosemite Mountaineering School** (Curry Village or Tuolomne Meadows; 209-372-8344; www.yosemitemountaineering.com).

Interpretive Programs & Activities

Ranger-led walks, lectures, campfire programs, children's programs, slide shows, films, pioneer demonstrations, stargazing, writing and poetry workshops, live performances, and guided snowshoe walks in winter are offered at Pioneer Village at Wawona, Yosemite Village Visitors Center, Curry Village Amphitheater, the Lodge at Yosemite Falls Amphitheater, the LeConte Lodge, and Parsons Lodge in Tuolomne Meadows. Check out Lee Stetson's enduring and well-informed impressions of John Muir, or see Ranger Shelton Johnson as Sgt. Elizy Bowman of the 9th Cavalry, at the handsome new Yosemite Theater behind the Yosemite Village Visitors Center. For details and the latest schedule, check the current issue of *Yosemite Today*, available at all entrance kiosks and visitors centers.

Horseback Riding & Mulepacking

Two-hour, four-hour, and all-day rides are available from the **Wawona Stable** (adjacent to Pioneer Village; 209-372-8348; www.yosemitepark.com), the **Valley Stable** (adjacent to North Pines Campground; 209-372-8427; www.yosemitepark.com), or the **Tuolomne Stable** (CA 120, at the turnoff to Tuolomne Meadows Lodge; 209-372-8427; www.yosemitepark.com). Custom multiday saddle trips and pack service are also available. Contact the **High Sierra Desk** (559-253-5674) for information on how to smuggle luxury items—beer, wine, fresh oysters, down comforters, ice cream, chaise longues (at $3 per pound)—to High Sierra Camps. Otherwise stop by the stable of your choice for more information. No children under seven years old or 44 inches tall are permitted. Maximum weight is 225 pounds. For trail and sleigh rides near the South Entrance, try **Yosemite Trails** (Fish Camp; 559-683-7611; www.yosemitetrails.com). See chapters 4 and 5 for a variety of private pack outfits into the Yosemite National Park backcountry from the east side of the range.

Mountain Biking

Off-road cycling is not allowed within the park, but the Sierra and Stanislaus National Forests, and the Merced River Recreation Area, offer hundreds of miles of logging roads and trails through the woods. **Tenaya Lodge** (1122 CA 41, Fish Camp; 1-888-514-2167; www.tenayalodge.com) and the **Evergreen** (33160 Evergreen Road, off CA 120; 209-379-2606; www.evergreenlodge.com) offer rentals and loads of good beta on local trails. The **Yosemite Bug** (CA 140, Midpines; 209-966-6666; www.yosemitebug.com) is another good base camp, with year-round riding. Bring your own bike. **Yosemite Bicycle and Sport** (40120 CA 41, Oakhurst, behind McDonald's; 559-641-BIKE; www.yosemitebicycle.com) is the nearest full-service bike shop to the park, offering rentals as well as guide and shuttle service.

Road Biking

The topography is terrific, the scenic value extraordinary, the traffic very often a bummer. Early-morning fast laps in Yosemite Valley (almost year-round), or the climb from Mono Lake to Tioga, and the long, gradual descent from Tuolomne to Crane Flat (spring to late fall) are hard to beat. The best time to ride all roads into the park is late fall—October and November, weather permitting—when the air is cool, the roads still dry, and the RVs stabled down south for the winter.

Rock Climbing & Mountaineering

"Climbers throughout the world have recently been expressing interest in Yosemite," wrote Yvon Chouinard (founder of Patagonia) in the *American Alpine Journal* of 1963, "although they know little about it." Those days are gone. Today, Yosemite is the most famous rock-climbing destination on the planet. Why? In part because of the array of characters who made the first ascents and changed the way climbing was done. But ultimate credit must be given to the rock itself—to the vast quantity of it, and to its quality. "Nowhere else in the world is the rock so exfoliated," wrote Chouinard, "so glacier-polished and so devoid of handholds." The valley is best known for its big-wall crack climbing—on any given day one can pull off at the turnout on Northside Drive, set up a lawn chair, crack a cold beer, and peer through binoculars at some miserable pair of sods toasting in the sun 15 pitches up the West Face of El Cap. If you're lucky, you can watch somebody do it without ropes. Bouldering is popular in the shade along the base of the cliffs, especially between Camp 4 and the Ahwahnee. In summer, when the valley heats up, most climbers—and the headquarters of the Yosemite Mountaineering School—pack up and move to the glorious granite-domeland paradise of Tuolomne Meadows. For those not quite so technically inclined, the range here offers many hundreds of fine and dramatic peaks that can be bagged John Muir–style with no more equipment than a pair of shoes and two good hands.

Southern Yosemite Mountain Guides (North Fork; 1-800-231-4575; www.symg.com). Scheduled and custom trips, classes. Climbing, hiking, backpacking, ski touring. Yosemite and points south.

Yosemite Mountaineering School (Curry Village, Tuolomne Meadows, Badger Pass; 209-372-8344; www.yosemitemountaineering.com). These are the people who trained Clint Eastwood for the 1975 movie *The Eiger Sanction,* the same people who invented and thankfully continue to profit from the world-famous Go Climb a Rock T-shirt (available at stores throughout the park). Classes and trips are scheduled year-round, and private instruction and custom guiding are available. Rock climbing, hiking, backpacking, ski touring, hut trips, and equipment rental.

Spa & Massage

✪ Spa Du Sureau (at the Chateau du Sureau, Oakhurst; 559-683-6193; www.chateau sureau.com). Film-noirish, lavender-scented, art deco pleasure palace, open to the public. Dry sauna, hydrostorm, lavishly appointed couple's room, facials, footbaths, marine therapy, the works.

Health Spa at the Yosemite Bug (CA 140, Midpines; 209-966-6666; www.yosemite bug.com/spa.htm). Massage therapy, spa treatments, sauna, and a stainless-steel outdoor hot tub. Tai Chi, yoga, and dance classes with a view.

Swimming

There are crowded swimming pools at the Lodge and at Curry Village that may come into their own during times of extreme drought (open to nonguests for a fee). Otherwise, with

Swimming in the Merced Burke Griggs

the crystalline water of the Merced and its plethora of swimming holes within strolling distance, the pool may not be the place. The antique cold tank at Wawona can hit the spot after a long drive up the Central Valley on a hot day. The small pool at the Ahwahnee is a convenient dip for hotel guests. It is illegal to put so much as toe in San Francisco's water supply at Hetch Hetchy, but higher up in the watershed, up the Tuolomne to the meadows and beyond, there are thousands of ice-cold bodies of water waiting to shock your system.

Tennis

There are courts near the Ahwahnee—like a secret garden, long-lost, neglected, and overgrown with vines—and behind the Wawona Hotel. Nonguests play for a nominal fee.

Skating at Curry Village, February 1939   Ralph Anderson, courtesy NPS, YNP

Winter Sports

Badger Pass Ski Area (Glacier Point Road; 209-372-8430; www.badgerpass.com), with its five lifts; lack of crowds; mellow, groomed terrain; and old-school laid-back atmosphere (the oldest ski area in California, since 1935), is a great place to work your telemark turns before heading into the backcountry, or to get the kids on skis without having to pull a third mortgage on the farm. There are **ski and snowboard rentals** (209-372-8438), **child care** (209-372-8430), **acclaimed ski school** (209-372-8430), **telemark and cross-country ski rentals** (209-372-8444), and **snow tubing** (209-372-8430). Season runs December to April, conditions permitting. Free shuttles daily to and from Curry Village, the Ahwahnee, and the Lodge at Yosemite Falls. For **sledding** try Crane Flat. If you're lucky enough to be in the valley when it snows, snowshoes or cross-country skis can be hired from the **Mountain Shop** at Curry Village (209-372-8396). Outdoor **ice skating** at Curry Village (209-372-8341) has been a favorite tradition since the 1920s. Open daily, December through March (weather permitting). Skate rental and hot chocolate available.

ANNUAL EVENTS

January
Chefs' Holidays (at the Ahwahnee; 559-252-2054; www.yosemitepark.com/chefs). Cooking demonstrations by award-winning chefs, kitchen tour, gala dinner, lodging packages.

February
Camp Mather lottery (San Francisco Recreation and Parks Department; 415-831-2715; www.services.sfgov.org/rpkcampdown.htm).

High Sierra Camps lottery results announced.

Yosemite Nordic Holiday (Badger Pass to Glacier Point; www.yosemitepark.com). Costumes, cross-country ski and telemark races.

March
Southern Yosemite Automotive Film Festival (Oakhurst; www.southernyosemite.com). Classic movies, cars, and guest appearances.

Spring Fest (Badger Pass; www.yosemitepark.com). Sun, slush, and general closing-day craziness.

April
Space-available reservations at High Sierra Camps (559-252-4848; www.yosemite park.com).

Earth Day Celebration (parkwide; www.yosemitepark.com). Crafts, film festival, hikes, walks, talks, children's activities.

May
Average Tioga Pass opening (209-372-0200; www.nps.gov/yose/planyourvisit/condi tions.htm).

Average peak waterfall flow.

Strawberry Music Festival (Camp Mather; 209-984-8630; www.strawberrymusic.com). California's favorite weekend-long, biannual, family-friendly outdoor acoustic-music camp-out extravaganza.

June
Average peak wildflower bloom.

Western Horse Show & Gymkhanas (Mariposa County Fairgrounds; 209-742-7162; www.mariposamountainriders.com).

Yosemite Indian Big Time (Yosemite Museum and Indian Village). Crafts, cultural activities, games, and dancing.

July
Fireworks (Mariposa County Fairgrounds; 209-966-2432).

August
Tuolomne Meadows Poetry Festival (Parsons Lodge).

Mariposa County Fair (Mariposa; 209-966-2432).

September
Strawberry Music Festival (Camp Mather; 209-984-8630; www.strawberrymusic.com). See May.

'49er Festival & Chili Cook-Off (Groveland; www.groveland.org/49er_festival.html). Parades, costumes, kids' activities, live music.

Mountain Heritage Days (Oakhurst; 559-683-6570; www.fresnoflatsmuseum.org).

Mariposa County Agricultural Tours (Mariposa; 209-377-8450; www.mariposa agtour.com). Harvest weekend in the country. Wineries, gardens, organic coffee roastery, bakery, olive orchard, pumpkin patch. Workshops, demonstrations, activities.

Requests accepted for High Sierra Camps lottery (559-252-4848; www.yosemite park.com).

October
Average peak fall colors.

Chocolate & Wine Festival (Oakhurst; 559-683-7766; www.oakhurstchamber.com).

Bugfest (at the Yosemite Bug; 209-966-6666; www.yosemitebug.com). The Bug's version of Oktoberfest. Live music and beer.

Annual Halloween Dance of the Dead (Evergreen Lodge; 209-379-2606; www.ever greenlodge.com/halloween.html). Four days of top-notch live music, revelry, and masquerade. Book early.

Vintners' Holidays (at the Ahwahnee; 559-253-2001; www.yosemitepark.com/vintners). Tastings, seminars, food, lodging packages.

November
Vintners' Holidays (at the Ahwahnee; 559-253-2001; www.yosemitepark.com/vintners). See October.

Ostrander Ski Hut lottery (209-372-0740; www.ostranderhut.com).

High Sierra Camps lottery (559-252-4848; www.yosemitepark.com).

Thanksgiving at the Evergreen (Evergreen Lodge; 209-379-2606; www.evergreenlodge .com/thanksgiving.html). In the woods, pilgrim-style, only with better food and good beer. Book early.

Tioga Pass closes (209-372-0200; www.nps.gov/yose/planyourvisit/conditions.htm).

December
Badger Pass opens (209-372-1114; www.yosemitepark.com)

Vintners' Holidays (at the Ahwahnee; www.yosemitepark.com/vintners; 559-253-2001). See October.

Bracebridge Dinner (at the Ahwahnee; 559-253-5604; www.yosemitepark.com). The ultimate Christmas pageant, since 1927. Lodging packages available. Reserve early.

Space-available reservations at Ostrander Ski Hut (209-372-0740; www.ostranderhut .com).

CA 168, Shaver Lake, June 2007.
Burke Griggs

PROTECT OUR FOREST
YOUR FUTURE HOMES

8

Information

Resources & Practical Matters

Agencies & Nonprofit Organizations
Banks & ATMs
Books
Hospitals & Emergency Medical Services
Kennels
Local Media
Lost & Found
Maps
Road & Auto Service
Tourist Information
Visitors Centers & Ranger Stations
Weather & Road Conditions

AGENCIES & NONPROFIT ORGANIZATIONS

City & County
County of Fresno: 2281 Tulare Street, Fresno; 559-488-1710; www.co.fresno.ca.us.

County of Inyo:
168 North Edwards Street, Independence; 760-878-0366; www.countyofinyo.org. Inyo County Water Department:
163 May Street, Bishop; 760-872-1168; www.inyowater.org.

County of Mariposa: 4982 10th Street, Mariposa; 209-966-3222; www.mari posacounty.org.

County of Mono: 452 Old Mammoth Road, Third Floor, Mammoth Lakes; 760-924-1700; www.monocounty.ca.gov.

County of Tulare: 2800 West Burrel Avenue, Visalia; 559-733-6531; www.co.tulare.ca.us.

Los Angeles Department of Water & Power: 300 Mandich Street, Bishop; 760-872-1104; www.laaqueduct.com.

San Francisco Recreation & Parks Department: 501 Stanyan Street, McLaren Lodge Annex Building, San Francisco; 415-831-2715; http://services.sfgov.org/rpkcampdown.htm

Town of Mammoth Lakes: 437 Old Mammoth Road, Suite R, Mammoth Lakes; 760-934-8989; www.ci.mammoth -lakes.ca.us.

State
Department of Conservation:
801 K Street, MS 24-01, Sacramento; 916-322-1080; www.consrv.ca.gov.

Department of Fish & Game:
1416 Ninth Street, Sacramento; 916-445-0411; www.dfg.ca.gov.

Bishop/East Side: 407 West Line Street, Bishop; 760-872-1171.
Central Region/West Side: 1234 East Shaw Avenue, Fresno; 559-243-4005.

Department of Water Resources: 1416 Ninth Street, Sacramento; 916-653-6192; www.water.ca.gov.

Environmental Protection Agency (CalEPA): 1001 I Street, Sacramento; 916-323-2514; www.calepa.ca.gov.

Federal
Army Corps of Engineers: 441 G Street, Washington, DC; 202-761-0010; www.usace.army.mil.

Bureau of Land Management: 2800 Cottage Way, Suite W-1834, Sacramento; 916-978-4400; www.ca.blm.gov.
Bakersfield: 3801 Pegasus Drive; 661-391-6000.
Bishop: 785 North Main Street, Suite E; 760-872-4881.
Ridgecrest: 300 South Richmond Road; 760-384-5400.

Bureau of Reclamation (Mid-Pacific Region): 2800 Cottage Way, Sacramento; 916-978-5100; www.usbr.gov.

Department of Transportation, National Scenic Byways Program: 1200 New Jersey Avenue SE, HEPN-50, Washington, DC; 202-366-1929; 1-800-4BYWAYS; www.byways.org.

Environmental Protection Agency: 75 Hawthorne Street, 13th Floor, San Francisco; 415-947-8000; 1-866-EPA-WEST; www.epa.gov.

Fish & Wildlife Service: 1849 C Street NW, Washington, DC; 1-800-344-WILD; www.fws.gov.

Geological Survey (Western Region Offices): Menlo Park Campus, Building 3, 345 Middlefield Road, Menlo Park; 650-853-8300; www.usgs.gov.

National Forest Service:
USDA–Pacific Southwest Region: 1323 Club Drive, Vallejo; 707-562-8737; www.fs.fed.us/r5/.
Humboldt-Toiyabe: 1200 Franklin Way, Sparks, NV; 775-331-6444; www.fs.fed.us/r4/htnf.
Inyo: 351 Pacu Lane, Suite 200, Bishop; 760-873-2400; www.fs.fed.us/r5/inyo.
Sequoia: 900 West Grand Avenue, Porterville; 559-784-1500; www.r5.fs.fed.us/sequoia.
Sierra: 1600 Tollhouse Road, Clovis; 559-297-0706; www.fs.fed.us/r5/inyo.
Stanislaus: 9777 Greenley Road, Sonora; 209-532-3671; www.fs.fed.us/r5/stanislaus.

National Interagency Fire Center: 2524 Mulberry Street, Riverside; 909-276-6721; www.nifc.gov.

National Park Service (NPS):
1849 C Street NW, Washington, DC; 202-208-6843; www.nps.gov.
Death Valley: Furnace Creek, CA 190, Death Valley; 760-786-2331; www.nps.gov/deva.
Devil's Postpile National Monument: Minaret Vista, CA 203; 760-934-2289; http://home.nps.gov/depo.
Manzanar National Historic Site: CA 395, 12 miles north of Lone Pine; 760-878-2932; www.nps.gov/manz.
Sequoia and Kings Canyon: 47050 Generals Highway, Three Rivers; 559-565-3341.
Yosemite: Park Headquarters, Yosemite Village; 209-372-0200; www.nps.gov/yose.

Utilities
Southern California Edison: 2244 Walnut Grove, Rosemead; 1-800-655-4555; www.sce.com.

Yosemite National Park Save-A-Bear Hotline: 209-372-0200 ext. 7, then 3.   Photo courtesy NPS, YNP

Nongovernment Organizations & Institutions

Audubon California: 765 University Avenue, Sacramento; 916-649-7600; www.audubon-ca.org.

California Native Plant Society: 2707 K Street, Suite 1, Sacramento; 916-447-2677; www.cnps.org.

California Wild Heritage Campaign: 916-442-3155; www.californiawild.org.

CalTrout: 870 Market Street, Suite 528, San Francisco; 415-392-8887; www.cal trout.org.

Death Valley Natural History Association: Furnace Creek Visitors Center; 1-800-478-8564; www.dvnha.org.

Environmental Defense Fund: 1875 Connecticut Avenue NW, Suite 600, Washington, DC; 1-800-684-3322; www.environmentaldefense.org.

Friends of the Inyo: 699 West Line Street, Suite A, Bishop; 760-873-6500; www.friendsoftheinyo.org.

Friends of the River: 915 20th Street, Sacramento; 916-442-3155; www.friends oftheriver.org.

Friends of the South Fork Kings: Carmichael, CA; 916-601-9954; www.sfk ingsriver.org.

Kings River Conservation Trust: www.elrioreyestrust.org.

Mammoth Lakes Trails & Public Access: 42 Davison, Apt. #2, Mammoth Lakes; 760-934-3154; www.mltpa.org.

Mono Lake Committee: CA 395 and Third Street, Lee Vining; 760-647-6595; www.monolake.org.

National Resources Defense Council:
40 West 20th Street, New York, NY;
212-727-2700; www.nrdc.org.

Owens Valley Committee: Bishop;
www.ovcweb.org.

Public Lands Interpretive Association:
6501 Fourth Street NW, Suite I,
Albuquerque, NM; 505-345-9498;
1-877-851-8946; www.publiclands.org.

**Sequoia Natural History Association
(SNHA):** 559-565-3759; www.sequoiahis
tory.org.

Sierra Club: 85 Second Street, Second
Floor, San Francisco; 415-977-5500;
www.sierraclub.org.

**Sierra Nevada Aquatic Research
Laboratory/Valentine Reserve:** 1016
Mount Morrison Road, Mammoth Lakes;
760-935-4334; http://vesr.ucnrs.org.

White Mountain Research Station:
3000 East Line Street, Bishop;
760-873-4344; www.wmrs.edu.

Wilderness Society: Presidio Building
1016, San Francisco; 415-561-6641;
www.wilderness.org.

Yosemite Association: P.O. Box 230,
El Portal 95318; 209-379-2646;
www.yosemite.org.

Banks & ATMs

Banks
Alta One (www.altaone.org)
Bishop: 462 North Main Street;
760-873-5626.

Kernville: 44 Big Blue Road; 760-376-2251.
Lone Pine: 111 Mount View Road;
760-876-4702.
Mammoth Lakes: 452 Old Mammoth Road;
760-934-3024.
Ridgecrest (Albertsons): 1301 North Norma
Street; 760-371-7000.

Bank of America
(www.bankofamerica.com)
Bishop: 536 North Main Street;
760-873-3551.
Carson City, NV: 947 Topsy Lane and US
395; 775-267-5842.
Gardnerville, NV: 1363 US 395;
775-783-1124.
Lake Isabella: 6212 Lake Isabella Boulevard;
1-800-338-5202.
Mammoth Lakes: 3069 Main Street;
760-934-6830.
Minden, NV: 1646 US 395; 775-688-8995.
Oakhurst: 40027 CA 49; 559-683-3981.
Visalia: 212 East Main Street;
559-635-3160.

Washington Mutual (www.wamu.com)
Bishop: 400 North Main Street;
760-873-5031.
Madera: 233 East Yosemite Avenue;
559-674-8574.
Oakhurst: 40003 CA 49; 559-642-1350.
Reno: 2295 South Virginia Street, #16;
775-823-2700.

Wells Fargo (www.wellsfargo.com)
Bishop: 1190 North Main Street;
1-800-869-3557.
Lake Isabella: 5610 Lake Isabella Boulevard;
760-379-4335.
Ridgecrest: 856C North China Lake
Boulevard; 1-800-869-3557.
Visalia: 414 West Main Street;
559-738-5820.

ATMs in the Parks

Death Valley: Furnace Creek Ranch (front desk), Stovepipe Wells (General Store).

Sequoia-Kings: Grant Grove, Cedar Grove, Lodgepole.

Yosemite: Yosemite Lodge registration, the Village Store, Curry Village Gift Shop, Wawona Store, adjacent to the Art Activity Center in Yosemite Village.

BOOKS

Primary Histories & Narratives

Bade, William Frederic. *The Life and Letters of John Muir.* Boston and New York: Houghton Mifflin, 1924.

Brewer, William Henry. *Up and Down California in 1860–1864: The Journal of William H. Brewer,* 4th ed. Edited by Francis P. Farquhar. Berkeley, Calif.: University of California Press, 2003.

Bunnell, Lafayette H., M.D. *Discovery of the Yosemite (& the Indian War of 1851 Which Led to That Event).* El Portal, Calif.: Yosemite Association, 1991.

Greeley, Horace. An Overland Journey from New York to San Francisco in the Summer of 1859. Lincoln, Neb.: University of Nebraska Press, 1999.

Grey, Zane. *Tales of Lonely Trails.* New York: Harper & Brothers, 1922.

Grooks, George R., ed. *The Southwest Expedition of Jedediah S. Smith.* Glendale, Okla.: Arthur H. Clark, 1977.

Gunsky, Frederick, R., ed. *South of Yosemite: Selected Writings of John Muir.* Berkeley, Calif.: Wilderness Press, 1988.

King, Clarence. *Mountaineering in the High Sierra.* El Portal, Calif.: Yosemite Association, 1997.

LeConte, Joseph. *A Journal of Ramblings Through the High Sierras of California.* El Portal, Calif.: Yosemite Association, 1994.

Olmsted, Frederick Law. *Yosemite and the Mariposa Grove: A Preliminary Report, 1865.* El Portal, Calif.: Yosemite Association, 1995.

Roper, Steve, ed. *Ordeal by Piton: Writings from the Golden Age of Yosemite Climbing.* Palo Alto, Calif.: Stanford University Press, 2003.

Steele, Carol MacRobert. *Pictorial History of Mono Hot Springs, California.* Privately printed, 2003. Available at Mono Hot Springs General Store.

Thompson, Hunter S. *Hell's Angels: A Strange and Terrible Saga.* New York: Random House, Inc., 1966.

Wright, James W. A. *The Lost Cement Mine.* Edited by Genny Smith. Mammoth Lakes, Calif.: Genny Smith Books, 1984.

Secondary Histories & General Interest

Beesley, David. *Crow's Range: An Environmental History of the Sierra Nevada.* Reno, Nev.: University of Nevada Press, 2004.

Caldwell, Gary. *Mammoth Gold.* Mammoth Lakes, Calif.: Genny Smith Books, 1990.

Carle, David. *Introduction to Water in California.* Berkeley, Calif.: University of California Press, 2004.

Chalfant, W. A. *Death Valley: The Facts.* Palo Alto, Calif.: Stanford University Press, 1930.

——. *Gold, Guns & Ghost Towns.* Palo Alto, Calif.: Stanford University Press, 1947.

——. *The Story of Inyo.* Revised ed. Bishop, Calif.: Chalfant Press, 1980.

Clifford, Hal. Downhill Slide: *Why the Corporate Ski Industry Is Bad for Skiing, Ski Towns, and the Environment.* San Francisco: Sierra Club Books, 2003.

Dilsaver, Lary M., and William C. Tweed. *Challenge of the Big Trees: A Resource History of Sequoia and Kings Canyon National Parks.* Three Rivers, Calif.: Sequoia Natural History Association, Inc., 1990.

Farquhar, Francis P. *History of the Sierra Nevada.* Berkeley, Calif.: University of California Press, 1965

Forstenzer, Martin. *Mammoth: The Sierra Legend.* Boulder, Colo.: Mountain Sports Press, 2002.

Ghiglieri, Michael P., and Charles R. "Butch" Farabee Jr. *Off the Wall: Death in Yosemite.* Flagstaff, Ariz.: Puma Press, 2007.

Hart, John. *Storm over Mono: The Mono Lake Battle and the California Water Future.* Berkeley, Calif.: University of California Press, 1996.

Hartesveldt, Richard J., H. Thomas Harvey, Howard S. Shellhammer, and Ronald E. Stecker. *The Giant Sequoia of the Sierra Nevada.* Washington, D.C.: U.S. Department of the Interior, National Park Service, 1975.

Hartesveldt, Richard J. *Yosemite Valley Place Names.* Yosemite Natural History Association, 1955.

Hundley, Norris Jr. *The Great Thirst: Californians and Water, A History.* Berkeley, Calif.: University of California Press, 2001.

Huth, Hans. "Yosemite: The Story of an Idea." *Sierra Club Bulletin* 33(3):47–78 (March, 1948).

Kroeber, A. L. *Handbook of the Indians of California,* Bulletin 78 of the Bureau of American Ethnology of the Smithsonian Institution, 1919.

McPhee, John. *Annals of the Former World.* New York: Farrar, Strauss & Giroux, 1981.

Morgan, Dale L. *Jedediah Smith and the Opening of the West.* Lincoln, Neb.: University of Nebraska Press, 1953.

O'Neill, Elizabeth Stone. *Meadow in the Sky: A History of Yosemite's Tuolomne Meadows Region.* Groveland, Calif.: Albicaulis Press, 1984.

Paden, Irene D., and Margaret E. Schlichtmann. *The Big Oak Flat Road.* San Francisco: Emil P. Schlichtmann, 1955.

Randl, Chad. *A-frame.* New York: Princeton Architectural Press, 2004.

Russell, Carl Parcher. *100 Years in Yosemite: The Story of a Great Park and Its Friends.* Berkeley, Calif.: University of California Press, 1947.

Smith, Genny, ed. *Sierra East: Edge of the Great Basin.* Berkeley, Calif.: University of California Press, 2000.

——. *Mammoth Lakes Sierra: A Handbook for Roadside and Trail.* Mammoth Lakes, Calif.: Genny Smith Books, 1993.

Snyder, Susan. *Past Tents: The Way We Camped.* Berkeley, Calif.: Heyday Books, 2006.

Snyder, Susan, ed. *Bear in Mind: The California Grizzly.* Berkeley, Calif.: Heyday Books, 2003.

Storer, Tracy I., and Lloyd P. Tevis Jr. *California Grizzly.* Berkeley, Calif.: University of California Press, 1955.

Trexler, Keith A. *The Tioga Road, A History: 1883–1961.* Revised ed. Yosemite Natural History Association, 1980.

Tweed, William C., Laura E. Souliere, and Henry G. Law. *Rustic Architecture: 1916-1942.* Washington D.C.: National Park Service, 1977.

Literary

Austin, Mary. *Land of Little Rain.* Boston and New York: Houghton Mifflin Company, 1903.

Hicks, Jack, James D. Houston, Maxine Hong Kingston, and Al Young, eds. *The Literature of California.* Berkeley: University of California Press, 2000.

Kerouac, Jack. *Dharma Bums.* New York: Harcourt Brace, 1958.

Twain, Mark. *Roughing It.* Berkeley, Calif.: University of California Press, 1995.

Art & Photography

Adams, Ansel. *Yosemite and the High Sierra.* Edited by Andrea G. Stillman. New York: Little, Brown & Co., 1994.

Curtis, Edward S. *The North American Indian.* Vol. 14. Norwood, Mass.: Plimpton Press, 1924. Digital version online at: http://curtis.library.north western.edu/curtis.

Denny, Glenn. *Yosemite in the Sixties.* n.p.: Patagonia and T. Adler Books, 2007.

Irwin, Sue. *California's Eastern Sierra: A Visitor's Guide.* Los Olivos, Calif.: Cachuma Press, 1992.

Rose, Gene. *Magic Yosemite Winters: A Century of Winter Sports.* Truckee, Calif.: Coldstream Press, 1999.

Scott, Amy. *Yosemite: Art of an American Icon.* Berkeley, Calif.: University of California Press, 2006.

Weamer, Howard. *The Perfect Art: The Ostrander Hut and Ski Touring in Yosemite.* Marceline, Mo. Walsworth Publishing Co., 1995.

Vintage Guidebooks

Adams, Ansel E., and Virginia Adams. *Illustrated Guide to Yosemite.* San Francisco: H. S. Crocker, 1940.

Chase, J. Smeaton. *Yosemite Trails: Camp and Pack Train in the Yosemite Region of the Sierra Nevada.* Boston and New York: Houghton Mifflin Company, 1911.

Hall, Ansel F. *Handbook of Yosemite National Park.* New York: G. P. Putnam's Sons, 1921.

——. *Guide to Sequoia & General Grant National Parks.* Berkeley, Calif.: National Parks Publishing House, 1930.

Hutchings, James Mason. *In the Heart of the Sierras: Yosemite, Big Trees, Etc.* Oakland, Calif.: Pacific Press Publishing House, 1886.

Muir, John. *The Yosemite.* New York: The Century Co., 1912.

——. *Our National Parks.* Boston and New York: Houghton, Mifflin & Company, 1901.

Putman, Jeff, and Genny Smith. *Deepest Valley: Guide To Owens Valley, Its Roadsides and Mountain Trails.* Reno, Nev.: University of Nevada Press, 1969.

Whitney, Josiah D. *The Yosemite Book.* Oakland, Calif.: Octavo Editions, 2003.

Works Progress Administration, Federal Writers' Project. *California: A Guide to the Golden State.* New York: Hastings House, 1939.

Contemporary Guidebooks

Flint, Wendell. *To Find the Biggest Trees.* Three Rivers, Calif.: Sequoia Natural History Association, Inc., 2002.

Gudde, Erwin C. *California Place Names: The Origin and Etymology of Current Geographical Names,* 4th ed. Revised and enlarged by William Bright. Berkeley, Calif.: University of California Press, 1998. Also available in a handy pocket edition: *1500 California Place Names.*

Holland, Dave. *On Location in Lone Pine: A Pictorial Guide to One of Hollywood's Favorite Movie Locations for 85 Years!* Santa Clarita, Calif: The Holland House, 1990.

Kaiser, Harvey H. *An Architectural Guidebook to the National Parks (California, Oregon, Washington).* Salt Lake City, Utah: Gibbs-Smith, 2002.

Roper, Steve. *Climber's Guide to the High Sierra.* San Francisco: Sierra Club Books. Handy, sturdy tote-book size.

Sharp, Robert P., and Allen F. Glazner. *Geology Underfoot in Death Valley and Owens Valley.* Missoula, Mont.: Mountain Press Publishing Company, 1997.

Storer, Tracy I., Robert L. Usinger, and David Lukas. *Sierra Nevada Natural History.* Revised ed. Berkeley, Calif.: University of California Press, 2004.

Sunderland, Bill. *Fly Fishing The Sierra Nevada.* n.p.: Aguabonita Books, 1999.

Hospitals & Emergency Medical Services

Death Valley & Eastern Sierra
Beatty Medical Clinic: 702 Irving Street, Beatty, NV; 775-553-2208.

Death Valley Health Center: CA 127, Shoshone; 760-852-4383.

Nye County Regional Medical Center: 825 Erie Main Street, Tonopah, NV; 775-482-6233; www.nyeregional.org.

Southern Inyo County Hospital: 501 East Locust Street, Lone Pine; 760-876-5501; www.sihd.org.

Mammoth Lakes Area
Mammoth Hospital: 85 Sierra Park Road, Mammoth Lakes; 760-934-3311; www.mammothhospital.com.

Sequoia/Kings
Kaweah Delta Hospital: 400 West Mineral King Avenue, Visalia; 559-624-2000; www.kaweahdelta.org.

Yosemite
Community Medical Center–Oakhurst: 48677 Victoria Lane, Oakhurst; 559-683-2992; www.communitymedical.org/295.htm.

Community Regional Medical Center: 2823 Fresno Street, Fresno; 559-459-6000; www.communitymedical.org/crmc.htm.

Sonora Community Hospital: 1000 Greenley Road, Sonora; 209-532-5000; www.sonoramedicalcenter.org.

Yosemite Medical Clinic: The Ahwahnee Road, behind Yosemite Village; 209-372-4637.

Kennels

Death Valley
Royal Canine Villa: 2480 Jayme Street, Pahrump, NV; 775-727-7977.

Eastern Sierra
Relaxing Furr Dogs: 751 Brockman Lane, Bishop; 760-872-7074; www.relaxingfurr.com.

Mammoth Lakes Area
Donna's Dogsitting: Old Mammoth Road, Mammoth Lakes; 760-934-2095.

Marta's Doggie Day Care: 1872 Old Mammoth Road, Mammoth Lakes; 760-WAG-PANT.

Sequoia/Kings
Pet Inn: 38 South Goddard Street, Visalia; 559-732-4803.

Yosemite
Elaine's Animal Inn & Spa–Fresno: 3912 North Hayston Avenue, Fresno; 559-227-5959; www.elainesanimalinn.com.

Elaine's Animal Inn–Madera: 40373 Brickyard Drive, Madera; 559-432-5959; www.elainesanimalinn.com.

University Pet Resort: 3789 East Yosemite Avenue, Merced; 209-722-5959; www.universitypetresort.com.

Yosemite Kennels: Yosemite Valley Stables; 209-372-8348.

LOCAL MEDIA

Death Valley & The Eastern Sierra

Death Valley Guide (www.americanpark
work.com). Available at visitors centers
and park entrance kiosks.

The Inyo Register (www.inyoregister.com).
The venerable local, published Tuesday,
Thursday, and Saturday; founded by P. A.
Chalfant in 1870.

Pahrump Valley Times (www.pahrumpvalley
times.com). Daily.

Visitor's Guide to Death Valley National Park
(www.nps.gov/deva). Best source for park
events, activities, news, and current conditions. Published seasonally. Available at
visitors centers and park entrance kiosks.

Mammoth Lakes Area

Mammoth Lakes Visitor Guide. Available at
the Mammoth Lakes Welcome Center.
Published seasonally.

Mammoth Local (www.mammothlocal.com).
Online only. Local news, events,
classifieds.

Mammoth Times
(www.mammothtimes.com). Weekly.

The Post (www.nps.gov/depo/photosmulti
media/visitor-newspaper.htm). Published
seasonally for Devil's Postpile National
Monument. Available at entrance station
and shuttle kiosk.

The Sheet (www.mammothsheet.com).
Ex–Royal Dishwasher John Domesick
Lunch III's mostly frequent, mostly irrev-
erent, always informative chronicle of local
politics and happenings in Mammoth
Lakes.

Sequoia/Kings

The Guide
(www.nps.gov/seki/parknews/newspaper
.htm). Best source for park events, activities, news, and current conditions.
Published seasonally. Available at visitors
centers and park entrance kiosks.

The Kaweah Commonwealth (www.kaweah
commonwealth.com). Weekly for Three
Rivers and surrounding communities.

Sequoia & Kings Canyon Guide (www.ameri
canparknetwork.com). Available at visitors
centers and park entrance kiosks.

Yosemite

Mariposa Gazette
(www.mariposagazette.com). Weekly.

Sierra Star (www.sierrastar.com). Published
Wednesday and Friday in Oakhurst.

Union Democrat
(www.uniondemocrat.com). Daily from
Sonora.

Yosemite Guide (www.americanparknet
work.com). Available at visitors centers
and park entrance kiosks.

Yosemite Today (www.nps.gov/yose/plan
yourvisit/today.htm). Best source for park
events, activities, news, and current conditions. Published monthly; bimonthly in
summer. Available at visitors centers and
park entrance kiosks.

LOST & FOUND

Death Valley
Closest visitors center or ranger station.

Mammoth Lakes Area
Lost and Found/Basket Check, Main Lodge: 760-934-0667.

Lost and Found/Basket Check, Canyon Lodge: 760-934-2571, ext. 3367.

Mammoth Lakes Welcome Center: 760-924-5500.

Sequoia/Kings
Closest ranger station or visitors center. Or contact the Property Office at Ash Mountain: 559-565-3181.

Yosemite
Yosemite Concession Services: 209-372-4357.

National Park Service Lost & Found: 209-379-1001.

MAPS

The best overall highway maps of California are those published by **Rand McNally** (www.randmcnally.com) and by the **American Automobile Association** (www.aaa-calif.com). AAA also publishes indispensable regional guide maps to Yosemite, the Eastern Sierra, and Death Valley. The most thorough and accurate overview information of back roads and campgrounds within each region can be found on the relevant **National Forest Service maps** (Inyo, Toiyabe, Sequoia, Sierra, Stanislaus), available at visitors centers and national forest ranger stations. **Tom Harrison** (1-800-265-9090; www.tomharrisonmaps.com) publishes a series of durable, waterproof, shaded-relief topographic maps covering trails and recreation sites from the Emigrant Wilderness to Death Valley, available at most regional bookstores. The most detailed maps for navigating on the ground are those in the USGS 7.5 minute, 1:24,000 quandrangle series, available at most regional visitors centers, specialty book-stores, and sporting goods stores. For map indexes and catalogs, and to order topo-graphic maps, or any USGS maps, contact USGS Information Services (303-202-4693; 1-888-ASK-USGS; http://ask.usgs.gov).

ROAD & AUTO SERVICE

AAA Emergency Road Service: 1-800-222-4357.

AAA Locations

Bakersfield: 1500 Commercial Way; 661-327-4661.

Bishop: 187 West Pine Street; 760-872-8241.

Carson City: 2901 South Carson Street; 775-883-2470.

Porterville: 24 West Morton Avenue; 559-784-6500.

Reno: 6795 South Virginia Street, Suite D; 775-826-8800.

Sonora: 1071 Sanguinetti Road; 209-532-3134.

Visalia: 300 South Mooney Boulevard; 559-732-8045.

Death Valley
Furnace Creek Chevron: 760-786-2345.

Eastern Sierra
Dave's Auto Parts: 430 North Main Street, Lone Pine; 760-876-5586.

Miller's Towing & Repair: 1506 South Main Street, Lone Pine; 760-876-4600.

Mr. K Automotive: 175 West Grove Street, Bishop; 760-873-9828; www.mrkautomotive.com.

Perry Motors: 310 South Main Street, Bishop; 760-872-4141; www.perrymotorsinc.com.

Mammoth Lakes Area
The Auto Doc: 159 Commerce Drive, #E8; 760-934-2211.

Norco/Goodyear Service Center: 3670 Main Street; 760-934-9693.

Sequoia/Kings
Lodgepole Garage: near Lodgepole Visitors Center; 559-565-4070.

Sierra Auto, Truck & Tractor Repair: 340 West Naranjo Boulevard, Woodlake; 559-564-0235.

Yosemite
Brand Automotive: 6008 Allred Road, Midpines; 209-966-5630.

Dan's Auto: 49329 Golden Oak Loop, Oakhurst; 559-683-6006; www.dansauto.com.

Napa Auto Parts: 4907 Joe Howard Road, Mariposa; 209-966-3697.

Sierra Auto Parts: 4985 CA 140, Mariposa; 209-966-4756.

Yosemite Village Garage: across from Yosemite Village Store; 209-372-8320.

TOURIST INFORMATION

Big Pine Chamber of Commerce and Visitor Center: 126 South Main Street, Big Pine; 760-938-2114; www.bigpine.com.

Bishop Area Chamber of Commerce and Visitors Center: 690 North Main Street, Bishop; 760-873-8405; 1-888-395-3952; www.bishopvisitor.com.

Death Valley Chamber of Commerce and Visitor Center: 117 CA 127, Shoshone; 760-852-4524; www.deathvalleychamber.org.

Fresno County Office of Tourism: 2220 Tulare Street, Eighth Floor, Fresno; 559-262-4271; www.gofresnocounty.com.

Independence Chamber of Commerce: 440 South Edwards, #1, Independence; 760-878-0084; www.independence-ca.com.

June Lake Chamber of Commerce: P.O. Box 2, June Lake 93529; www.junelakeloop.org.

Lee Vining Chamber of Commerce: CA 395 and Third Street; 760-647-6629; www.leevining.com.

Lone Pine Chamber of Commerce and Inyo County Film Commission: 126 South Main Street, Lone Pine; 760-876-4444; 1-877-253-8981; www.lonepinechamber.org.

Mammoth Lakes Tourism & Recreation: 2520 Main Street (CA 203), Mammoth Lakes; 760-934-2712; 1-888-GO-MAMMOTH; www.visitmammoth.com.

Mono County Tourism & Film Commission: P.O. Box 603, Mammoth Lakes 93546; 1-800-845-7922; www.monocounty.org.

Oakhurst Area Chamber of Commerce: 49074 Civic Circle, Oakhurst; 559-683-7766; www.oakhurstchamber.com.

Sequoia Foothills Chamber of Commerce:
42268 Sierra Drive, Three Rivers;
559-561-3300; www.threerivers.com.
Yosemite Chamber of Commerce:
18583 CA 120, Groveland; 209-962-0429;
www.groveland.org.
**Yosemite/Mariposa County Chamber of
Commerce:** 5158 CA 140, Mariposa;
209-966-2456; 1-866-425-3366;
www.mariposachamber.org.

VISITORS CENTERS & RANGER STATIONS

Death Valley National Park
**Eastern Sierra Interagency Visitors
Center:** CA 395 and 136, Lone Pine;
760-876-6222.

Furnace Creek Visitor Center: North of
Furnace Creek Ranch; 760-786-3244.

Devil's Postpile National Monument
Ranger Station: 760-934-2289.

Inyo National Forest
**Ancient Bristlecone Pine Forest Visitor
Center–Schulman Grove:** 10 miles north
of CA 168 East, on White Mountain Road;
760-873-2500.

**Eastern Sierra Interagency Visitors
Center:** CA 395 and 136, Lone Pine;
760-876-6222.

**Mammoth Ranger Station and Welcome
Center:** CA 203, Mammoth Lakes;
760-924-5500.

**Mono Basin Scenic Area Ranger Station &
Visitor Center:** CA 395, Lee Vining;
760-647-3044.

Mount Whitney Ranger Station:
640 South Main Street, Lone Pine;
760-876-6200.

White Mountain Ranger Station:
798 North Main Street, Bishop;
760-873-2500.

Sequoia National Forest/National Monument
Cannell Meadow Ranger District Office:
105 Whitney Road, Kernville;
760-376-3781.

Hume Lake Ranger District Office:
35860 East Kings Canyon Road, Dunlap;
559-338-2251.

**Kern River Ranger District–Kernville
Office:** 105 Whitney Road, Kernville;
760-376-3781.

**Tule River/Hot Springs Ranger District
Office:** 32588 CA 190, Springville;
559-539-2607.

Sequoia–Kings Canyon National Park
Cedar Grove Visitor Center: Cedar Grove
Village; 559-565-3793.

Foothills/Ash Mountain Visitor Center:
47050 Generals Highway; 559-565-3135.

Grant Grove Visitor Center: Grant Grove
Village; 559-565-4307.

Lodgepole Visitors Center: Lodgepole
Village; 559-565-4436.

Mineral King Ranger Station: Mineral
King; 559-565-3768.

Road's End Permit Station: Kings Canyon;
no phone.

Sierra National Forest

Bass Lake Ranger District Office: 57003 Road 225, North Fork; 559-877-2218.
High Sierra Ranger District Office: 29688 Auberry Road, Prather; 559-855-5355.

High Sierra Ranger Station: Kaiser Pass; 559-877-7173.

Stanislaus National Forest

Groveland Ranger District Office: 24545 CA 120, Groveland; 209-962-7825.

Mi-Wok Ranger District Office: 24695 CA 108, Mi-Wuk Village; 209-586-3234.

Summit Ranger District Office: 1 Pinecrest Lake Road, Pinecrest; 209-965-3434.

Yosemite National Park

Badger Pass Ranger Station A-Frame: Glacier Point Road; 209-372-0409.

Big Oak Flat Station: CA 120, at the park entrance; 209-379-1899.

Hetch Hetchy Station: Hetch Hetchy Entrance Station; 209-379-1928.

Tuolumne Meadows Visitors Center & Ranger Station: Tuolomne Meadows; 209-372-0263.

Wawona Information Station: Hill's Studio, adjacent to Wawona Hotel; 209-375-9531.

Yosemite Valley Visitors Center & Ranger Station: Yosemite Village; 209-372-0299.

Yosemite Valley Wilderness Center: Yosemite Village, next to Ansel Adams Gallery; 209-372-0740.

WEATHER & ROAD CONDITIONS

Caltrans Statewide Road Conditions: 916-445-7623; 1-800-427-7623; www.dot.ca.gov/hq/roadinfo.

Death Valley Conditions: www.dvnha.org/morning_report/Morning.pdf.

High Sierra Avalanche & Snowpack Information: http://patrol.mammoth mountain.com; www.esavalanche.org.

Long Valley Volcanic Conditions: http://lvo.wr.usgs.gov.

Mammoth Ski & Snow Report: 760-934-6166; 1-888-SNOWRPT; www.mammothmountain.com.

Mammoth Weather Conditions: 760-934-7669; www.mammothweather.com.

Sequoia-Kings Road Conditions: 559-565-3341, ext. 941.

Wildfire Conditions: http://inciweb.org/.

Yosemite Road Conditions: 209-372-0200; www.nps.gov/yose/plan yourvisit/conditions.htm.

INDEX

A

AAA (Bishop), 141

Adams, Ansel, 65, 142, 263, 266, 267

Adams, James Capen ("Grizzly"), 44

Aerie Crag camping area (Mammoth Lakes), 162

Aerohead Cycles (Bishop), 141, 147

agencies and nonprofit organizations, 317–318

Agnew Meadows camping areas (Mammoth Lakes), 162

Aguereberry Point (Panamint/Saline area), 100

Ahwahneechee Indians, 24

The Ahwahnee Hotel (Yosemite Valley)
annual events, 313, 315; Bar, 301; Dining Room, 300–301; history, 306; lodging, 299; Sweet Shop, 302

air travel
international airports, 53–56; municipal and local airports, 56

Alabama Hills (Lone Pine)
annual events, 148; Café & Bakery, 130; hunting, 146; points of interest, 132–134

Alabama Spillway (Owens Valley), 109–110

Alamo car rental, 65

Allen Outdoor Products, Sierra Saddlery & Feed, 141

The Alpine Approach (Mammoth Town), 186

Alta California, 23–26

Alta Peak hiking (Generals Highways area), 254

Amargosa Basin & Range (Death Valley), 92–94

Amargosa Hotel & Opera House (Death Valley Junction), 92
Gift Shop, 90

American Factors, Inc. (Amfac), 86

American River Touring Association, Inc. (ARTA), 307

America the Beautiful - National Parks and Federal Recreation Lands Pass, 72

AMTRAK, 59

Ancient Bristlecone Pine Forest (Big Pine), 137

Anderson, George, 304–305

Angel's (Mammoth Town), 176

Anne Lang's Emporium (Three Rivers), 221

annual events
Death Valley, 106–107; Mammoth Lakes and Mono Country, 205–207; Owens Valley & Eastern Sierra, 148–149; Sequoia/Kings Canyon, 258; Yosemite, 313–315

Ansel Adams Gallery (Yosemite Village), 302–303, 307

Anza, Juan de, 25

après ski. See taverns, saloons, roadhouses

Argus Range, 38

Army Corps of Engineers, 318

Art & Education Center (Yosemite Village), 307

art education, Yosemite, 307

Ashford Mill (French Creek area), 98

Ash Meadows National Wildlife Refuge (Death Valley), 92
bird-watching, 103; Christmas Bird Count, 107

Ash Mountain (Three Rivers), 223–224

Aspen camping area (Mammoth Lakes), 163

Aspendell (Owens Valley/Eastern Sierra), horseback riding, 145

Aspen Hollow camping area (Sequoia/Kings Canyon), 217

Aspen Park camping area (Mammoth Lakes), 162

Assembling California (McPhee), 18

Astorga's Mexican Grill (Bishop), 139

ATVs (all-terrain vehicles), trails for, 73

Atwell Mill & Skinner Grove (Mineral King area), 225–226

Audubon California, 319

The Auld Dubliner (Mammoth Town), 182

Austin, Mary, 14, 116–117, 122, 124, 130, 136

Austria Hof (Mammoth Town), 176

automobile transportation. See driving

avalanche/snowpack information, 177

Avis car rental, 66

Ayres, Thomas, 48, 49, 262

Azalea camping area (Sequoia/Kings Canyon), 217

B

Babbitt, Bruce, 65

backcountry skiing/snowboarding, 73, 198

Badger Pass Ski Area (Yosemite)
activities, 312; annual events, 313, 315; Sport Shop, 279

Badwater (French Creek area)
Badwater Ultra-Marathon, 106, 149; points of interest, 96

Badwater Saloon (Stovepipe Wells), 89

Baker Creek camping area (Eastern Sierra), 123

bakeries, sandwiches, takeout
Mammoth Lakes and Mono Country, 184–185; Owens Valley & Eastern Sie rra, 140; Sequoia/Kings Canyon, 221–222; Yosemite, 301–302

Bakersfield (BFL) airport, 56

Balch Park Pack Station (Sequoia/Kings Canyon), 254

Bald Mountain Lookout (Owens Valley/Eastern Sierra), 125–126

Ballarat (Death Valley)
general store, 92; history, 10, 76; points of interest, 101

Banff Mountain Film Festival (Bishop), 148

banks/ATMs, 320–321

Bardini Foundation (Bishop), 147

Bartlett Glass Plant (Owens Lake), 127

Base Camp Café & Coffee Bar (Mammoth Town), 176–180

Bass Lake (Yosemite), 279

Bear in Mind: The California Grizzly (ed. Snyder), 44–45

Bearpaw High Sierra Camp (High-Country Sequoia), 227, 230–231

Beatty Information Center (Death Valley), 89

Beetle Rock Nature Center (High-Country Sequoia), 231

Belknap camping area (Sequoia/Kings Canyon), 217

Belladonna (Mammoth Town), 204

Belle Vous Day Spa & Salon (Bishop), 147

Ben & Jerry's (Mammoth Town), 185

Benton Hot Springs (Owens Valley/Eastern Sierra) lodging, 119, 121–222; spa, 148

Benton (Owens Valley/Eastern Sierra), 165

Bessley, David, 18

Best Western Creekside Inn (Bishop), 119

Beverly & Jim Rogers Museum of Lone Pine Film History, 131

Beyond the Mississippi (Richardson), 263

bicycling. *See also* mountain biking; road biking Death Valley, 103; Owens Valley & Eastern Sierra, 146; Yosemite, 307

Bierstadt, Albert, 262

Big Bend camping area (Mammoth Lakes), 163

Big Meadow camping area (Mammoth Lakes), 162

Big Meadows camping area (Sequoia/Kings Canyon), 217

Big Meadows Guard Station (High-Country Sequoia), 229

Big Oak Flat Road area (Yosemite) bookstores, maps, & information, 290; camping areas, 271; dining, 288–289; food & beverage purveyors, 290; general information, 285–286; lodging, 287; points of interest, 291; shopping, 290–291; taverns, saloons, roadhouses, 289–290

Big Pine Creek camping area (Eastern Sierra), 123

Big Pine (Owens Valley/Eastern Sierra) camping areas, 123; general store, 136; horseback riding, 146; lodging, 119; points of interest, 136–137

Big Sandy camping area (Yosemite), 271

Big Springs camping area (Mammoth Lakes), 162

Big Trees camping area (Eastern Sierra), 123

bird-watching Death Valley, 103; Mammoth Lakes and Mono Country, 198; Owens Valley & Eastern Sierra, 144; Sequoia, Kings Canyon & the Great Western Divide, 250

Bishop Motosports, 146

Bishop (Owens Valley/Eastern Sierra) annual events, 148–149; bakeries, sandwiches, takeout, 140; bookstores, maps, & information, 141; camping areas, 123; Chamber of Commerce/Visitors Bureau, 141; clothing stores, 141; coffee, tea, 140; dining, 139; galleries, 142; golf, 144–145; horseback riding, 146, 202; lodging, 119; meats, smokehouses, 140–141; motorsports, 146; mountaineering, 147; photography supplies, 142; points of interest, 142–143; rock climbing equipment, 147; spas, yoga & massage, 147; taverns, saloons, roadhouses, 140

Bishop Pack Outfitters (Aspendell), 145

Bishop Peak camping area (Eastern Sierra), 123

Bishop Yoga & Massage Center, 147

Bitterbush camping area (Eastern Sierra), 123

Black Sheep Espresso Bar (Bishop), 140

BLM Wild Horse & Burro Adoption Facility (Panamint/Saline area), 102

Blue Heron Sports (Mariposa), 284

Bluesapalooza & Festival of Beers (Mammoth Lakes), 206

boating and floating Mammoth Lakes and Mono Country, 198–200; Owens Valley & Eastern Sierra, 144; Sequoia, Kings Canyon & the Great Western Divide, 250; Yosemite National Park, 307

Bodie State Historical Park (Lee Vining), 197–198

Bonanza Family Restaurant (Lone Pine), 130

books about the area, 321–323

bookstores, maps, & information Death Valley, 89–90; general resources, 326; Mammoth Lakes and Mono Country, 185, 196; Owens Valley & Eastern Sierra, 131–132, 141; Sequoia/Kings Canyon, 222, 225, 231, 249; Yosemite, 278, 284, 290, 295, 302

Booky Joint (Mammoth Town), 185

Borax Museum (Death Valley), 94

borax production, 77–78, 114, 194

Boulder camping area (Mammoth Lakes), 163

Bower, David, 65

Boyden Caverns (Grant Grove area), 240

Bracebridge Dinner (Yosemite Valley), 315

Brewer, William Henry, 165, 194, 207

Breyfogle, Charles, 75–76

Brian's Bicycles and Cross Country Skis (Mammoth Town), 187

Bridalveil Creek camping area (Yosemite), 271

Bridalveil Fall (Yosemite Valley), 46–47, 53, 286, 297, 308

Bridgeport (Mammoth Lakes), horseback riding, 202

Bridger, Jim, 32

The Bridges (Mammoth Town), 175

Bristlecone Forest camping areas (Eastern Sierra), 123

bristlecone pines, 137

Brock's Flyfishing Specialists (Bishop), 144

Brower, David, 65

Browne, J. Ross, 42

Bryan, William Jennings, 289

Buckeye Flat (Sequoia/Kings Canyon) camping area, 217; trailhead, swimming, 256

Buckeye Tree Lodge (Three Rivers), 219–220

Buck Rock camping area (Sequoia/Kings Canyon), 217

Buck Rock Lookout (High-Country Sequoia), 234 Open House/4th of July Celebration, 258

Budget car rental, 66

Bug Fest (Midpines), 314

Bug Store (Midpines), 284

Bunnell, Lafayette, 45, 263

Burbank/Bob Hope (BUR) airport, 53

Burney, James, 44

burros, wild, 96–97
bus tours, guided (Yosemite Valley), 308
bus travel, 60–63
Busy Beez General Store (Mammoth Town), 183–184
Buz Beszek's Fly Shop (Visalia), 253

C

Café at the Bug (Midpines), 283–284
Caldera Kayaks (Mammoth Lakes), 198
California Department of Conservation, 317
California Department of Fish & Game, 317
California Department of Water Resources, 317
California Environmental Protection Agency, 317
California grey wolf, 45
California grizzly, 44, 45, 241
California Magazine, 262
California Native Plant Society, 319
California State Mining & Mineral Museum
    (Mariposa), 285
California Tunnel Tree (Yosemite), 279
California utility companies, contact information, 318
California Wild Heritage Campaign, 319
California Wild Horse and Burro Show (Bishop), 149
Caltrans, road condition information, 58
Camp 4 camping area (Yosemite), 271
Camp High Sierra camping area (Mammoth Lakes),
    162
camping areas. *See also* lodging
    Death Valley, 87; High Sierra Camps (Yosemite),
    294; Mammoth Lakes and Mono Country,
    162–163; Owens Valley & Eastern Sierra,
    122–123; permits for, 73; reservations, 163, 270;
    Sequoia/Kings Canyon, 217; Yosemite, 271
Camp Mather (Hetch Hetchy region)
    annual events, 313; lodging, 272; lottery for, 313
Camp Nelson General Store (Camp Nelson), 245
Camp Nelson Lodge (Great Western Divide Highway),
    243
Canyon Lodge (Mammoth Mountain), 178–179
Canyon View camping area (Sequoia/Kings Canyon),
    217
car rentals, 53–56. *See also* driving
Carroll's Market (Big Pine), 136
Carson & Colorado narrow-gauge railway, 127, 135
Carson, Kit, 30, 93, 110
Cartago (Owens Valley/Eastern Sierra), 127
Casa Diablo (Mammoth Lakes), 166–167
Case Mountain Area (Sequoia/Kings Canyon)
    hiking, 253; mountain biking, 252
Castle, Kari, hang gliding, 144–145
Cathy's Candy (June Lake), 193
Cattleguard camping area (Mammoth Lakes), 163
Cedar Grove (Kings Canyon)
    camping areas, 217; Lodge, 238; Market, 238;
    Pack Station, 254; Snack Bar, 238
Cedar Slope (Sequoia/Kings Canyon), tavern, 245
Celebration of Sequoias Festival (Sequoia/Kings
    Canyon), 258

Central California Cyclists, 252
Central Reservations of Mammoth, 174
Central Valley, 9, 26, 28, 29
Cerro Gordo (Keller), lodging, 119
C'est Si Bon Café (Shosone), 88
Chalfant House (Bishop), 119
Chalfant, P. A., 74–75
Chalfant, W. A., 17–18, 78, 109
chambers of commerce, 327–328
Charles Brown Company Market (Shoshone), 91
Charles Street Dinner House (Mariposa), 283
Charlito (Sequoia/Kings Canyon), rock climbing, 256
Charlotte Domes (Sequoia/Kings Canyon), rock
    climbing, 256
Chateau du Sureau (Oakhurst)
        lodging, 273–274; spa, 311
Chato (Mammoth Town), 185
Chefs Holidays (Yosemite Valley), 313
Cherry Valley camping area (Yosemite), 271
Chidago Canyon Petroglyphs (Bishop), 143
Chimney Creek camping area (Eastern Sierra), 123
Chimney Rock Challenge (Sequoia/Kings Canyon), 258
China Ranch Date Farm (Tecopa), 93–94, 103
Chloride City (Death Valley), 76
Chocolate & Wine festival (Oakhurst), 314
Chowchilla Indians, 39–40
city entities, contact information, 317
Civilian Conservation Corps (CCC), 33, 80
Clark, Galen, 48, 263
    cabin, 281
climate. *See also* weather information
        average temperature and precipitation, 56; Death
        Valley, 28, 79; diversity of, 10; flood and drought
        cycles, 28–29; Mammoth Lakes region, 158; win-
        ter conditions, 57–58
climbing. *See* rock climbing
Clinton, Bill, 80, 95
Clocktower Cellar (Mammoth Town), 182
clothing stores
        Mammoth Town, 185; Owens Valley & Eastern
        Sierra, 141
Clyde Glacier camping area (Eastern Sierra), 123
Clyde Pack Outfit (Sequoia/Kings Canyon), 254
Cobbleknoll Trail (Sequoia/Kings Canyon), swim-
    ming, 256
coffee, tea
        Mammoth Lakes and Mono Country, 183, 193,
        196; Owens Valley & Eastern Sierra, 130, 140;
        Sequoia/Kings Canyon, 221; Yosemite, 284, 301
Cold Springs camping area (Sequoia/Kings Canyon),
    217
Coldwater camping area (Mammoth Lakes), 162
Coleman, William Tell, 77–78
Comfort Inn & Suites (Three Rivers), 219
Comfort Inn (Lone Pine), 119
Community Center Park Municipal Courts (Mammoth
    Town), 205
Concert in the Rocks (Alabama Hills), 148

condos, town houses, vacation rentals, 174–176
confederated tribes, 39–40
Conness, John, 261, 263
Converse Basin, Chicago Stump & Boole Tree (Grant Grove area)
    mountain biking, 252; points of interest, 239
Convict Lake (Mammoth Lakes/Mono Country)
    camping area, 162; Convict Lake Marina, 199; Convict Lake Resort, 166, 201; dining, 164
Corkscrew Saloon (Death Valley), 89
Coronado, Francisco Vásquez de, 23–25, 96
Cort Gallery (Three Rivers), 222
Cottonwood Lakes camping area (Eastern Sierra), 123
Cottonwood Lakes Road (Lone Pine), 134
Cottonwood Pack Station (Horseshoe Meadows), 145
Cottonwood Pass camping area (Eastern Sierra), 123
Country Kitchen Herb Farm (Mariposa), 284
county entities, contact information, 317
courses and seminars
    Sequoia/Kings Canyon, 251–252; Yosemite Village, 307
Cove camping area (Sequoia/Kings Canyon), 217
Coy Flat camping area (Sequoia/Kings Canyon), 217
Crane Flat (Yosemite)
    camping areas, 271; general store, 291; points of interest, 291; sledding, 312
Creekside Corner at Double Edge (June Lake), 193
Creekside Spa at Double Eagle Resort (June Lake), 204
Crest/Inyo Mono Transit, 60–61
Crestview camping areas (Mammoth Lakes), 162
cross-country skiing. See skiing
Crowley Lake (Mammoth Lakes)
    camping areas, 162; Fish Camp Marina, 198
Crow's Range (Beesley), 42
Crystal Cave (High-Country Sequoia), 232–234
Crystal Geyser Bottling Plant (Olancha), 127
Crystal Springs camping area (Sequoia/Kings Canyon), 217
Curry Bar (Yosemite Valley), 301
Curry Village Pavilion, 300, 301
    bicycle cruising, 307; boat rentals, 307
Curry Village (Yosemite Valley)
    bicycle cruising, 307; boat rentals, 307; bookstores, maps, & information, 302; dining, 300; food & beverage purveyors, 301–302; general information, 272; Gift & Grocery, 303; guide services, 309; Recreation Center, 307; taverns, saloons, roadhouses, 301; winter sports, 312

D

Dante's View (Death Valley), 94
Darwin (Death Valley), 103
David Moss Fly Fishing (Mammoth Lakes), 200
David Neal, Reel Mammoth Adventures (Mammoth Lakes), 200
Deadman camping area (Mammoth Lakes), 162
Death Valley
    annual events, 106–107; bookstores, maps, & information, 89; dining, 87–89; emergency road service, 326; history, 37–38, 74–80; hospitals and medical services, 324; kennels, 324; local media, 325; lodging, 82–86; lost and found, 326; map, 81; movies shot in, 91; points of interest, 92–103; ranger and interpretative programs, 105; recreational activities, 103–105; shopping, 90–92; taverns, saloons, roadhouses, 89; traveling to, 80–82; when to visit, 79
Death Valley Days, 94
Death Valley '49ers, 37
Death Valley '49ers Encampment, 107
Death Valley Junction
    general information, 82; history, 74, 78; points of interest, 92; shopping, 90
Death Valley National Park
    access and amenity fees, 72; camping, 87; history, 80; lodging, 83–85; traveling to, 79–82; visitors centers, ranger stations, 328
Death Valley Natural History Association, 90, 319
Death Valley Railroad (DVRR) narrow-gauge railway, 74, 80
Death Valley View Hotel, 78
Degnan's Café/Deli (Yosemite Village), 301, 302
delicatessens. See bakeries, sandwiches, take out
Devil's Golf Course (French Creek area), 96
Devil's Hole (Death Valley), 93
Devil's Postpile National Monument (Mammoth Lakes)
    camping area, 162; points of interest, 190; visitors centers, ranger stations, 328
Diaz Lake camping area (Eastern Sierra), 123
Didion, Joan, 32
Digger Indians, 134
Dimond "O" camping area (Yosemite), 271
dining
    Death Valley, 87–89; Mammoth Lakes and Mono Country, 164, 176–182, 192–193, 196; Owens Valley & Eastern Sierra, 122–123, 126, 135, 139; price codes, 13; Sequoia/Kings Canyon, 221, 225, 229–230, 238, 243, 248–249; Yosemite, 272, 283–284, 288–289, 295, 300–301
Dining Room at the Wuksachi (High-Country Sequoia), 230
Dinkey Creek (Kaiser Pass Road), 249
Dirt Flat camping area (Yosemite), 271
DJ's Snowmobile Adventures (Smokey Bear Flat), 202
doctors, 324
dogsledding, 200
Do It Center (Mammoth Town), 186
Dollar car rental, 66
Dolomite Marble Mine (Owens Valley/Eastern Sierra), 129
Don Cecil Trail (Kings Canyon), 254
Donner Party, 32–34
Doorstep Dinner delivery service (Mammoth Town), 182
Dorst camping area (Sequoia/Kings Canyon), 217

Double Eagle Spa & Resort (June Lake)
  Creekside Spa, 204; lodging, 192
Dowd, Augustus T., 233
downhill skiing. *See* skiing
Dow Villa Hotel & Motel (Lone Pine), 120
Dow, Walter, 120
driving
  Badwater to Bridalveil loop, 53; car rentals,
  65–66; to Death Valley, 79–82; distances and
  driving times, 66–67; Eastern Sierra Scenic
  Byway, 126; emergency road service, 326–327;
  general information, 63–65; June Lake Loop,
  192; from Las Vegas and points east, 68–69; from
  Los Angeles and points south, 70–71; to
  Mammoth Lakes and Mono Country, 158;
  Mammoth Lakes Scenic Loop, 165; off-highway,
  105; to Owens Valley & Eastern Sierra, 117; from
  points west, 70; from Reno, 70; road condition
  information, 58, 177, 329; from San
  Francisco/Oakland, 71; from San Jose/Monterey,
  71; Tioga Road area (Yosemite), 291; winter driving, 58; to Yosemite National Park, 268
Dry Creek Bar (Mammoth Town), 182
Dry Gulch camping area (Yosemite), 271

E

Eagle Lodge (Mammoth Mountain), 179
Eagle Run (Mammoth Town), 175
Eagle's Landing (June Lake), 192–193
Early Opener Trout Derby (Lone Pine), 148
Earth Day Celebration (Yosemite), 313
Earthquake Fault (Mammoth Town), 188
Easter Festivities & Pond Skim (Mammoth Mountain),
  205–207
Eastern California Museum (Independence), 136
Eastern Sierra
  camping chart, 123; emergency road service,
  326–327; height of, 114–115; hospitals and med-
  ical services, 324; kennels, 324; local media, 325
Eastern Sierra Audubon Society, 144, 198
Eastern Sierra Birding Trail Map, 198
Eastern Sierra Gem & Mineral Show (Bishop), 148
Eastern Sierra Guide Service (Mammoth Lakes), 200
Eastern Sierra Interagency Visitors Center (Lone
  Pine), 90, 131
Eastern Sierra Scenic Byway, 126
Eastern Sierra Tri-County Fair (Bishop), 149
East Fork camping area (Mammoth Lakes), 162
Eaton, Frank, 14
Eaton, Fred, 111–114
Ebbetts Pass, winter closure, 58
The 1849 (Mammoth Town), 175
1872 earthquake, 17–18
1872 Earthquake Graveyard (Lone Pine), 134
El Capitan (Yosemite), 16, 46, 115, 297
Elevation (Lone Pine), 132, 147
elk, wild, 138
Ellery Lake camping area (Mammoth Lakes), 163

El Mono Motel (Mono Lake), 195
El Portal Road area (Yosemite)
  bookstores, maps, & information, 284; camping
  areas, 271; dining, 283–284; food & beverage
  purveyors, 284; general stores, 282–283; lodging,
  283; points of interest, 285; shopping, 285
emergency information. *See also* resources/informa-
tion
  road service, 326–327; weather/road conditions,
  58, 329
Emerson, Ralph Waldo, 9, 46
Emigrant Canyon Road (Panamint/Saline area), 100
Emigrant (Death Valley), camping, 87
Emigrants' Guide to California and Oregon (Hastings),
  30–31
Enterprise car rental, 66
Environment Defense Fund, 319
Erick Schat's Bakkery (Bishop), 140
Erna's Elderberry House (Oakhurst), 277
Ernie's Tackle & Ski Shop (June Lake), 193
Eshom Creek camping area (Sequoia/Kings Canyon),
  217
Espresso Parlor (Lone Pine), 130
Eureka Dunes (French Creek area), 99
Evergreen General Store & Gift Shop, 290
Evergreen Lodge (Groveland)
  annual events, 314–315; general store/gift shop,
  290; lodging, 287; mountain biking, 310; restau-
  rant at, 289–290; tavern, 290; Yosemite Valley
  guide services, 308
Ewing's On The Kern (Kernville), 243
EZ Mountain Vacations (Mammoth Town), 174

F

Fairview camping area (Sequoia/Kings Canyon), 217
fall colors, peak at Yosemite, 314
Fall Death Valley Century and Double Century,
  106–107
Fall Kick-Off Golf Tournament (Furnace Creek),
  106–107
Farquhar, Francis, 48
fast food. *See* bakeries, sandwiches, take out
Father Crowley Point (Panamint/Saline area), 103
Fat Tire Classic (Springville), 258
federal entities, contact information, 317–318
Feinstein, Dianne, 289
Ferguson camping area (Eastern Sierra), 123
festivals. *See* annual events
fiber optics, 78
Fir camping area (Sequoia/Kings Canyon), 217
fires
  controlled burning, 24; Mammoth Lakes fire
  information, 160
First Falls camping area (Eastern Sierra), 123
First Street Leather & Troppe Borse (Mammoth Town),
  185
Fish Camp (Yosemite)
  lodging, 274; mountain biking, 310

Fish Creek camping area (Eastern Sierra), 123

fishing

Mammoth Lakes and Mono Country, 200–201; Owens Valley & Eastern Sierra, 144; Sequoia, Kings Canyon & the Great Western Divide, 252–253; trout season, 148–149; Yosemite National Park, 307–308

Fish Slough Road (Bishop), 142–143

5 Boroughs Pizza (Mammoth Town), 184

flood and drought cycles, 28–29

Florence Lake Ferry (Sequoia/Kings Canyon), 251

Florence Lake Store (Kaiser Pass Road), 249

Florence Reservoir (Sequoia/Kings Canyon), swimming, 257

Font, Pedro, 25

food & beverage purveyors

Mammoth Lakes and Mono Country, 183–185, 193, 196; Owens Valley & Eastern Sierra, 140–141; Sequoia/Kings Canyon, 221; Yosemite, 278, 284, 290, 295, 301–302

Food Court at the Lodge (Yosemite Valley), 301

Foothills/Ash Mountain Visitor Center (Three Rivers), 222

Footloose Sports (Mammoth Town), 187

Ford Mammoth Motocross (Mammoth Lakes), 206

Forest Service

cabin or lookout rentals, 243; firefighting activities, 24

Forks camping area (Eastern Sierra), 123

Forstenzer, Martin, 154–155

Fort Independence camping area (Eastern Sierra), 123

'49er Festival & Chili Cook-Off (Groveland), 314

49er (Mariposa), 284

Forty-Niner Café (Furnace Creek), 88

Fossil Falls (Little Lake)

camping area, 123; climbing, 126

Four Jeffrey camping area (Eastern Sierra), 123

Fourth of July Celebrations, Mammoth Lakes and Mono Country, 206

Fox car rental, 66

Fred Harvey Company, 86

Frémont, John C., 30, 44, 110, 138, 233, 263

French Camp camping area (Mammoth Lakes), 162

Fresno, California

Fresno County contact information, 317; Fresno-Yosemite (FYI) airport, 53; sporting gear & equipment, 268

Fresno Dome camping area (Yosemite), 271

Friends of Last Chance Canyon, 102

Friends of the Inyo, 319

Friends of the River, 319

Friends of the South Fork Kings, 319

Frog Meadow camping area (Sequoia/Kings Canyon), 217

Frontier Pack Station (Bishop), 146, 201–202

Fry, Walter, 235

Furnace Creek (Death Valley)

annual events, 106–107; camping, 87; gasoline

and water, 82; points of interest, 94–100; temperatures, 79; trails to, 37; traveling to, 80–81; Visitor Center, 89–90; winter temperatures, 79

Furnace Creek 508 (Death Valley), 106–107

Furnace Creek Inn

construction of, 78; Dining Room, 88; gift shop, 90

lodging, 78–80, 83–84

Furnace Creek Invitational Golf Tournament, 106

Furnace Creek Ranch

bird-watching, 103; Corkscrew Saloon, 89; Forty-Niner Café, 88; general store, 91; golf, 90, 103–104; lodging, 84; Wrangler Buffet & Steakhouse, 88

Furnace Creek Stables, 104

G

Gaines, David, 195

Gallerie Barjur (Mammoth Town), 186

galleries

Mammoth Town, 186; Owens Valley & Eastern Sierra, 142; Sequoia/Kings Canyon, 222; Yosemite, 302

Garfield Grove (Sequoia/Kings Canyon), hiking, 253

gasoline, Death Valley, 82

Gateway Restaurant (Three Rivers), 221

gear. See Gear, Guides and Outfitters index; sporting gear & equipment

Gediman, Scott, 304

Gem-O-Rama (Trona), 106–107

General Grant Tree (Grant Grove area), 239

General Sherman Tree (High-Country Sequoia), 213, 232, 235

Generals Highway/High-Country Sequoia area (Sequoia/Kings Canyon)

bookstores, maps, & information, 231; camping areas, 217; hiking, 254; history, 226; lodging, 226–229; points of interest, 231–235; shopping, 231

general stores

Death Valley, 91–92; Mammoth Lakes and Mono Country, 186, 196; Owens Valley & Eastern Sierra, 132, 135, 136; Sequoia/Kings Canyon, 222–223, 225, 231, 238, 245, 249; Yosemite, 279, 290, 296

geocaching, 308

geology, geological formations, 10, 19–21. See also specific locations

George Bush Tree (Great Western Divide Highway)

mountain biking trails, 252; points of interest, 245

geothermal energy, 166–167

Giant Forest (High-Country Sequoia)

Ex-Village, 231–232; general information, 211; Museum, 231; snowfall, 28

Giant Sequoia National Forest/Monument

North and South camping areas, 217; prescribed fire program, 24

Gibson, Jim, 155
gifts. *See* souvenirs, gifts, sundries
Glacier Lodge (Big Pine), 119
Glacier Pack Train (Big Pine), 146
Glacier Point (Yosemite)
 Glacier Point Lodge, 275–276; points of interest,
 281–282; winter travel, 58
Glacier View camping area (Eastern Sierra), 123
Glass Creek camping area (Mammoth Lakes), 162
Glen Aulin (Yosemite) backcountry campsite, 294
Goldedge camping area (Sequoia/Kings Canyon), 217
Golden Trout camping area (Eastern Sierra), 123
Golden Trout Pack Trains (Great Western Divide
 Highway), 255
Gold Rush, the, 34–38
Goldwell Open Air Museum (Death Valley), 93
golf
 Death Valley, 103–104; Mammoth Lakes and
 Mono Country, 201; Owens Valley & Eastern
 Sierra, 144–145; Sequoia/Kings Canyon, 253;
 Yosemite, 308
Goodale Creek camping area (Eastern Sierra), 123
The Good Life Café (Mammoth Town), 180
Good Ole Days (Laws), 149
Grand Havens (Mammoth Town), 174
Grandview camping area (Eastern Sierra), 123
Grant Grove Village (Kings Canyon), 237
 camping areas, 217; Gift Shop, 238; Restaurant,
 237–238; Stables, 254; Village Market, 238;
 Visitor Center, 238
Grant Grove/Kings Canyon Scenic Byway
 bookstores, maps, & information, 238; history,
 236–237; lodging, 237–238; points of interest,
 239–240; shopping, 238
Grapevine Canyon (Death Valley), 90
Great Basin Air Pollution Control District, 114
Great Basin Bakery (Bishop), 140
Great Western Divide Highway area (Sequoia/Kings
 Canyon)
 camping areas, 217; dining, 243; history, 241;
 horseback riding, 255; lodging, 241–242; map,
 242; points of interest, 245–246; taverns,
 saloons, roadhouses, 245
Greeley, Horace, 262
Greenland Ranch, 79
Greenwater (Death Valley), 76
Gregory, Rusty, 156
Greyhound bus service, 61
Greys Mountain camping area (Yosemite), 271
Grey, Zane, 74, 79, 80
Grizzly Bar (Mammoth Town), 182
grizzly bears, 44, 45, 241
Grizzly Giant sequoia (Yosemite), 279
groceries. *See also* general stores
 Mammoth Town, 183–184; Owens Valley &
 Eastern Sierra, 130, 141; Sequoia/Kings Canyon,
 221; Yosemite, 278, 284, 290
Groveland Hotel
 dining, 289; lodging, 287

Groveland Mercantile, 290
Groveland (Yosemite)
 annual events, 314–315; bookstores, maps, &
 information, 290; food & beverage purveyors,
 290; golf, 308; lodging, 287; mountain biking,
 310; shopping, 290–291; taverns, saloons,
 289–290
Groveland Yosemite Gateway Museum, 290
guided bus tours, Yosemite National Park, 308
guides. *See* Gear, Guides and Outfitters Index; outfitters
Gull Lake camping area (Mammoth Lakes), 162
Gull Lake Marina (June Lake Loop), 199

H

Hackfield, Heinrich, 86
Haines, Asa, 37
Half Dome (Yosemite Valley), 304–305
Hall, Ansel, 289
Halloween Dance of the Dead (Groveland), 315
Handbook of Yosemite (Hall), 289
hang gliding, 144–145
Happy Burger Diner (Mariposa), 283
Happy Isles Nature Center (Curry Village), 302
Happy Isles Snack Stand (Curry Village), 302
Harmony Borax Works (French Creek area), 98
Harrison, Benjamin, 211, 265
Harrison, Tom, 309
Hartley Springs camping area (Mammoth Lakes), 162
Harvey, Frederick Henry, 86
Harvey, Walter, 47–48
Hastings, Lansford W., 30–32, 138
Hayden Cabin/Mammoth Museum (Mammoth Town),
 189
Healing Arts (Mammoth Town), 204
Health Spa at the Yosemite Bug (Midpines), 311
Hearst, William Randolph, 45, 289
In the Heart of the Sierras (Hutchings), 51, 266, 282, 298
Herb Bauer (Fresno), 268
Hertz car rental, 66
Hess Park (Mono Lake area), 197
Hetch Hetchy area (Yosemite), lodging, 272
Hetch Hetchy reservoir (Yosemite National Park), 29,
 288–289
High Country Health Food & Café (Mariposa), 284
High-Country Sequoia area. *See* Generals
 Highway/High-Country Sequoia area
High Sierra Brine Shrimp (Mono Lake), 197
High Sierra Camps (Tioga Pass Road)
 dining, 295; hiking trails, 309; horseback riding,
 309; lodging, 293; lottery, 313, 315
High Sierra Fall Century Ride (Mammoth Lakes), 206
High Sierra Pack Station (Sequoia/Kings Canyon), 255
High Sierra Ranger Station (Kaiser Pass Road), 249
High Sierra Trail, 73
hiking
 backcountry, permits for, 73; Death Valley, 104;
 Mammoth Lakes and Mono Country, 201; Owens

Valley & Eastern Sierra, 145; Sequoia/Kings Canyon, 253–254; Yosemite, 308–309
Hill's Studio & Information Station (Wawona), 278
Hill, Thomas, 262
history
Alta California, 23–26; Death Valley, 74–80; earliest human settlement, 22–23; early promotors, promotions, 30–31, 48; early travelers and travel routes, 26–30, 51–52; Generals Highway/High-Country Sequoia area, 226; the Gold Rush era, 34–49; Grant Grove area, 236–237; Great Western Divide Highway area, 241; Hetch Hetchy reservoir, 288–289; Mammoth Lakes and Mono Country, 151–157; Mineral King area, 224; Mono Lake & Lee Vining, 194–195; Owens Valley & Eastern Sierra, 109–116; rail travel, 58; Sequoia/Kings Canyon, 209–211, 233, 246–247; timeline of events, 1775-2005, 40–41; Xanterra Parks & Resorts, 86; Yosemite, 261–268, 291–292
History of Fresno County (Elliott), 47
Hi-Tec Boot Outlet (Oakhurst), 278
Hodel Donald, 289
Hodgdon Meadow camping area (Yosemite), 271
Hoffman, Charles, 165
Holey Meadow camping area (Sequoia/Kings Canyon), 217
Holiday camping area (Mammoth Lakes), 162
Honeymoon Point Cabin (Mineral King area), 226
horseback riding
Death Valley, 104; Mammoth Lakes and Mono Country, 201–202; Owens Valley & Eastern Sierra, 145; Sequoia/Kings Canyon, 254–255; Yosemite, 309
Horse Corral Pack Station (Sequoia National Park), 255
Horse Meadon camping area (Eastern Sierra), 123
Horseshoe Lake Tree Kill (Mammoth Town), 189
Horseshoe Meadow camping area (Eastern Sierra), 123
Horseshoe Meadows (Lone Pine)
horseback riding, 145; points of interest, 134
Horton Creek camping area (Eastern Sierra), 123
Hospital Flat camping area (Sequoia/Kings Canyon), 217
Hospital Rock Picnic Area (Three Rivers), 223–224
Hospital Rock (Sequoia/Kings Canyon), rock climbing, 256
hospitals, medical care, 324
Hot Chicks Rotisserie (Mammoth Town), 184
Hot Creek Geological Site, 166–167
Hot Creek Ranch (Mammoth Lakes), 163–164
Hot Creek State Fish Hatchery (Mammoth Lakes), 166
Hotel Creek-Lewis Creek loop (Kings Canyon), 254
Housekeeping Camp (Southside Drive area), 272
Hume Lake (Grant Grove area)
camping area, 217; mountain biking trails, 252; points of interest, 239–240; swimming, 256
hunting, 146
Hunt, Jefferson, 35
Hutchings, James Mason, 14, 24, 48, 51, 262, 266, 282, 298
Hutchings Orchard (Yosemite Valley), 306

I
Ice Cream & Coffee Corner (Curry Village), 301
ice skating
Mammoth Lakes and Mono Country, 202; Yosemite National Park, 312
Illustrated Handbook of American Travel (Richardson), 262
Imperial County, 115–116
Imperial Gourmet (Bishop), 139
Independence Creek camping area (Eastern Sierra), 123
Independence Day Celebration, 149
Independence (Owens Valley/Eastern Sierra)
annual events, 149; camping areas, 123; dining, 135; general stores, 135; horseback riding, 146; lodging, 119, 120–121; points of interest, 136–137
Indian Field Days, 25
Indian Palace (Bishop), 139
Indian Wells Brewing Company (Owens Valley/Eastern Sierra), 122–124
Intake 2 camping area (Eastern Sierra)s, 123
interpretative programs. *See* ranger and interpretative programs
Inyo County, 115–116
contact information, 317
Inyo County Courthouse (Independence), 136
Inyo Craters (Mammoth Town), 189
Inyokern (IYK) airport, 56
Inyo National Forest
access and amenity fees, 72; history, 112; visitors centers, ranger stations, 141, 328
Iris meadow camping area (Mammoth Lakes), 162
Iron Door Saloon (Groveland), 289–290

J
J & R Crowbar Café & Saloon (Shoshone), 89
Jake's Saloon (Lone Prine), 130
James, George, 115
January Midweek Madness (Mammoth Mountain), 205–207
Jawhawkers, 35–37
Jazzaffair (Three Rivers), 258
Jazz Jubilee (Mammoth Lakes), 206
Jefferson, Thomas, 32
Jennie Lakes Wilderness hiking (Generals Highways area), 254
Jerseydale camping area (Yosemite), 271
John Muir Lodge (Grant Grove area), 238
John Muir Trail (Yosemite Valley), 73, 309
Joseph House Inn (Bishop), 119
Joseph's Bi-Rite
Bishop, 141; Lone Pine, 130
Joshua Trees (Owens Valley/Eastern Sierra), 124
Juarez, José, 39–40, 43–44
July 4th celebrations (Mariposa), 314
Junction camping area (Mammoth Lakes), 163
Junction View (Grant Grove area), 240
June Lake Junction general store, 193

June Lake (Mammoth Lakes/Mono Country)
 camping areas, 162; dining, 192–193; guides,
 198; lodging, 192; General Store, 193; Marina,
 199; tavern, 193
June Lake Triathlon, 206
June Mountain ski area, 207
Juniper Springs Resort (Mammoth Town), 173

K

Kaiser Pass Road area (Sequoia/Kings Canyon)
 history, 246–247; lodging, 248; map, 247; points
 of interest, 249; ranger station, 249
Kaweah Colony Post Office (Three Rivers), 223
Kaweah Co-operative Commonwealth, 211, 218
Kaweah General Store (Three Rivers), 222
Kaweah River (Sequoia/Kings Canyon)
 fishing, 252; Kaweah River Page web site, 250;
 Marina, 250; swimming, 256
Kaweah Whitewater Adventures (Sequoia/Kings
 Canyon), 250
kayaking. see boating and floating
Keeler (Owens Valley/Eastern Sierra), 127–128
Keeley, C. Clarke, 158
Kelty Meadow camping area (Yosemite), 271
Kennedy Meadows camping area (Eastern Sierra), 123
Kennedy Meadows General Store (Owens
 Valley/Eastern Sierra), 125
kennels, 324
Keogh's Hot Springs (Owens Valley/Eastern Sierra),
 148
Kern Regional Transit, 61
Kern River Brewing Company (Kernville), 245
Kern River Festival (Kernville), 258
Kern River (Sequoia/Kings Canyon)
 boating, 250–251; swimming, 257
Kern River Valley Museum (Kernville), 245–246
Kern Valley Hummingbird Celebration, 258
Kern Valley Spring Nature Festival, 258
Kernville (Sequoia/Kings Canyon)
 annual events, 258–259; dining, 243; lodging,
 243; points of interest, 245–246; taverns,
 saloons, roadhouses, 245
Keseburg, Louis, 34
Ketch Hetchy camping area (Yosemite), 271
Kevin Peterson's Fly Fishing Adventures (Mammoth
 Lakes), 201
King, Clarence, 128–129, 212–213, 263
King, Joseph Starr, 14
Kings Canyon (Grant Grove area)
 hiking, 254; rock climbing, 256
Kings Canyon Lodge (Grant Grove area), 238, 240
Kings River Conservation Trust, 319
Kings River Expeditions (Sequoia/Kings Canyon), 250
Kings River (Sequoia/Kings Canyon), swimming, 256
Knight Wheel (Mammoth Town), 189–190
Kroeber, A. L., 23

L

Labor Day Festival of the Arts (Mammoth Lakes), 206
Ladybug Waterfall (Sequoia/Kings Canyon), hiking,
 253
Lakanuki (Mammoth Town), 182
Lake Crowley (Mammoth Lakes/Mono Country), 164
Lake Elowin Resort (Three Rivers), 219–220
Lakefront Restaurant (Mammoth Town), 180
Lake George (Mammoth Lakes)
 boat rentals, 200; camping areas, 162
Lake Kaweakh Recreation Area (Sequoia/Kings
 Canyon), 250
Lake Mary (Mammoth Lakes)
 camping areas, 162; marina, 199
Lakes Trail hiking (Generals Highways area), 254
Lake Tenaya (Yosemite), 296
Lake Thomas A. Edison (Kaiser Pass Road), 249
Land of Little Rain (Austin), 116, 136
Landslide camping area (Sequoia/Kings Canyon), 217
La Quinta Inn (Bishop), 119
Last Chance Canyon Petroglyphs (Panamint/Saline
 area), 102
Las Vegas, Nevada
 driving from, 68–69; Las Vegas/McCarran (LAS)
 airport, 53–54
Latte Da Coffe Cafe (Lake Mono), 196
Lawson, Andrew, 289
Laws (Owens Valley/Eastern Sierra), annual events,
 149
Laws Railroad Museum & Historical Site (Bishop), 142
Lazy J Ranch Motel (Three Rivers), 219
Learning Express Toys (Mammoth Town), 186
Leavis Flat camping area (Sequoia/Kings Canyon), 217
Lebrado, Maria, 24
LeConte, Joseph, 14
LeConte Memorial Lodge (Yosemite Valley), 303
Lee's Frontier Store (Lone Pine), 132
Lee Vining (Mammoth Lakes/Mono Country)
 camping areas, 163; winter travel from, 58
Leonard, Zenas, 233
Lert, Jim, 156
Limestone camping area (Sequoia/Kings Canyon), 217
The Lingerie Lounge (Mammoth Town), 185–186
Lions Team Roping (Three Rivers), 258
Lippincott, Joseph B., 111
Little Baldy (Generals Highway area)
 hiking, 254; rock climbing, 256
Little Lake (Eastern Sierra)
 camping areas, 123; points of interest, 126–127
Little Lake to Owens Lake area (Owens Valley/Eastern
 Sierra)
 dining, 126; points of interest, 126–127
The Lodge at Yosemite Falls (Yosemite Valley)
 dining, 301; lodging, 300; lounge, 301
Lodgepole camping area (Sequoia/Kings Canyon), 217
Lodgepole Market, Deli & Gift Shop (High-Country
 Sequoia), 231
Lodgepole Visitors Center (High-Country Sequoia), 231

lodging. *See also* camping areas
backcountry lodging, 294; Death Valley, 82–86; Mammoth Lakes and Mono Country, 163–164, 166, 171–176, 195–196; Owens Valley & Eastern Sierra, 117–122; price codes, 13; Sequoia/Kings Canyon, 219–221, 224–225, 226–229, 237–238, 241–242, 248; Yosemite, 273–277, 283, 287, 292–294, 299–300
Logger flat camping area (Sequoia/Kings Canyon), 217
Lone Pine Chamber of Commerce, Film Commission & Tourist Information Center, 131
Lone Pine Film Festival, 149
Lone Pine (Owens Valley/Eastern Sierra)
annual events, 148–149; bookstores, maps, & information, 90, 131; camping area, 123; coffee, tea. etc., 130; dining, 130; golf, 144; groceries, 130; horseback riding, 145; lodging, 119, 120; points of interest, 132–135; rock climbing equipment, 147; Rocks & Gifts, 132; shopping, 132; Sporting Gear, 132
Lone Pine Pheasant Club (Alabama Hills), 146
Lone Pine Station, 135
Lone Pine Time Trials (Manzanar), 148
Long Meadow camping area (Sequoia/Kings Canyon), 217
Long Valley Caldera, 166–167
Long Valley camping area (Eastern Sierra), 123
Looney Bean
Bishop, 140; Mammoth Town, 183
Los Angeles, California. *See also* history
driving from, 70–71; Los Angeles (LAX) airport, 54
Los Angeles Department of Water and Power, 317
Lost Claim camping area (Yosemite), 271
Lower Grays Meadow camping area (Eastern Sierra), 123
Lower Lee Vining camping area (Mammoth Lakes), 163
Lower Peppermint camping area (Sequoia/Kings Canyon), 217
Lower Pines camping area (Yosemite), 271
lowest point in North America, 79, 96
Lucas, George, 80
Lumsden camping area (Yosemite), 271
Lundy Canyon camping area (Mammoth Lakes), 163

M

Maclean, Norman, 24
Mahogany Flat (Death Valley) camping area, 87
Main Lodge (Mammoth Mountain), 178
Main Street Market (Groveland), 290
Mairs Market (Independence), 135
Mammoth Accommodation Center, 174
Mammoth Air Charter, 56
Mammoth Brewing Company (Mammoth Town), 183
Mammoth Festival of Wine, Music & Food (Mammoth Mountain), 206
Mammoth Film Festival (Mammoth Town), 207

Mammoth Five Star Lodging reservations, 174
Mammoth Front Desk reservations, 174
Mammoth Gallery (Mammoth Town), 186
Mammoth Lakes and Mono Country
annual events, 205–207; bookstores, maps, & information, 185; camping areas, 162; camping, camping chart, 160–162; dining, 161, 164, 176–182, 192–193, 196; emergency road service, 327; food & beverage purveyors, 183–185, 193; history, 151–157; hospitals and medical services, 324; June Lake Loop, 192–193; kennels, 324; local media, 325; lodging, 158–160, 163–164, 195; lost and found, 326; Mammoth Lakes, 167–191; map, 159; Mono Lake & Lee Vining, 194–205; points of interest, 164–167, 187–191, 197–198; recreational activities, 147, 198–205; Rock Creek to Casa Diablo, 161–167; shopping, 185–187, 193; spas, yoga & massage, 192, 204; taverns, saloons, roadhouses, 182–183, 193; traveling to, 158; volcanoes, 165; Welcome Center, tourist information, 185
Mammoth Lakes Nordic Trail System, 200
Mammoth Lakes Pack Outfit, 202
Mammoth Lakes Town, contact information, 317
Mammoth Lakes Trails & Public Access, 319
Mammoth Lakes Transit, 61
Mammoth Luxury Outlets (Mammoth Town), 185–186
Mammoth Memories (Mammoth Town), 186
Mammoth Mines (Mammoth Town), 189
Mammoth Mountaineering (Mammoth Town), 147, 187, 198
Mammoth Mountain Fumarole, 189
The Mammoth Mountain Inn (Mammoth Town), 171
Mammoth Mountain ski resort
Adventure Center, 204; annual events, 205–207; Canyon Lodge, 178–179; Eagle Lodge, 179; early development, 153–156; general information, 177; Main Lodge, 178; McCoy Station, 179; mountain biking, 202–203; Mountain Center at the Village Gondola, 179; opening/closing days, 206, 207; Outpost 14, 179; reservations, 174; Sierra Star golf course, 201; Stump Alley, 178; Top of the Sierra, 179
Mammoth Mountain Wine & Jazz, 206
Mammoth Pacific Geothermal, 167
Mammoth Premiere Reservations, 174
Mammoth Property Reservations, 174
Mammoth Sierra Reservations, 174
Mammoth Ski & Racquet (Mammoth Town), 175
Mammoth: The Sierra Legend (Forstenzer), 154
Mammoth Town
bookstores, maps, & information, 185; camping areas, 162; clothing stores, 185; condos, town houses, vacation rentals, 174–176; delivery service, 182; dining, 176–182; food & beverage purveyors, 183–185; galleries, 186; general information, 167–169; general store, 186; lodging, 163–164, 171–176; map, 169; points of interest, 187–191; taverns, saloons, roadhouses, 182–183

Mammoth-Yosemite (MMH), 56

Manly, William Lewis, 35, 38

Mann brothers, 48

Manson, Charles, 80, 102, 103, 136

Manzanar Interpretive Center (Owens Valley/Eastern Sierra), 132

Manzanar National Historic Site (Lone Pine), 134, 148

Map of Mexico, Louisiana, & the Missouri Territory (Robinson), 26

maps. *See also* bookstores, maps, & information; resources/information

    approaches to the Sierra from the east, 69; approaches to the Sierra from the west, 70; Death Valley National Park, 81; Eastern Sierra, 118; Great Western Divide Highway, 242; Kaiser Pass Road area, 247; Mammoth Lakes and Mono overview, 159; overall area, 6; regional overview, 52; Yosemite National Park, 269; Yosemite Valley, 298

Marble Fork (Sequoia/Kings Canyon), swimming, 256

Marge's (Kernville), 243

Margie's Merry Go Round (Lone Pine), 130

Mariposa Batallion, 24, 45–47

Mariposa Big Tree Grove (Yosemite South Entrance), 279–281

Mariposa Coffee Company, 284

Mariposa County Agricultural Tours (Mariposa), 314

Mariposa County, contact information, 317

Mariposa County Courthouse (Mariposa), 285

Mariposa County Fair (Mariposa), 314

Mariposa County Visitors Center (Mariposa), 284

Mariposa Grove Museum (Yosemite Valley), 279–281

Mariposa Grove trailhead (Yosemite Valley), 309

Mariposa Museum & History Center, 284

Mariposa (Yosemite)

    annual events, 313–314; bookstores, maps, & information, 284; dining, 283; food & beverage purveyors, 284; points of interest, 285; shopping, 284

Marshall, James, 34

Mary Austin House (Independence), 136

Masters Race Camp Week (Mammoth Mountain), 207

Maturango Museum & Death Valley Tourist Center (Ridgecrest), 90

May Lake backcountry campsite (Yosemite), 294

McCabe Flat camping area (Yosemite), 271

McCoy, Dave, 152–156

McCoy Sports & Wilderness Outfitters (Mammoth Town), 187

McCoy Station (Mammoth Mountain), 179

McGee Creek (Mammoth Lakes)

    camping area, 162; Pack Station, 202; points of interest, 164

McPhee, John, 18, 21

Meadow Farms Country Smokehouse (Bishop), 141

Meadow Resort (Mammoth Mountain), 190

The Meat House (Bishop), 140

meats, smokehouses, 140–141

medical services, 324

Merced Lake (Yosemite) backcountry campsite, 294

Merced River (Yosemite), 26, 44

    swimming, 311

Merlin Dome (Sequoia/Kings Canyon) rock climbing, 256

Mesquite Spring (Death Valley), camping area, 87

Metrolink, 61

Middle Fork (Sequoia/Kings Canyon), swimming, 256

Midpines (Yosemite)

    annual events, 314; bookstores, maps, & information, 284; dining, 283–284; food & beverage purveyors, 284; lodging, 283; mountain biking, 310; spa, 311

Miller's Mountain Sports (Oakhurst), 278

Millpond Music Festival (Bishop), 149

Millpond Recreation Area camping area (Eastern Sierra), 123

Minaret Falls camping area (Mammoth Lakes), 162

Mineral King (Sequoia/Kings Canyon)

    bookstores, maps, & information, 225; camping area, 217; dining, 225; general stores, 225; history, 224; lodging, 224–225; points of interest, 225–226; Ranger Station, 225; ski resort, 155

mining. *See also* history

    in Death Valley, 74–78; Mammoth Lakes area, 151–152

Mirror Lake (Yosemite Valley), 303–305

missions, Spanish, 25

Mist Falls (Kings Canyon), 254

Modesto (MOD) airport, 56

Mono Basin Scenic Area Visitor Center (Lee Vining), 196–197

Mono County, contact information, 317

Mono Hot Springs (Kaiser Pass Road)

    General Store, 249; swimming, 257

Mono Hot Springs Resort, 248

Mono Indians, 48

Mono Inn Roadhouse (Lee Vining), 196

Mono Lake & Lee Vining

    bird-watching, 198; bookstores, maps, & information, 196–197; dining, 196; food & beverage purveyors, 196; history, 194–195; lodging, 195; points of interest, 197–198; remnants of volcanoes, 165

Mono Lake Bird Chatauqua, 206

Mono Lake Committee

    bookstore, 197; contact information, 319

Mono Market (Mono Lake), 196

Mono Trail, 30

Montecito Lake Resort (High-Country Sequoia), 228

Montecito-Sequoia Lodge (High-Country Sequoia), 230–231

Montecito-Sequoia Ski Resort (High-Country Sequoia), 258

Moore Creek camping area (Yosemite), 271

Moore, Tredwell, 47, 194

Moraine camping area (Mammoth Lakes), 163

Moraine camping area (Sequoia/Kings Canyon), 217

Moro Rock-Crescent Meadow Road (High-Country Sequoia)
points of interest, 232; rock climbing, 256

Mosquito Flat camping area (Mammoth Lakes), 162

Mother Lode, 21

motor sports
Mammoth Lakes and Mono Country, 202; Owens Valley & Eastern Sierra, 146

Mountain and River Adventures (Sequoia/Kings Canyon), 250–251, 252

mountain biking
general information, 73; Mammoth Lakes and Mono Country, 202–203; Sequoia/Kings Canyon, 252; Yosemite, 310

The Mountain Center at the Village Gondola (Mammoth Mountain), 179

mountaineering
Mammoth Lakes and Mono Country, 198; Owens Valley & Eastern Sierra, 147; Yosemite, 310

Mountain Glen camping area (Eastern Sierra), 123

Mountain Heritage Days (Oakhurst), 314

Mountain Light Gallery (Bishop), 142

Mountain Mobile Massage (Mammoth Lakes), 204

mountain peaks, highest, 125

Mountain Room Lodge (Yosemite Valley), 301

Mountain Room Restaurant (Yosemite Valley), 301

Mountain Sage (Groveland), 290

Mountain Shop (Curry Village), 303

Mountainside Grill (Mammoth Town), 180

Mountain View Grocery (Midpines), 284

Mount Whitney, 125, 128–129

Mount Whitney Classic, 149

Mount Whitney Fish Hatchery (Independence), 136

Mount Whitney Golf Club (Bishop), 144

Mount Whitney Military Reservation, 129

Mount Whitney Pack Trains (Bishop), 146

Mount Whitney Rally & Poker Run (Lone Pine), 149

Mount Whitney Trail, permits, 73

movies shot in area
Death Valley, 91; Kings Canyon area, 241; Mammoth Lakes and Mono Country, 168; Owens Valley, 133

Muir, John. *See also* history
on allowing cars into Yosemite, 65; ascent of Half Dome, 304; on 1872 earthquake, 18; first visits to Yosemite, 9–11, 51, 265–266; Mount Whitney climb, 129; on mountain passes, 71; on "openness" of the woods, 24; opposition to Hetch Hetchy reservoir, 288–289; on sequoias, 212, 213, 235

Muir Trail Ranch (Kaiser Pass Road), 248

Mule Days (Bishop), 148

mulepacking, 309

Mulholland, William, 111, 113, 152

Munchkins (Mammoth Town), 185–186

Murphy, Landrum, 34

N

Narrow Gauge Inn (Fish Camp), 274

National car rental, 66

National Forest Service, 318

National Interagency Fire Center, 318

National Park Service (NPS), 318. *See also specific parks*
controlled burning, 24; Xanterra Parks & Resorts, 86

National Park Week (Sequoia/Kings Canyon), 258

National Recreation Reservation System, 270

National Scenic Byways Program, 318

Native Americans. *see specific Indian tribes*

Nativearth (Mariposa), 284

natural fire zones, 24

Natural Resources Defense Council, 319

The Nature Shop (Yosemite Valley), 303

Navy Public Affairs Office, 102

The Needles (Great Western Divide Highway), 245

Nelder Grove camping area (Yosemite), 271

Nelson camping area (Eastern Sierra), 123

Nevados (Mammoth Town), 180

New Shady Rest camping area (Mammoth Lakes), 162

Nidever, George, 44–45

Nik & Willie's (Mammoth Town), 184

Nine Mile Canyon (Owens Valley/Eastern Sierra), 124

Nohara, Hirofumi, 304

nongovernment organizations, listing of, 319–320

Noren camping area (Eastern Sierra), 123

North Fork (Yosemite), mountaineering guides, 310

North Lake camping area (Eastern Sierra), 123

North Pines (Yosemite)
camping area, 271; horseback riding, 309

Northrop, Jack, 152–153

Novak, Rocky, 101

Nugget Gift Shop (Stovepipe Wells), 90

O

Oak Creek camping area (Eastern Sierra), 123

Oakhurst (Yosemite)
amenities, 273; annual events, 313–314; bookstores, maps, & information, 278; dining, 277; Fruit Stand, 278; lodging, 273–274; mountain biking, 310; shopping, 278–279; spas, 311

Oakland (OAK) airport, 54

O.A.R.S. (Yosemite Valley), 307

Obsidian Flat camping area (Mammoth Lakes), 162

off-highway driving, Death Valley, 105

Oh! Ridge camping area (Mammoth Lakes), 162

Oktoberfest (Mammoth Lakes), 207

Olancha (Owens Valley/Eastern Sierra)
dining, 126; points of interest, 126–127

Old Colony Mill Road (Sequoia/Kings Canyon), hiking, 253

Old Corral Grocery & Tackle Shop (Oakhurst), 278

Old Guest House Museum (Trona), 90

Old House at Benton Hot Springs, 119, 121–122

Old New York Deli & Bagel Co., 184

Old School House Museum (Hess Park), 197
Old Shady Rest camping area (Mammoth Lakes), 162
Olmsted, Frederick Law, 261–262, 263–264, 298
Olmsted Point trail (Yosemite Valllley), 309
101 Great Escapes (Mammoth Town), 174
Onion Valley camping area (Eastern Sierra), 123
Ontario (ONT) airport, 55
O'Shaughnessy Dam (Hetch Hetchy), 291
Ostrander Lake, lodging, 276–277
Ostrander Ski Hut
    lodging, 276–277; lottery for, 315
Otis, Harrison Gray, 112
outfitters. *See also* Gear, Guides and Outfitters Index
    Lone Pine, 132; Mammoth Lakes and Mono
    Country, 187, 190, 201–202, 250; Owens Valley &
    Eastern Sierra, 141–142, 145–146; Sequoia/Kings
    Canyon, 254–255
Outpost 14 (Mammoth Mountain), 179
The Outpost (Ballarat), 92
Out Post General Store (Ballarat), 101–102
Owens Lake (Owens Valley/Eastern Sierra), 114,
    126–129
Owens, Richard, 110
Owens River, 29, 38, 110
Owens Valley & Eastern Sierra
    annual events, 148–149; Big Pine area, 136–139;
    Bishop area, 139–143; books, maps & informa-
    tion, 141; camping, 122–123; dining, 122–124,
    126, 130, 135, 139; East of Owens Lake area,
    127–129 ; environmental problems, 114; food &
    beverage purveyors, 140–141; geological forma-
    tions, 18; history, 17–18, 109–116, 117;
    Independence area, 135–136; Little Lake to
    Owens Lake area, 126–127; lodging, 117–122;
    Lone Pine area, 130–135; map, 118; movies shot
    in, 133; Owens Lake area, 127–129; points of
    interest, 124, 126–129, 132–135, 136–139,
    142–143; recreational activities, 144–148; shop-
    ping, 132, 135, 136, 141–142; spas, yoga & mas-
    sage, 147–148; taverns, saloons, roadhouses, 130,
    140; traveling to, 117; Walker Pass to Sherman
    Pass area, 122–124
Owens Valley Committee, 319
Owens Valley Native Fish Sanctuary (Bishop), 143
Owens Valley Radio Observatory (Big Pine), 136–137

P

Pacific Crest National Scenic Trail, 71–72
Pacific plate, 19–21
pack animals, 73
Paiute Indians, 18–19, 134
Palisade camping area (Mammoth Lakes), 162
Palisade Glacier (Big Pine), 139
Palisade Glacier camping area (Eastern Sierra), 123
Palmer, Harold, 65
Panache (Mammoth Town), 186
Panamint City (Death Valley), 76

Panamint Springs/Panamint Valley (Death Valley)
    camping, 87; gasoline and water, 82; history, 33;
    points of interest, 100–103; Resort, 85–86;
    saloon, 89
paragliding, 144–145
Parcher's Resort (Bishop), 119
Parsons Memorial Lodge (Tuolomne Meadows), 296
passes, to national parks and forests, 72
Pastel's Bistro (Tecopa Hot Springs), 87–88
Pat Yaeger's Eastern Sierra Guide Service, 144
Paul Schat's Bakkery (Mammoth Town), 184–185
Pear Lake Ski Hut (High-Country Sequoia), 227–228
Pearsonville (Owens Valley/Eastern Sierra), 124
Peppermint camping area (Sequoia/Kings Canyon),
    217
Performance Anglers (Mammoth Lakes), 201
Perry's Italian Café (Mammoth Town), 181
Petra's Bistro & Wine Bar (Mammoth Town), 180–181
petroglyphs, 102, 129, 143
pets, traveling with, 63
Phillips Camera House (Bishop), 142
photography supplies, Owens Valley & Eastern Sierra,
    142
photography, Yosemite National Park, 306–307
Pichot, Gifford, 289
Pierpont Springs Resort (Great Western Divide
    Highway)
        dining, 243; lodging, 243
Pilgrimage to Manzanar, 148
Pinchot, Gifford, 24
Pine City camping area (Mammoth Lakes), 162
Pine Creek Pack Station (Owens Valley/Eastern
    Sierra), 146
Pine Glen camping areas (Mammoth Lakes), 162
Pine Grove camping area (Mammoth Lakes), 162
Pine Mountain Lake Golf Club (Groveland), 308
The Pines camping areas (Yosemite), 271
Pioneer Gift & Grocery (Wawona), 279
Pioneer Market (Mariposa), 284
Pioneer Village & Yosemite History Center (Wawona),
    281
The Pita Pit (Mammoth Town), 184
Pizza Deck (Curry Village), 301–302
Pizza Parlor (Grant Grove Village), 238
Pleasant Valley Pit camping area (Eastern Sierra), 123
points of interest
        Death Valley, 92–103; Mammoth Lakes and Mono
        Country, 164–167, 187–191, 197–198; Owens
        Valley & Eastern Sierra, 124, 126–127, 132–135,
        136–139, 142–143; Sequoia/Kings Canyon,
        223–226, 231–235, 239–240, 245–246, 249;
        Yosemite, 279–282, 284, 291, 296, 303–306
Pokobe Resort (Lake Mary), 199
Polar Dip River Swim (Three Rivers), 258
Polk, James, 34–35
Ponderosa Lodge (Great Western Divide Highway)
        lodging, 243; saloon, 245
Pony Expresso (Mariposa), 284

Porcupine Flat camping area (Yosemite), 271

Portagee Joe camping area (Eastern Sierra), 123

Potwisha camping area (Sequoia/Kings Canyon), 217

Potwisha trailhead (Sequoia/Kings Canyon), swimming, 256

precipitation
average monthly, 56; Death Valley, 28, 79; Mammoth Lakes region, 158; Sierra Nevada, 28

price codes, 13

Princess camping area (Sequoia/Kings Canyon), 217

P-3 (Mammoth Town), 187

Public Lands Interpretive Association, 319

Pumice Flat camping areas (Mammoth Lakes), 162

Pumpkin Hollow Bridge, return of swallows to (Sequoia/Kings Canyon), 258

Q

Quaking Aspen Cabin (Great Western Divide Highway), 243

Quaking Aspen camping area (Sequoia/Kings Canyon), 217

R

The Racetrack (French Creek area), 99

Railroad Flat camping area (Yosemite), 271

rail travel
AMTRAK, 59; Carson & Colorado narrow-gauge railway, 127, 135; Death Valley Railroad narrow-gauge railway, 74, 80; Yosemite Mountain Sugar Pine Railroad, 59

Rainbow Pack Outfitters (Bishop), 146, 255

Raley's Superstore (Oakhurst), 278

The Ranch House Café (Olancha), 126

ranger and interpretative programs
Death Valley, 105; Owens Valley & Eastern Sierra, 147; Yosemite, 309

Raymond, Israel Ward, 262, 263

Raymond's Deli (Bishop), 140

recreational activities. *See also specific activities*
Death Valley, 103–105; Mammoth Lakes and Mono Country, 147, 198–205; Owens Valley & Eastern Sierra, 144–148; Sequoia/Kings Canyon, 250–257; Yosemite, 306–312

Redbud Arts & Crafts Festival (Three Rivers), 258

Red Hill Cinder Cone (Olancha), 126

Reds Meadows/Agnew Meadows Pack outfit (Mammoth Lakes), 202

Reds Meadows (Mammoth Lakes)
camping areas, 162; points of interest, 190

Redwood Meadow camping area (Sequoia/Kings Canyon), 217

Redwood Mountain Grove (High-Country Sequoia), 235

Reed, James, 60

Reimer's Candies & Gifts (Three Rivers), 222

Reno, Nevada
driving from, 70; Reno-Tahoe (RNO) airport, 55

Rent-4-Less car rental, 66

reservations
Death Valley National Park camping, 87; Mammoth Lakes and Mono Country condos, 174; Mammoth Lakes camping, 163; Yosemite camping, 270

resources/information. *See also* books, maps & information
agencies and nonprofit organizations, 317–318; banks/ATMs, 320–321; books about the area, 321–323; emergency road service, 326–327; hospitals and medical services, 324; kennels, 324; local media, 325; lost and found, 326; non-government organizations, 319–320; visitors centers, ranger stations, 328–329; visitor/tourist information, 327–328; weather information/road conditions, 329

The Restaurant at Convict Lake, 164

Restaurant Lulu (Mammoth Town), 181

Reversed Creek camping area (Mammoth Lakes), 162

Rey, José (King Joseph), 39–40, 44–45

Rhyolite (Death Valley), 76, 93

Richardson, T., 262, 263

Ridgecrest (Death Valley), bookstores, maps, & information, 90

River Road (Grant Grove area), 240

The River Rock Café (Mono Hot Springs), 248–249

River View Lodge (Kernville), 243

Riverview Restaurant & Lounge (Three Rivers), 221

road biking
Mammoth Lakes and Mono Country, 203; Owens Valley & Eastern Sierra, 147; Sequoia/Kings Canyon, 255–256; Yosemite, 310

road condition information, 58, 177, 329. *See also* weather information

roadhouses. *See* taverns, saloons, roadhouses

Road's End Permit Station (Kings Canyon), 238

road service, emergency, 326–327

Roberto's (Mammoth Town), 181

rock climbing
Mammoth Lakes and Mono Country, 198, 204; Owens Valley & Eastern Sierra, 147; Sequoia/Kings, 256; Yosemite, 310

Rock Creek Lake camping areas (Mammoth Lakes), 162

Rock Creek Lakes Resort (Mammoth Lakes), 161

Rock Creek Lodge (Mammoth Lakes)
dining, 164; lodging, 163

Rock Creek Pack Station (Mammoth Lakes), 202

Rock Creek to Casa Diablo (Mammoth Lakes/Mono Country)
camping areas, 162; dining, 161, 164; overview, 161; points of interest, 164–167

Rock Creek to Convict Lake area (Mammoth Lakes)
camping sites, 139–143

Rocky Mountain Chocolate Factory (Mammoth Town), 185

Rogers, John, 38

Rogers, Will, 86

Roosevelt, Franklin, 33

Roosevelt, Teddy, 9, 14, 24, 112, 266

Rowell, Galen, 142

The Rubber Room (Bishop), 147

Russell, Carl, 42

Rusty's saloon (Bishop), 140

RV travel, 60

Ryan (Death Valley), history, 78

S

Sabrina (Eastern Sierra)
    boat landing, 144; camping area, 123

Sacramento (SMF) airport, 55

Saddlebag Lake camping area (Mammoth Lakes), 163

Saddlebag Trailhead camping area (Mammoth Lakes), 163

Sage Flat camping area (Eastern Sierra), 123

Sage to Summit (Bishop), 142

Saline Valley (Death Valley)
    points of interest, 103; taverns, saloons, road-
    houses, 245

saloons. *See* taverns, saloons, roadhouses

Salsa's (Mammoth Town), 185

Sal's (Mariposa), 283

Salt Creek
    Death Valley, points of interest, 98;
    Sequoia/Kings Canyon, hiking, 253

sandwiches. *see* bakeries, sandwiches, takeout

San Francisco/Oakland, California. *See also* Hetch
    Hetchy reservoir; history
    driving from, 71; Recreation & Parks
    Department, 317; San Francisco (SFO) airport,
    56

San Joaquim valley, 26, 28

San Joaquin line (AMTRAK), 59

San Joaquin River (Sequoia/Kings Canyon), swim-
    ming, 257

San José/Monterey, California
    driving from, 71; San José/Norman Y. Mineta air-
    port, 55–56

Saratoga Springs (Death Valley), bird-watching, 103

Savage, James D. (Jim), 39–48

Savage's Trading Post site (El Portal Road area), 285

Savoury's (Mariposa), 283

Sawmill camping area (Mammoth Lakes), 163

Scenes of Wonder and Curiosity in California
    (Hutchings), 14

Schoenherr, Allan, 138

Scorpion Cocktail recipe, 88

Scott, Walter, 99

Scotty's Castle (Grapevien Canyon), 99
    Bookstore & Visitors Center, 90; gift shop, 92

seasonal events. *see* annual events

Senior Pass, Lifetime, 72

Sentinel camping area (Sequoia/Kings Canyon), 217

Sequoia and General Grant National Parks
    camping areas, 217; history, 211

Sequoia Field Institute (Sequoia/Kings Canyon), 252

Sequoia Gifts & Souvenirs (Three Rivers), 222

The Sequoia High Sierra Camp (High-Country
    Sequoia)
    dining, 230; lodging, 229

Sequoia, Kings Canyon & the Great Western Divide
    annual events, 258; bookstores, maps, & infor-
    mation, 222, 230, 238, 249; camping areas, 215,
    216; courses and seminars, 251–252; dining,
    216–218, 221, 225, 229–230, 243, 248–249;
    emergency road service, 327; food & beverage
    purveyors, 221–222; Generals Highway/High-
    Country Sequoia area, 226–235; Grant
    Grove/Kings Canyon Scenic Byway, 236–240;
    Great Western Divide Highway area, 241–246;
    history, 209–211, 233, 236–237, 241, 246–247;
    hospitals and medical services, 324; Kaiser Pass
    Road area, 246–250; kennels, 324; local media,
    325; lodging, 215, 219–221, 224–225, 226–229,
    237–238, 241–242, 248; lost and found, 326;
    maps, 242, 247; Mineral King area, 224–226;
    points of interest, 223–224, 225–226, 231–235,
    239–240, 245–246, 249; recreational activities,
    250–257; shopping, 222–223, 225, 231, 238, 245,
    249; taverns, saloons, roadhouses, 221; Three
    Rivers area, 218–224; traveling to, 214–215

Sequoia-Kings Canyon National Parks
    access limits and amenity fees, 72–73; fishing,
    252–253; General Sherman Tree, 213; history, 33,
    211–212; horseback riding, 255; map, 213;
    Mineral King ski resort, 155; natural fire zone,
    24; road condition information, 58; visitors cen-
    ters, ranger stations, 328; winter closures, 58,
    212

Sequoia-Kings Pack Trains (Independence), 146

Sequoia National Forest/National Monument
    access and amenity fees, 72; visitors centers,
    ranger stations, 328

Sequoia Natural History Association, 222, 319

sequoias, 212, 233, 235, 239

Sequoia Shuttle Bus, 59

Sequoia Tours (Sequoia/Kings Canyon), 254

Sequoia Village Inn (Three Rivers), 220–221

Serrano's (Three Rivers), 221

Sheep Creek camping area (Sequoia/Kings Canyon),
    217

Sherman Pass (Eastern Sierra)
    camping areas, 123; general information, 117;
    winter closure, 58

Sherwin Creek camping area (Mammoth Lakes), 162

Sherwin's Folly (Mammoth Town), 183

Shogun (Mammoth Town), 181

shopping
    Death Valley, 90–92; Mammoth Lakes and Mono
    Country, 185–187, 193; Owens Valley & Eastern
    Sierra, 132, 141–142; Sequoia/Kings Canyon,
    222–223, 231, 238, 245; Yosemite, 278–279, 284,
    290–291, 296, 302–303

Shoshone (Death Valley)

annual events, 107; bookstores, maps, & information, 89; dining, 88, 89; shopping, 91
Shoshone Museum, 89, 91
Shoshone Old West Days, 107
shuttle buses, 60–63
Side Door Bistro (Mammoth Town), 182
Sierra Club, 9, 14, 65, 250, 296, 303. *See also* Hetch Hetchy reservoir; Muir, John
  contact information, 319
Sierra Country Canoes & Kayaks, 199
Sierra Drifters Guide Service (Mammoth Lakes), 201
Sierra Engine (Mammoth Lakes), 202
Sierra Meadows Ranch Equestrian Center (Mammoth Lakes), 202
Sierra Mountain Center (Bishop), 147
Sierra Mountaineering International (SMI) (Bishop), 147
Sierra Mountain Guides (June Lake), 198
Sierra National Forest
  access and amenity fees, 72; visitors centers, ranger stations, 329
Sierra Nevada. *See also* history
  American Indian populations, 26; average temperatures and precipitation, 28; early crossings, 30–33, 35–38; High Sierra Trail, 73; John Muir Trail, 73; Mount Whitney Trail, 73; natural history, 18–22; Pacific Crest National Scenic Trail, 71–72; peaks, heights of, 125; sequoias, 212–213; as single mountain range, 14; timeline of events, 1775-2005, 40–41
Sierra Nevada Aquatic Research Laboratory, 319
Sierra Restaurant (Fish Camp), 277
Sierra Rock Climbing School (Bishop, Mammoth Lakes), 204
Sierra South Mountain & Paddle Sports (Sequoia/Kings Canyon), 251, 252
Sierra Star golf course (Mammoth Mountain), 201
  opening events, 205
Sierra Subs & Salads (Three Rivers), 221–222
Sierra Sundance Earth Foods (Mammoth Town), 184
Sierra Wave T-Shifts & Gifts (June Lake), 193
Silver City General Store (Mineral King area), 225
Silver City Resort (Mineral King area), 224–225
Silver City Restaurant & Bakery (Mineral King area), 225
Silver Lake (Mammoth Lakes)
  camping area, 162; general store, 193
Silver Lake Resort, 192, 199
Skadi (Mammoth Town), 181
skateboarding, 204
Skidoo (Panamint/Saline area), 100
ski equipment. *See* outfitters; sporting gear & equipment
skiing
  Badger Pass Ski Area, 312–313, 315; June Mountain ski area, 207; Mammoth Lakes and Mono Country, 200; Mammoth Mountain Ski Resort, 153–156, 177–179, 201–207; Yosemite, 312

Ski Museum (Mammoth Town), 187–188
sledding, 312
Sledz (Mammoth Town), 205
sleigh rides, Yosemite Valley, 309
Slick Rock Recreation Area (Sequoia/Kings Canyon), swimming, 256
Slocum's Grill (Mammoth Town), 181
Smith, Jedediah Strong, 26–27
Smokey Bear Flat (Mammoth Lakes/Mono Country), 202
snorkeling, 204–205
Snowbird Condominiums (Mammoth Town), 175
snowboarding
  Mammoth Lakes and Mono Country, 200; Yosemite National Park, 312
Snowcreek Resort (Mammoth Town)
  golf course, 201; lodging, 175–176
snowfall, 28, 158
snowmobile trails, 73
snowplay, 205
snowshoeing, 200
snow tubing, 312
Snyder, Susan, 44
Sommermeyer, Michael, fishing Web site, 144
Sonora Pass, winter closure, 58
Soquel camping area (Yosemite), 271
Southern California Edison, 318
Southern Sierra Nevada
  CCC maintenance work, 33; diversity of, 10; geographical boundaries, 12
Southern Yosemite Automotive Film Festival (Oakhurst), 313
Southern Yosemite Mountain Guides (North Fork), 308, 310
South Fork camping area (Yosemite), 271
South Fork (Sequoia/Kings Canyon)
  camping area, 217; trailhead, swimming hole, 256
South Lake (Owens Valley/Eastern Sierra), boat landing, 144
Southside Drive area (Yosemite), lodging, 272
South Tufa (Lee Vining), 197
souvenirs, gifts, sundries
  Death Valley, 90; Mammoth Lakes and Mono Country, 186, 193; Owens Valley & Eastern Sierra, 132; Sequoia/Kings Canyon, 222, 231, 238; Yosemite, 284, 290, 303
Spa Du Sureau (Oakhurst), 311
Spanish settlement, 23–26
spas, yoga & massage
  Mammoth Lakes and Mono Country, 192, 204; Owens Valley & Eastern Sierra, 147–148; Yosemite National Park, 311
Spellbinder Books (Bishop), 141
sporting gear & equipment. *See also* Gear, Guides and Outfitters index
  Death Valley, 90; June Lake, 193; Lone Pine, 132; Mammoth Town, 186–187; Owens Valley &

Eastern Sierra, 141; Yosemite, 268, 278–279, 284, 296, 302–303
Sportsman's Inn (Kernville), 245
Spring Death Valley Century and Double Century, 106
Spring Fest (Badger Pass), 313
Spring Fest (Mammoth Mountain), 205–207
Springville Apple Festival, 258
Springville Inn (Great Western Divide Highway), 241–242
Springville (Sequoia/Kings Canyon), annual events, 258–259
Springville Sierra Rodeo, 258
Stagecoach Bar & Grill (Great Western Divide Highway), 243
Stanislaus National Forest. *See also* Groveland mountain biking, 310; visitor center, ranger station, 329
state entities, California, contact information, 317–318
State Water Project (SWP), 29
steamboats, 51
Stegner, Wallace, 10, 15
Stellar Brew (Mammoth Town), 183
Stephenson, Nathan, 235
Still Life Café (Independence), 135
Stony Creek (Sequoia/Kings Canyon)
    camping area, 217; swimming, 256
Stony Creek Village (High-Country Sequoia), 231
The Stove (Mammoth Town), 181
Stovepipe Wells (Death Valley)
    Badwater Saloon, 89; camping, 87; gasoline and water, 82; general store, 92; lodging, 84–85; shopping, 90; Toll Road Restaurant, 88–89; trails to, 37
Strawberry Music Festival (Camp Mather), 313, 314
Stump Alley (Mammoth Mountain), 178
Summerdale camping area (Yosemite), 271
Summit camping area (Yosemite), 271
The Summit (Mammoth Town), 176
Sunrise (Yosmite) backcountry campsite, 294
Sunset camping area (Sequoia/Kings Canyon), 217
Sunset (Death Valley), camping, 87
Surefoot (Mammoth Town), 187
Surprise Canyon (Death Valley), history, 76
Sutter, Johann, 30
sweets
    Mammoth Lakes and Mono Country, 185, 193; Sequoia/Kings Canyon, 222; Yosemite, 302
Sweetwater camping area (Yosemite), 271
swimming
    Mammoth Lakes and Mono Country, 204–205; Sequoia/Kings Canyon, 256–257; Yosemite, 311

T

Table Mountain camping area (Eastern Sierra), 123
Taboose Creek camping area (Eastern Sierra), 123
take out. *see* bakeries, sandwiches, take out
Tallus (Mammoth Town), 176
Tamarack Flat camping area (Yosemite), 271

Tamarack Lodge & Resort (Mammoth Town), 171–172
    Cross Country Ski Center, 200, 207
Tavern at the Green (Groveland), 290
taverns, saloons, roadhouses
    Death Valley, 89; Mammoth Lakes and Mono Country, 182–183, 193; Owens Valley & Eastern Sierra, 122–124, 130, 140; Sequoia/Kings Canyon, 221, 245; Yosemite, 290–291, 301
Tecopa Hot Springs (Death Valley)
    dining, 87–88; points of interest, 93–94
Tehachapi Pass, 117
Telebration (Mammoth Mountain), 205–207
Telescope Peak (Panamint/Saline area), 100–101
temperature
    average monthly, 56; Death Valley, 79; Mammoth Lakes region, 158
Tenaya Lodge (Fish Camp)
    dining, 277; lodging, 274; mountain biking, 310
Tenaya (Yosemite Chief), 24, 46–47, 48
Tenmile camping area (Sequoia/Kings Canyon), 217
Tenmile Creek to Quail Flat bike route (Sequoia/Kings Canyon), 256
tennis
    Death Valley, 104; Mammoth Lakes and Mono Country, 205; Yosemite, 311
Texas Flat camping area (Yosemite), 271
Texas Spring camping area (Death Valley), 87
Thanksgiving at Evergreen (Groveland), 315
Tharp, Hale D., 218
Thomas Edison Reservoir (Sequoia/Kings Canyon), swimming, 257
Thoreau, Henry, 9
Thorndike camping area (Death Valley), 87
3 Rivers Cyber Café, 221–222
Three Rivers area (Sequoia/Kings Canyon)
    annual events, 258–259; camping areas, 217; dining, 221; food & beverage purveyors, 221–222; golf, 253; history, 218–224; lodging, 219–221; points of interest, 223–224; shopping, 222–223; taverns, saloons, roadhouses, 221
Three Rivers Historical Museum, 223
Three Rivers Mercantile, 222–223
Three Rivers Public Golf Course, 253
Three Rivers Village Market, 221
Thrifty car rental, 66
The Tiger Bar (June Lake), 193
Timber Ridge (Mammoth Town), 176
Timbisha Homeland Act (2000), 95
Timbisha Shoshone Indians, 79, 95
timeline of events, 1775-2005, 40–41
Tinemaha Creek camping area (Eastern Sierra), 123
Tinemaha (Paiute chief), 134
Tioga Gas Mart (Lee Vining), 196
Tioga Lake camping area (Mammoth Lakes), 163
Tioga Lodge (Mono Lake), 195
Tioga Pass
    average closing date, 207; opening, 205; winter closure, 58, 315

Tioga Pass Entrance Station (Yosemite), 296
Tioga Pass Resort (TPR) (Yosemite Tioga entrance)
    dining, 295; lodging, 292
Tioga Road/Tuolomne Meadows area (Yosemite)
    bookstores, maps, & information, 295; camping
    areas, 271; dining, 295; food purveyors, 295; his-
    tory/general information, 291–292; lodging,
    292–294; points of interest, 296; shopping, 296
Tioga Toomey's Whoa Nelly Deli (Lee Vining), 196
Tokopah Falls hiking (Generals Highway area), 254
Toll Road Restaurant (Stovepipe Wells), 88–89
Tom's Place (Crowley Lake), 161
Tonik (Mammoth Town), 186
Top of the Sierra (Mammoth Mountain), 179
topography, 18–22, 114–115
Totem Café (Lone Pine), 130
Totem Trading Post (Lone Pine), 132
tourism, history of, 48–49, 65, 78–80
tourist information. see visitor information
town houses. see condos, town houses, vacation rentals
trail bicycles, trails for, 73
Trail of 100 Giants (Great Western Divide Highway),
    245
transportation. See also driving
    air travel, 53–58; buses and shuttles, 60–63;
    early travel routes, 51–52; modern routes, 52–53;
    rail travel, 58–60
Trek to the Nation's Christmas Tree (Grant Grove), 258
Trona (Death Valley)
    annual events, 107; bookstores, maps, & infor-
    mation, 90; points of interest, 100
Trona Pinnacles National Natural Landmark, 100
trona production, 114
The Troutfitter Fly Shop (Mammoth Town), 201
Troutstock Eastern Sierra, 206
Trout Town Joe (June Lake), 193
Troy Meadow camping area (Eastern Sierra), 123
Trumball Lake camping area (Mammoth Lakes), 163
Tubbs' Saloon and Whorehouse, 78
tubing, 205
Tuff camping area (Mammoth Lakes), 162–163
Tulare County, contact information, 317
Tule elk, 138
Tule Indians, 233
Tule River (Sequoia/Kings Canyon), swimming, 257
Tuolomne Grove of Big Trees (Crane Flat), 291
Tuolomne Meadows Grill, 295
Tuolomne Meadows Lodge
    dining, 295; lodging, 293
Tuolomne Meadows (Yosemite)
    bookstores, maps, & information, 295; camping
    area, 271; dining, 295; food & beverage purvey-
    ors, 295; horseback riding, 309; lodging, 293;
    Poetry Festival, 314; points of interest, 296;
    shopping, 296; Store & Gas Station, 296; Visitors
    Center, 295
Tuolomne Stable (Tuolomne Meadows), 309
Tusks Bar (Mammoth Town), 183

Twain, Mark (Samuel Clemens), 51, 151, 194
Twin Lake camping area (Mammoth Lakes), 162
Twin Lakes Store (Mammoth Lakes), 199

U

Ubehebe Crater (French Creek area), 99
ulexite, 77–78
Upper Grays Meadow camping area (Eastern Sierra),
    123
Upper Kern River (Sequoia/Kings Canyon) camping
    areas, 217
Upper Pine Grove camping area (Mammoth Lakes),
    162
Upper Pines camping area (Yosemite), 271
Upper Sage Flat camping area (Eastern Sierra), 123
Upper Soda Springs camping area (Mammoth Lakes),
    162
Upper Stony Creek camping area (Sequoia/Kings
    Canyon), 217
Upper Yosemite Falls Trail (Yosemite Valley), 309
U.S. Bureau of Land Management, 318
U.S. Bureau of Reclamation, 318
U.S. Department of Transportation, 318
U.S. Environmental Protection Agency, 318
U.S. Fish & Wildlife Service, 318
U.S. Naval Museum Of Armament & Technology
    (Panamint/Saline area), 102
U.S. Park Service, General Management Plan, 65
utility companies, contact information, 318

V

vacation rentals. See condos, town houses, vacation
    rentals
Vacation trailer Rentals (Mammoth Lake), 160–161
Val d'Isere (Mammoth Town), 176
Valentine Reserve (Mammoth Town), 188
Valley Stable (Yosemite Valley), 309
Valley Visitors Center (Yosemite Village), 302
Vance, R. H., 262
Vermilion (Kaiser Pass Road), shopping, 249
Vermilion Valley Ferry & Resort Rentals
    (Sequoia/Kings Canyon), 251
Vermilion Valley Resort (Lake Thomas A. Edison), 249
Vermillion Camp Store, 249
Vern Clevenger Gallery (Bishop), 142
The Victorian Room Restaurant (Groveland), 289
Viewpoint Condominiums (Mammoth Town), 176
The Village at Mammoth (Mammoth Town), 172–173
The Village Café (Bishop), 139
Village Grill (Yosemite Village), 302
Village Sport Shop (Yosemite Village), 302
Village Sports (Mammoth Town), 187
Vining, Leroy, 48, 194
Vintners' Holidays (Yosemite Valley), 315
Virginia Lakes Pack Outfit (Bridgeport), 202
Visalia (Sequoia/Kings Canyon), fishing/guides, 253
Visalia (VIS) airport, 56

visitor information. *See also* resources/information
 chambers of commerce, 327–328; Death Valley,
 89–90; Mammoth Lakes and Mono Country, 185,
 196; Owens Valley & Eastern Sierra, 131, 141;
 Sequoia/Kings Canyon, 222, 225, 231, 238, 249;
 visitors centers, ranger stations, 328–329;
 Yosemite, 278, 284, 302, 309
Volcam Peanut Butter & Rail Jam (Mammoth
 Mountain), 207
Volcano Hazards Program's Long Valley Observatory,
 165
volcanoes, 20–21, 165
Volcom Brothers Skatepark (Mammoth Town), 204
Vons grocery
 Bishop, 141; Mammoth Town, 184; Oakhurst, 278

W

Walker Canyon camping area (Mammoth Lakes), 162
Walker, Joseph R., 30, 32, 110, 194, 233
Walker Pass to Sherman Pass area (Owens
 Valley/Eastern Sierra)
 dining, 126–128; points of interest, 117, 124–125;
 winter travel, 58
Walter Fry Nature Center (High-Country Sequoia), 232
water, drinking and irrigation, 28–29, 82, 111–114
waterfalls, peak flow (Yosemite), 313
watermelon snow, 226
Watkins, Carleton, 262
Wave Rave (Mammoth Town), 187
Wawona Hotel, 274–275
 Dining Room, 278
The Wawona Road area (Yosemite)
 bookstores, maps, & information, 278; camping
 areas, 271; dining, 277–278; food & beverage pur-
 veyors, 278; general information, 273; history,
 48; lodging, 273–277; points of interest,
 279–282; shopping, 278–279
Wawona Stable, 309
Wawona Tunnel Tree (Yosemite), 279
Wawona (Yosemite)
 bookstores, maps, & information, 278; Golf
 Course and Shop, 279, 308; horseback riding,
 309; lodging, 274–275; points of interest, 281;
 shopping, 279
weather information, 329
 Death Valley, 79; Mammoth Mountain, 177
Weed, Charles, 262
Wellsville Saloon (Cedar Slope), 245
Western Horse Show & Gymkhanas (Mariposa), 313
The Westin Monache Resort (Mammoth Town),
 173–174
West Side Road (French Creek area), 96
We Three Bakery/Café (Three Rivers), 221
Whiskey Creek (Bishop), 139
Whiskey Creek Mountain Bistro (Mammoth Town),
 183

Whiskey Flat Days (Kernville), 258
Whispering Pines Lodge/B&B (Kernville), 243
Whitebark Restaurant (Mammoth Town), 182
White Mountain Ranger Station (Bishop), 141
White Mountain Research Station (Bishop), 137, 319
White Mountains camping areas (Eastern Sierra), 123
White River camping area (Sequoia/Kings Canyon),
 217
White Wolf camping area (Yosemite), 271
White Wolf Lodge (Tioga Pass Road)
 dining, 295; lodging, 293
Whitmore Pool (Mammoth Town), 205
Whitney, Josiah D., 14, 17, 128, 263
Whitney Portal (Lone Pine)
 camping, 123; points of interest, 134; store, 132
Wild Burro Rescue (Olancha), 127
Wilderness Center (Yosemite Village), 302
Wilderness Outfitters (Mammoth Town), 201
Wilderness Society, 319
Wildflower Show (Ridgecrest), 106
wildflowers, peak bloom (Yosemite), 313
Wild Free-Roaming Horse and Burro Act (1971),
 96–97
Wild Horse and Burro Corrals, 96
Wildrose (Death Valley)
 camping areas, 87; Charcoal Kilns, 100
Wild, Wild West Marathon, 148
Williams Cutoff, 35
Willow camping area (Eastern Sierra), 123
Willow Placer camping area (Yosemite), 271
Wilson's Eastside Sports (Bishop), 142, 147
Wilson's Eastside Sports (Bishop), 148
Wilson, Woodrow, 289
Winnedumah Hotel (Independence), 119, 120–121
Winnedumah (Paiute), legend of, 134
winter conditions
 Death Valley, 79; driving, 58; Mammoth Lakes
 and Mono Country, 165; 19th century crossing
 attempts, 31–33; preparing for, 57; seasonal clo-
 sures, 58
Winters, Aaron and Rosie, 77–78
winter sports
 Owens Valley & Eastern Sierra, 148;
 Sequoia/Kings Canyon, 257; Yosemite National
 Park, 312
Wishon camping area (Sequoia/Kings Canyon), 217
Woods Lodge (Lake George), 200
Wooster, J.M., 233
Wrangler Buffet & Steakhouse (Furnace Creek), 88
Wright, James W. A., 151, 152
Wukashi Gift Shop (High-Country Sequoia), 231
Wuksachi Lodge (High-Country Sequoia), 228

X

Xanterra Parks & Resorts, 86

Y

Yamatani (Bishop), 139
Yosemite Association
    contact information, 319; Yosemite Village bookstore, 302
Yosemite Bicycle and Sport (Oakhurst), 279, 310
Yosemite Bug (Midpines), 59
    dining, 283–284; lodging, 282; mountain biking, 310; spa, 311
Yosemite Cemetery (Yosemite Village), 306
Yosemite Creek camping area (Yosemite), 271
Yosemite Creek trailhead (Yosemite Valley), 309
Yosemite Forks Mountain House Restaurant (Oakhurst), 277
Yosemite Gifts (Mariposa), 284
Yosemite High Country Trail Map (Harrison), 309
Yosemite Indian Big Time (Yosemite Village), 314
Yosemite Indians, 40, 42–43, 46–47
The Yosemite Lodge (Yosemite Valley)
    facilities, 297; Nature Shop, 303; Store, 303
Yosemite Mountaineering School & Outdoor Shop (Yosemite Valley), 296, 309, 310–311
Yosemite Mountain Sugar Pine Railroad, 59, 279
Yosemite Museum and Indian Village (Yosemite Village), 306
Yosemite National Park
    access limits and fees, 72; annual events, 313–315; bookstores, maps, & information, 278, 284, 290, 295, 302; Campground Offices, 271; camping areas, 271; CCC work at, 33; dining, 272, 283–284, 288–289, 295, 300–301; El Portal Road area, 282–285; emergency road service, 327; food & beverage purveyors, 278, 284, 295, 301–302; guided bus tours, 308; Hetch Hetchy reservoir, 29; history, 261–268, 291–292; hospitals and medical services, 324; interpretive programs, 309; kennels, 324; limits on wheeled and motorized vehicles, 73; local media, 325; lodging, 268–270, 273–277, 283, 287, 292–294, 299–300; lost and found, 326; map, 269; points of interest, 279–282, 285, 291, 296, 303–306; prescribed fire program, 24; recreational activities, 306–312; road condition information, 58; shopping, 278–279, 284, 290–291, 296, 302–303; spas, yoga & massage, 311; taverns, saloons, roadhouses, 289–290, 301; Tioga Road/Tuolomne Meadows area (Yosemite), 291–296; traveling to, 268; visitors centers, ranger stations, 329; Wawona Road area, 273–282; Yosemite Valley area, 297–306
Yosemite Nordic Holiday, 313
Yosemite Shuttle, 63
Yosemite Sierra Visitors Bureau (Oakhurst), 278
Yosemite, The (Muir), 10
Yosemite Trails sleigh rides, 309
Yosemite Valley Railroad (YVRR), 58
Yosemite Valley
    bookstores, maps, & information, 302; camping areas, 271; dining, 300–301; 1872 earthquake, 18; food & beverage purveyors, 301–302; general information, 297–299; lodging, 299–300; map, 298; naming of, 46–47; points of interest, 303–306; shopping, 302–303; taverns, saloons, roadhouses, 301; winter travel and closures, 58
Yosemite Village (Yosemite Valley)
    annual events, 314; art education, 307; bookstores, maps, & information, 302; food & beverage purveyors, 301–302; points of interest, 306
Young Men and Fire (Maclean), 24
Yucca Point (Grant Grove area), 240

Z

Zabriskie Point (Death Valley), 94
Zephyr Whitewater Expeditions
    Sequoia/Kings Canyon, 250; Yosemite Valley, 307
Zumwalt Meadow (Grant Grove area), 240

Lodging by Price

Inexpensive: Up to $75
Moderate: $75 to $125
Expensive: $125 to $200
Very Expensive: $200 and up

Death Valley

Moderate
Panamint Springs Resort, 85-86
Stovepipe Wells Village, 84–85

Moderate to Expensive
Furnace Creek Ranch, 84

Very Expensive
Furnace Creek Resort, 83–84

Mammoth Lakes & Mono Country

Inexpensive to Moderate
El Mono Motel, 195

Moderate to Expensive
Tioga Lodge, 195

Moderate to Very Expensive
Rock Creek Lodge, 163

Expensive
Hot Creek Ranch, 163–164
The Village at Mammoth, 172–173

Expensive to Very Expensive
Juniper Springs Resort, 173
The Mammoth Mountain Inn, 171
Tamarack Lodge & Resort, 171–172

Very Expensive
The Westin Monache Resort, 173–174

Owens Valley & Eastern Sierra

Inexpensive to Moderate
Dow Villa Hotel & Hotel, 120

Moderate
Cerro Gordo, 119
Old House at Benton Hot Springs, 121–222
Winnedumah Hotel, 120–121

Sequoia, Kings Canyon & the Great Western Divide

Inexpensive
Pear Lake Ski Hut, 227–228
Quaking Aspen Cabin, 243

Inexpensive to Moderate
Grant Grove Village, 237–238
Mono Hot Springs Resort, 248
Silver City Resort, 224–225

Moderate
Big Meadows Guard Station, 229
Buckeye Tree Lodge, 220
Comfort Inn & Suites, 219
Lazy J Ranch Motel, 219
River View Lodge, 243

Moderate to Expensive
Cedar Grove Lodge, 237–238
Sequoia Village Inn, 220–221
Montecito Lake Resort, 228

Moderate to Very Expensive
Wuksachi Lodge, 228
Lake Elowin Resort, 219–220
Whispering Pines Lodge/B&B, 243

Expensive
Camp Nelson Lodge, 243
John Muir Lodge, 237–238
Springville Inn, 241–242

Very Expensive
Bearpaw High Sierra Camp, 227
Muir Trail Ranch, 248
The Sequoia High Sierra Camp, 229

Yosemite

Inexpensive
Camp Mather, 272
Housekeeping Camp, 272
Ostrander Ski Hut, 276–277

Inexpensive to Moderate
White Wolf Lodge, 293
Yosemite Bug, 283

Moderate
Curry Village, 272
Evergreen Lodge, 287
Tuolomne Meadows Lodge, 293

Moderate to Expensive
Narrow Gauge Inn, 274
Tioga Pass Resort, 292
Wawona Hotel, 274–275

Expensive
The Lodge at Yosemite Falls, 300

Expensive to Very Expensive
Glacier Point Lodge, 275–276
Groveland Hotel, 287

Very Expensive
Chateau du Sureau, 273–274
High Sierra Camps, 294
Tenaya Lodge, 274
The Ahwahnee Hotel, 299

Gear, Guides and Outfitters

Death Valley
Furnace Creek Pro Shop, 90

Mammoth Lakes & Mono Country
The Alpine Approach, 186
Brian's Bicycles and Cross Country Skis, 187
Caldera Kayaks, 198
Convict Lake Resort, 201
Crowley Lake Fish Camp Marina, 198
David Moss Fly Fishing, 200
David Neal, Reel Mammoth Adventures, 200
DJ's Snowmobile Adventures, 202
Eastern Sierra Guide Service, 200
Ernie's Tackle & Ski Shop (June Lake), 193
Footloose Sports, 187
Frontier Pack Station, 201–202
Kevin Peterson's Fly Fishing Adventures, 201
Mammoth Lakes Pack Outfit, 202
Mammoth Mountain Adventure Center, 204
Mammoth Mountaineering, 187, 198
McCoy Sports & Wilderness Outfitters, 187
McGee Creek Pack Station, 202
P-3, 187
Performance Anglers, 201
Reds Meadows/Agnew Meadows Pack outfit, 202
Rock Creek Pack Station, 202
Sierra Drifters Guide Service, 201
Sierra Engine, 202
Sierra Meadows Ranch Equestrian Center, 202
Sierra Mountain Guides, 198
Sierra Rock Climbing School, 204
Smoke Bear Flat, 202
Surefoot, 187
The Troutfitter Fly Shop, 201
Village Sports, 187
Virginia Lakes Pack Outfit, 202
Wave Rave, 187
Wilderness Outfitters, 201

Owens Valley & Eastern Sierra
Aerohead Cycles, 141
Allen Outdoor Products, Sierra Saddlery & Feed, 141
Bardini Foundation, 147
Bishop Pack Outfitters, 145
Brock's Flyfishing Specialists, 144
Elevation, 147
Frontier Pack Station, 146
Glacier Pack Train, 146
Interagency Visitor Center, 147

Mammoth Mountaineering, 147
Michael Sommermeyer Web site, 144
Mount Whitney Pack Trains, 146
Pat Yaeger's Eastern Sierra Guide Service, 144
Pine Creek Pack Station, 146
Rainbow Pack Outfitters, 146
Sage to Summit, 142
Sequoia-Kings Pack Trains, 146
Sierra Mountain Center, 147
Sierra Mountaineering International (SMI), 147
The Rubber Room, 147
White Mountain Ranger Station, 147
Wilson's Eastside Sports, 142, 147, 148

Sequoia, Kings Canyon & the Great Western Divide
Balch Park Pack Station, 254
Buz Beszek's Fly Shop, 253
Cedar Grove Pack Station, 254
Clyde Pack Outfit, 254
Golden Trout Pack Trains, 255
Grant Grove Stables, 254
High Sierra Pack Station, 255
Horse Corral Pack Station, 255
Kaweah Whitewater Adventures, 250
Kings River Expeditions, 250
Mountain and River Adventures, 250–251, 252
Rainbow Pack Outfitters, 255
Sierra South Mountain & Paddle Sports, 251, 252
Zephyr Whitewater Expeditions, 250

Yosemite
American River Touring Association, Inc. (ARTA), 307
Badger Pass Sport Shop, 279
Blue Heron Sports, 284
Evergreen Lodge, 308
Herb Bauer, 268
Hi-Tec Boot Outlet, 278
Miller's Mountain Sports, 278
Mountain Shop, 303
O.A.R.S., 307
REI, 268
Southern Yosemite Mountain Guides, 308, 310
Village Sport Shop, 302
Wawona Golf Shop, 279
Yosemite Bicycle and Sport, 279, 310
Yosemite Mountaineering School & Outdoor Shop, 296, 309, 310–311
Zephyr Whitewater Expeditions, 307

Spas and Golf

Spas

Mammoth Lakes & Mono Country
Belladonna, 204
Creekside Spa at Double Eagle Resort, 204
Healing Arts, 204
Mountain Mobile Massage, 204

Owens Valley & Eastern Sierra
Belle Vous Day Spa & Salon, 147
Benton Hot Springs, 148
Bishop Yoga & Massage Center, 147
Keogh's Hot Springs, 148

Yosemite
Spa Du Sureau, 311

Golf

Death Valley
Furnace Creek Ranch, 103–104

Mammoth Lakes & Mono Country
Sierra Star, 201
Snowcreek Golf Course, 201

Owens Valley & Eastern Sierra
Bishop County Club, 144–145
Mount Whitney Golf Club, 144

Sequoia, King's Canyon & the Great Western Divide
Three Rivers Public Golf Course, 253